Thermal Analysis with SOLIDWORKS Simulation 2026 and Flow Simulation 2026

Paul M. Kurowski, Ph.D., P.Eng.

SDC PUBLICATIONS

SDC Publications
P.O. Box 1334
Mission, KS 66222
913-262-2664
www.SDCpublications.com
Publisher: Stephen Schroff

ISBN-13: 978-1-63057-796-4
ISBN-10: 1-63057-796-0

Printed and bound in the United States of America.

About the Author

Dr. Paul Kurowski received his MSc and PhD in Applied Mechanics from Warsaw University of Technology and completed postdoctoral work at Kyoto University. He is Professor Emeritus in the Faculty of Engineering at the University of Western Ontario. Prior to joining academia, he spent two decades in industry, working as a design and research engineer in sectors including heavy equipment, automotive, and defense. His teaching has included Finite Element Analysis, Computer-Aided Engineering, Product Design, Dynamics of Machines, Mechanical Vibrations, and Reverse Engineering.

Dr. Kurowski has published numerous books and technical papers and has delivered professional development seminars for the Society of Automotive Engineers, the American Society of Mechanical Engineers, Professional Engineers Ontario, Parametric Technology Corporation, Rand Worldwide, SolidWorks Corporation, and other organizations.

Table of Contents

Before You Start

Learning Path

Thermal analysis problems in this book are introduced progressively. The first part focuses on heat transfer in solids modeled with finite element analysis, where convection is represented by boundary conditions. The second part extends these models by including radiation. The third part introduces CFD, where convection is computed from fluid motion and conjugate heat transfer can be analyzed. The final chapter applies these methods to benchmark problems with known reference solutions. Detailed descriptions are given at the beginning of each part.

Models

To support the learning progression outlined above, each chapter includes prepared models created in SOLIDWORKS. These models allow students to focus on the analysis procedures rather than spending time constructing geometry. In each chapter, a primary model is solved step by step to demonstrate the techniques being introduced. Additional practice models are provided so that readers can repeat the analysis using the same methods and further develop their understanding of the simulation workflow.

All exercises in this book use **SOLIDWORKS** models which can be downloaded from www.SDCpublications.com. Exercises do not contain any **Simulation** studies or **Flow Simulation** projects; readers will be asked to solve problems themselves.

You may find your results slightly different from results presented in this book. This is because numerical results may differ slightly depending on software service pack.

Explore each exercise beyond its description by investigating other options, other menu choices, and other ways to present results. Use additional practice models and create your own problems. You will soon discover that the same simple logic applies to all functions in structural, thermal or flow analysis.

This book is not intended to replace software manuals. The knowledge acquired by the reader will not be strictly software specifics. The same concepts, tools and methods apply to every FEA and CFD program.

Functionality of Simulation and Flow Simulation

This book uses SOLIDWORKS add-ins: Simulation and Flow Simulation. Information on these applications is available at: https://www.solidworks.com/domain/simulation

Prerequisites

"**Thermal Analysis with SOLIDWORKS Simulation**" is not an introductory text. Rather, it picks up Thermal Analysis from where it was left in the textbook "Engineering Analysis with SOLIDWORKS Simulation."

If you are new to SOLIDWORKS Simulation, we recommend using "Engineering Analysis with SOLIDWORKS Simulation" to gain essential familiarity with Finite Element Analysis and with SOLIDWORKS Simulation.

The following pre-requisites are recommended:

- An understanding of Heat Transfer Analysis
- An understanding of Structural Analysis
- Familiarity with SOLIDWORKS
- Familiarity with SOLIDWORKS Simulation to the extent covered in "Engineering Analysis with SOLIDWORKS Simulation" or an equivalent experience

Selected terminology

The mouse pointer plays a very important role in executing various commands and providing user feedback. The mouse pointer is used to execute commands, select geometry, and invoke pop-up menus. We use Windows terminology when referring to mouse-pointer actions.

Item	Description
Click-inside	Click the left mouse button. Wait a second, and then click the left mouse button inside the pop-up menu or text box. Use this technique to modify the names of folders and icons in SOLIDWORKS Simulation Manager.
Drag and drop	Use the mouse to point to an object. Press and hold the left mouse button down. Move the mouse pointer to a new location. Release the left mouse button.
Right-click	Click the right mouse button. A pop-up menu is displayed. Use the left mouse button to select a desired menu command.

SOLIDWORKS file names appear in CAPITAL letters, even though the actual file names may use a combination of capital and small letters. Selected menu items and **SOLIDWORKS Simulation** commands appear in **bold**; **SOLIDWORKS** configurations, **SOLIDWORKS Simulation** folders, icon names and study names appear in *italics* except in captions and comments to illustrations. Bold font may also be used to draw the reader's attention to a particular term.

1: Introduction

- Heat transfer by conduction
- Heat transfer by convection
- Heat transfer by radiation
- Thermal boundary conditions
- Numerical tools used in analysis of heat transfer
- Analogies between thermal and structural analysis
- Thermal elements: solids and shells
- Scalar and vector entities
- Presenting results
- Steady state thermal analysis
- Transient thermal analysis
- Linear thermal analysis
- Nonlinear thermal analysis

What is Thermal Analysis?

Thermal analysis deals with heat transfer in solid bodies. We approach thermal analysis from the perspective of a user experienced in structural analysis such as static, modal, buckling etc. as implemented in SOLIDWORKS Simulation. You will soon note that experience in structural analysis is transferable to thermal analysis because of the close analogies between structural and thermal analyses. Selected analogies are summarized in Figure 1-1.

Structural Analysis	**Thermal Analysis**
Hooke's law $\sigma = E\frac{du}{dx}$	Fourier's law $q = -k\frac{dT}{dx}$
Displacement [m]	Temperature [K]
Strain [1]	Temperature gradient [K/m]
Stress [N/m^2]	Heat flux [W/m^2]
Load [N] [N/m] [N/m^2] [N/m^3]	Heat source [W] [W/m] [W/m^2] [W/m^3]
Displacement [m]	Temperature [K]
Pressure [N/m^2]	Heat flux [W/m^2]

Figure 1-1: Selected analogies between structural and thermal analyses.

All units are in SI system.

The primary unknown in structural analysis is displacement; the primary unknown in thermal analysis is temperature. This leads to an important difference between structural and thermal analysis performed with the finite element method. Displacement, which is a vector and includes both translation and rotation, requires up to six degrees of freedom per node. The number of degrees of freedom in structural analysis depends on the type of elements; for example, solid elements have three degrees of freedom per node and shell elements have six degrees of freedom per node. Two-dimensional structural elements have two degrees of freedom per node. Temperature is a scalar and requires only one degree of freedom per node, regardless of element type. This makes thermal problems much easier to solve because thermal models typically have fewer degrees of freedom as compared to structural models.

Another conceptual difference is that thermal analysis is never a "static" analysis. If heat flow does not change, then the problem is "steady state analysis" and not static because heat flow never stops. If heat flow changes with time, then the problem is called transient.

Mechanisms of heat transfer

Conduction

Conduction is responsible for heat transfer in solid bodies. In a solid body, the energy is transferred from a high temperature region to a low temperature region. The rate of heat transfer per unit area is proportional to the material thermal conductivity, cross sectional area and temperature gradient in the normal direction; it is inversely proportional to the distance (Figure 1-2). This mode of heat transfer is referred to as conduction:

$$Q_{COND} = kA(T_{HOT} - T_{COLD})/L$$

Where:

Q_{COND} – Heat transferred by conduction [W]

k – Thermal conductivity [W/m/K]

A – Area [m^2]

T_{HOT} – Temperature on the hot side [K]

T_{COLD} – Temperature on the cold side [K]

L – Distance of heat travel [m]

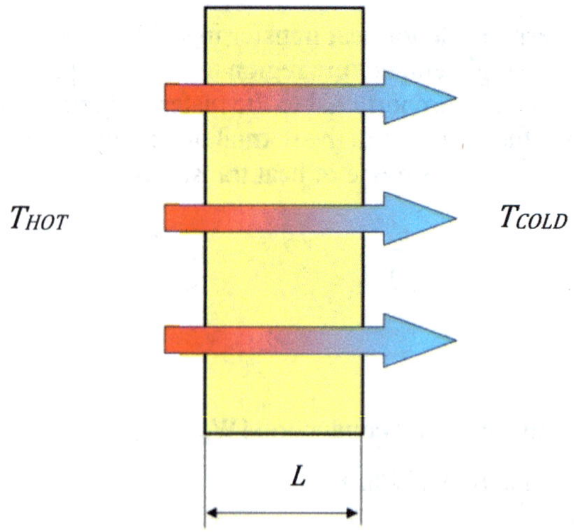

Figure 1-2: Heat transfer by conduction.

Conduction is responsible for heat transfer in solid bodies.

Thermal conductivity is very different for different materials as shown in Figure 1-3.

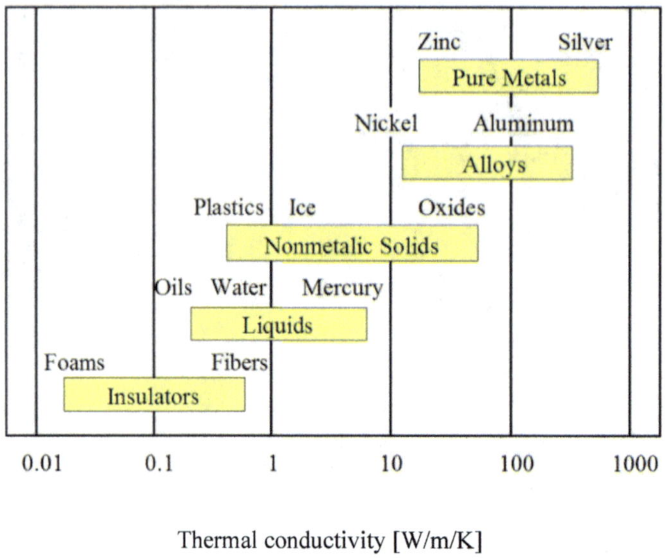

Figure 1-3: Thermal conductivity for different materials.

There are five orders of magnitude difference in thermal conductivity between conductors and insulators.

Convection

Convective heat transfer is the heat flow between a solid body and the surrounding fluid (either liquid or gas). Convective heat transfer can be either natural convection where the fluid flow is due to the variation in specific weight of a hot and cold fluid or forced convection where the fluid is forced to flow past the solid body. Therefore, natural convection requires gravity (Figure 1-4), and forced convection does not require gravity (Figure 1-5). Since fluid (air, water, steam, oil etc.) is required for heat transfer by convection, this type of heat transfer cannot happen in a vacuum. Heat exchanged by convection is expressed as:

$$Q_{CONV} = hA(T_S - T_F)$$

Where:

Q_{CONV} – Heat transferred by convection [W]

h – Convection coefficient [W/m^2/K]

A – Surface area [m^2]

T_S – Surface temperature [K]

T_F - Fluid bulk (ambient) temperature [K]

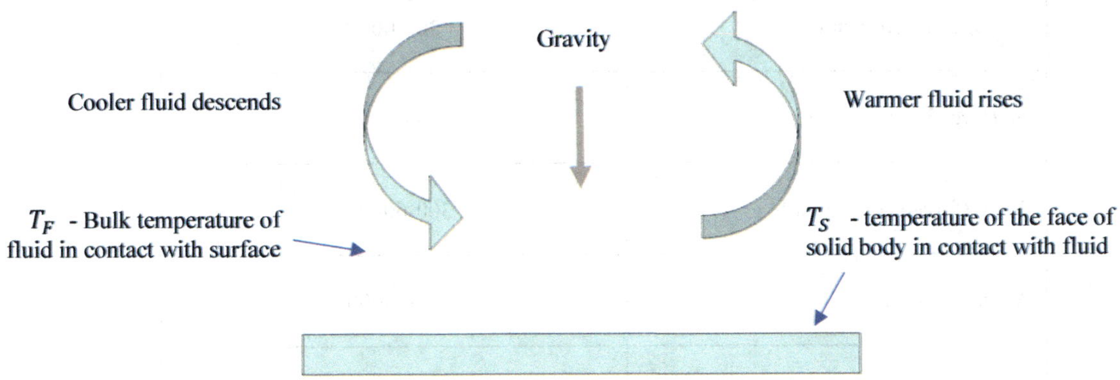

Figure 1-4: Heat transfer by natural convection.

Convective heat transfer can take place only in the presence of fluid and gravity.

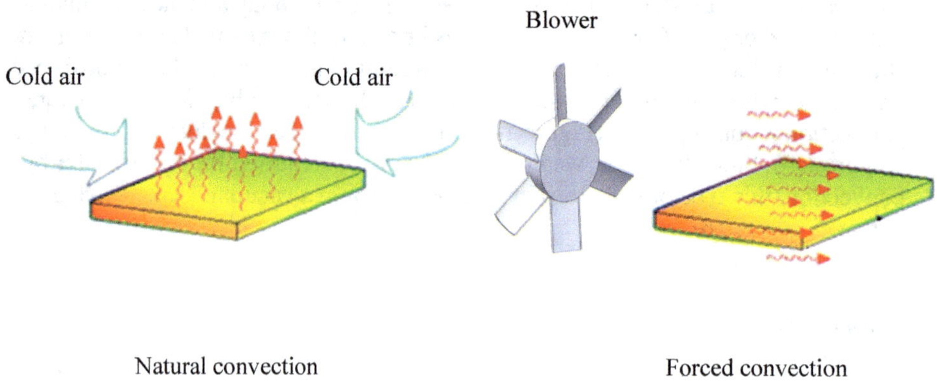

Figure 1-5: Natural convection and forced convection.

Natural convection requires gravity; forced convection does not require gravity.

The magnitude of the convection coefficient strongly depends on the medium (fluid) surrounding a solid body (Figure 1-6).

Medium	**Convection coefficient** W/m^2/K
Air (natural convection)	5-25
Air/superheated steam	20-300
Oil (forced convection)	60-1800
Water (forced convection)	300-6000
Water (boiling)	3000-60000
Steam (condensing)	60000-120000

Figure 1-6: Convection coefficient for different media.

There are five orders of magnitude difference in convection coefficients depending on media and type of convection.

Radiation

Radiative heat transfer occurs between a solid body and the ambient or between two solid bodies without presence of any medium (fluid). Radiative heat transfer may occur in a vacuum because heat flows by electromagnetic radiation. The upper limit to radiative emissive power is a Black Body radiating heat and is described by the Stefan-Boltzmann law:

$$q = \sigma T_s^4$$

Where:

q – Heat flux (heat emitted by radiation per unit of area) [W/m^2]

σ – Stefan-Boltzmann constant = 5.67037×10^{-8} [W/m^2/K^4]

T_s – Surface temperature [K]

The heat flux emitted or received by a real surface is less than that of a Black Body at the same temperature. It is given as:

$$q = \varepsilon \sigma T_s^4$$

where ε is a radiative property of a surface called emissivity. Values of ε are in the range of $0 \leq \varepsilon \leq 1$ and provide a measure of how well the surface emits or receives radiant energy in comparison to a black body. It depends on the surface material and finish. For example, a polished aluminum surface has an emissivity of about 0.05; an oxidized aluminum surface has an emissivity of 0.25. The emissivity also depends on the temperature of the face participating in heat exchange by radiation.

In heat transfer by radiation, heat may be radiated out to space by a single body; it may be exchanged between two bodies, or it may be exchanged between two bodies as well as radiated out to space (Figure 1-7).

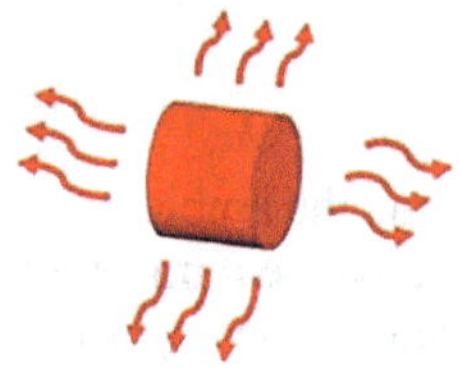

(1)
Heat radiated out to space

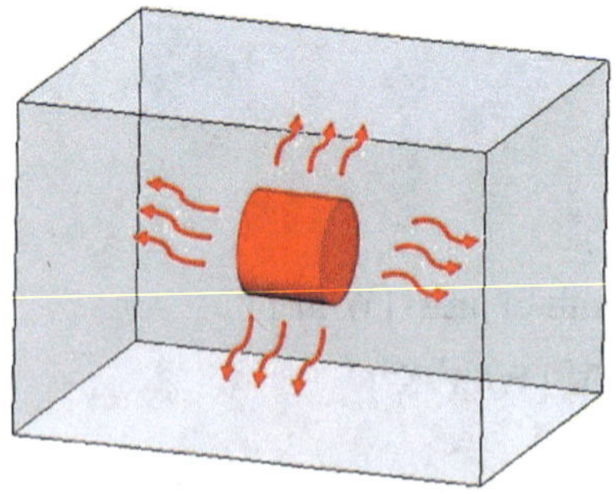

(2)
Heat radiated from one body to another body. The cylinder is fully surrounded by the box.

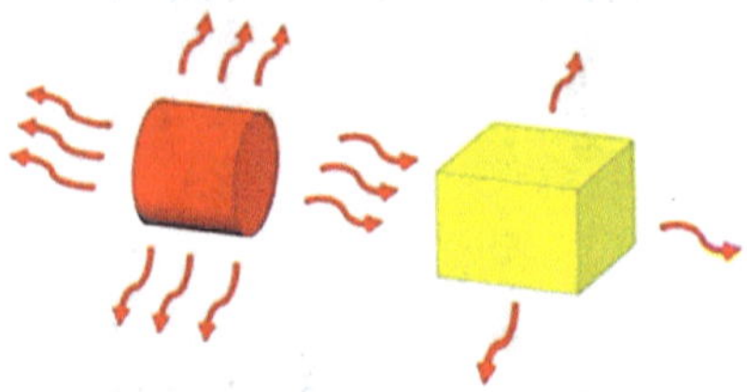

(3)
Heat radiated from one body to another body and to space.

Figure 1-7: Different cases of heat transfer by radiation.

If heat is exchanged between two bodies only and not radiated out to space, then one body must be fully enclosed by the other body (case 2). Heat gained by radiation may be radiated out again into space (case 3).

Having introduced the three mechanisms of heat transfer, it is important to clarify the scope and limitations of the tools used in this book. **SOLIDWORKS Simulation**, which is intended for the analysis of solid bodies, can model convective heat transfer only through assumed boundary conditions. In contrast, **SOLIDWORKS Flow Simulation**, a tool for analyzing fluid motion, allows convective heat transfer between a fluid and a solid to be modeled directly, without prescribing convective boundary conditions. This topic is discussed in greater detail in Chapters 14 - 19.

The next two examples show how a prescribed temperature, convection, and heat load work together to induce heat flow inside a solid body. These examples are not hands-on exercises. Hands-on exercises will start in Chapter 2.

Heat Flow Induced by Prescribed Temperatures

Just like stresses may be caused by prescribed displacement, heat flow may be induced by temperature differences defined by prescribed temperatures. Consider the model BRACKET TH with different temperatures defined on two faces as shown in Figure 1-8. Note that the temperature field establishes itself in the model, but heat flow continues due to temperature gradients. Also note that no heat escapes from the model because we have not defined any mechanism to exchange heat through any surfaces other than the two faces with prescribed temperatures. This implies that the model is perfectly insulated, except for two faces where prescribed temperatures are defined and may correspond to a situation where the bracket holding a hot pipe is mounted on a cold surface and heat escaping through faces exposed to air is negligible.

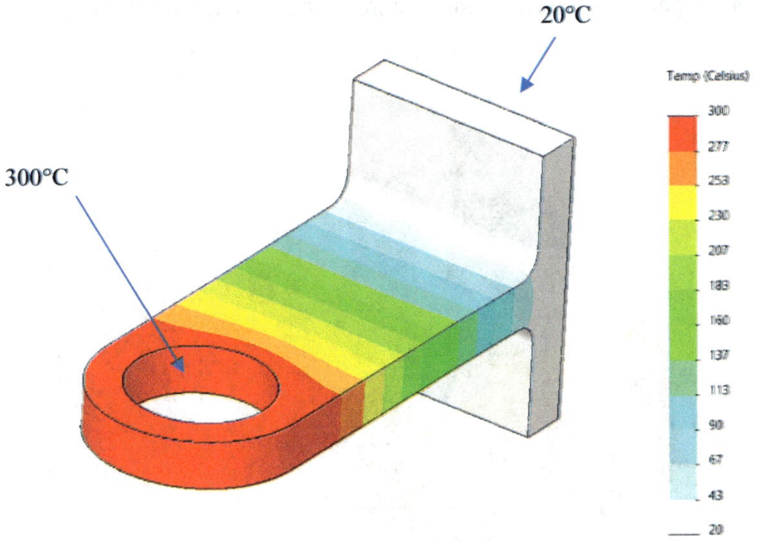

Figure 1-8: Temperature in the model where heat flow is induced by prescribed temperatures.

A temperature of 300°C is applied to the cylindrical face, and a temperature of 20°C is applied to the back face.

Plot in Figure 1-8 uses custom colors (grey substituted for blue) to improve readability. Custom colors will be used frequently to show fringe plots in this book. Custom colors may be defined in Chart Options in plot settings.

Heat flow induced by heat load and convection

Heat flow can also be induced by the applied heat load. Heat flowing through an imaginary section is also called heat flux. Total heat applied to a volume or face is called heat power. Note that since thermal analysis deals with heat flow, a mechanism for that heat flow to occur must be in place. In the heat sink problem HEAT SINK01, shown in Figure 1-9, heat enters the radiator through the base, as defined by the applied heat power which is a close analogy to force load in structural analysis. Convection coefficients [W/m^2/K], also called film coefficients, are defined for all remaining surfaces and provide the way to remove heat from the model; ambient temperature must also be defined.

In summary, heat enters the model through the base where heat power is defined and escapes the model through faces where convective boundary conditions are defined. Definition of convective boundary conditions consists of convection coefficients and ambient temperature, which is temperature of the surrounding fluid.

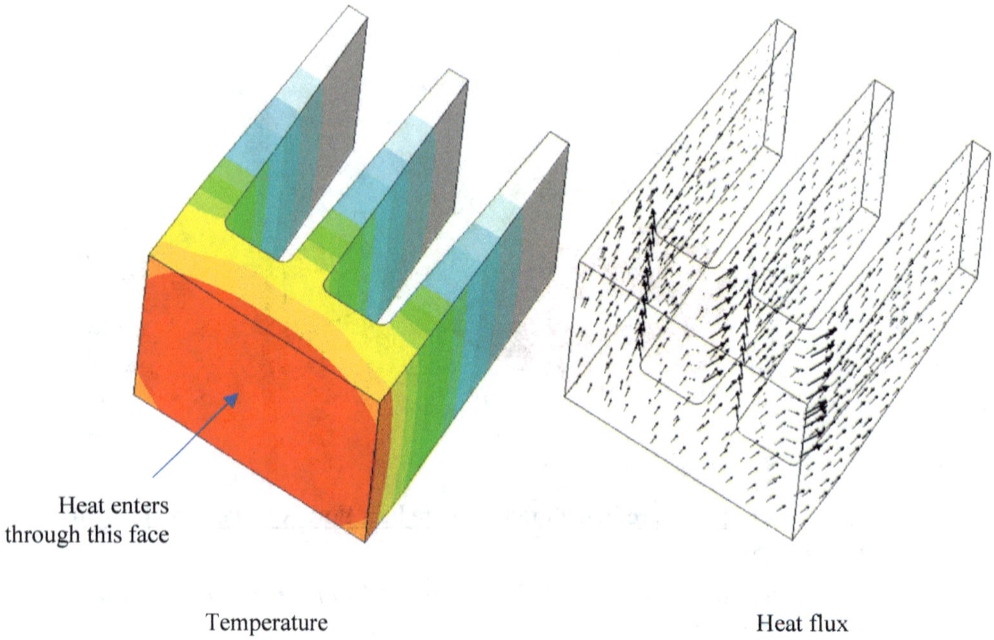

Figure 1-9: Temperature distribution and heat flux in a heat sink model.

A temperature being a scalar quantity can only be shown using a fringe plot. Heat flux is a vector quantity and can be illustrated either by a fringe plot or by a vector plot. Note that arrows "coming out" of the walls illustrate heat that escapes the model because of convection.

Convection coefficients are analogous to elastic supports offered by distributed springs. Just like supports and/or prescribed displacements are necessary to establish model equilibrium in a structural analysis problem, convection coefficients and/or prescribed temperatures are necessary to establish heat flow in a thermal analysis problem.

An attempt to run thermal analysis with heat loads but with no convection coefficients or prescribed temperatures (no mechanism to remove heat) results in an error similar to the one caused by the absence of supports in structural analysis.

Modeling considerations in thermal analysis

Symmetry boundary conditions can be used in thermal analysis based on the observation that if symmetry exists in both geometry and boundary conditions, then there is no heat flowing through a plane of symmetry. After simplifying the model to ½ in case of single symmetry or to ¼ in case of double symmetry (Figure 1-10), nothing needs to be done to surfaces exposed by cuts. No convection coefficients defined for those surfaces mean that no heat flows across them.

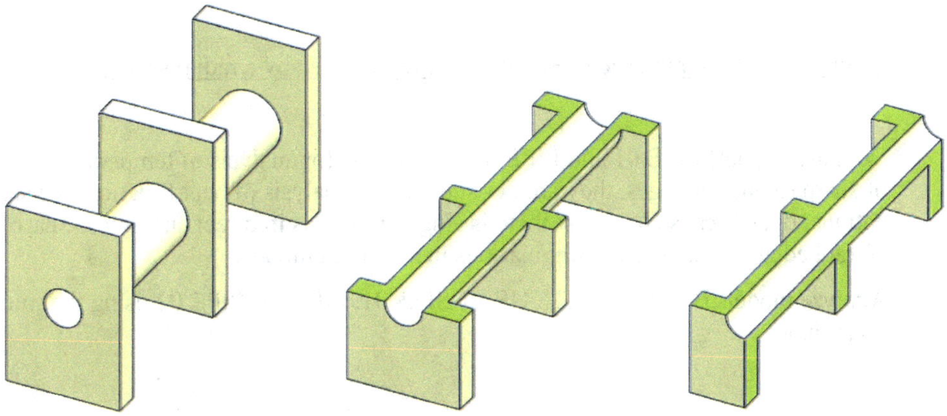

Full model ½ model ¼ model

Figure 1-10: Model PIPE 01 with double symmetry can be analyzed using ¼ of the model.

No thermal boundary conditions are applied to faces in the planes of symmetry.

Axisymmetric problems may be represented by 2D models (Figure 1-11).

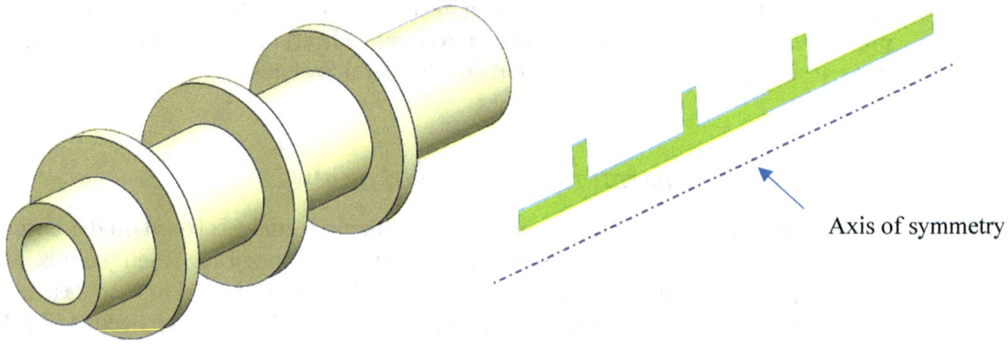

Full model Radial section

Figure 1-11: Axisymmetric model PIPE 02 represented by a radial section.

Note that models PIPE 01 and PIPE 02 are suitable for analysis of temperature, but because of sharp re-entrant edges, they are not suitable for analysis of heat flux near the sharp re-entrant edges because heat flux there is singular. This is in direct analogy to sharp re-entrant edges causing stress singularities in structural models.

Analyze models BRACKET TH, HEAT SINK01, PIPE 01, PIPE 02 using thermal input of your choice.

Let's wrap up this review with an important observation which will serve as a guide to all thermal analysis problems. In structural analysis we define a load path by defining loads and supports. In a heat transfer problem, we define a mechanism of heat transfer; we must know how heat enters the model, how it travels through the model and how it exits the model.

Types of thermal analysis

Thermal analysis may be linear or nonlinear, steady state or time dependent as shown in Figure 1-12.

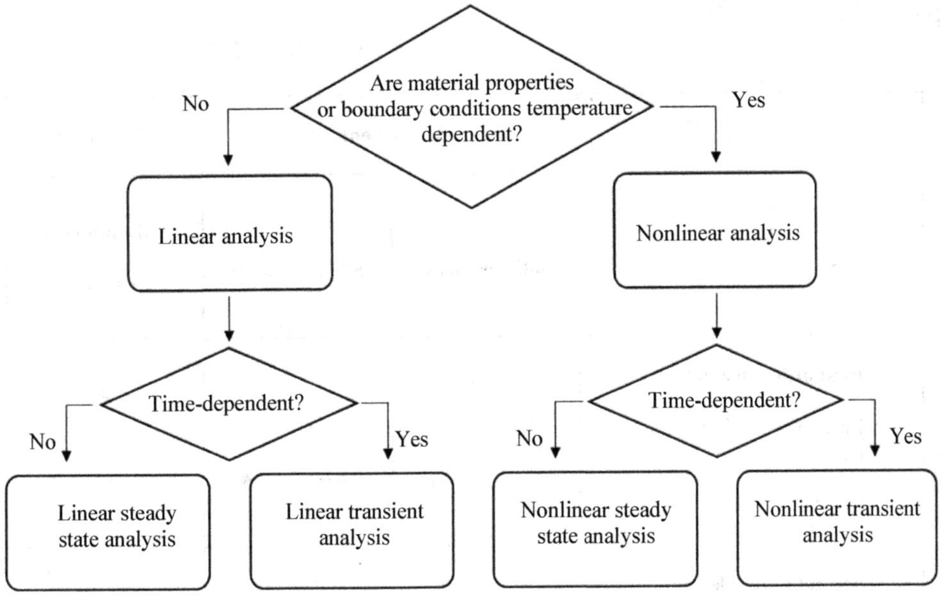

Figure 1-12: Types of thermal analyses.

In linear analysis, the conductivity matrix does not change during the solution process; in nonlinear analysis it must be modified because material properties and/or boundary conditions are temperature dependent. In steady state analysis, material conditions and boundary conditions do not change with time; in time dependent (transient) they do change.

Thermal analysis with SOLIDWORKS Simulation

SOLIDWORKS Simulation uses Finite Element Method to solve both structural and thermal problems. CAD models prepared in SOLIDWORKS are discretized (meshed) into finite elements which type depends on the type of geometry prepared in SOLIDWORKS. Solid bodies are meshed into solid elements. Surface bodies are meshed into shell elements. 2D axisymmetric and extruded models may be meshed with corresponding 2D elements. Types of finite elements, meshing techniques and other mesh specific considerations are discussed in detail in the pre-requisite text "Engineering Analysis with SOLIDWORKS Simulation."

Elements available in thermal analysis with SOLIDWORKS Simulation are shown in Figure 1-13.

	3D elements		**2D elements**
	Solid elements	**Shell elements**	**Axisymmetric** **Extruded**
First order element Linear (first order) temperature field Constant heat flux field	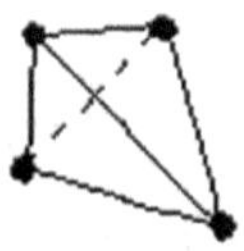	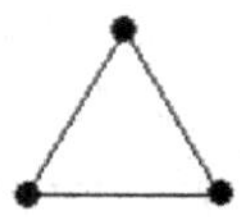	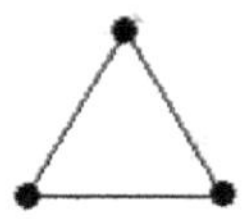
Second order element Parabolic (second order) temperature field Linear heat flux field	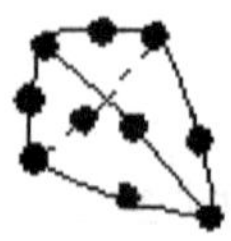	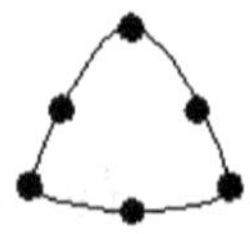	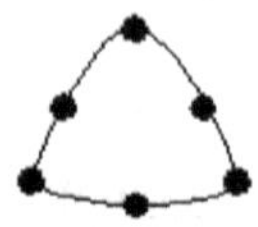

Figure 1-13: Elements available in thermal analysis with SOLIDWORKS Simulation.

Most analyses use the second order solid tetrahedral elements.

First order elements do not offer any advantages in either structural or thermal analysis and beam elements are neither applicable nor available in thermal analysis. Therefore, we are left with second order solids and second order shells to model 3D problems and second order plate elements to model 2D axisymmetric or extruded problems.

Prior to commencing work with thermal problems, make sure that **Solid Bodies** and **Surface Bodies** are visible in the SOLIDWORKS Feature Manager (Figure 1-14).

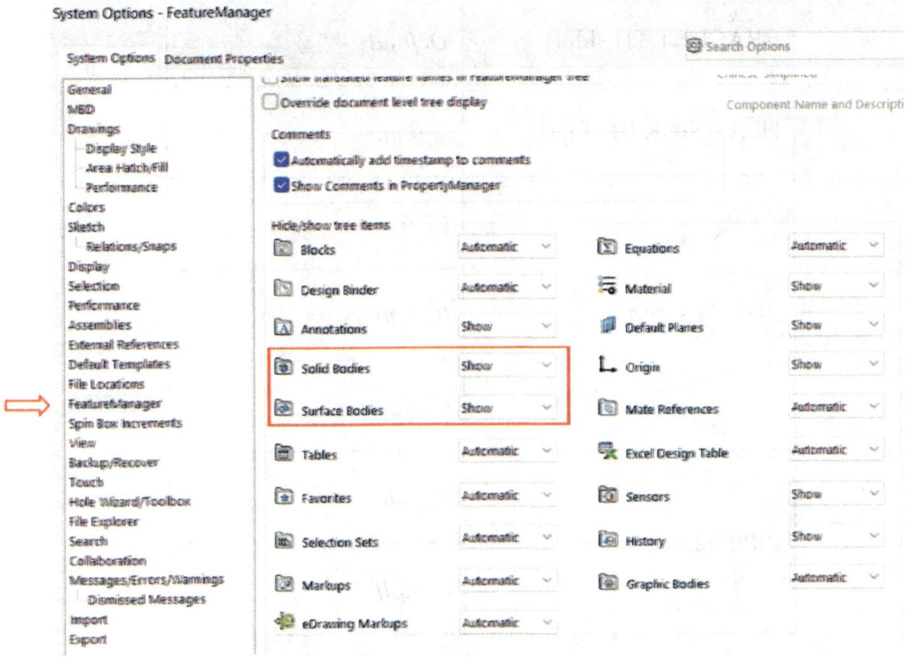

<u>Figure 1-14: Settings of Feature Manager.</u>

To facilitate working with Simulation models make Solid Bodies, Surface Bodies and Material always visible.

Models used in this chapter

Analyze these models using input data of your choice.

Model	Configurations
BRACKET TH.sldprt	*Default*
HEAT SINK 01.sldprt	*Default*
PIPE 01.sldprt	*01 full*
	02 half
	03 quarter
PIPE 02.sldprt	*01 full*
	02 half

Part 1

Heat Transfer with Finite Element Analysis

Thermal analysis using SOLIDWORKS Simulation is introduced. Heat conduction within solids is modeled directly with the finite element method, while convection is represented through boundary conditions.

The primary goal is to establish the basic workflow of thermal simulation: defining materials, applying thermal loads and boundary conditions, generating meshes, and interpreting temperature and heat-flux results. To keep the focus on fundamental modeling techniques, radiation is not yet included, and convection is introduced as a boundary condition.

These chapters provide the foundation for the rest of the book, where progressively more complete physical descriptions of heat transfer will be introduced.

2: Hollow plate

- Heat transfer by conduction
- Heat transfer by convection
- Different ways of presenting results of thermal analysis
- Convergence analysis in thermal problems
- Solid elements in heat transfer problems
- Shell elements in heat transfer problems

Project description

We will conduct thermal analysis of a simple model to study the effects of discretization error and the use of different types of elements. We start with HOLLOW PLATE TH.

Open model HOLLOW PLATE TH and review the two configurations: *01 solid* where the model is represented as a solid body and *02 shell* where the model is represented as a surface body. Use *01 solid* configuration to create a thermal study called *01 solid.* Apply the prescribed temperature boundary conditions as shown in Figure 2-1; these prescribed temperatures will induce heat flow from hot to cold.

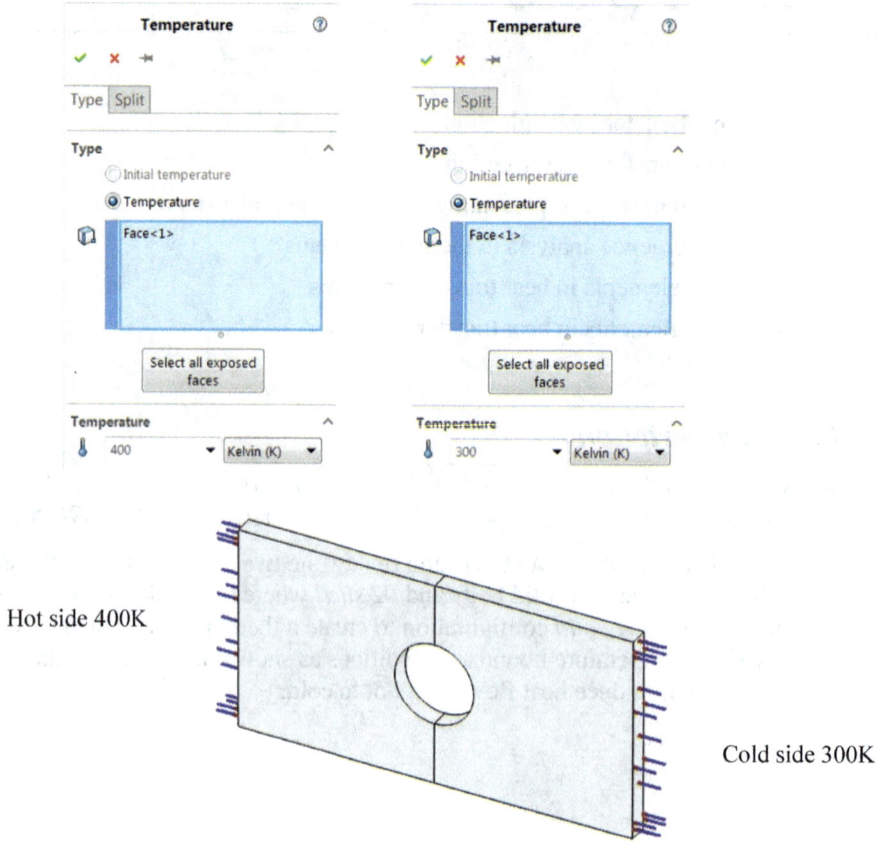

Figure 2-1: Prescribed temperatures are applied to two end faces.

No convection is defined anywhere in the model meaning that all faces are insulated except where temperature boundary conditions are defined. Split lines and split faces are used to facilitate probing of results.

Define prescribed temperature as shown in Figure 2-1. Mesh the model with a coarse mesh as shown in Figure 2-2.

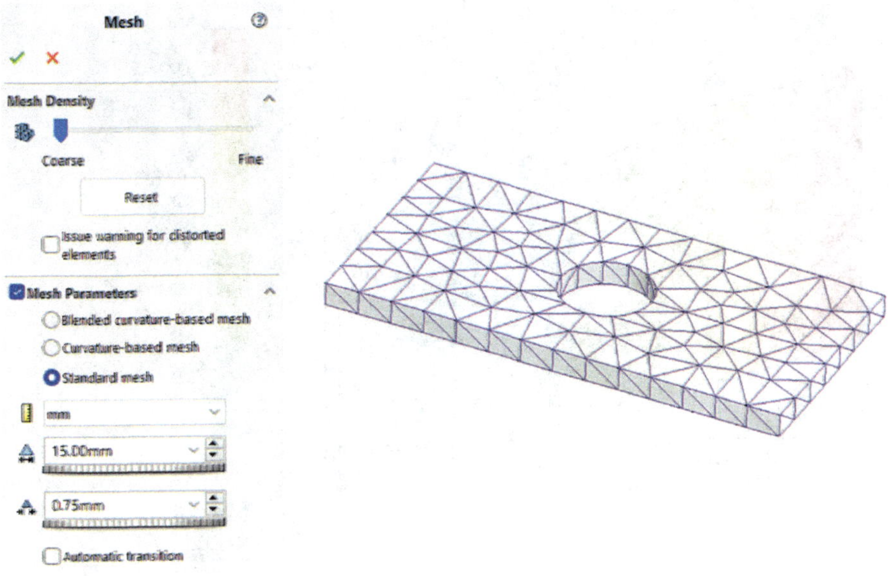

Figure 2-2: Coarse Standard mesh created with 15mm element size.

Use Standard mesh with High quality elements. This mesh is coarse; it is used as the first step in the convergence analysis.

Run the solution and create two plots: **Temperature** and **Resultant Heat Flux**, and probe results as shown in Figure 2-3 and Figure 2-4.

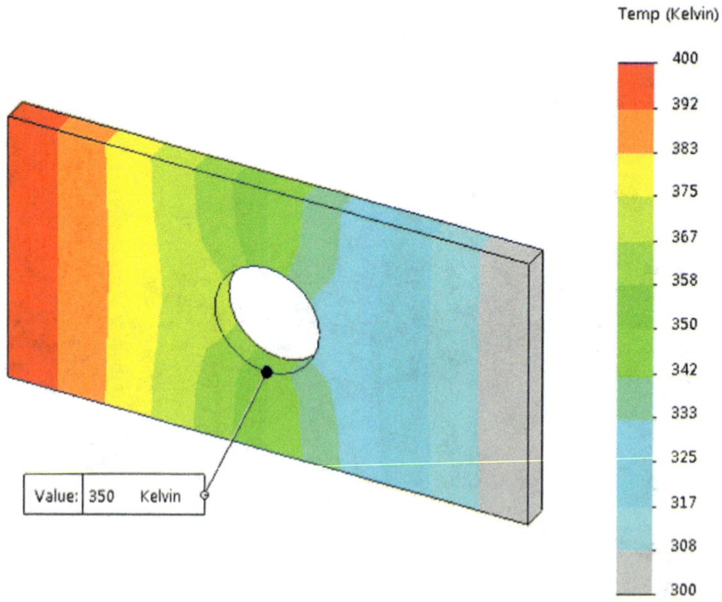

Figure 2-3: Temperature results: 350K in the probed location.

Probe at the vertex created by the split line.

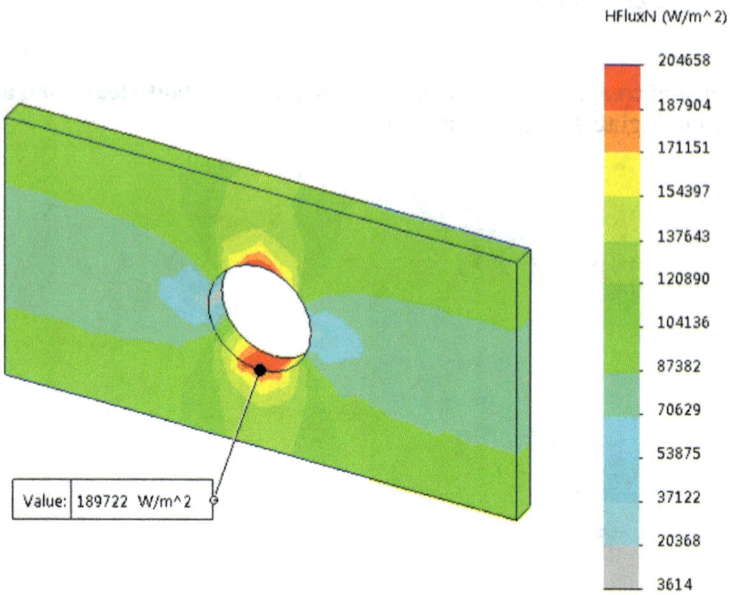

Figure 2-4: Resultant heat flux results: 189722W/m^2 in the probed location.

Probe at the vertex created by the split line. Your result may be slightly different depending on the solver and service pack used. This applies to all Simulation results presented in this book.

Repeat the analysis using a mesh of default size 5.72mm (study *02 solid*) and a fine mesh with element size 2mm (study *03 solid*). Optionally try meshing the model with 1mm element size but be prepared for a long run (study *04 solid*). Note that while temperature results are almost insensitive to mesh refinement, the maximum resultant heat flux changes with mesh refinement as shown in Figure 2-5.

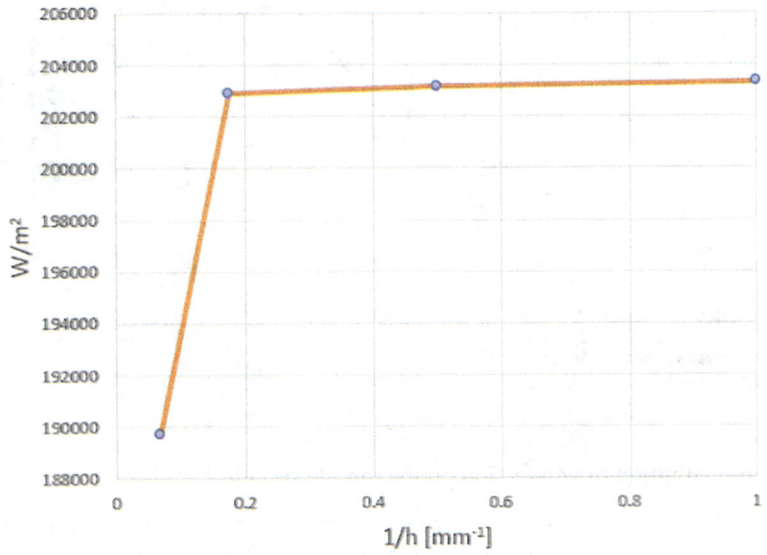

Figure 2-5: Resultant heat flux in the probed location as a function of the inverse of the element size.

The second point corresponds to default element size. Four points are connected by straight lines to visually enhance the graph.

As the graph in Figure 2-5 demonstrates, the heat flux converges to a finite value, and the default element size produces acceptable results. Every given mesh introduces artificial thermal resistance; the coarser the mesh, the larger that added resistance is, and that causes lower heat flux. This is the effect of discretization error in direct analogy to structural models where artificial stiffness is added to the model by meshing.

Copy study *02 solid* (the one with the default mesh) into study *05 solid convection.* We will use it to demonstrate convective heat transfer out of the plate. Delete prescribed temperature on the cold side. In its place, define **Convection** as shown in Figure 2-6.

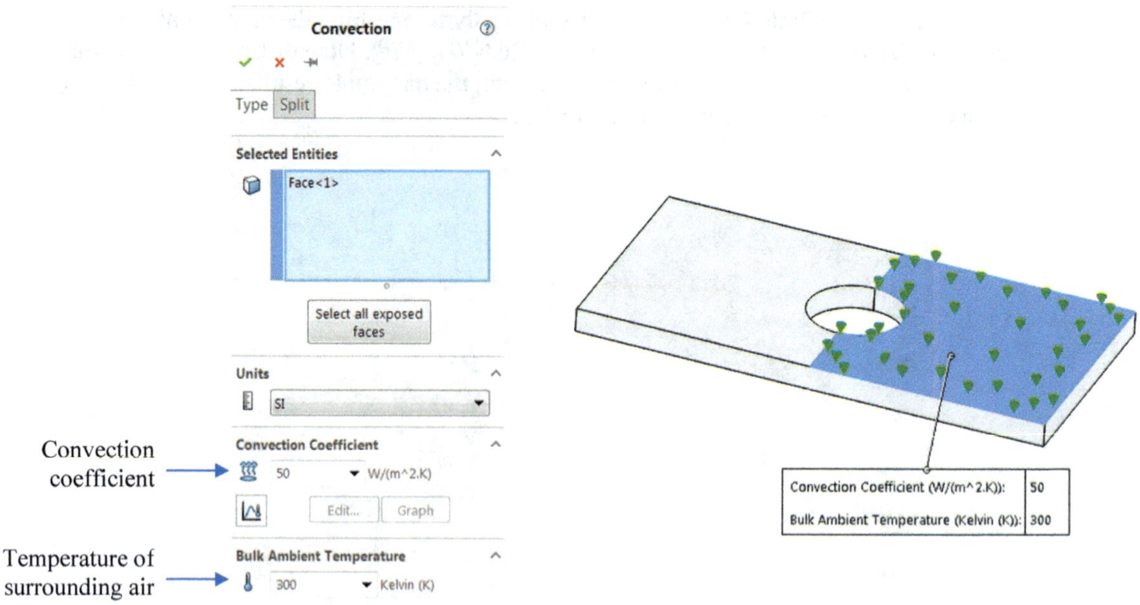

Figure 2-6: Definition of convection on the top of one side.

As always, definition of convection requires a convection coefficient and a bulk temperature, which is the temperature of the fluid surrounding the model.

A convection coefficient of 50W/m^2/K models free convection with air as medium.

Use a default element size to mesh the model.

Run the solution of study *05 solid convection* and review results shown in Figure 2-7.

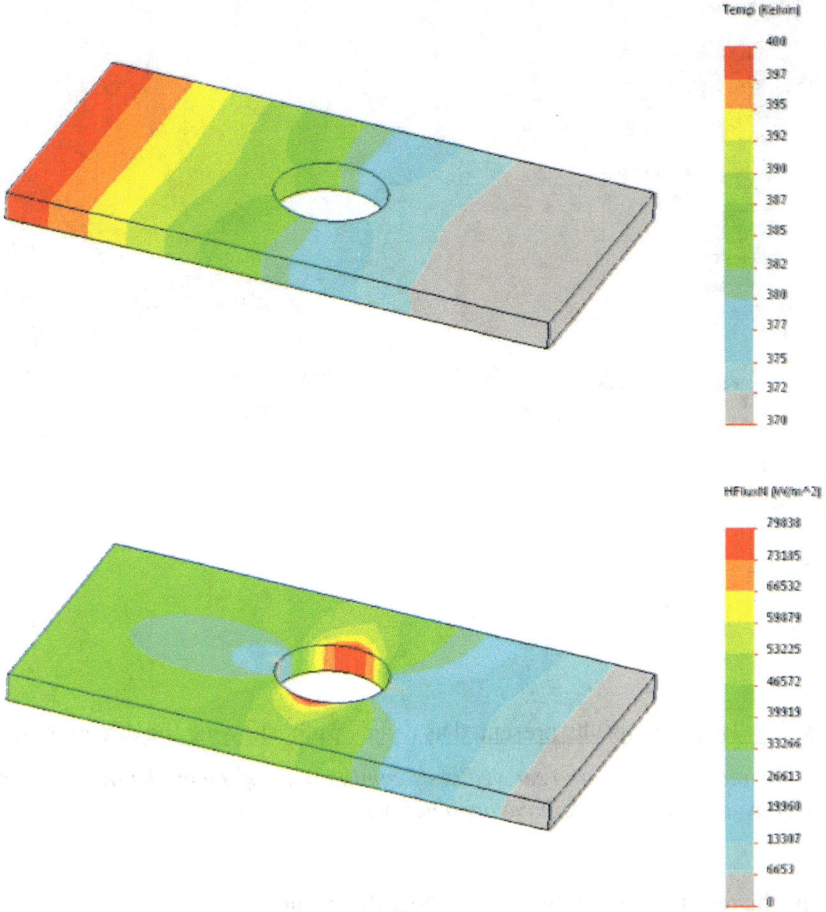

Figure 2-7: Temperature and heat flux results in the presence of convection.

Temperature is a scalar value; it can be plotted only using a fringe plot as shown above. Heat flux is a vector value; presenting it as a fringe plot shows only the magnitude but not the direction of heat flow.

Modify the heat flux plot into a vector plot as shown in Figure 2-8.

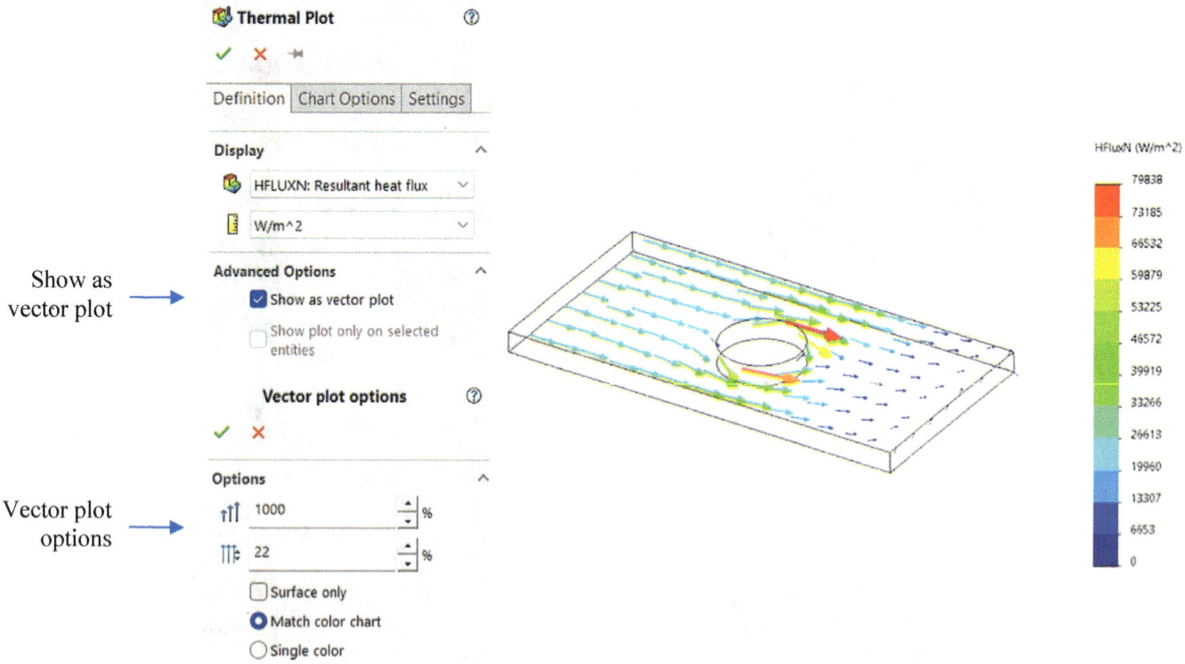

Figure 2-8: Heat flux results presented as a vector plot showing the direction of heat flow.

Rotate the plot as required to see vectors "coming out" of the model through the face where convection conditions have been defined.

Review the results of other studies with heat flux results shown as a vector plot.

Having demonstrated analogies between the convergence process in structural and thermal analyses using solid elements, we will now study the use of shell elements in thermal analysis.

Stay with model HOLLOW PLATE TH but switch to *02 surface* configuration. Create a thermal study *06 surface convection*. Exclude the Solid Body from analysis and define the surface thickness as shown in Figure 2-9.

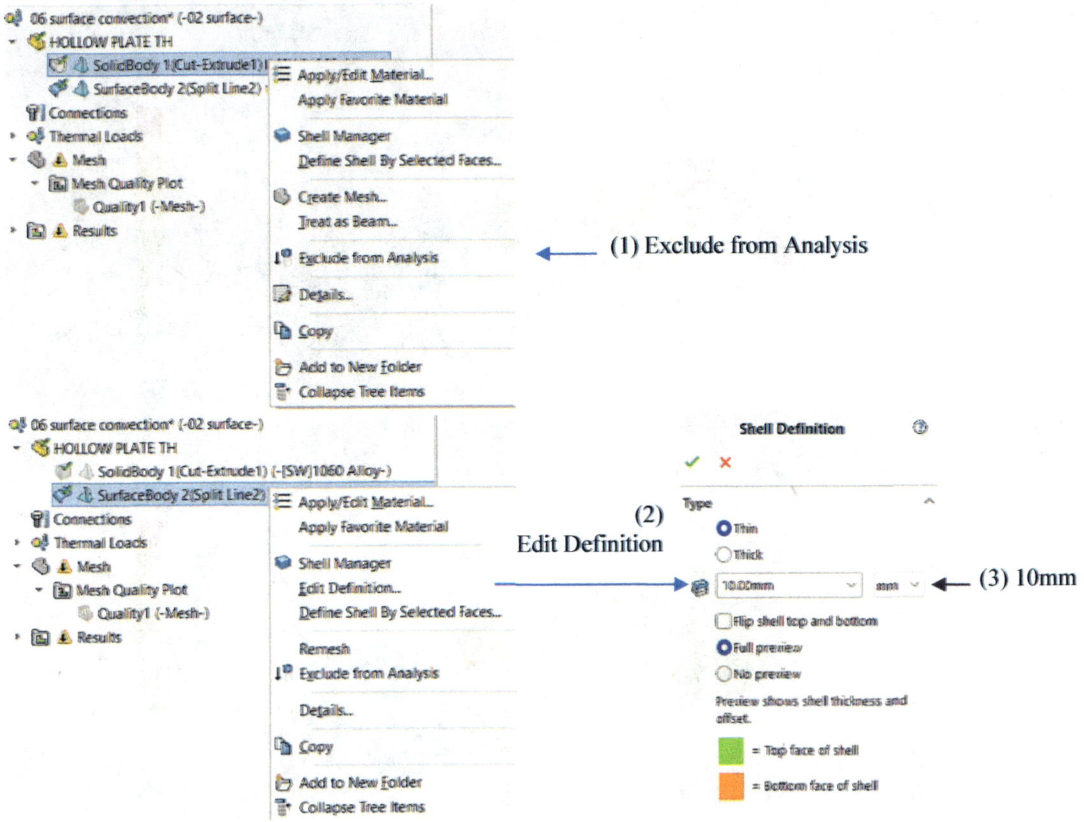

Figure 2-9: Definition of surface thickness.

Even though the Solid Body is invisible, it needs to be excluded from the analysis.

The definition of thickness (Figure 2-9) is required because thickness is not specified in the surface model.

Apply thermal boundary conditions as in study *05 solid convection*: a prescribed temperature of 400K on the hot side (the edge) and convection to the side face as shown in Figure 2-6. Use the default element size to mesh the model into shell elements, obtain a solution and present **Temperature** and **Heat Flux** results using fringe plots (Figure 2-10).

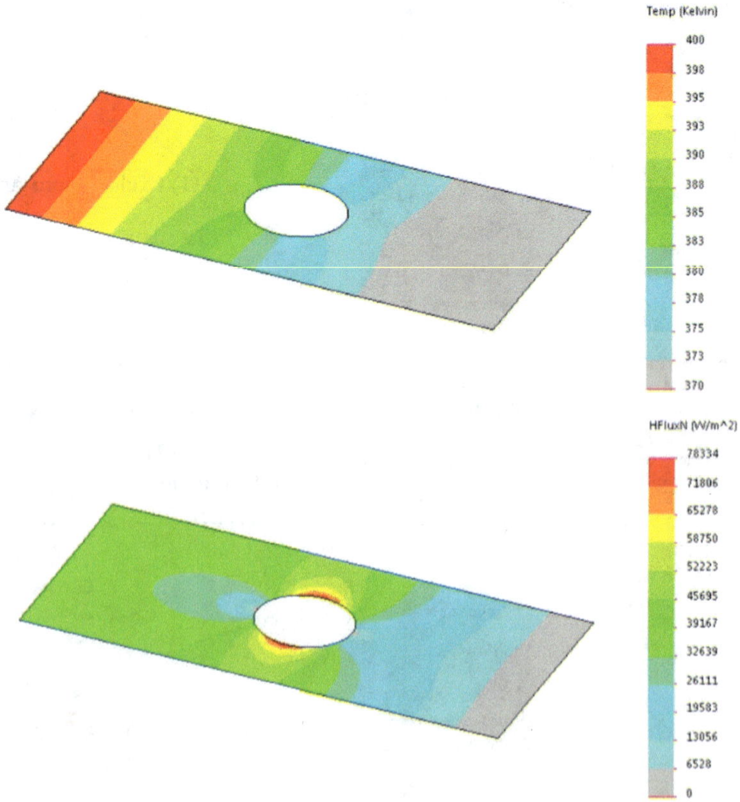

Figure 2-10: Temperature and heat flux results in the shell element model presented as fringe plots.

These results are very similar to the results produced by the solid element model.

While fringe plots show little difference between results obtained from the solid element and shell element models, vector plots do show important differences (Figure 2-11).

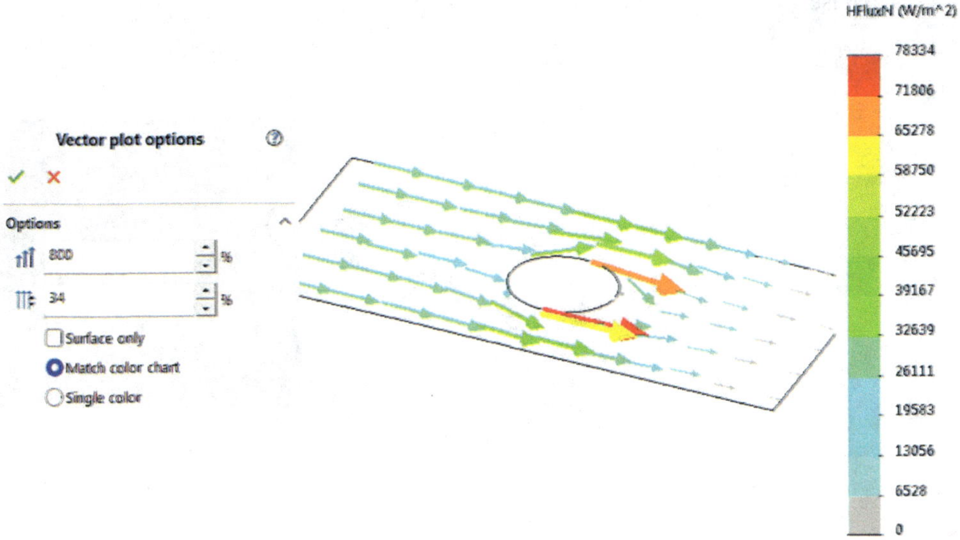

Figure 2-11: Heat flux results in the shell element model presented using vector plot.

Rotate the plot to see that heat flux vectors do not "come out" of the model. They just "face-out".

In structural analysis, shell elements differentiate between top and bottom and different stress results are read on opposite sides. In thermal analysis, shell elements do not differentiate between sides. Therefore, the shell element model cannot show to which side heat escapes from the model. As shown in Figure 2-11, heat flux vectors diminish without "coming out" of the model.

Since in thermal analysis shell elements do not differentiate between sides, you cannot apply different thermal boundary conditions to two sides of a face meshed with shell elements.

Additional practice models

To reinforce the concepts presented in this chapter, repeat the analysis using the additional practice models. Define project input data following the approach used in the main exercise.

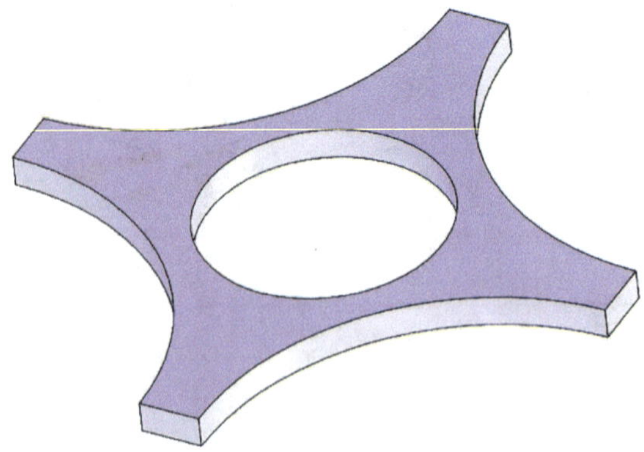

Figure 2-12: CROSS part model.

Figure 2-13: WAVE part model.

Models in this chapter

Model	**Configuration**	**Study Name**	**Study Type**
HOLLOW PLATE TH.sldprt	*01 solid*	*01 solid*	Thermal
		02 solid	Thermal
		03 solid	Thermal
		04 solid	Thermal
		05 solid convection	Thermal
	02 surface	*06 surface convection*	Thermal
CROSS.sldprt	Additional practice model		
WAVE.sldprt	Additional practice model		

Notes:

3: L bracket

- Heat transfer by conduction
- Use of 2D simplification
- Singularities in thermal problems

Project description

We will conduct a thermal analysis of a simple model to study heat flux singularities. Demonstration of heat flux singularities requires the use of very small elements, consequently models are large and expensive to solve. However, our model lends itself toward a 2D representation. Using 2D thermal elements, we will demonstrate a heat flux singularity at a fraction of the computational effort that would be required if a 3D analysis were performed.

Open model L BRACKET TH shown in Figure 3-1; use *01 sharp edge* configuration.

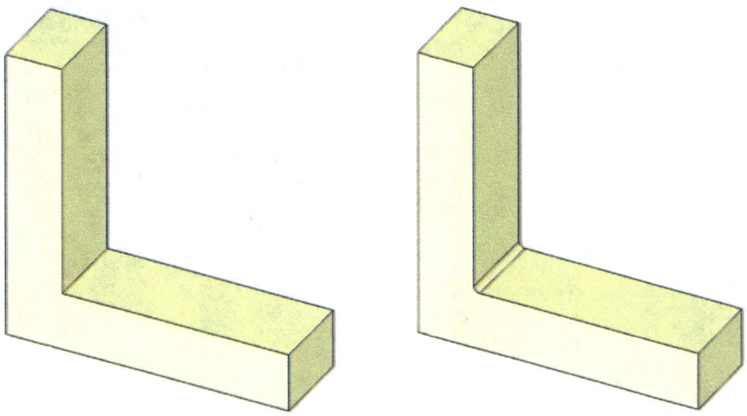

Configuration *01 sharp edge*

Configuration *02 round edge*

Figure 3-1: Model L BRACKET TH has two configurations.

Heat flux singularities are demonstrated in 01 sharp edge configuration.

Create thermal study *01 sharp* using 2D Simplification (Figure 3-2).

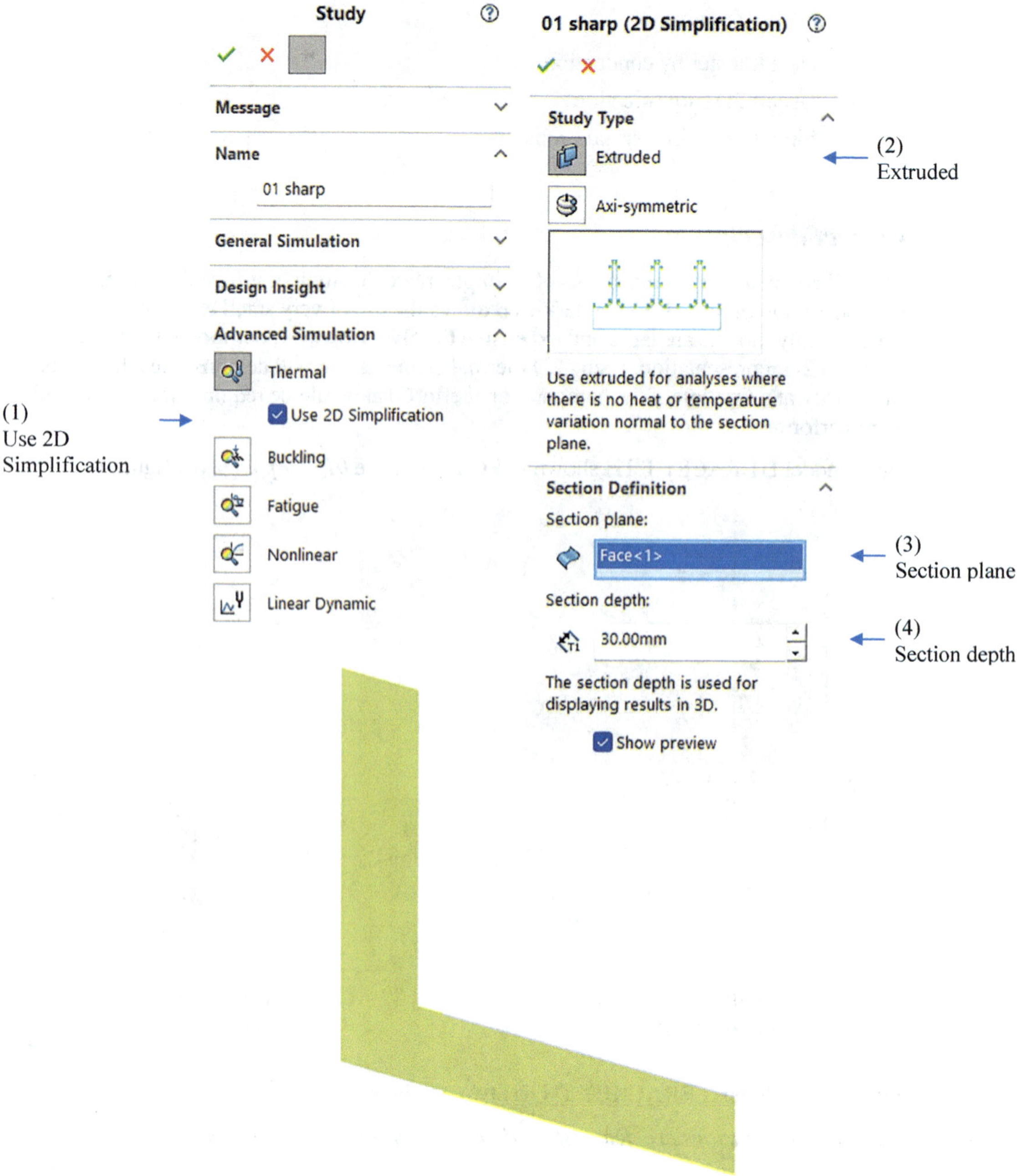

Figure 3-2: Model L BRACKET TH modeled using 2D simplification.

The side face is the section plane. Section depth 30mm is the thickness of 3D model.

To demonstrate the heat flux singularity, we must induce heat flow in the model. Here, we define boundary conditions in the form of prescribed temperatures (Figure 3-3).

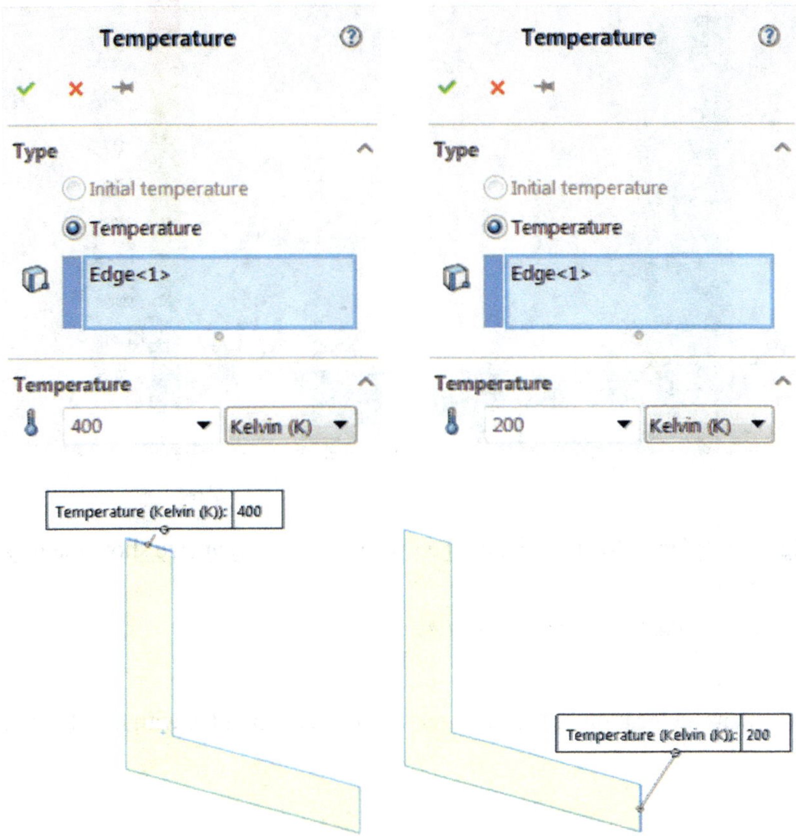

Figure 3-3: Definition of prescribed temperatures in 2D model.

The temperature 400K is defined on the top horizontal edge; the temperature of 200K is defined on the right vertical edge.

Mesh the model with an element size of 2mm, run the solution and display a resultant **Heat Flux** plot (Figure 3-4).

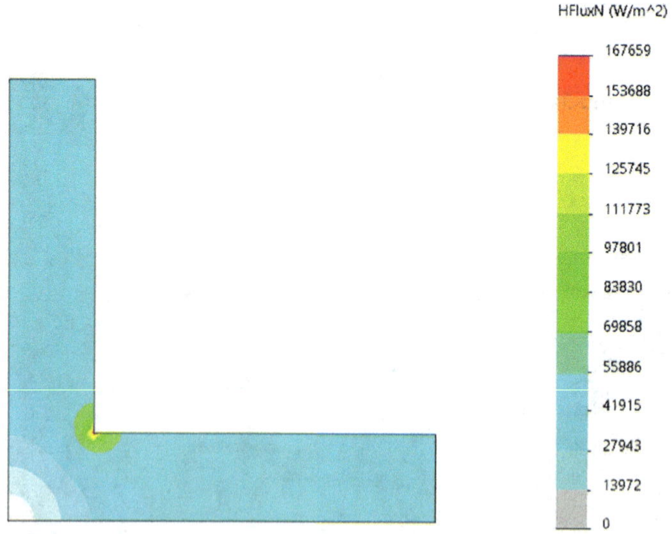

Figure 3-4: Heat flux results obtained with 2mm element size show the maximum heat flux 168kW/m^2.

Review this plot using vector display.

Note that the location of the maximum heat flux coincides with the sharp corner.

Copy study *01 sharp* into study *02 sharp* and apply global mesh refinement with element size 1mm. Then, execute two more global mesh refinements: study *03 sharp* with element size 0.5mm and *04 sharp* with element size 0.25mm.

Collect the maximum Heat Flux results from four studies and present a summary of results (Figure 3-5).

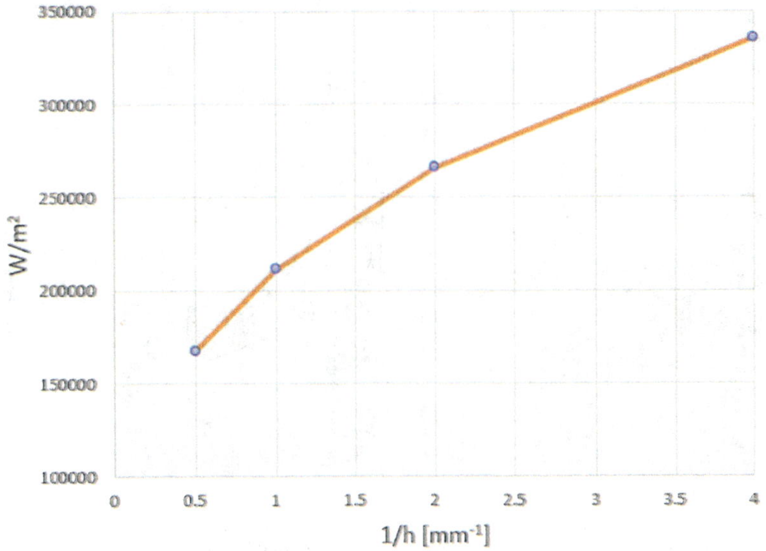

Figure 3-5: Maximum heat flux as a function of the inverse of the element size h.

Four points are connected by straight lines to visually enhance the graph.

The summary of results presented in Figure 3-5 demonstrates divergence of Heat Flux results in the presence of a sharp corner. This is in direct analogy to divergence of stresses in sharp corners in 2D models or sharp edges in 3D models.

Repeat the analysis using configuration *02 round* edge to see convergence of heat flux results.

Additional practice model

To reinforce the concepts presented in this chapter, repeat the analysis using the additional practice models. Define project input data following the approach used in the main exercise.

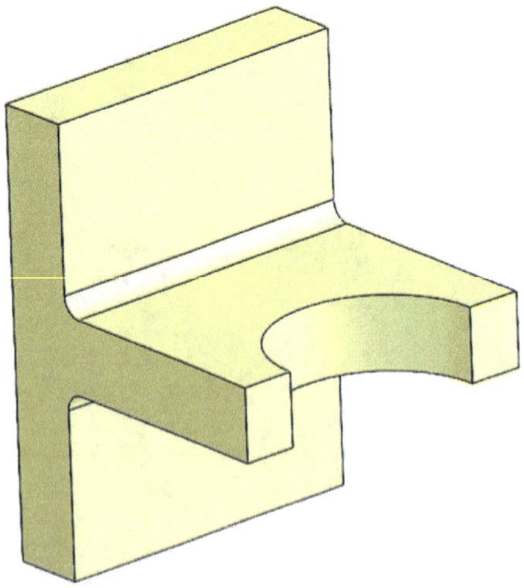

Configuration *01 fillet*

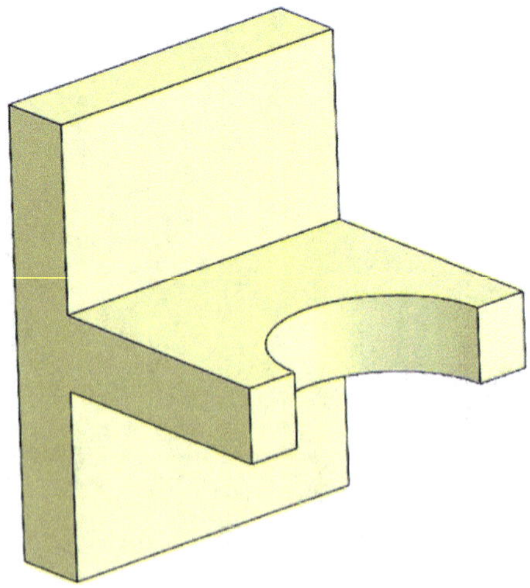

Configuration *02 no fillet*

Figure 3-6: BRACKET 10 part model.

This model has two configurations.

Models in this chapter

	Configuration	Study Name	Study Type
L BRACKET TH.sldprt	*01 sharp edge*	*01 sharp*	Thermal
		02 sharp	Thermal
		03 sharp	Thermal
		04 sharp	Thermal
	02 round edge		
BRACKET 10.sldprt	Additional practice model		

Notes:

4: Round bar

- Heat transfer by conduction
- Thermal conductivity
- Heat transfer by convection
- Convective boundary conditions
- Thermal resistance
- Prescribed temperature boundary conditions
- Heat power
- Heat flux

Project description

A round steel rod is represented by STEEL ROD part model; it has one end in boiling water at 100°C and the other end in melting ice at 0°C. The cylindrical face is insulated; no heat is exchanged through that face (Figure 4-1).

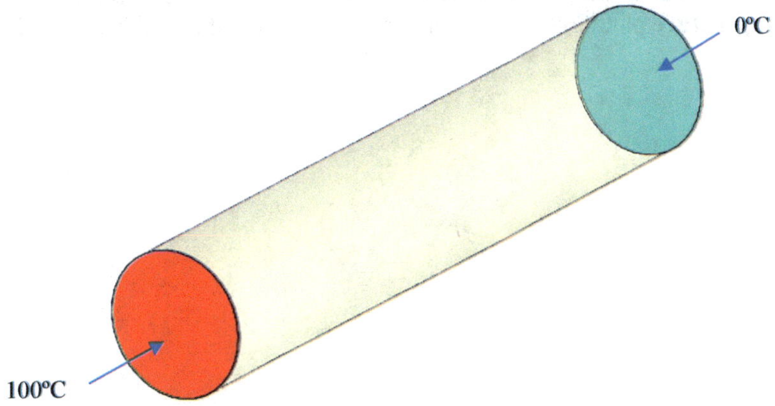

Figure 4-1: STEEL ROD model with prescribed temperatures on both ends.

The model is shown in a transparent view. The cylindrical face is insulated; no boundary conditions are defined on that face. Prescribed temperatures are defined on the end faces.

Our objective is to find the total heat transferred from the hot to the cold side. Conduction is the only heat transfer mechanism present in the model.

Create a thermal study *01 conduction* and define prescribed temperatures on both end faces (Figure 4-2).

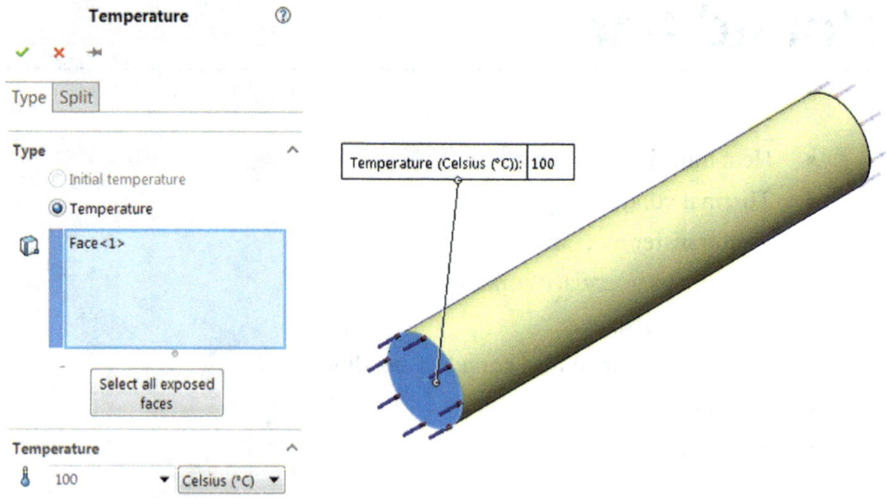

Figure 4-2: Prescribed temperature of 100°C defined on the hot side of the rod.

Define a prescribed temperature of 0°C on the other side.

Obtain a solution using a Standard mesh with default element size and review the **Temperature** plot. Follow steps in Figure 4-3 to find the total heat traveling through the rod.

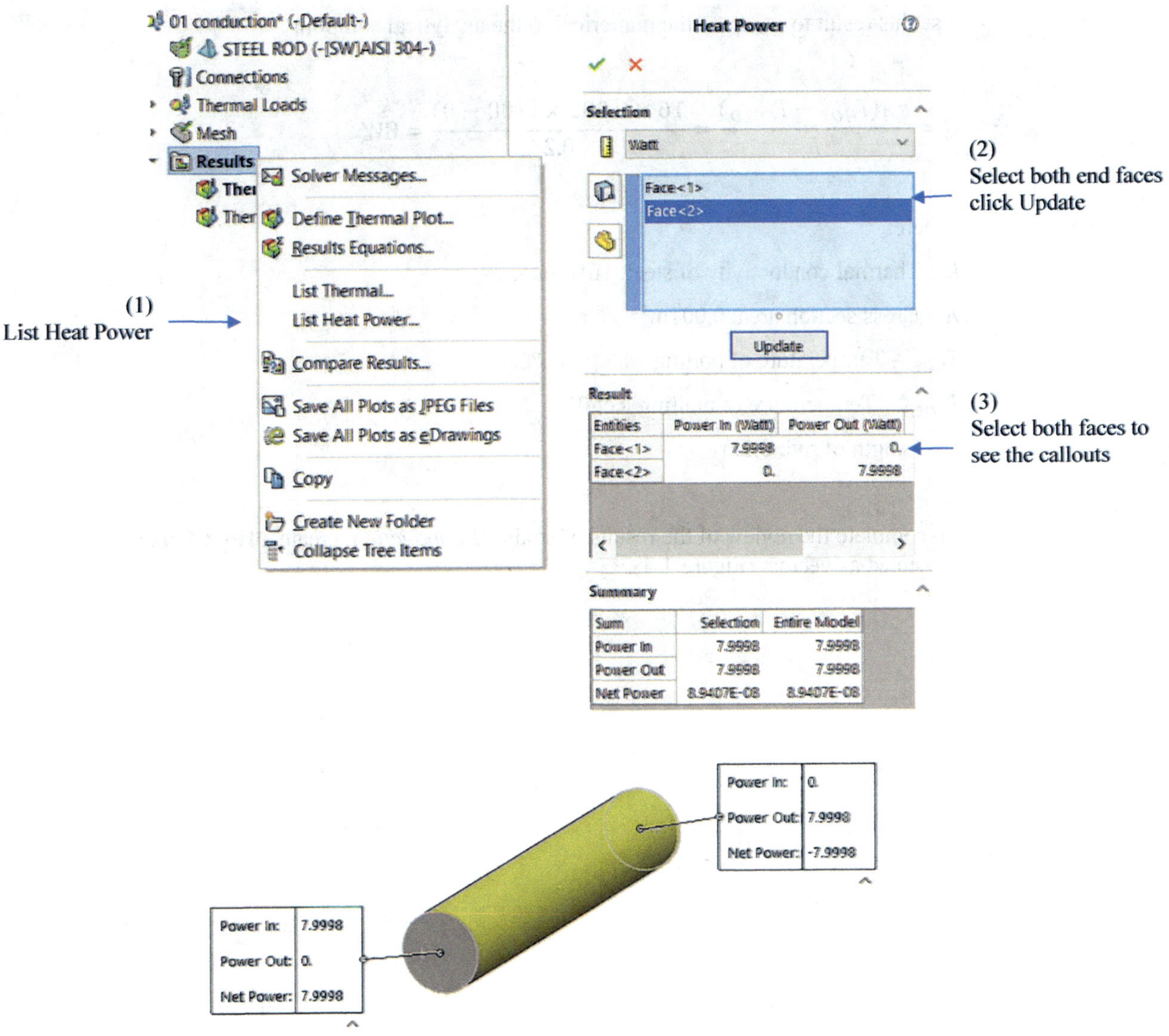

Figure 4-3: Listing Heat Power.

Heat power entering the model is +8W; heat power exiting the model is -8W.

Use this result to compare the numerical to the analytical solution:

$$Q = \frac{kA(T_{HOT} - T_{COLD})}{L} = \frac{16 \times 0.001 \times (100 - 0)}{0.2} = 8W$$

Where:

k – Thermal conductivity of steel: 16W/m/K

A – Cross section area: 0.001m^3

T_{HOT} – Temperature of boiling water: 100°C

T_{COLD} – Temperature of melting ice: 0°C

L – Length of rod: 0.2m

To complete the review of the results of study *01 conduction*, create a **Heat Flux** plot presented as vectors (Figure 4-4).

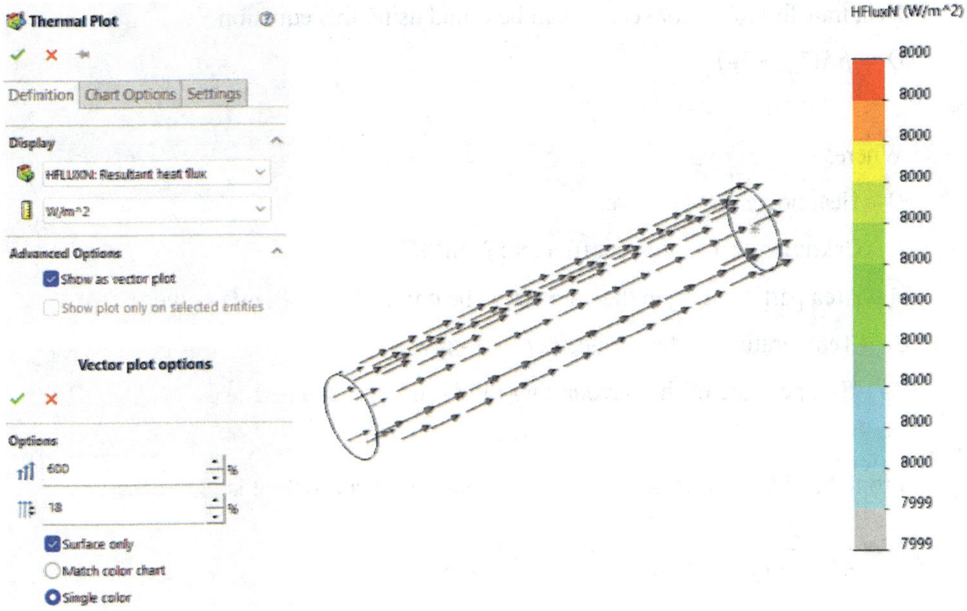

Figure 4-4: The resultant heat flux plot using vector display.

Heat flux is uniform throughout the model as shown by the numbers on the color bar. The only reason for minute differences is a discretization error introduced by meshing.

Next, we introduce heat transfer through convection. Copy *study 01 conduction* into *02 convection* and delete the prescribed temperature on the cold side. We want to replace this prescribed temperature boundary condition with a convection boundary condition that will give the same temperature distribution along the length of the rod and the same heat flow 8W. What should be the convection coefficient?

First, let us consider what ambient temperature should be defined. We want the cold end of the rod to be at 0°C (273K). If we defined the ambient temperature equal to the previously used prescribed temperature 0°C (273K), then the convection coefficient would have to be infinitely large. The ambient temperature must be lower than 0°C. The lower the ambient temperature, the lower the required convection coefficient will be while 8W of heat power travels through the rod. Let us assume the ambient temperature is -10 °C.

Heat transferred by convection can be found using this equation:

$$Q = hA(T_S - T_F)$$

Where:

Q – Heat power (8W) - given

h – Unknown convection coefficient [W/m^2/K]

A – Area participating in the convective heat transfer (0.001m^2) - given

T_S – Temperature of the surface (273 K) - given

T_F – Temperature of the surrounding fluid (263K) - assumed

From the above equation, the required convection coefficient is:

$$h = \frac{Q}{A(T_S - T_F)} = \frac{8}{0.001 \times 10} = 800 \frac{W}{m^2K}$$

Using this result, define the convection coefficient as shown in Figure 4-5.

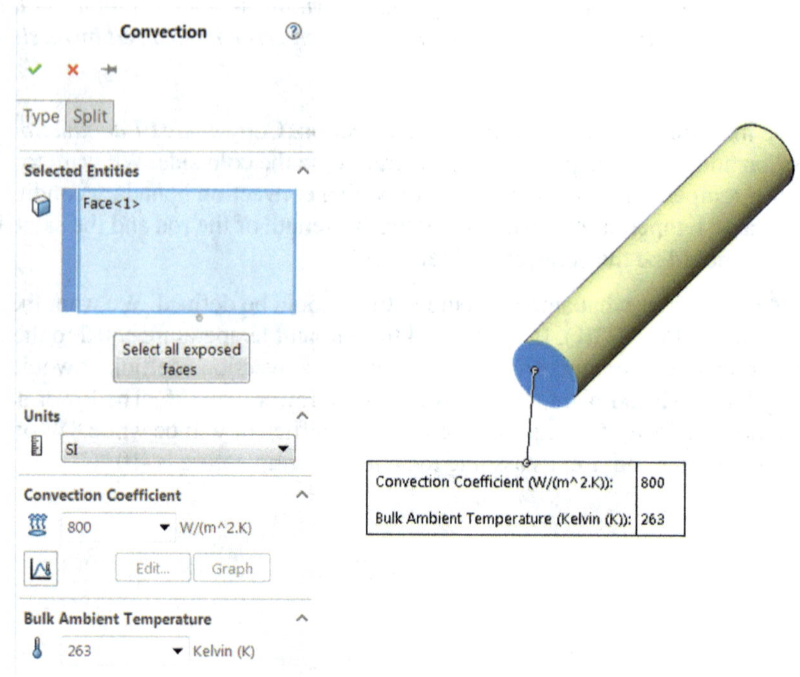

Figure 4-5: Convective boundary conditions on the cold side.

The convection coefficient replaces the previously used prescribed temperature boundary condition. Keep the prescribed temperature 100°C on the opposite side.

Obtain the solution and review the temperature plot shown in Figure 4-6.

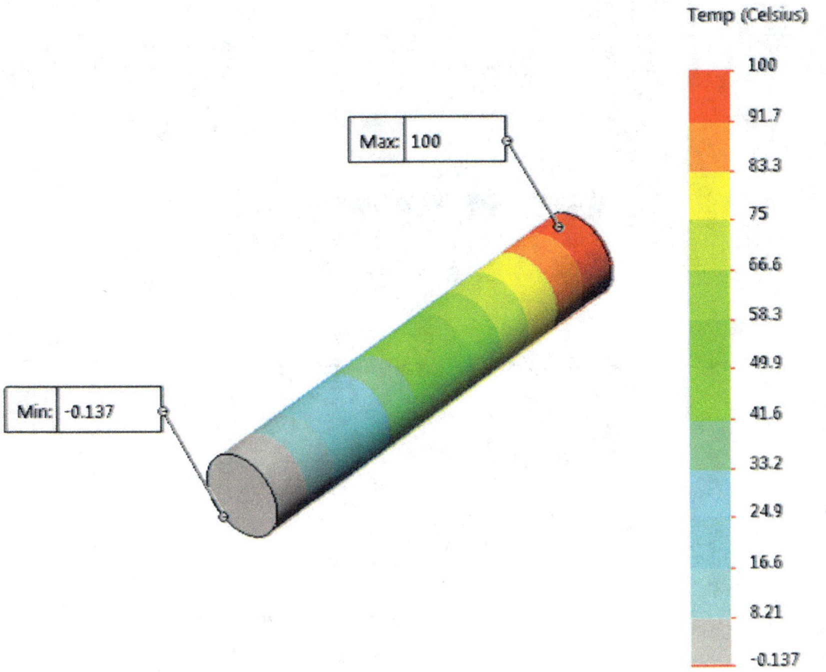

Figure 4-6: Temperature plot; the callouts indicate the minimum and the maximum temperature in the rod.

The maximum temperature is equal to the prescribed temperature of 100°C; the minimum temperature is close to 0°C.

Note a linear distribution of temperature along the length of the rod; this is because no heat is exchanged through the cylindrical face.

Find the heat power as shown in Figure 4-7.

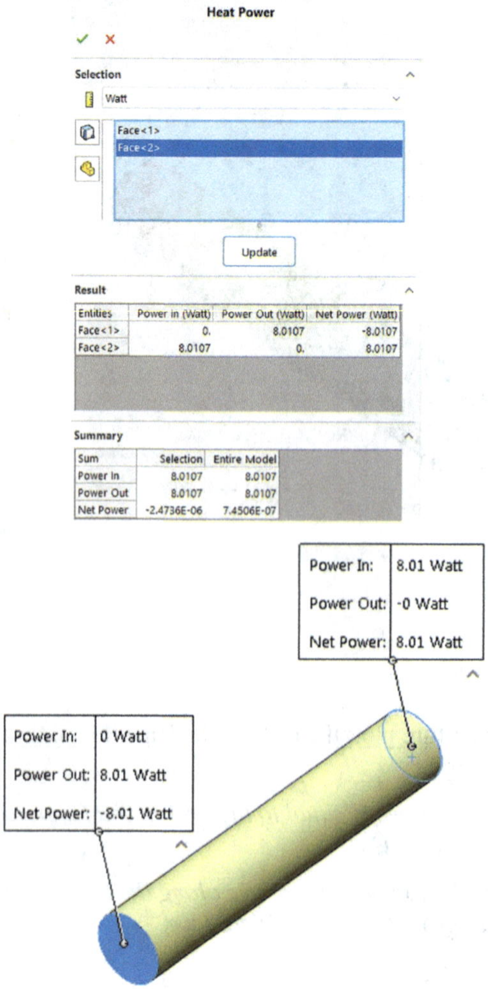

Figure 4-7: Heat power in model with prescribed temperature on the hot side and convection on the cold side.

Compare this to the results shown in Figure 4-3.

As Figure 4-6 shows, the convection coefficient of $800\text{W/m}^2\text{/K}$ combined with the temperature of surrounding fluid -10°C (263K) is equivalent to the prescribed temperature of 273K.

Open assembly TWO RODS; the assembly consists of two identical Copper rods 100mm long glued by a layer of epoxy resin. The thickness of the glue is 0.5mm (Figure 4-8).

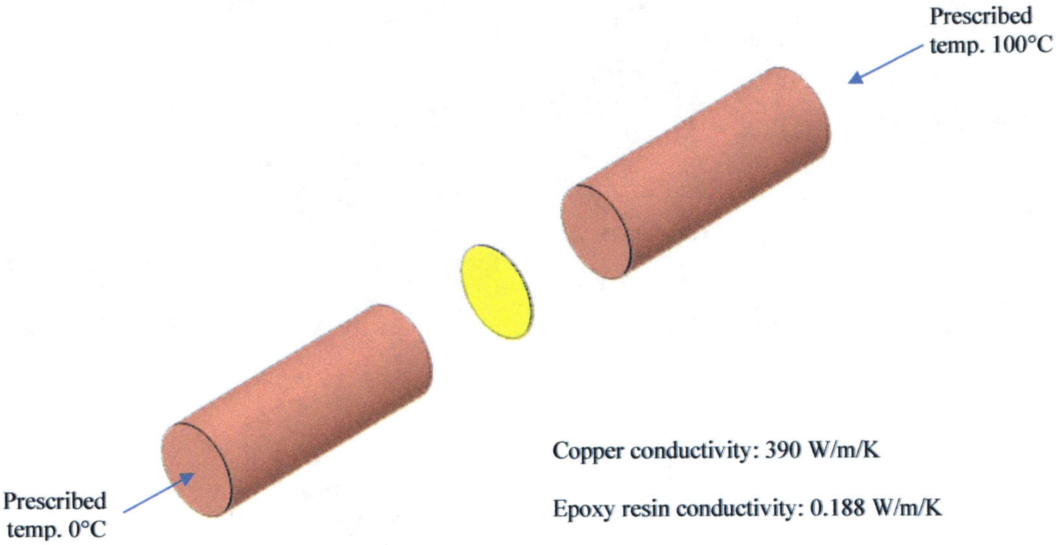

Figure 4-8: TWO RODS model has two copper rods glued by epoxy glue. Prescribed temperatures on both end and material conductivities are shown.

The rod material (copper) and glue material (epoxy resin) have vastly different thermal conductivities. Assembly is shown in an exploded view.

Our objective here is to study the effect of thermal resistance caused by the layer of epoxy. Even though the layer of epoxy is very thin, it has a major effect on the heat transfer through the assembly because of its low thermal conductivity. The thinness of the epoxy layer will cause significant meshing difficulties.

Use the assembly in *01 glue* configuration and create a thermal study called *01 glue.* To ensure correct aspect ratio of elements meshing the glue layer, apply a **Mesh Control** to the glue component as shown in Figure 4-9.

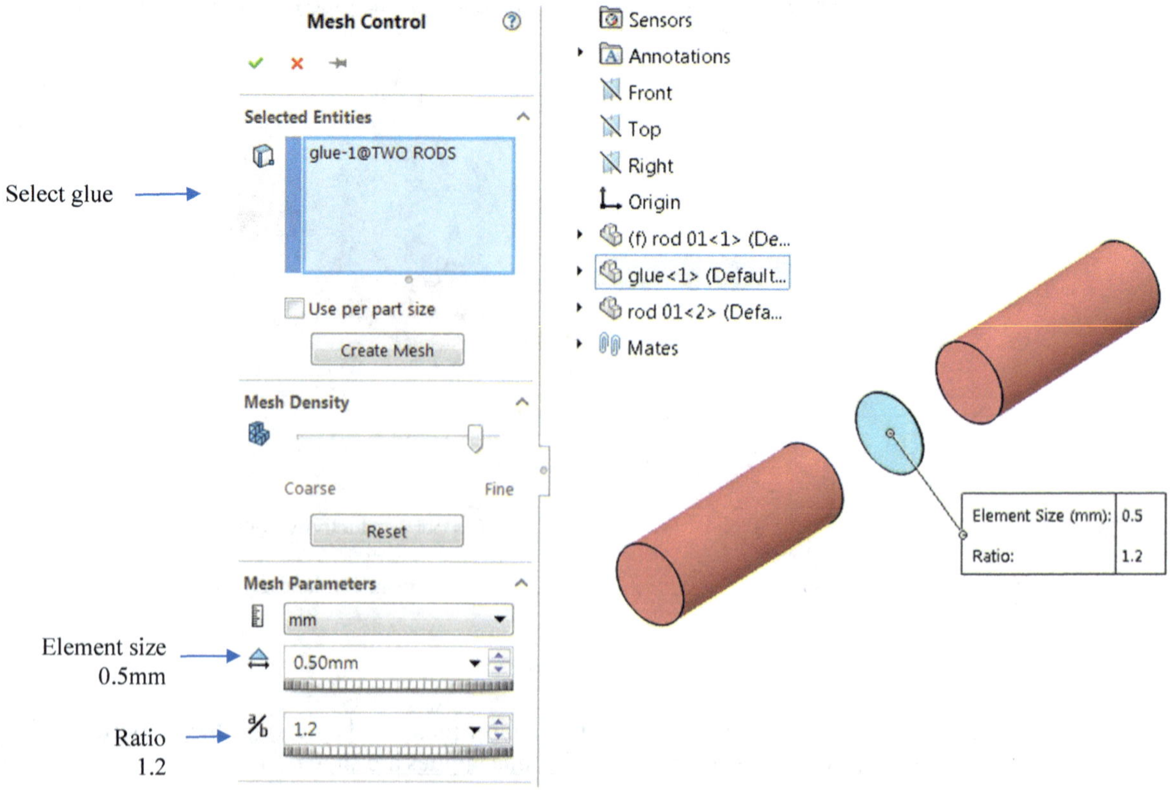

Figure 4-9: Mesh Control applied to glue assembly component.

A low a/b ratio assures a smooth transition between large elements that mesh the rods, and small elements that mesh the glue. Assembly shown in exploded view.

The mesh control shown in Figure 4-8 produces one layer of elements in the glue. Second order elements model second order temperature distribution. Given the expected linear temperature drop across the epoxy layer, one layer of elements will suffice.

Mesh the assembly with a default element size. Apply prescribed temperatures identical to the STEEL ROD exercise: 100°C on one end, 0°C on the other end (Figure 4-8).

Run the solution and review the **Temperature** plot. Note the temperature drop of 8°C over the distance of 100mm in the bar. Compare that to the drop of 84°C over the distance of 0.5mm in glue (Figure 4-10).

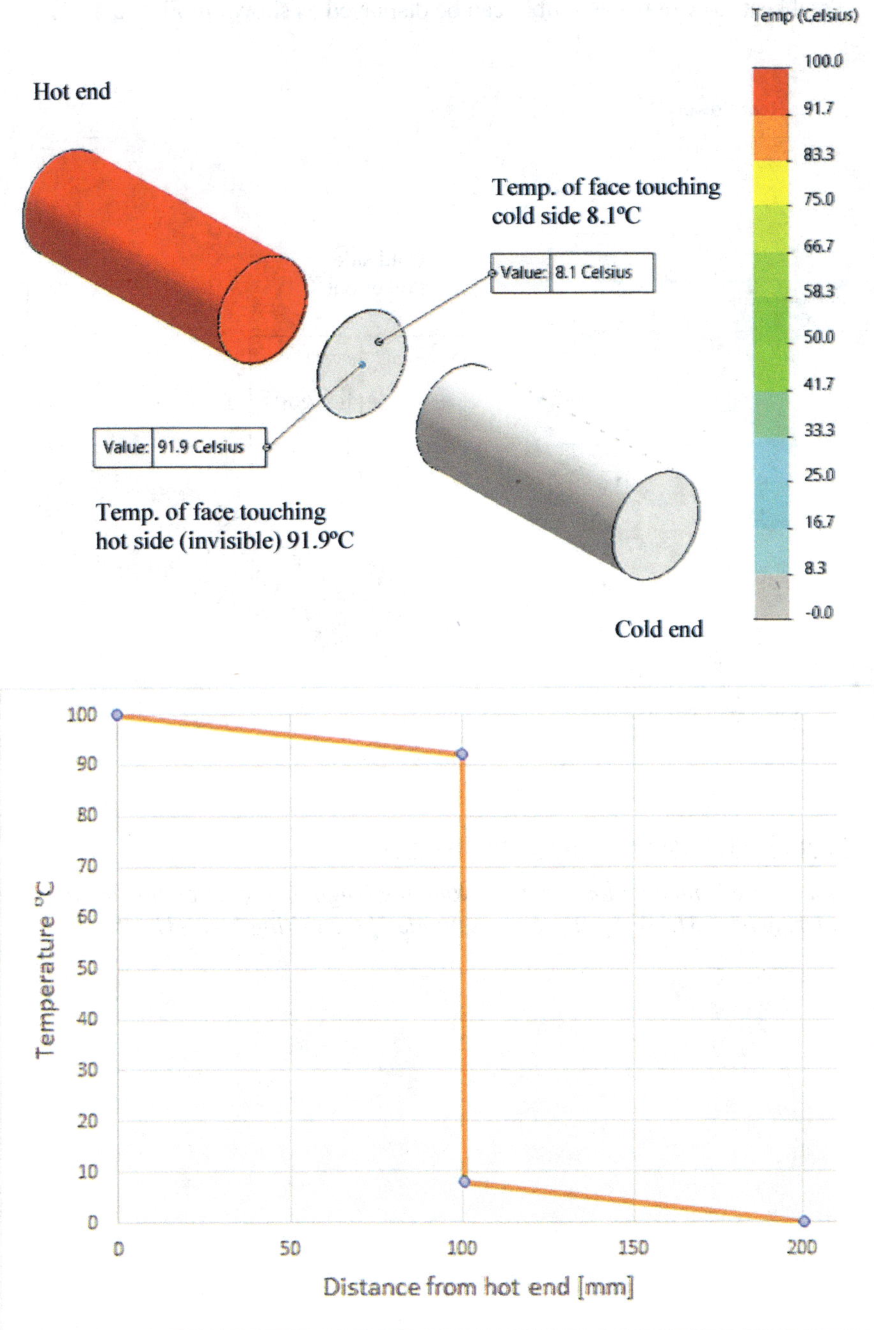

Figure 4-10: Temperature drop along the length of the assembly.

A rapid temperature drop is caused by a low thermal conductivity of epoxy glue.

Total heat flow in the assembly can be displayed as shown in Figure 4-11.

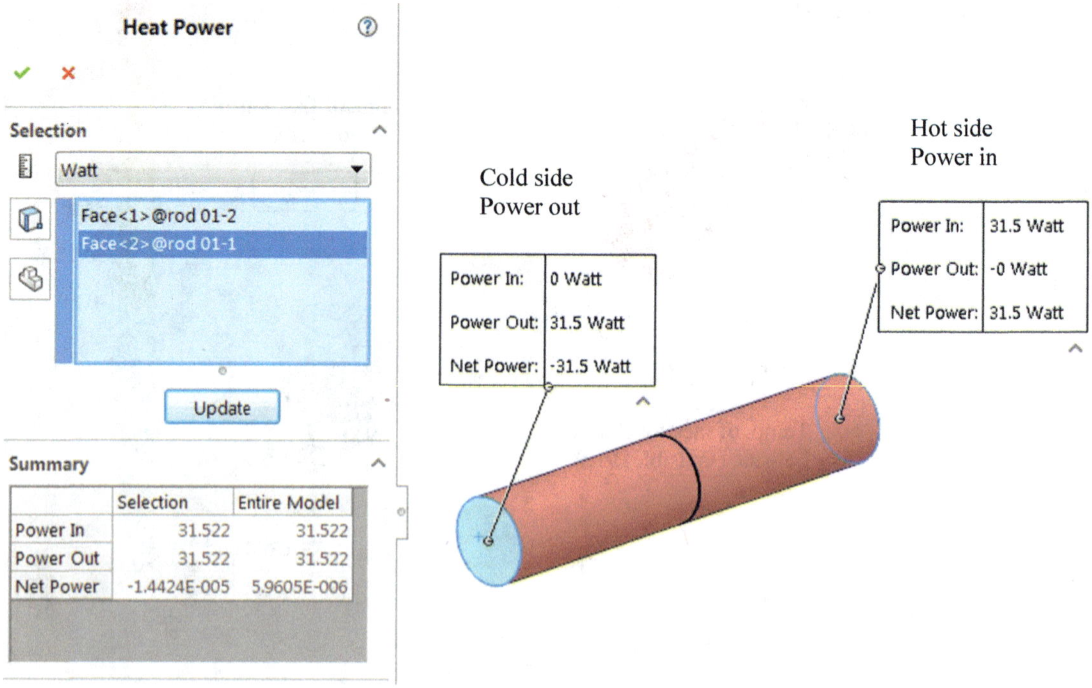

Figure 4-11: Heat flow through the assembly.

Since there is no heat loss or gain along the length of the assembly, the magnitude of the entering heat 31.5W equals the magnitude of the exiting heat -31.5W.

The thermal resistance of epoxy causes a temperature a drop of 83.8°C over the distance of 0.5mm. Heat flowing through the epoxy is 31.5W. The cross sectional area of the epoxy is 1000mm^2.

Knowing the above we may calculate the distributed thermal resistance of the epoxy layer:

$$R = \frac{\Delta TA}{P} = \frac{83.8 \times 0.001}{31.5} = 0.00266\frac{Km^2}{W}$$

Where:

R – Distributed (per area) thermal resistance Km^2/W

ΔT – Temperature drop across the layer: 83.8K

A – Cross sectional area: 0.001m^2

P – Heat flow (heat power) through the layer: 31.5W

Similarly, we may calculate the total thermal resistance of the epoxy layer:

$$R = \frac{\Delta T}{P} = \frac{83.8}{31.5} = 2.66\frac{K}{W}$$

The glue part of the assembly is very small in comparison to the rods, yet it causes a major obstacle in heat flow because of its low heat conductivity. It also poses major modeling difficulties; we had to apply a mesh control that increased the number of elements in the model very significantly.

The objective of this exercise is to introduce the concept of the layer of thermal resistance. We saw that explicit modeling of the layer of thermal resistance is difficult and gets even more so when the layer gets very thin. We will now use a better way of modeling layers of thermal resistance.

Stay with the TWO RODS assembly but switch to the *02 no glue* configuration. The assembly now consists of two parts only. Create a thermal study *02 thermal resistance distributed*. The layer of thermal resistance will be modeled as a **Contact Condition**. Follow Figure 4-12 to define a **Thermal Resistance Contact Condition**.

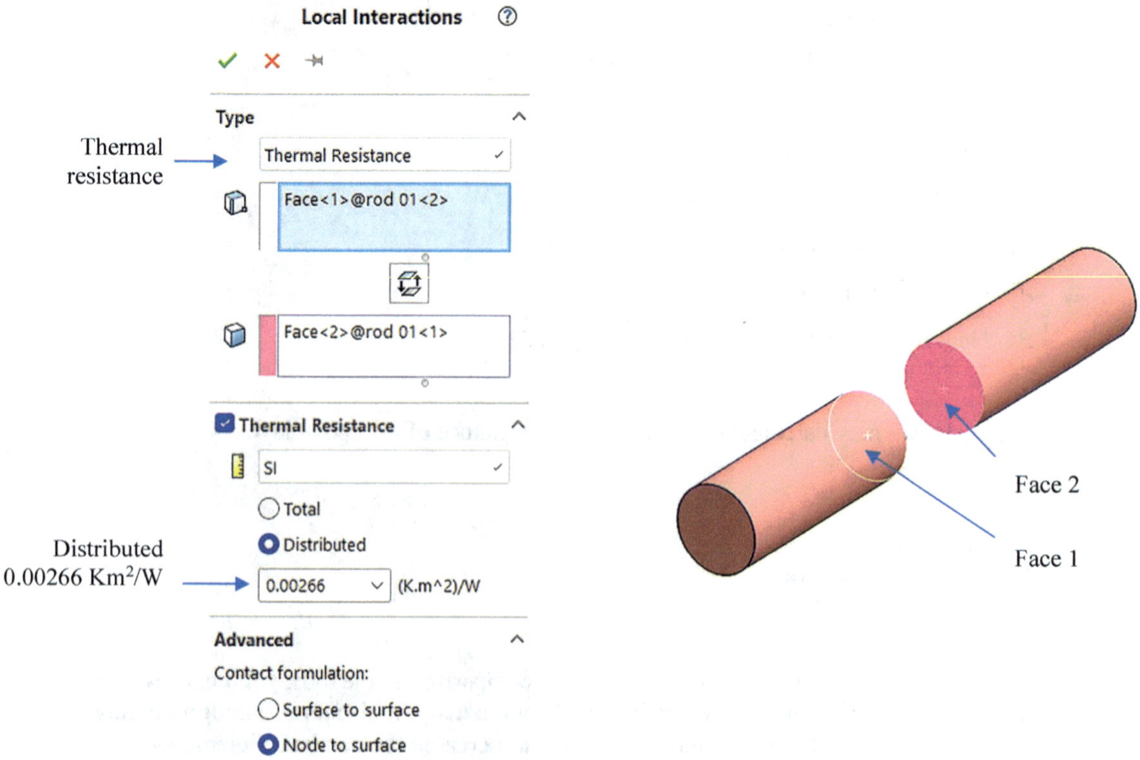

Figure 4-12: Definition of a Thermal Resistance Contact Condition.

Thermal Resistance is the only type of contact condition available in a thermal analysis. Use exploded view.

The value of thermal resistance, 0.00266 Km^2/W, comes from a calculation based on the results of the previous study where the layer of thermal resistance was modeled explicitly.

Mesh the assembly with the Standard mesh with default element size; no mesh control is needed. Obtain a solution and review the **Temperature** plot.

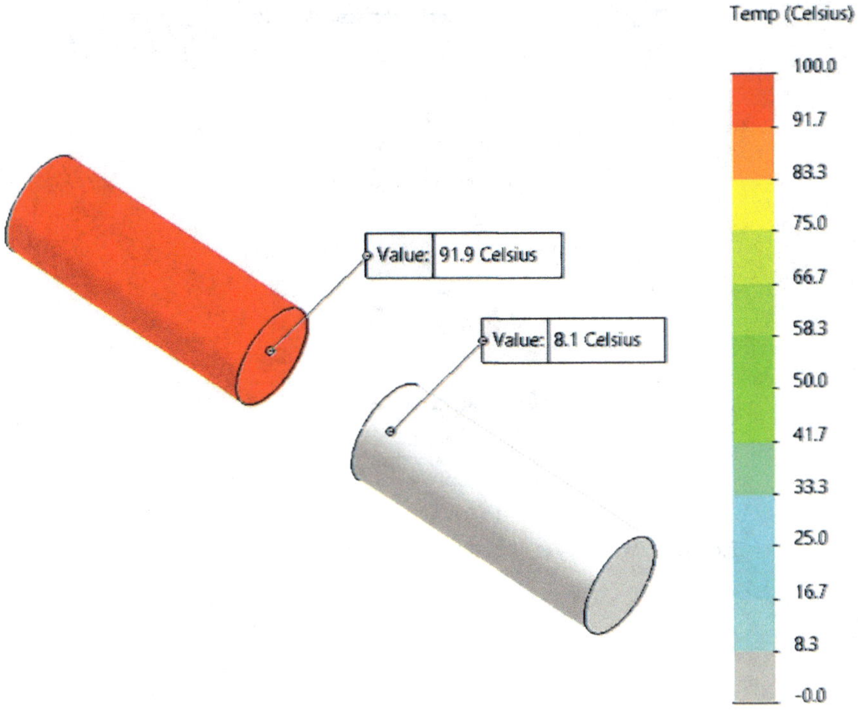

Figure 4-13: Temperature results in the model with a layer of thermal resistance.

The temperature drop across the layer of thermal resistance is 83.8°C.

The results of study *01 glue* (Figure 4-10) and study *02 thermal resistance distributed* (Figure 4-13) are the same. The layer of epoxy glue produces the same temperature drop when modeled either explicitly or as a layer of thermal resistance.

Copy study *02 thermal resistance distributed* into study *03 thermal resistance total*. Change the definition of thermal resistance from **Distributed** to **Total** (Figure 4-14).

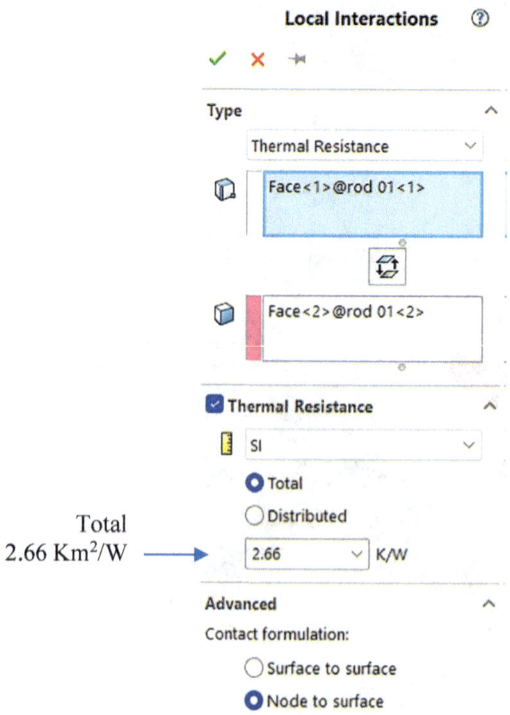

Figure 4-14: Definition of Total Thermal resistance.

This definition is equivalent to the definition of Distributed Thermal Resistance shown in Figure 4-12.

Run study *03 thermal resistance total* to see the same results as in study *02 thermal resistance distributed.*

The use of **Thermal resistance Contact Conditions** allows for a very significant simplification of the model, and a faster solution time compared to explicit modeling, if the value of thermal resistance is known. If it is not known, it can be found using simple models such as TWO RODS in the *01 glue* configuration.

Additional practice model

To reinforce the concepts presented in this chapter, repeat the analysis using the additional practice models. Define project input data following the approach used in the main exercise.

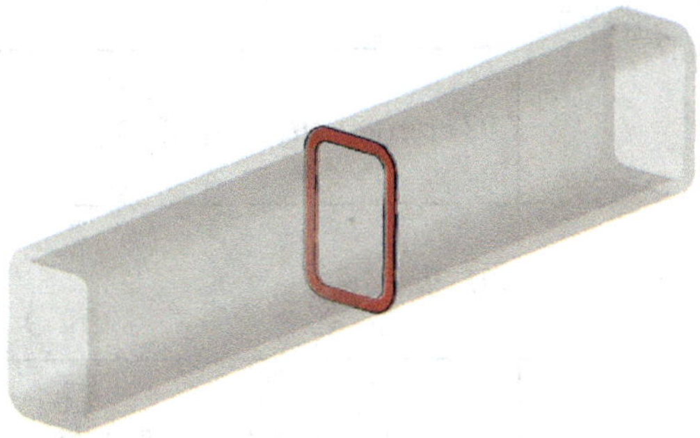

Configuration *01 glue*

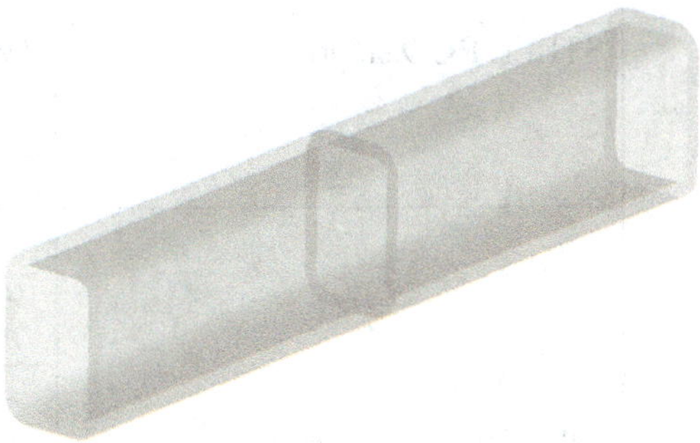

Configuration *02 no glue*

Figure 4-15: RECTANGULAR TUBES assembly model.

The assembly has two configurations.

Summary of studies completed

Model	Configuration	Study Name	Study Type
STEEL ROD.sldprt	*Default*	*01 conduction*	Thermal
		02 convection	Thermal
TWO RODS.sldasm	*01 glue*	*01 glue*	Thermal
	02 no glue	*02 thermal resistance distributed*	Thermal
		03 thermal resistance total	Thermal
RECTANGULAR TUBES.sldasm	Additional practice model		

5: Heating ducts

- Heat transfer by conduction
- Heat transfer by convection
- Temperature boundary conditions
- Convective boundary conditions
- Heat power
- Heat flux
- Heat flux singularities

Project description – part 1

A ceramic floor panel used to heat a room is modeled as assembly HEATING DUCTS. Hot air flows in the ducts transferring heat to the panel. Heat is dissipated by top faces. We assume that the side and bottom faces are insulated, therefore no thermal boundary conditions are defined there: no prescribed temperature, no convection coefficient and no radiation. We will study heat flow induced by prescribed temperatures shown in Figure 5-1.

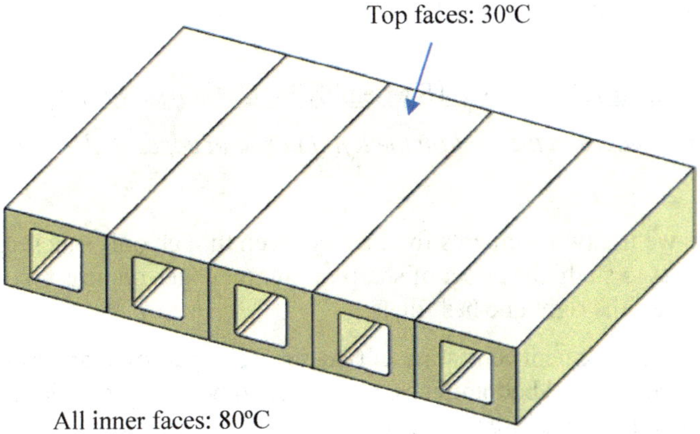

Figure 5-1: HEATING DUCTS assembly model.

The assembly consists of five identical parts. The model is shown in 01 CAD configuration.

We will perform a thermal analysis of this floor panel to find out how much heat is transferred to the room. Because of repetitive geometry, analysis could be conducted on one segment. Since there is no temperature gradient along the length of ducts (uniform prescribed temperature is defined), the analysis can be further simplified by using a 2D model.

Switch to *02 Analysis Part 1* configuration and review the model (Figure 5-2).

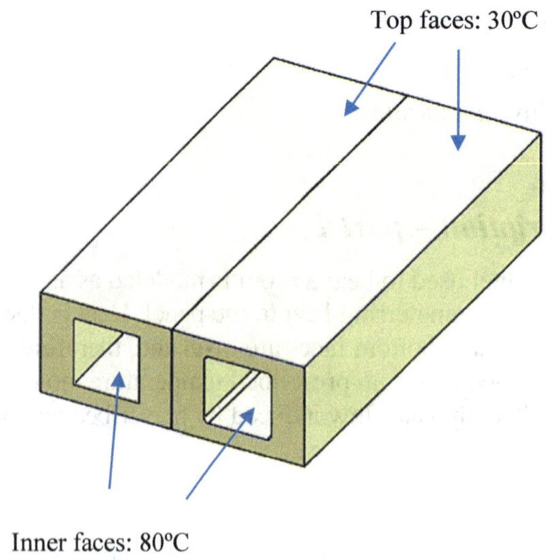

Figure 5-2: HEATING DUCTS assembly in *02 Analysis Part 1* configuration.

Note sharp edges in the duct on the left and round edges in the duct on the right.

Why do we use two segments for analysis even though only one segment could be used? We do that to study the effect of sharp re-entrant edges on heat flux; the left segment has sharp edges; the right one has fillets.

The analyzed segment consisting of two ducts is a part of a larger assembly. No heat flows through the side and bottom faces; therefore, no boundary conditions are defined there. The side and bottom faces are treated as insulated.

Procedure

Change to configuration *02 Analysis Part 1* and define a thermal study *01 2D* using 2D Simplification. Follow the steps shown in Figure 5-3.

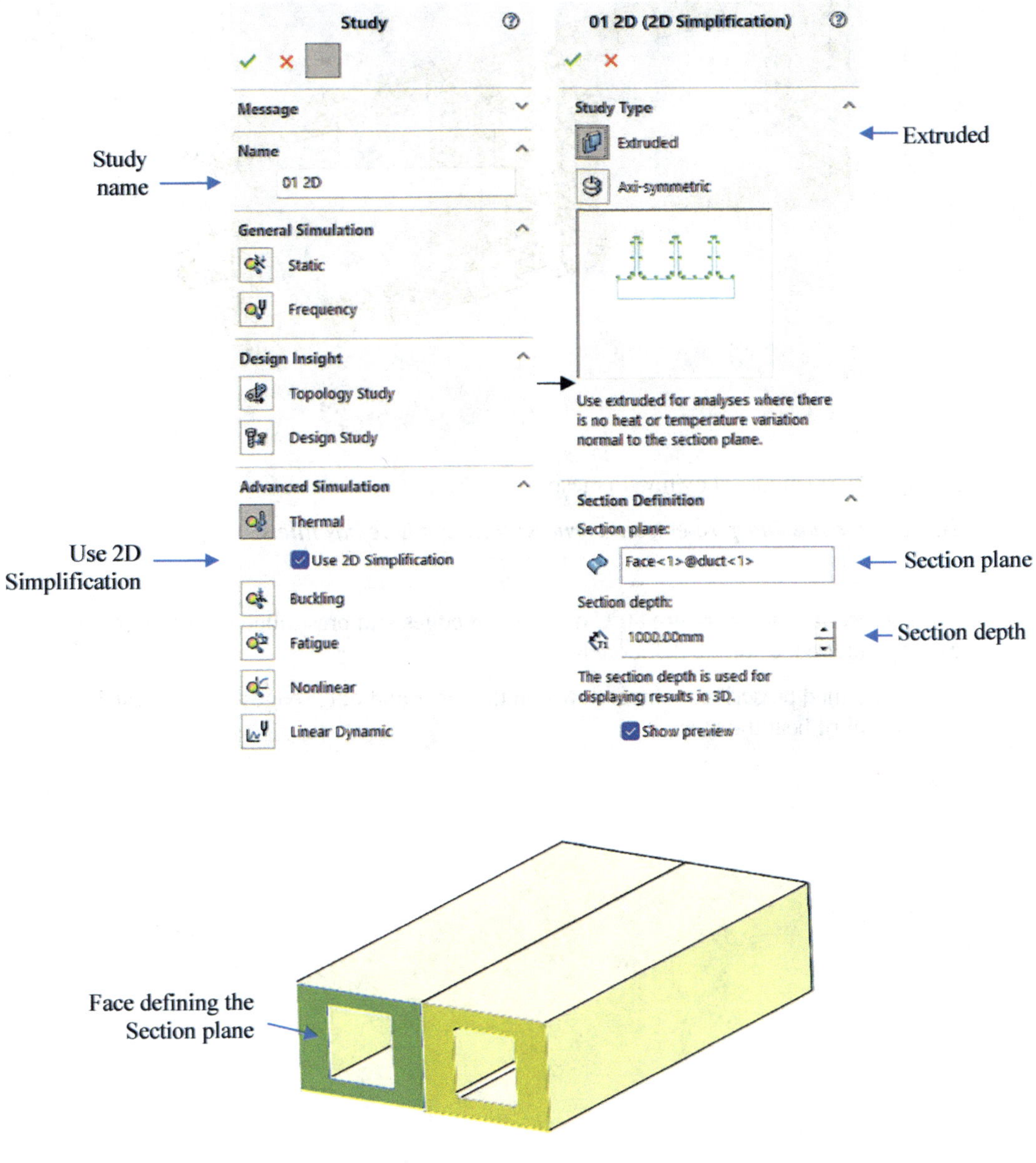

Figure 5-3: Thermal study definition using 2D Simplification.

Front face defines section plane. Section depth is equal to the length of the floor panel: 1000mm.

Mesh the model using Standard mesh with a default element size (Figure 5-4).

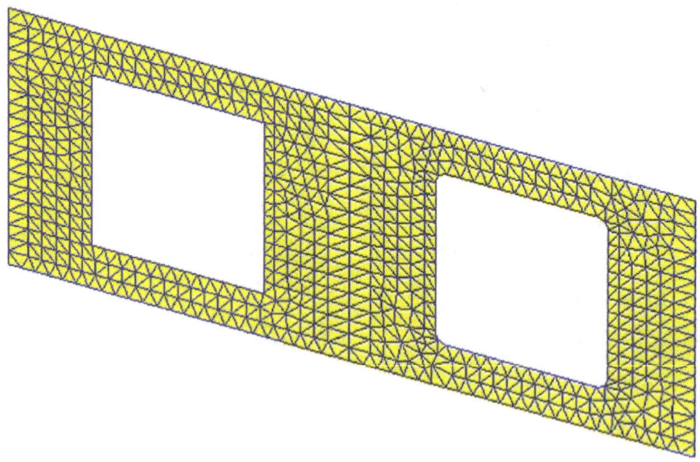

Figure 5-4: 2D model shown with mesh.

The left hole has sharp re-entrant corners; the right hole has fillets.

Apply prescribed temperature 80°C on all inner edges and prescribed temperature 30°C on two top outer edges of the 2D model.

Having defined prescribed temperatures on the inner and outer edges we have established a mechanism of heat transfer.

Obtain a solution noticing almost instantaneous results; 2D thermal models solve very fast because there is only one degree of freedom (temperature) per node in thermal models. Temperature results are shown in Figure 5-5.

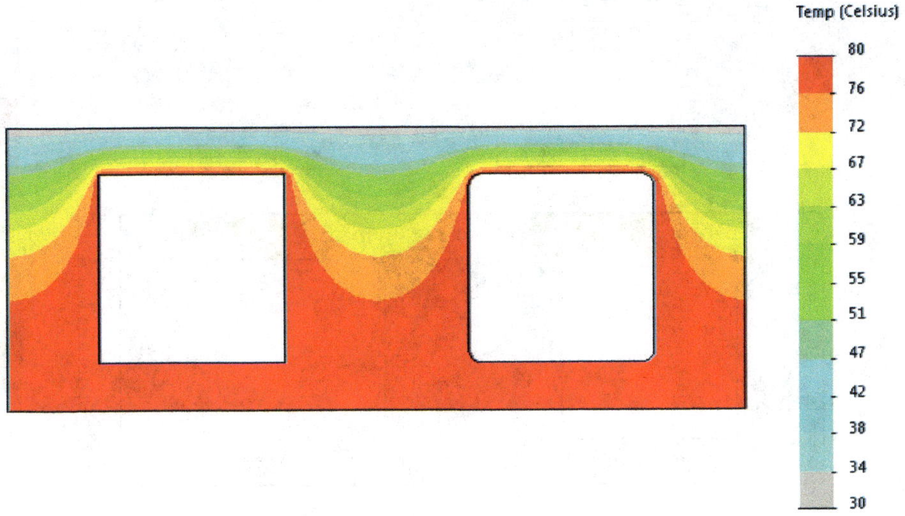

Figure 5-5: Temperature results in study *2D thermal 01*.

Temperature is a scalar value; temperature results can be presented only as a fringe plot.

As Figure 5-5 illustrates, there is little difference between sharp and round corners. The temperature on the inner edges is equal to 80°C; the temperature on the outer edges is equal to 30°C. Everywhere else, a steady state temperature establishes itself because of heat flow from hot (80°C) to cold (30°C) edges.

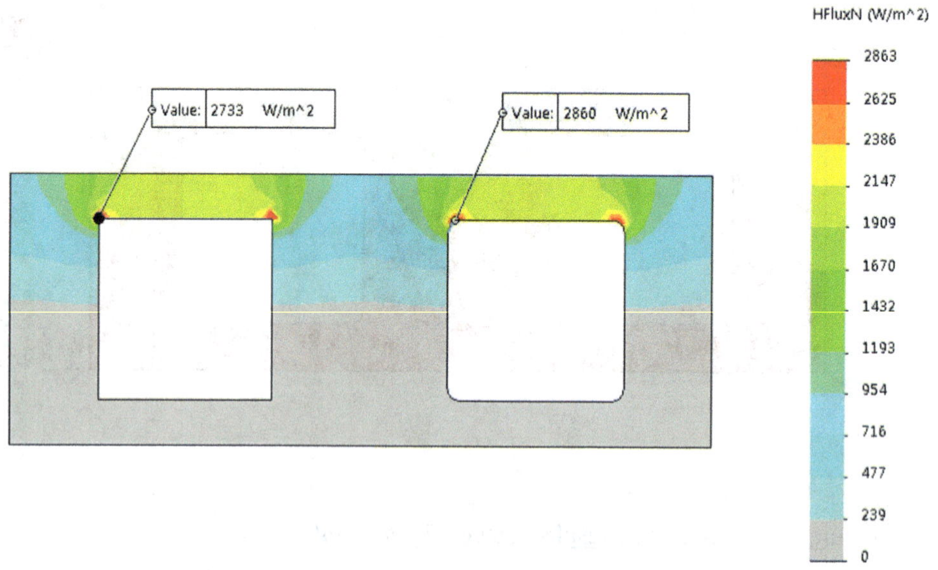

Figure 5-6: Heat Flux results from study *2D thermal 01*. The probed result in the sharp corner is 2733W/m^2; the probed result in the round corner is 2860W/m^2.

The fringe plot is used to present Heat Flux results.

Now, create Heat Flux plot as shown in Figure 5-7. Note small differences in Heat Flux between the sharp and the round corners, but this will change once we use a more refined mesh.

Heat Flux is a vector value; fringe plots show the magnitude but not the direction. To see the direction of heat flow, use a vector plot.

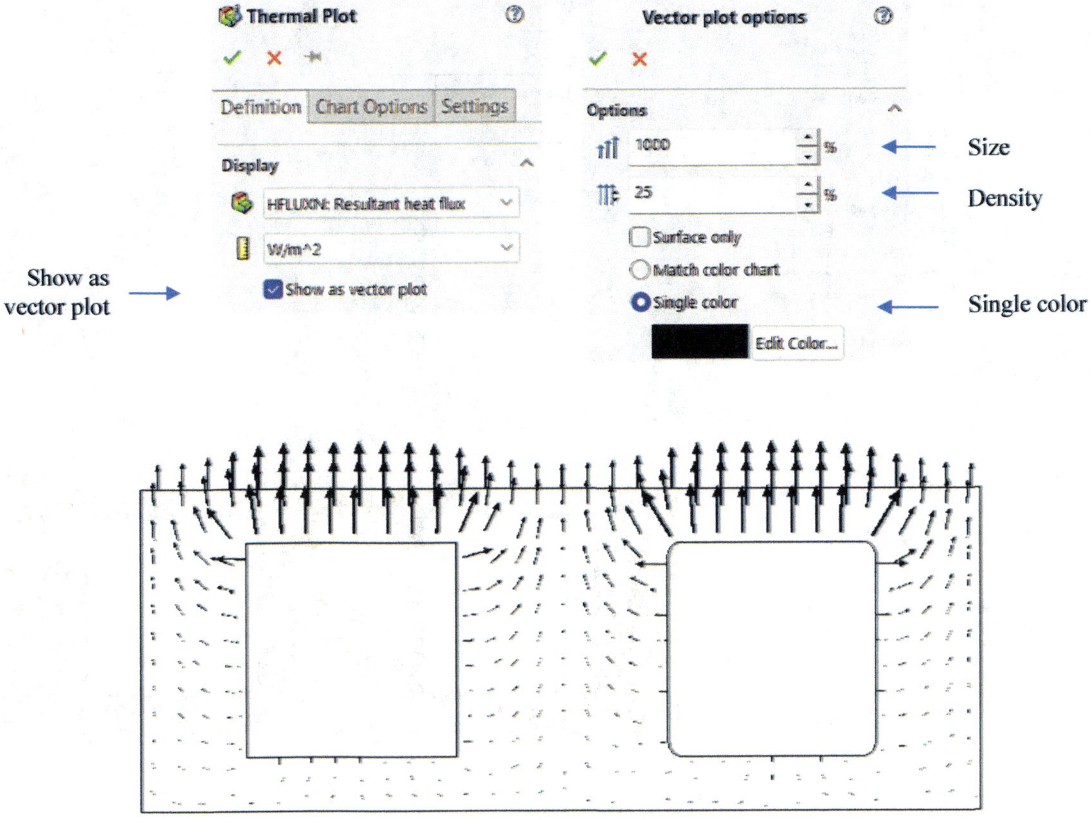

Figure 5-7: Heat Flux results in study *2D thermal 01.*

The vector plot may be modified using Vector plot options. The color information is suppressed.

Figure 5-7 makes it clear that heat enters and escapes the model only through the edges where prescribed temperatures have been defined. No heat enters or escapes the model through the bottom or side edges.

Copy study *01 2D* into *02 2D* and add mesh controls (Figure 5-8).

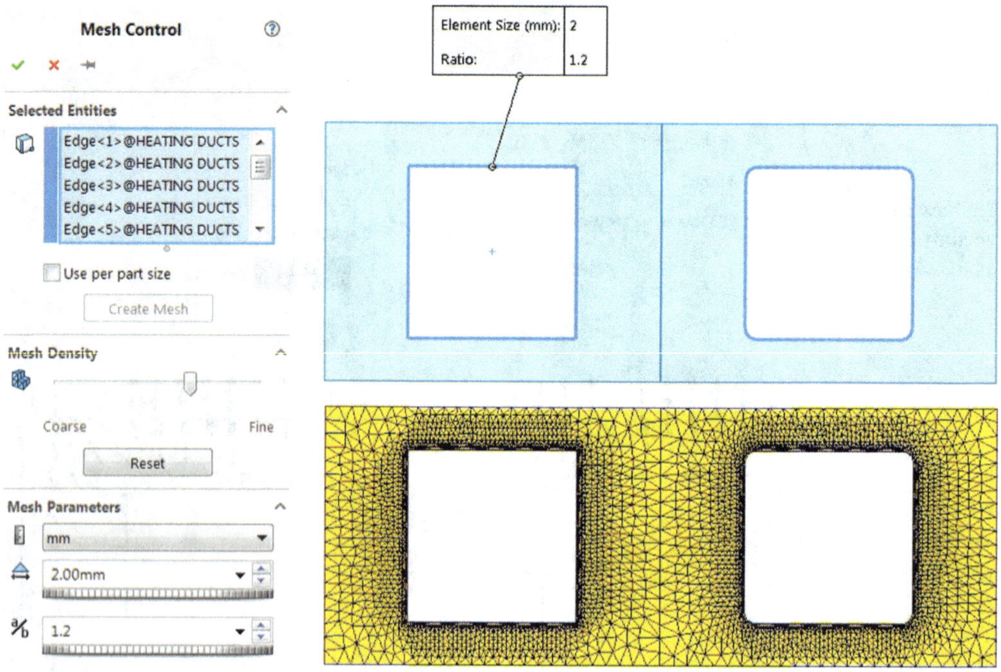

Figure 5-8: Mesh controls and mesh in study *02 2D.*

An element size of 2mm is defined on all edges of both holes. A transition ratio of 1.2 creates a large transition zone.

Using a small element size as shown in Figure 5-8 will demonstrate an important difference in the results of heat flow in the presence of a sharp and round corner. Obtain the solution of *02 2D* and review the Temperature and Heat Flux results shown in Figure 5-9 and Figure 5-10.

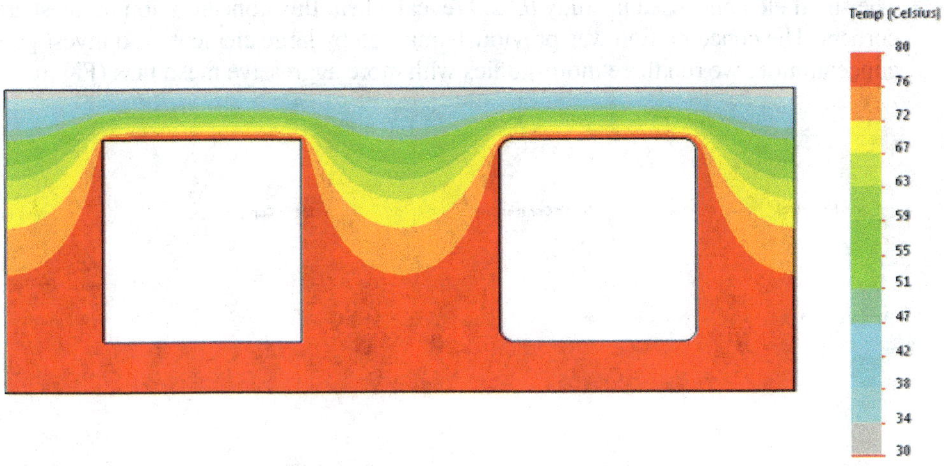

Figure 5-9: Temperature results in study 02 *2D.*

These results are indistinguishable from the results of study 2D thermal 01.

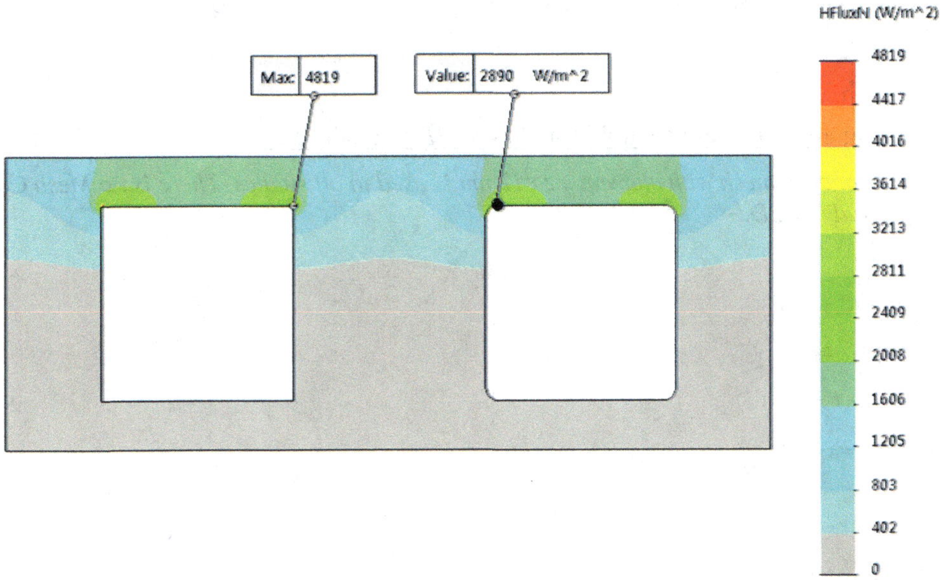

Figure 5-10: Heat Flux results from study 02 *2D.* The maximum value coincides with the sharp corner and reads 4819 W/m^2. A probed result in the round corner shows 2890W/m^2.

Due to high Heat Flux gradients in sharp corners and in round corners, the magnitude displayed by probing strongly depends on the location of probing. You may see your results slightly different from what is shown here.

The small elements used in study *02 2D* reveal a heat flux concentration in the sharp corners. The concentration was previously masked by large elements. To investigate this concentration, we run three more studies with more aggressive mesh bias (Figure 5-11).

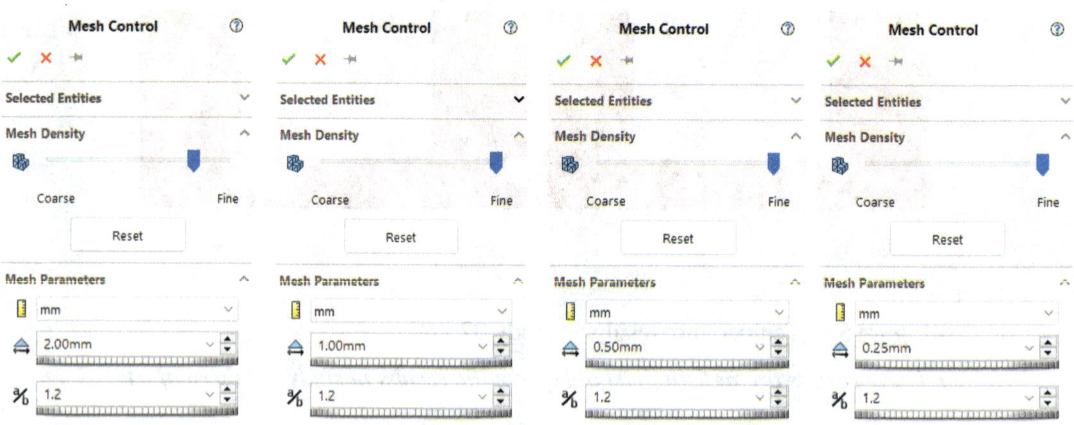

Study *02 2D* | Study *03 2D* | Study *04 2D* | Study 05 *2D*

<u>Figure 5-11: Mesh control in studies *02 2D* through *05 2D*.</u>

Standard mesh with element size 12mm is used in all studies. There is no Mesh Control in study 01 2D.

The summary of results is shown in Figure 5-12.

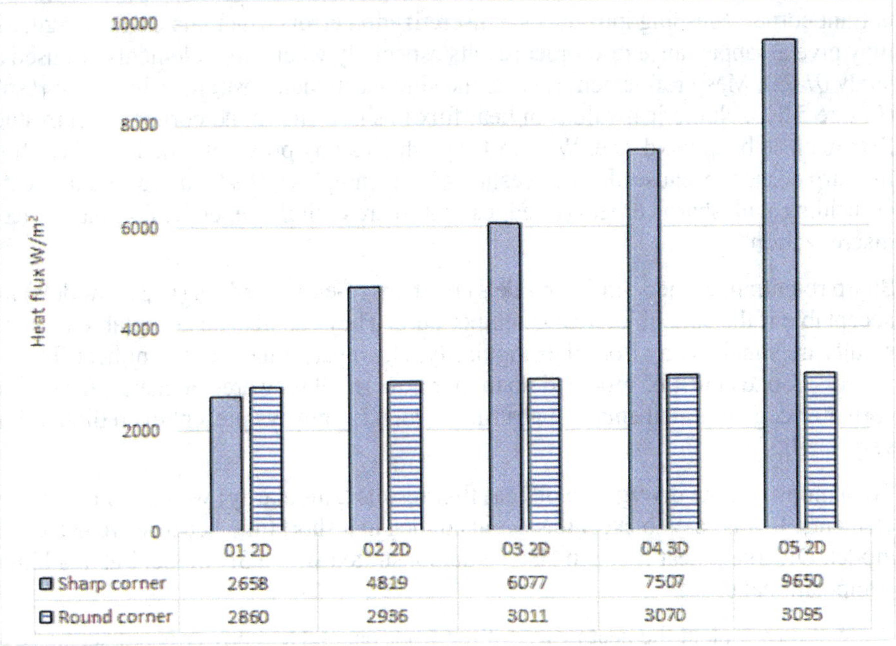

<u>Figure 5-12: Heat Flux results in sharp corner and in round corner in five studies.</u>

The Heat Flux magnitude diverges with mesh refinement in the sharp corner. Mesh refinement has little effect on Heat Flux in the round corner.

Divergent heat flux results in a sharp corner are caused by a singularity. The mathematical model has no heat flux solution in a sharp corner; a mathematician would say that the solution is singular there; an engineer would say that heat flux is infinite in a sharp re-entrant corner. Meshing introduces a discretization error, which masks the singularity and may give an appearance of correct results especially when large elements are used as in study *01 2D*. Mesh refinement reveals the singularity demonstrating divergent results (Figure 5-12). Numerical values of heat flux in sharp and round corners seen in study *01 2D* are close by coincidence. We can't say which study provides "the best" heat flux results in sharp corners because all these results are meaningless. Heat flux results in locations coinciding with sharp corners (or edges in 3D) are entirely dependent on the choice of discretization.

Sharp re-entrant corners (in 2D models) or sharp re-entrant edges (in 3D models) may be acceptable if the data of interest is temperature. They can also be acceptable if heat flux results are sought away from the singularity. However, if the maximum heat flux is of interest, rounds must be modeled no matter how small they are. A sharp (zero-radius) corner or edge is a mathematical abstract; a round is always present even though it may be very small.

To demonstrate the divergence of heat flux results (singularity) we had to use very small elements. It was easy to execute several studies in a short time because we used a 2D model. Divergent heat flux can also be demonstrated with a 3D model but at a higher computational effort.

We will now look at the heat power of the floor panel. Heat power is not sensitive to mesh refinement or heat flux singularities so we may use any of the five studies created so far. Heat power is analogous to the reaction force in a structural analysis.

To list heat power for two segments we use results from study *01 2D* and follow the steps shown in Figure 5-13.

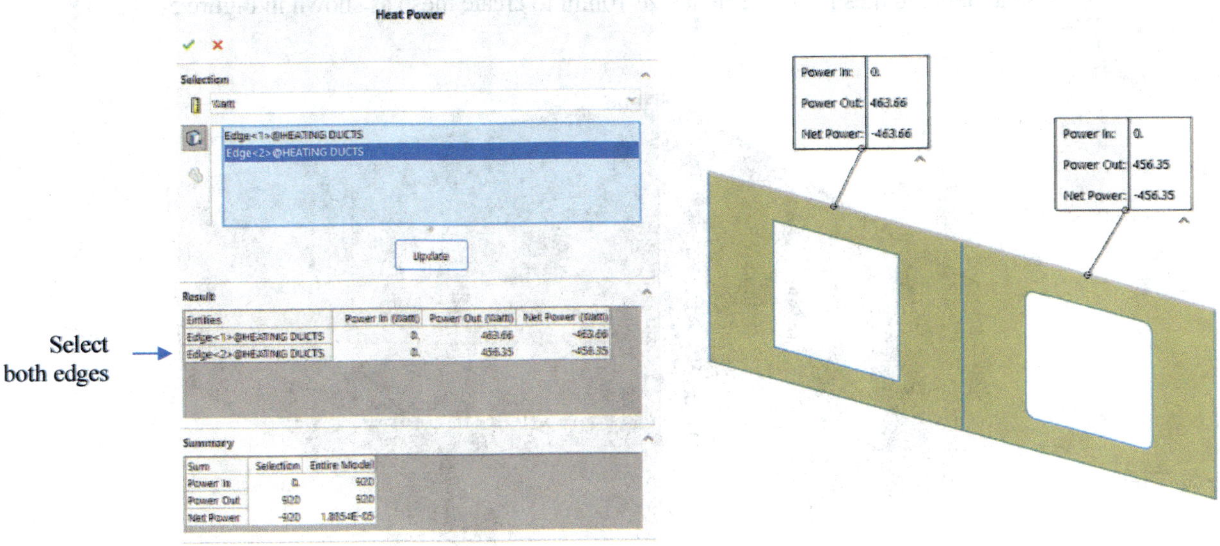

Figure 5-13: Listing heat power of two segments.

Select both edges from Results table to see the callouts.

As shown in Figure 5-13, the heat power of the segment with sharp corners is 463.7W and the heat power of the segment with round corners is 456.4W. The difference in heat power is due to the different amount of conducting material (fillets). The total heat power of the two segments is 920W.

To wrap up the analysis of the floor panel with prescribed temperatures used as boundary conditions we will create one more study: *06 3D* where a 3D model will be analyzed to find the total heat power.

Use a Standard mesh with element size 10mm to create mesh as shown in Figure 5-14.

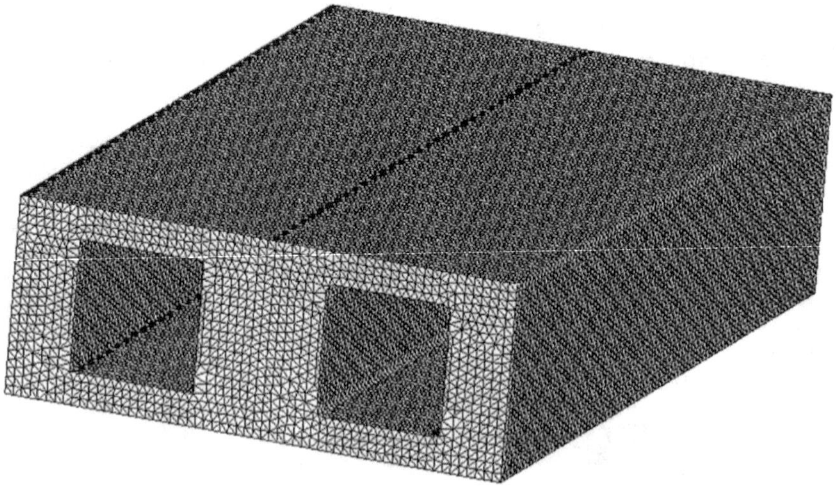

Figure 5-14: Solid element mesh of the 3D model with two segments.

Small elements are used to avoid high element distortions in the round corners. Using global mesh refinement instead of mesh controls is acceptable because large thermal models still solve fast.

Heat Power results are shown in Figure 5-15.

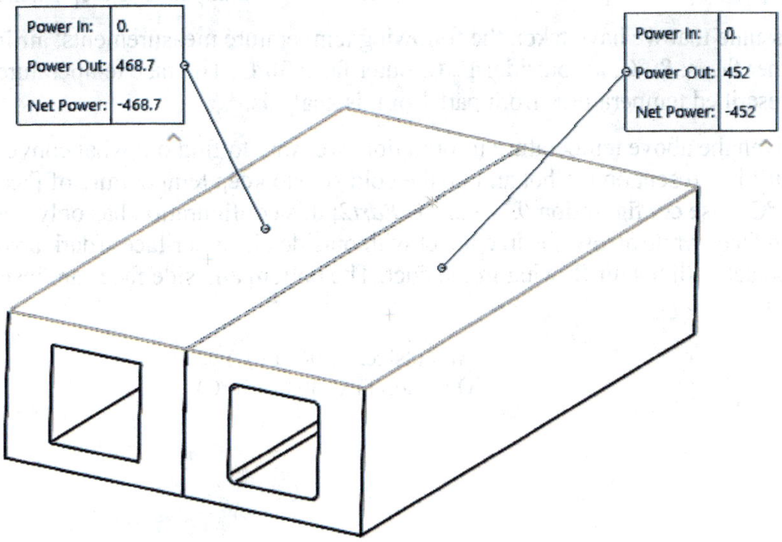

Figure 5-15: The heat power of the segment with sharp edges is 468.7W; the heat power of the segment with round edges is 452W.

Small differences in results between the 2D model (Figure 5-16) and the 3D model (Figure 5-15) are caused by discretization error that are different between 2D and 3D models.

Project description – part 2

We have completed part 1 of analysis of the floor heat panel modeling heat flow induced by prescribed temperatures. Now, we will take this analysis one step further.

Assume that we have taken the following temperature measurements: air inside: 85 °C, inner faces: 80°C, air outside: 17°C, outer face: 30°C. The face temperatures are the prescribed temperatures from part 1 of this analysis.

Given the above temperature information, we want to find out what convection conditions must be present on the hot and on the cold side to keep temperature of faces at 80°C and 30°C . Use configuration *03 Analysis Part2*; this configuration has only one segment. The top face (white arrows) is in contact with outside air. Inner faces (dark arrows) are in contact with hot air flowing in the duct. The bottom and side faces are insulated (Figure 5-16).

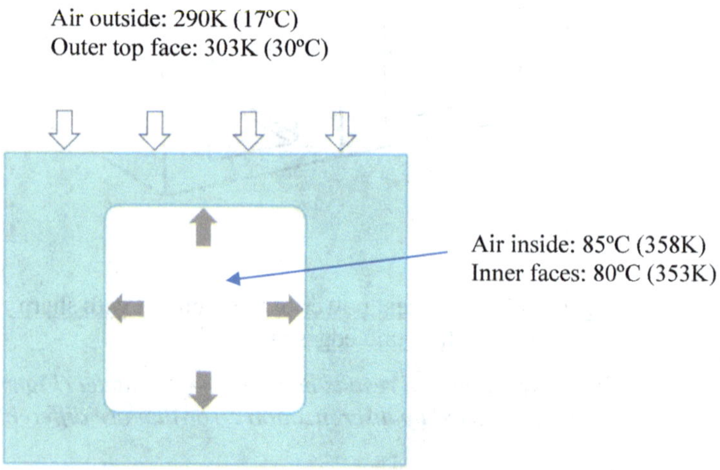

Figure 5-16: HEATING DUCTS assembly model in 03 Analysis Part3 configuration. A 2D Simplification of one segment with round edges is used.

Faces are represented by edges.

The bottom outer face is assumed to be insulated, and side faces don't exchange heat because this segment is a part of the larger assembly; therefore, no thermal boundary conditions are defined on these faces. We will proceed in two steps.

Step 1 (study *07 2D*):

Thermal boundary conditions on the inner edges are prescribed temperatures of 80°C; this is unchanged from part 1. The convection coefficient on the outer edge will be changed in steps from 10W/m²/K to 1000W/m²/K to determine for what value of convection coefficient the temperature of the top face will be 30°C. This will require several runs of study *07 2D*.

Step 2 (study *08 2D*):

The convection condition on the outer edge will be the one found in step 1. The convection coefficient on the inner edges will change in steps from 10W/m²/K to 1000W/m²/K to determine for what value of convection coefficient the temperature of the internal edge will be 80°C.

Once the convection coefficients on both sides have been found, we won't need prescribed temperatures, and heat flow will be modeled more realistically.

To prepare study *07 2D*, use 2D simplification. Define Convection as shown in Figure 5-17. Define a prescribed Temperature of 80°C on the inner edges as in part 1 of this exercise. Use default standard mesh.

Figure 5-17: Convective boundary conditions on the outer edge.

A value of 100W/m²/K is shown.

Using default element size run study *07 2D* for the following values of convection coefficients on the outer edge: 10, 50, 100, 200, 300, 500, $1000 Wm^{-2}K^{-1}$. For each value, find the average temperature on the outer edge as shown in Figure 5-18.

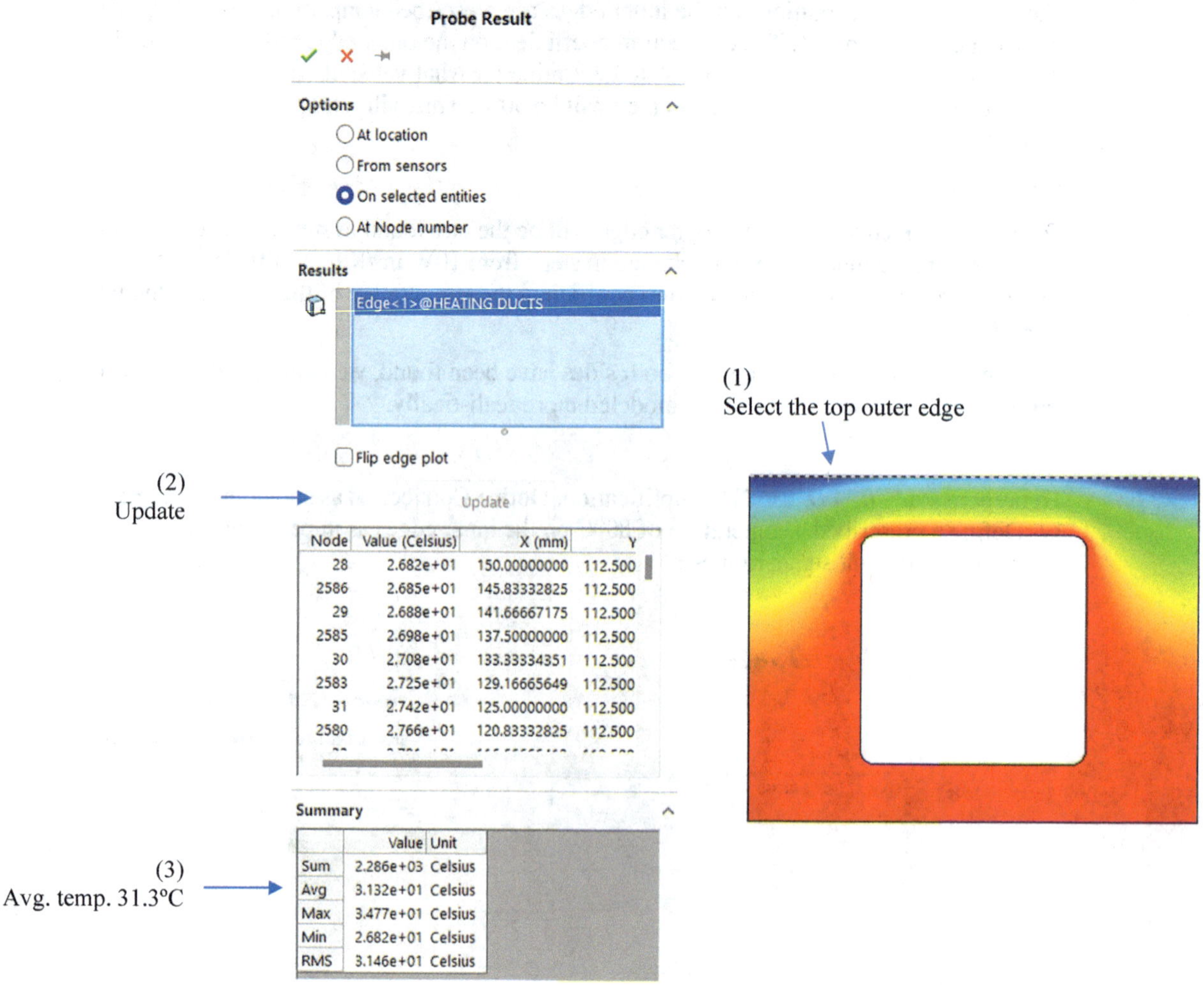

Figure 5-18: Average temperature on the outer edge.

With a convection coefficient of 100W/m²/K, the average temperature of the outer edge is 31.3°C.

The summary of all runs with convection coefficients on the outer edge of 10, 50, 100 and 200Wm^{-2}K^{-1}is shown in Figure 5-19.

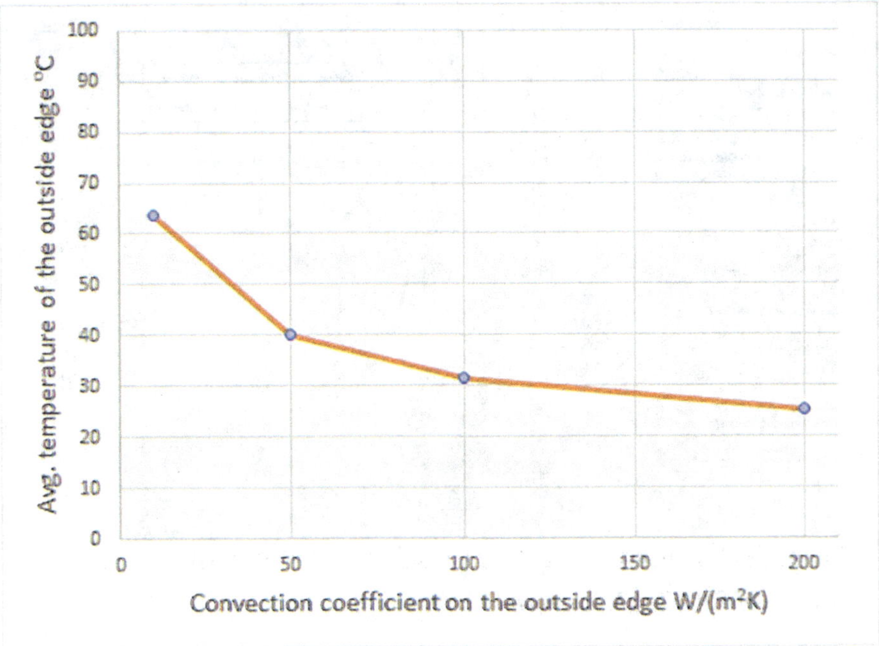

Figure 5-19: Average temperature on the top outer edge as a function of convection coefficient.

A convection coefficient of 100W/m^2/K in combination with an ambient temperature of 290K results in an average temperature of the outer edge of approximately 30°C.

We find that a convection coefficient of 100W/m^2/K in combination with an ambient temperature of 290K results in an average temperature of the outer edge of approximately 30°C.

Having found the convection coefficient on the outer edge, proceed to finding convection coefficient on the inner edges. Copy study *07 2D* into *08 2D* and delete the prescribed temperature on the inner edges. Define convection on the outer edge with the convection coefficient 100W/m^2/K and the ambient temperature 290K and keep that unchanged throughout the analysis.

Run study *08 2D* for the following values of convection coefficients on the inner edges: 10, 50, 100, 200, 300, 500, and 1000 $Wm^{-2}K^{-1}$.

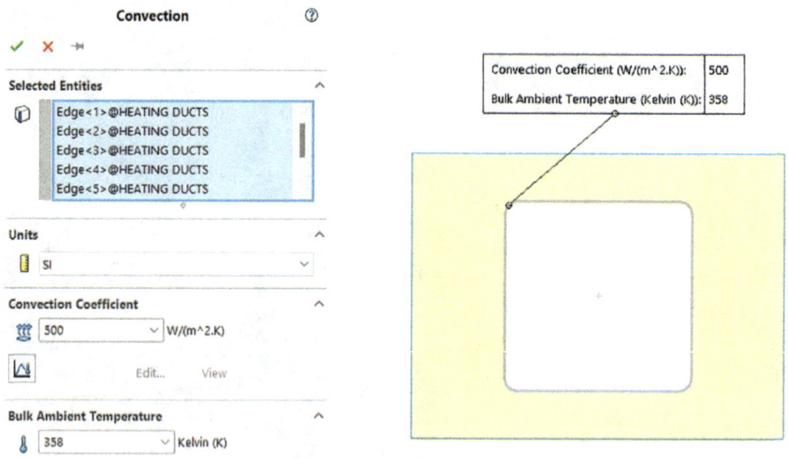

Figure 5-20: Convective boundary conditions on the inner edges.

A value of 500W/m²/K is shown.

For each value of convection coefficient find the average temperature on all the inner edges following the same steps as shown in Figure 5-18.

A summary of all runs for convection coefficients on the inner edges of 100, 200, 300, and $500Wm^{-2}K^{-1}$ is shown in Figure 5-21.

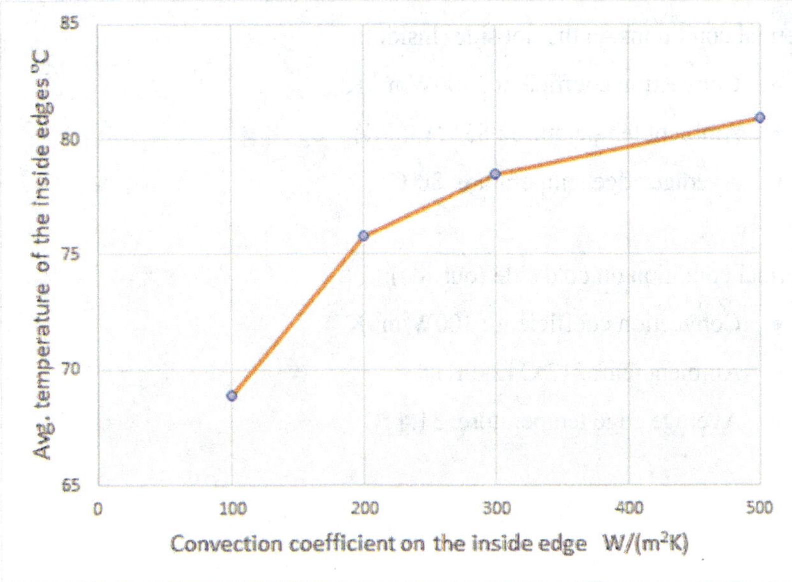

Figure 5-21: Average temperature on the top inner edge as a function of convection coefficient.

A convection coefficient of 400W/m²/K gives an average temperature close to 80°C on the inner edge. Compare this with Figure 6-6 showing results for 500W/m²/K.

Run study *08 2D* one more time with a convection coefficient of 400W/m²/K on the top outer edge and see that the average temperature is 31.4 °C.

In summary, we have found the convective boundary conditions that approximate the prescribed temperature boundary conditions used in part 1.

Thermal conditions on the hot side (inside):

- Convection coefficient : $400 W/m^2/K$
- Ambient temperature : 85°C (358K)
- Average edge temperature: 80°C

Thermal condition on cold side (outside):

- Convection coefficient : $100 W/m^2/K$
- Ambient temp. 17°C (290K)
- Average edge temperature: 31.4 °C

The important difference is that in part 1, the prescribed temperature along the edges is uniform. Using convective boundary conditions, temperature along the edges is not uniform, which is more realistic.

Heat Power in the presence of convection on hot and cold sides is shown in Figure 5-22.

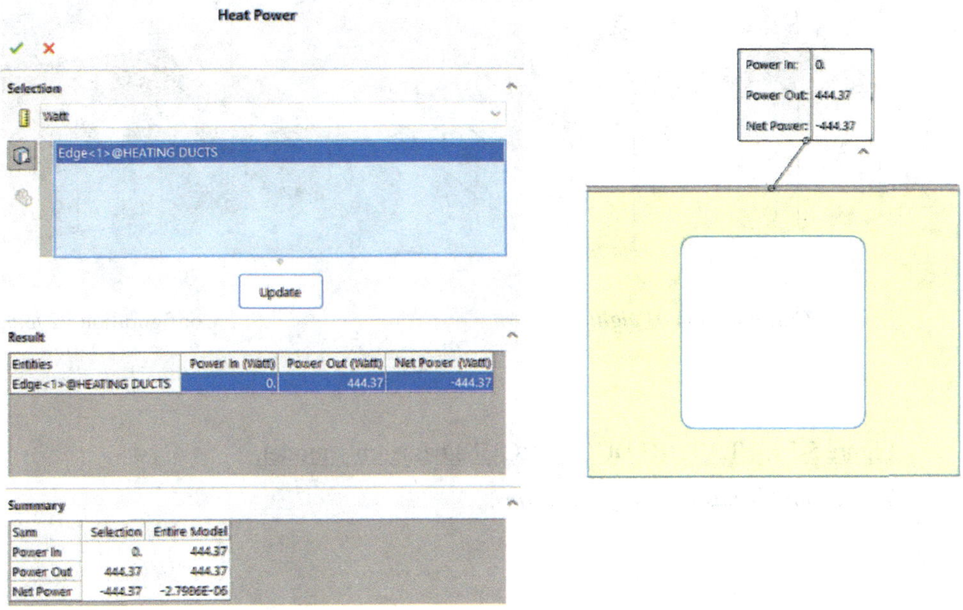

Figure 5-22: Heat power of one segment.

Each segment transfers 444W heat power.

Additional practice model

To reinforce the concepts presented in this chapter, repeat the analysis using the additional practice models. Define project input data following the approach used in the main exercise.

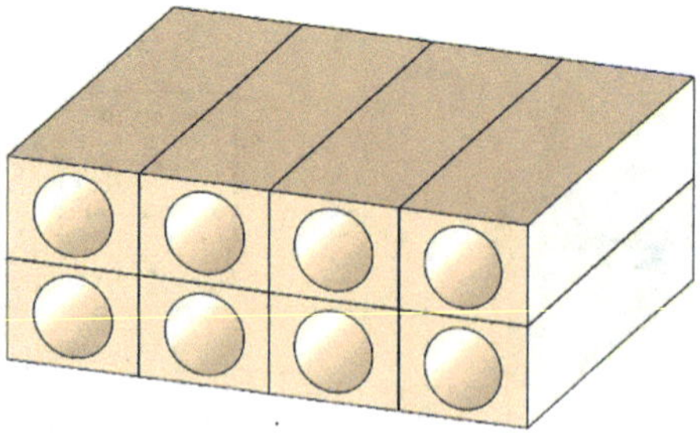

Configuration *01 eight*

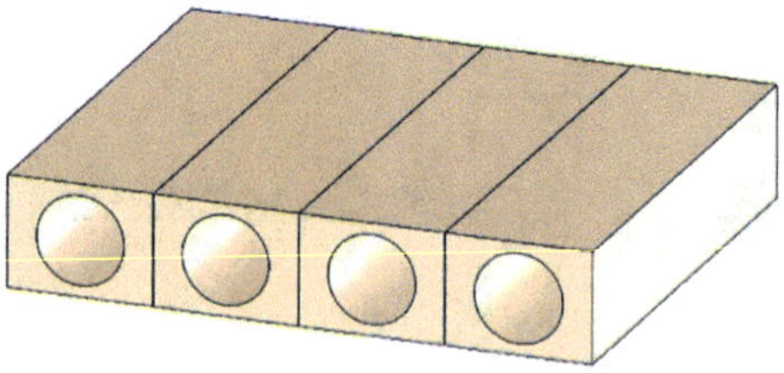

Configuration *02 four*

Figure 5-23: HEATING DUCTS ROUND assembly model.

This assembly has two configurations.

Models in this chapter

Model	Configuration	Study Name	Study Type
HEATING DUCTS.sldasm	*02 Analysis Part 1*	*01 2D*	Thermal
		02 2D	Thermal
		03 2D	Thermal
		04 2D	Thermal
		05 2D	Thermal
		06 3D	Thermal
	03 Analysis Part 2	*07 2D*	Thermal
		08 2D	Thermal
HEATING DUCTS ROUND.sldasm	Additional practice model		

Notes:

6: Hot plate

- Transient thermal analysis
- Conductive heat transfer
- Convective heat transfer
- Heat power
- Thermostat
- Thermal inertia

Project description

A ceramic housing has an embedded heating element producing 1000W of thermal power. The power can be cycled on and off by a thermostat, so the plate keeps the surface temperature at about 100°C. We will study temperature fluctuations with time for given thermostat settings.

Procedure

Open assembly model HOT PLATE (Figure 6-1).

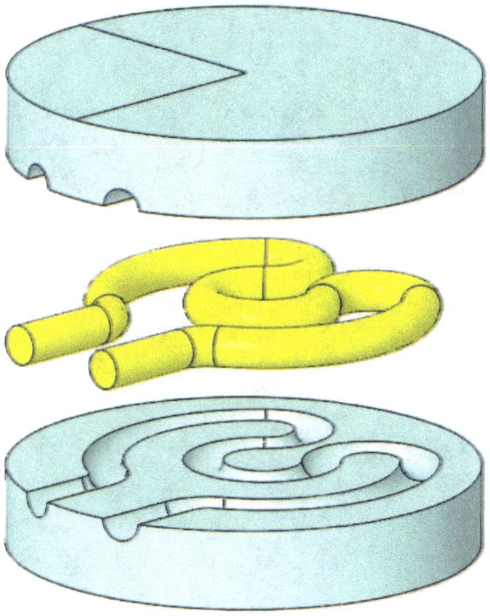

Figure 6-1: HOT PLATE assembly in an exploded view.

The assembly consists of two identical halves of ceramic plate that encase a heating element. The split line on the top face is there to position a thermostat.

Analysis of temperature fluctuations, while power is cycled on and off, requires transient thermal analysis. Create a transient Thermal study and set the parameters (Figure 6-2).

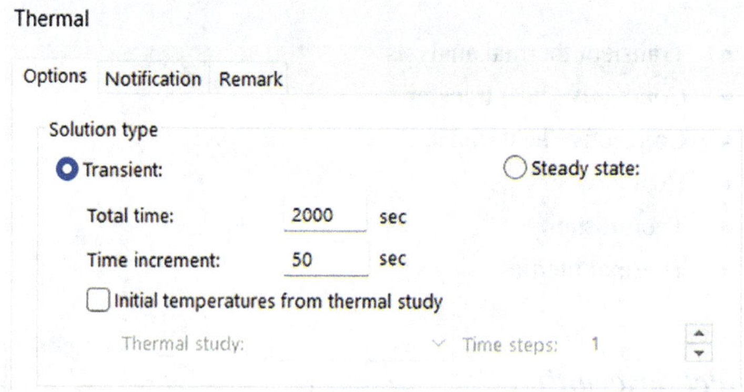

Figure 6-2: Properties of the transient thermal study: total time 2000s, time step 50s.
Setting the duration and time step requires trial runs.

Using the transient study settings shown in Figure 6-2, the analysis duration is 2000s, completed in 40 steps with increments of 50s.

Define **Heat Power** and a **Thermostat** as shown in Figure 6-3.

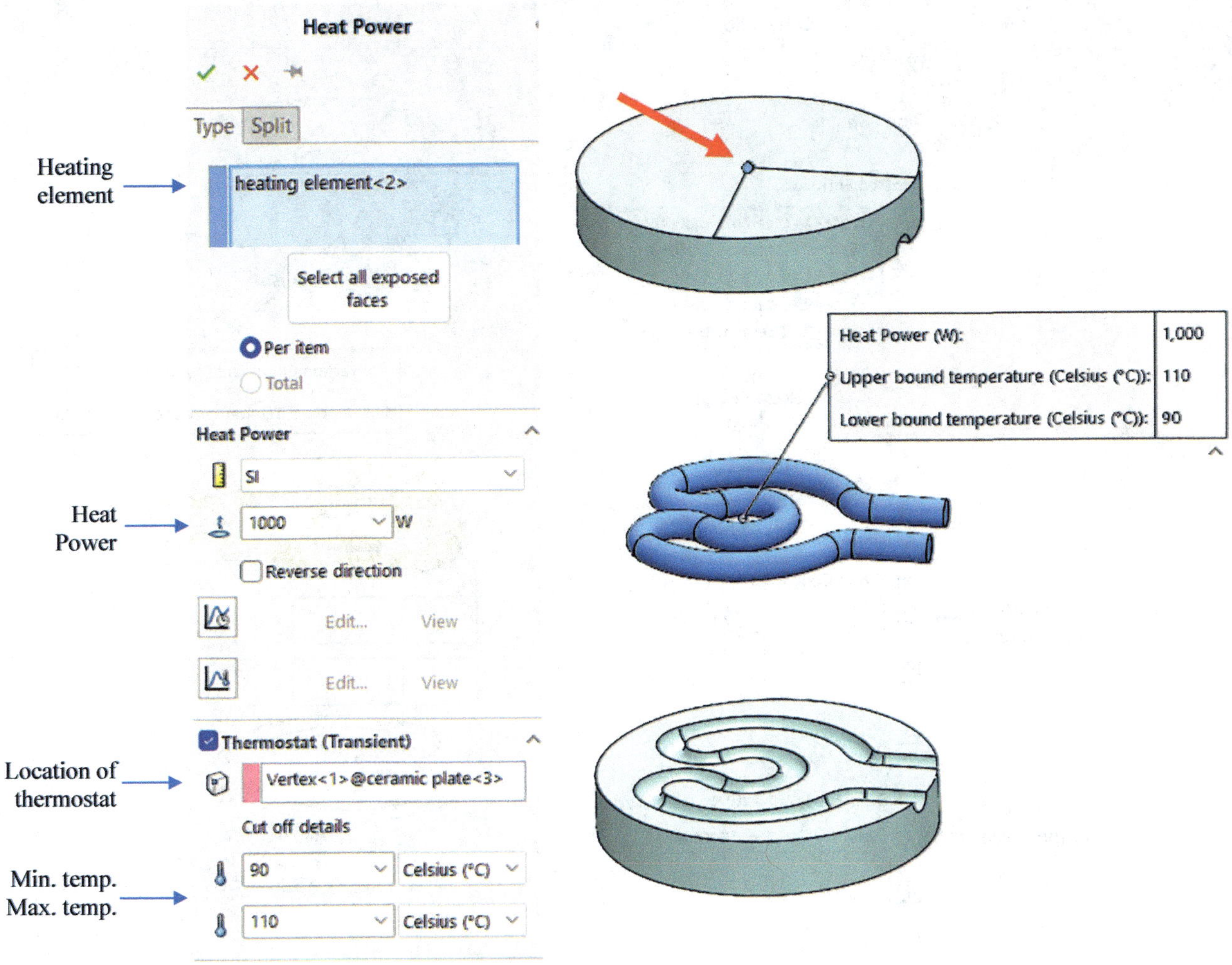

Figure 6-3: Definition of Heat Power controlled by a Thermostat. The temperature of the thermostat controls the power switch on and off.

Select the heating element part from the fly-out menu. Place the thermostat as indicated by the red arrow.

With the **Thermostat** setting as in Figure 6-3, the power is turned on at time t = 0 and it stays on until the temperature reaches 110°C. At 110°C power is turned off until the temperature drops down to 90°C, then the power is turned on again.

Define **Convection**, select all external faces of the ceramic plates (Figure 6-4).

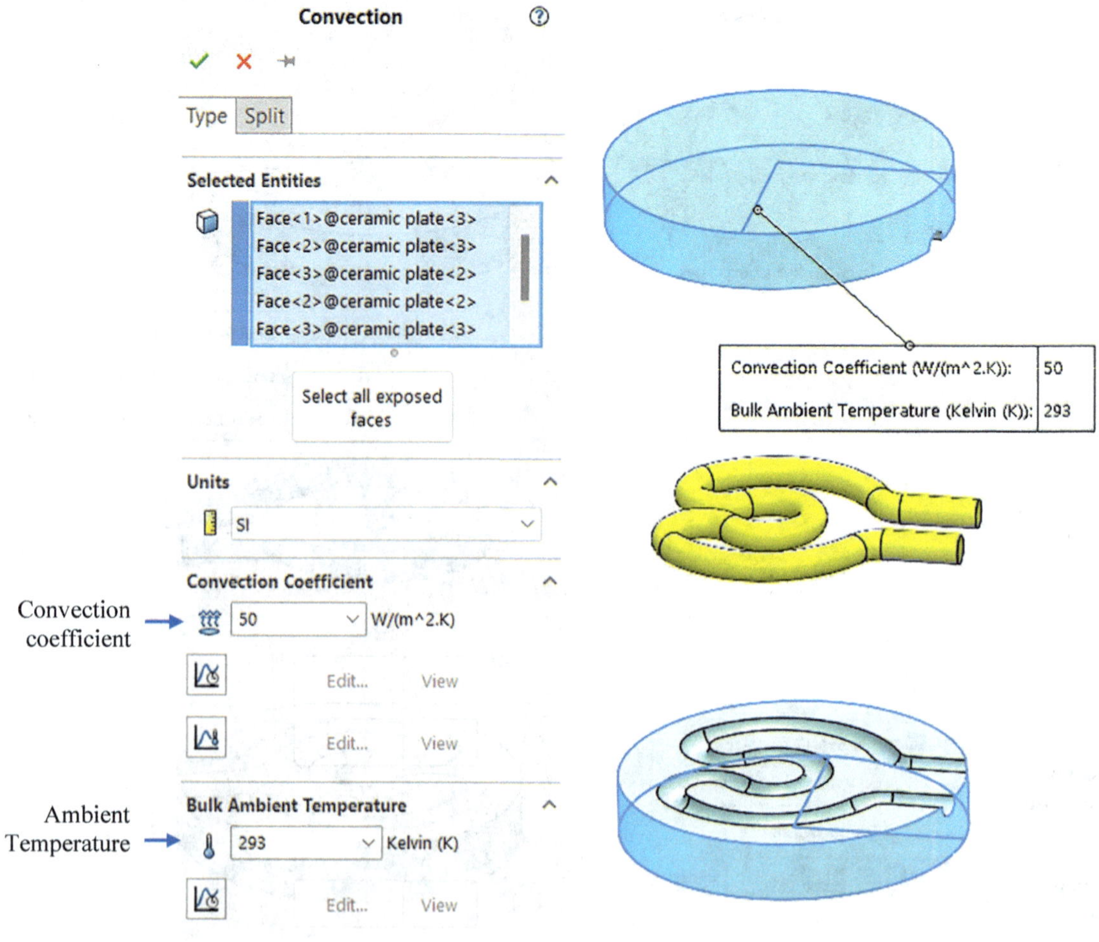

Figure 6-4: Definition of Convection conditions.

The faces of the heating element that stick out of the housing are insulated; do not define convection conditions there.

Define an **Initial temperature** to all assembly components as shown in Figure 6-5.

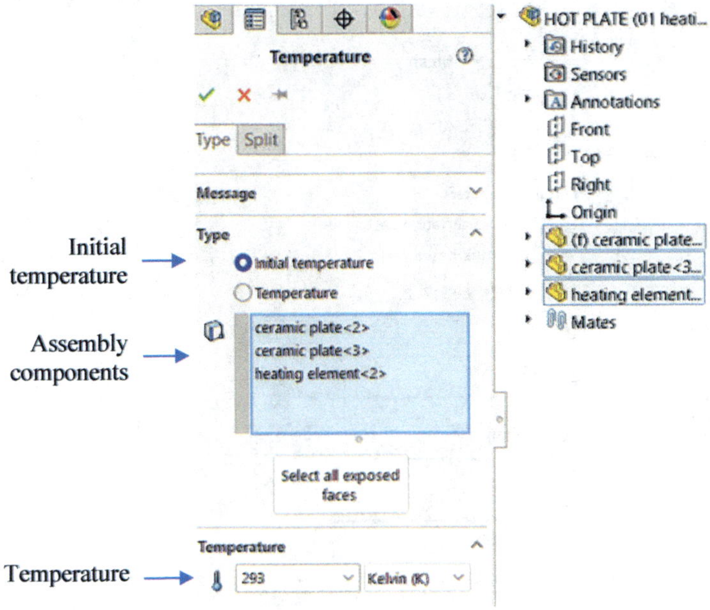

Figure 6-5: Definition of the Initial temperature.

Select all three assembly components from the fly-out menu.

Initial temperature must be defined in **Transient** thermal analysis but not in **Steady State** thermal analysis.

Mesh the assembly with a **Curvature based mesh** using settings shown in Figure 6-6.

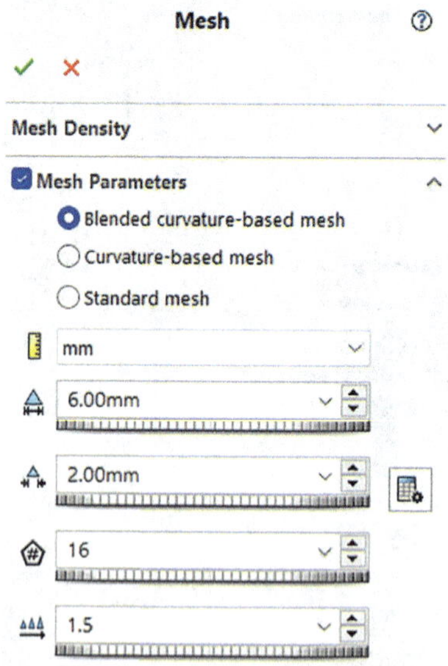

Figure 6-6: Blended curvature-based mesh settings.

The maximum element size is 6mm. A minimum of 16 elements in a circle gives an element turn angle of 22.5°.

A **Curvature based mesh** is used because of the many curved faces present in the model. Review the mesh using exploded view to see how the heating element has been meshed.

We assume an ideal bond between the heating element and ceramic plate; therefore, no thermal resistance is defined there.

The transient solution completes in 50 steps. If you want to reduce the solution time, use a less demanding mesh setting and/or switch to Standard mesh. You may also reduce the time of analysis. Once solution completes, show the Temperature plot and follow the steps in Figure 6-7 to create a **Temperature Time History** graph.

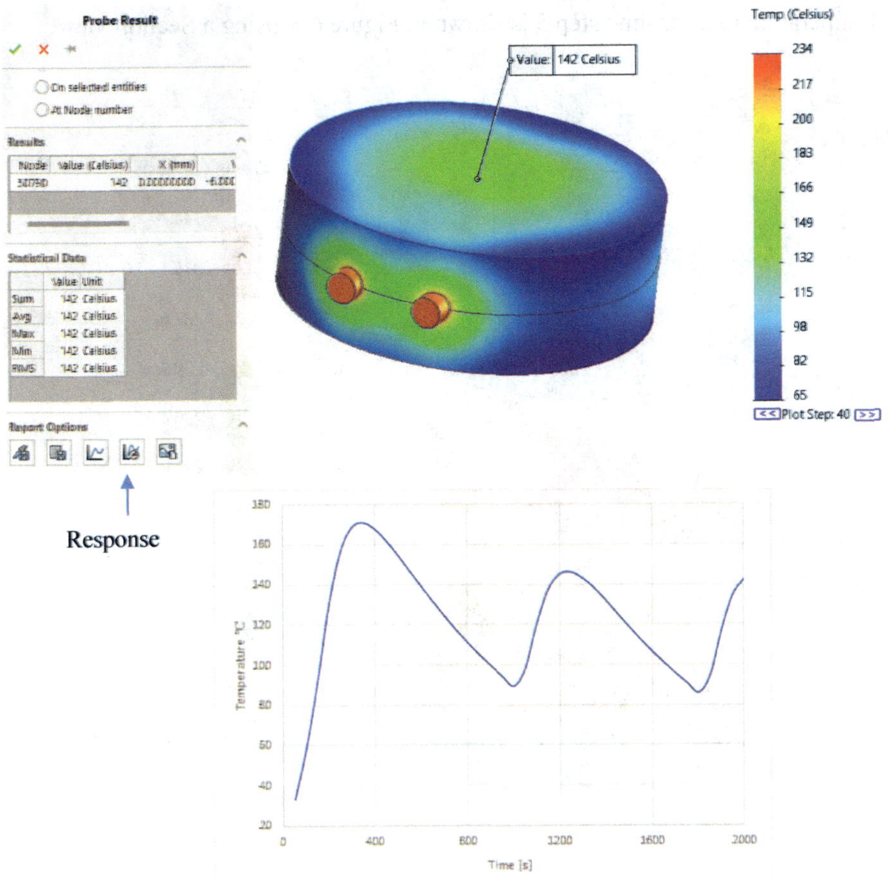

Figure 6-7: Temperature time history at the Thermostat location during 2000s.

Probe temperature plot in the sensor location and select Response to see the temperature time history graph. You can probe plots from any time step; it does not have to be the last one. Try probing other locations. The graph has been formatted in Excel.

As the graph in Figure 6-7 indicates, after the initial warm-up period, the temperature fluctuates between 85C° and 145°C. Note that the range of temperature fluctuation of 85C° to 145°C is wider than what we have defined in Thermostat. This is caused by thermal inertia; after power has been turned off, the temperature in the thermostat location keeps on climbing for a while. After power has been turned on, the temperature keeps on dropping for a while.

Temperature plot for time step 5 is shown in Figure 6-8 using a Section view.

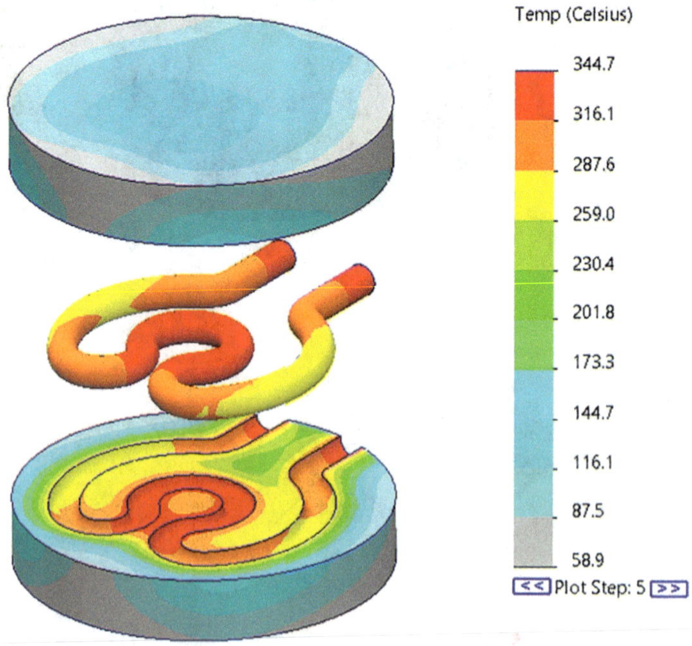

Figure 6-8: Temperature plots at time step 5 corresponding to time 250s.

The temperature of the heating element is not uniform. Custom colors are used.

Repeat the analysis with different Heat Power and Thermostat settings to see the effects of different settings on the temperature time history.

Additional practice models

To reinforce the concepts presented in this chapter, repeat the analysis using the additional practice models. Define project input data following the approach used in the main exercise.

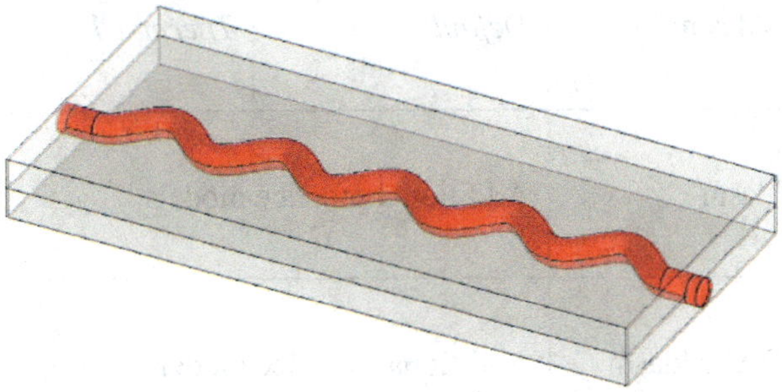

Figure 6-9: HPLATE10 assembly model.

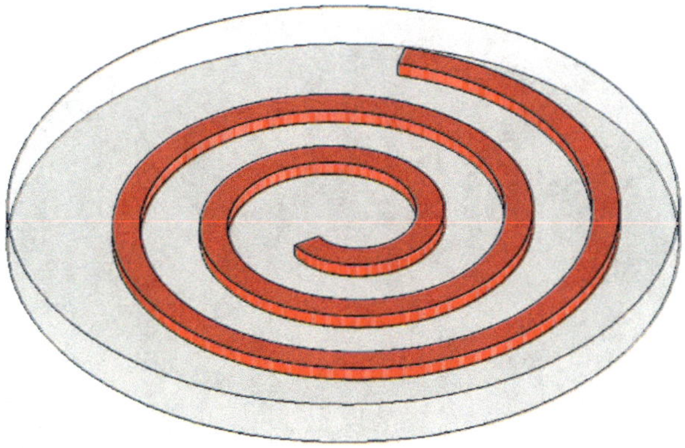

Figure 6-10: HPLATE SPIRAL assembly model.

Models in this chapter

Model	**Configuration**	**Study Name**	**Study Type**
HOT PLATE.sldasm	*Default*	*Thermal 1*	Thermal
HPLATE10.sldasm	Additional practice models		
HPLATE SPIRAL.sldasm	Additional practice models		

7: Coffee mug

- Transient thermal analysis
- Thermal stress analysis
- Thermal symmetry boundary conditions
- Structural symmetry boundary conditions
- Use of soft springs

Project description

A ceramic coffee mug at room temperature is filled with boiling water for long enough to reach a steady state temperature, then the water is poured out, and the mug is left to cool down. We will find thermal stresses in the mug.

Procedure

Open MUG part model and review two configurations (Figure 7-1).

Configuration *01 full* Configuration *02 half*

Figure 7-1: Coffee mug model in two configurations.

Configuration 02 half will be used for analysis.

First, we conduct a **Steady state** thermal analysis to find the initial temperature conditions for the cool down process. Taking advantage of symmetry, we will use the *02 half* configuration. Switch to *02 half* configuration and create a **Thermal** study called *01 steady state*. Due to a high convection coefficient between water and porcelain, the inside of the mug will reach almost 100ºC, the temperature of boiling water. This can be modeled as a prescribed temperature (Figure 7-2).

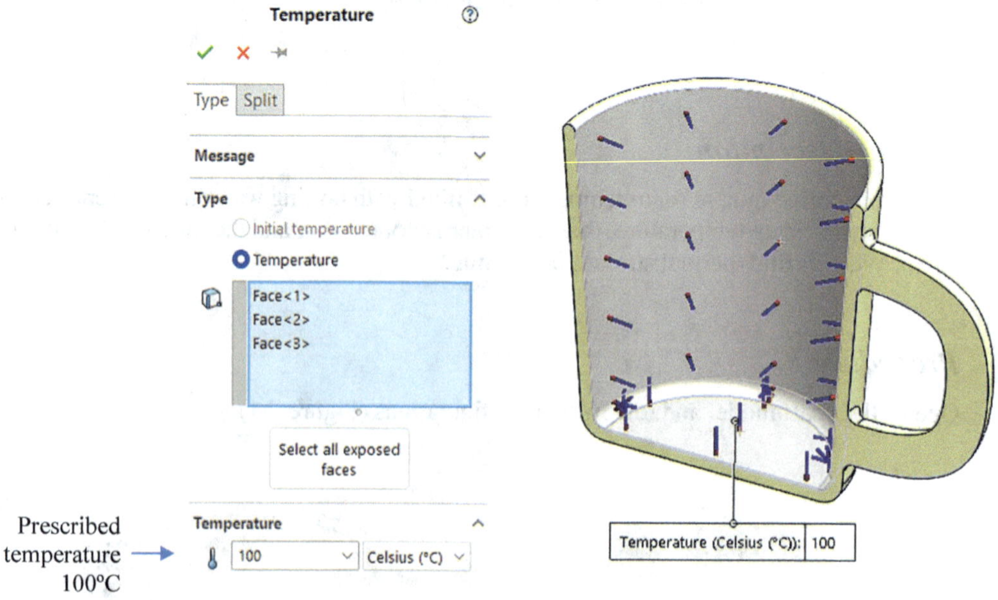

Figure 7-2: Prescribed temperature definition on the inner faces of the coffee mug.

A prescribed temperature is defined on three inner faces. No thermal conditions are defined on the faces in the plane of symmetry.

Heat enters the mug through faces where prescribed temperature is defined, travels by conduction through the porcelain, and exits to the surrounding air by convection. Define convective boundary conditions on the outer faces including the top face as shown in Figure 7-3.

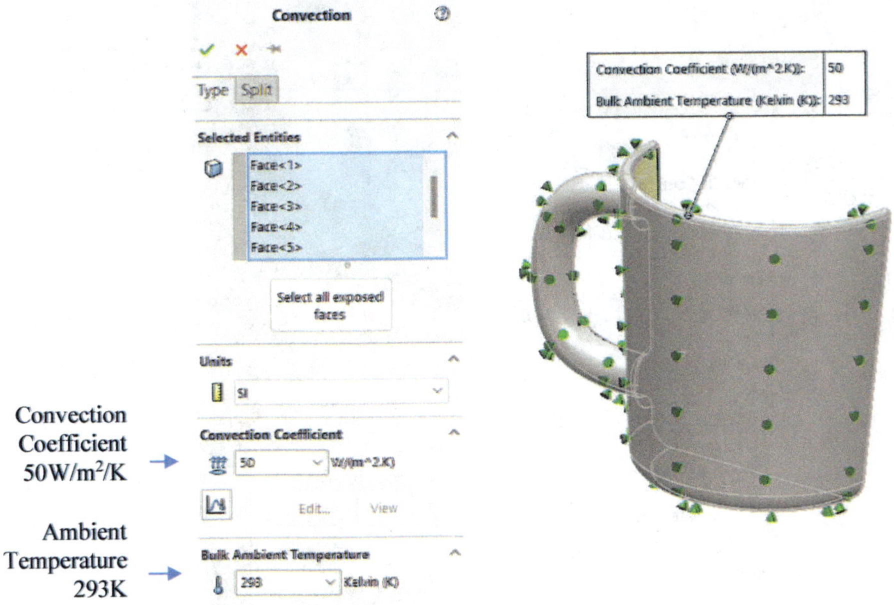

Figure 7-3: Convective boundary conditions on the outer faces of the coffee mug.

No convective boundary conditions are defined on the faces in the plane of symmetry.

Thermal symmetry boundary conditions require that no heat flows in the direction normal to the plane of symmetry. By not defining any convection conditions on the faces in the plane of symmetry, we enforce thermal symmetry boundary conditions.

Before meshing the model, we must remember that after thermal analysis completes, we will conduct the analysis of thermal stresses. In thermal analysis we study temperatures and that usually doesn't require highly refined mesh. It is analogous to the analysis of displacements only (and not stresses) in structural analysis. However, in thermal stress analysis, which is a structural analysis, we will study stresses. The mesh must be identical in thermal and thermal stress analyses and therefore, it must satisfy the more demanding requirements of the thermal stress analysis.

Define mesh controls on rounds where stress concentrations are expected (Figure 7-4).

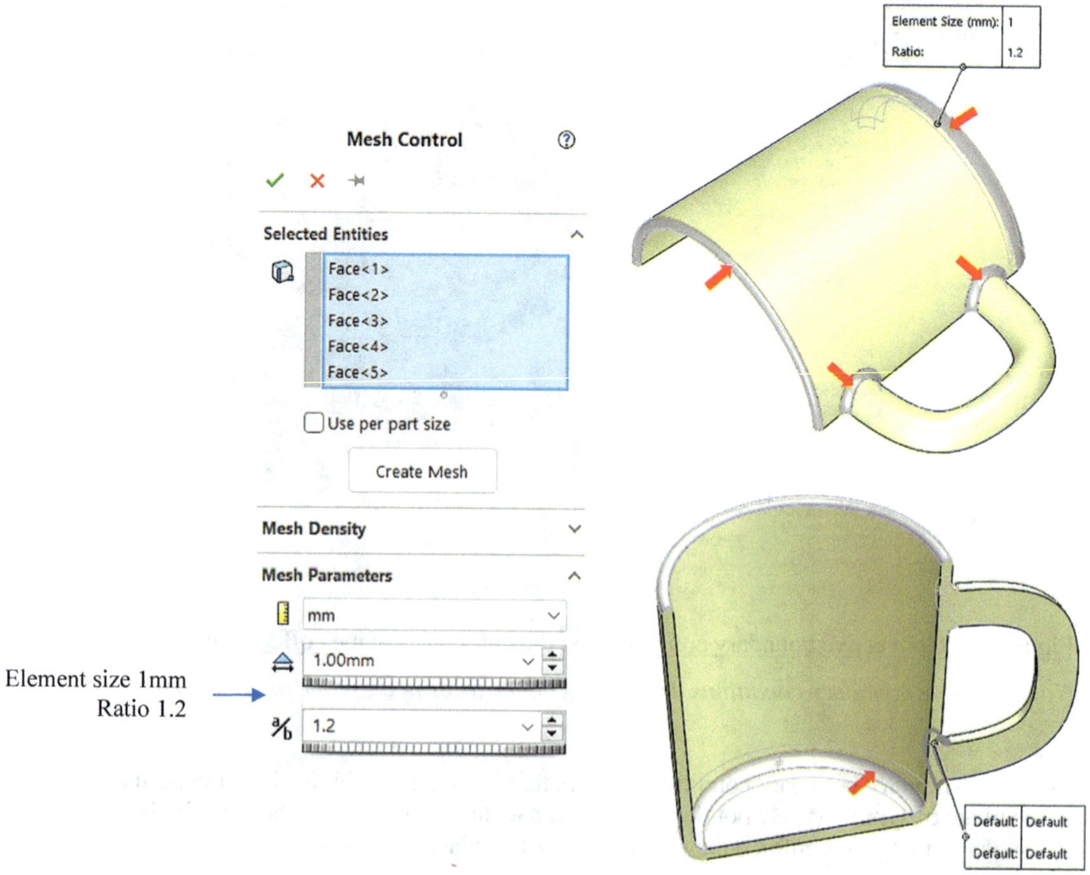

Figure 7-4: Mesh controls are defined on fillets where the ear connects to cup, on the rim and on the bottom of the mug on the outside and the inside round face as indicated by arrows.

1mm element size ensures low turn angle; a 1.2 transition ratio a/b ensures a smooth transition between locally refined mesh and the rest of the model.

Use a Standard mesh with global element size of 1.8mm to create two elements across the wall thickness. Run the solution of study *01 steady state* and review **Temperature** results (Figure 7-5).

Figure 7-5: Steady state temperature results.

Note a low temperature gradient across the mug wall as shown in the probed locations. Custom colors are used.

The temperature from the steady state thermal analysis conducted in study *01 steady state* is the initial conditions for transient thermal analysis.

Copy study *01 steady state* into *02 transient*. Define the study properties as shown in Figure 7-6.

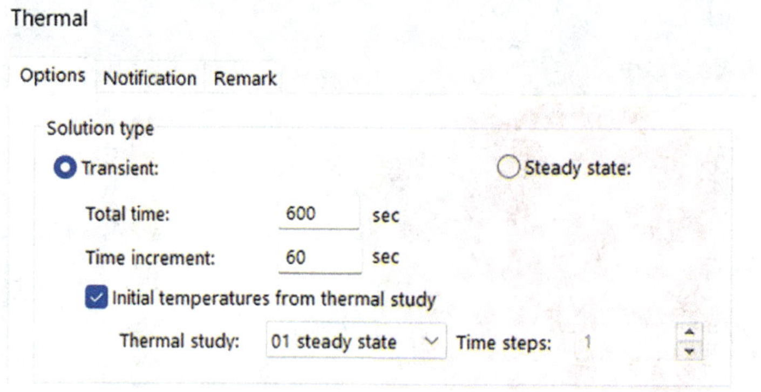

Figure 7-6: Properties of *02 transient* study: duration 600s and time step: 60s. The initial temperature conditions are taken from the completed steady state study *01 steady state.*

A total time of 600s and a time step of 60s mean that the analysis will be completed in 10 steps.

Delete the prescribed temperature (water has been poured out) and edit convection conditions to include faces where prescribed temperature was defined before (the inside faces are now exposed to air).

Run the transient solution and display a **Temperature** plot for step 4 or other step(s) of your choice (Figure 7-7).

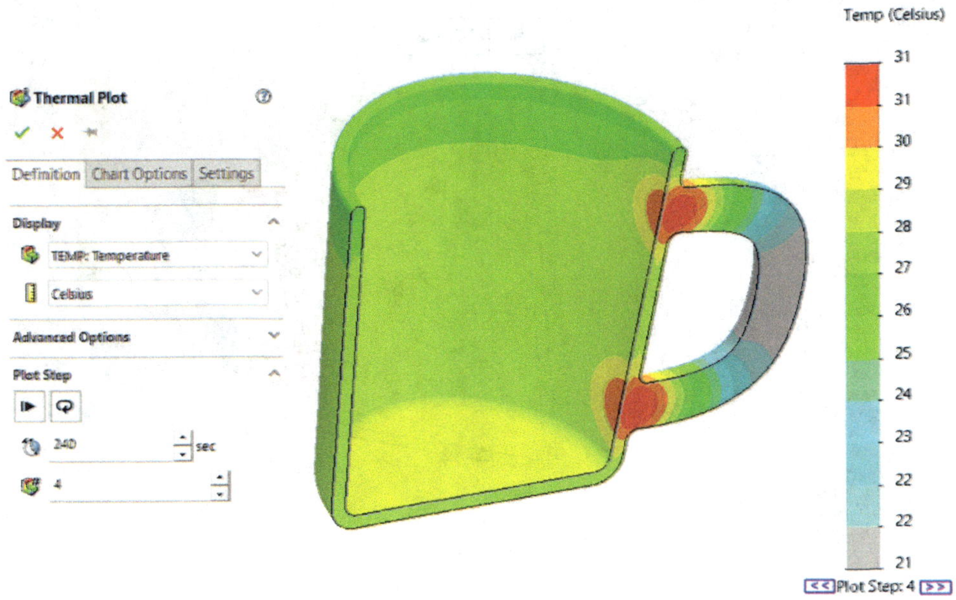

Figure 7-7: Temperature plot intime step 4.

Review other steps to see the change of temperature distribution over time.

Probe a temperature plot from any time step to produce temperature time history as shown in Figure 7-8.

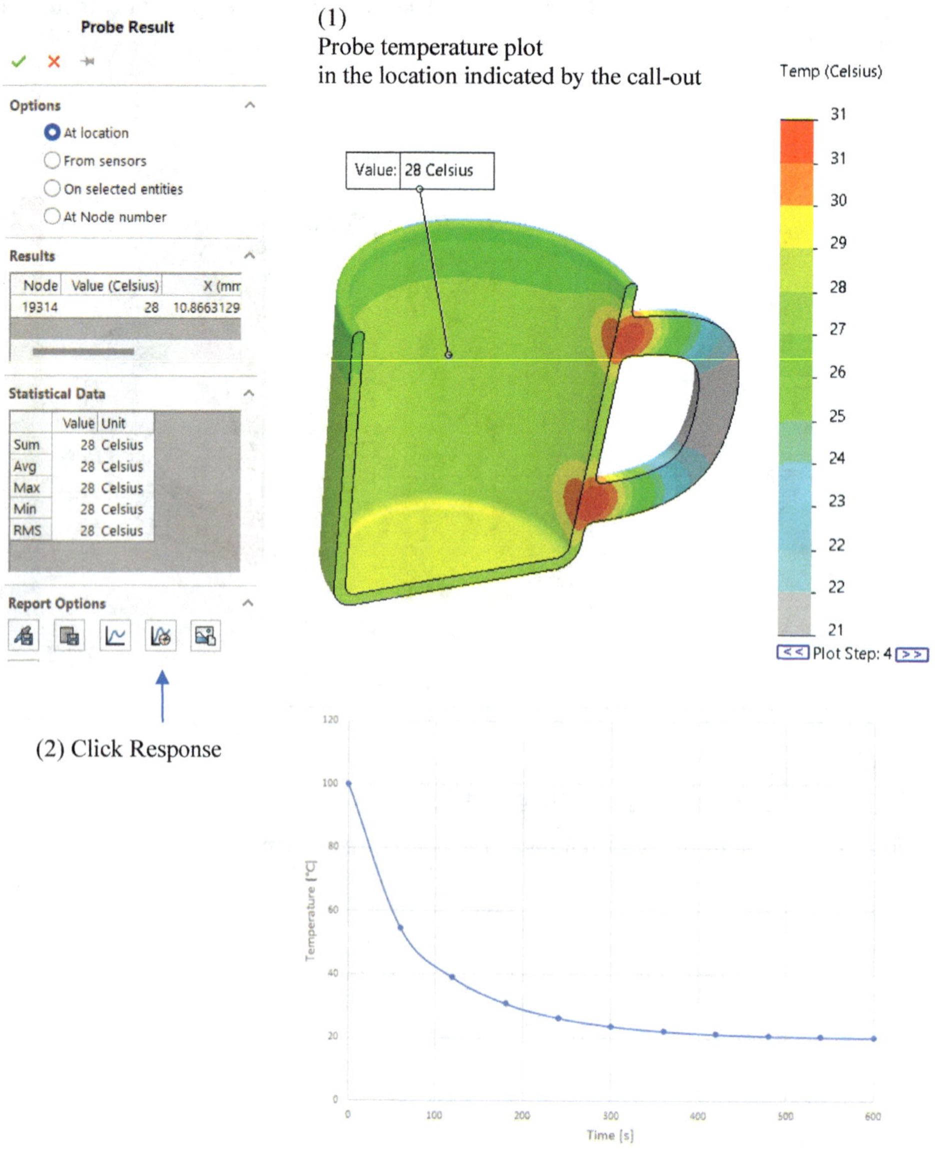

Figure 7-8: Temperature time history during 600s of the cooling down time.

After 600s the mug cools down to an ambient temperature. The graph has been formatted in Excel, the first point (0s, 100°C) has been added.

With temperature results from all 10 steps, we may now find how thermal stresses change over time. Create a static study *03 stress step 1* and define study properties as shown in Figure 7-9.

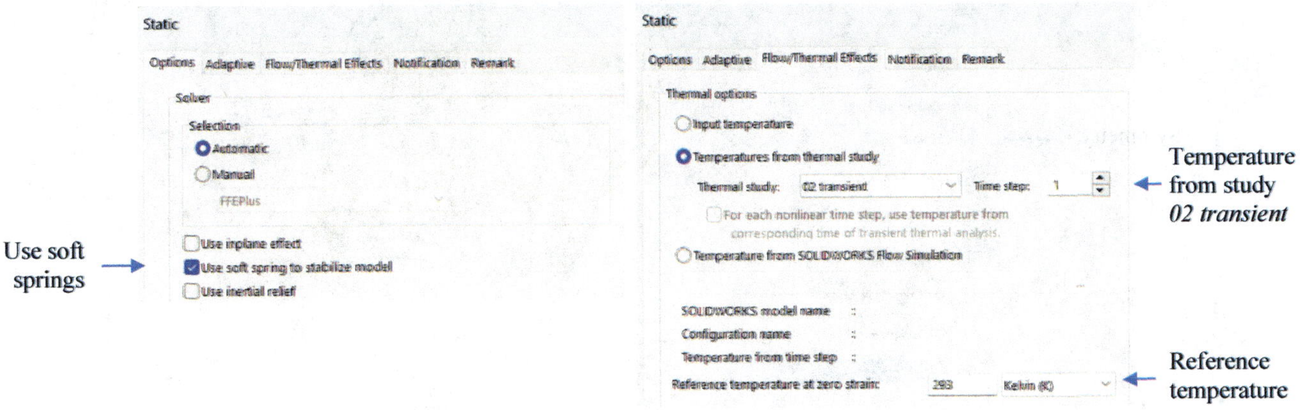

Options　　　　Flow/Thermal Effects

Figure 7-9: Properties of a static study used for analysis of thermal stresses.

Select Use soft springs to stabilize the model. The reference temperature at zero strain equals the ambient temperature used in thermal studies (293K).

While thermal boundary conditions require no action (nothing is defined on the face of symmetry), structural boundary conditions must be defined to eliminate out-of-plane motions. Follow Figure 7-10 to define structural symmetry boundary conditions.

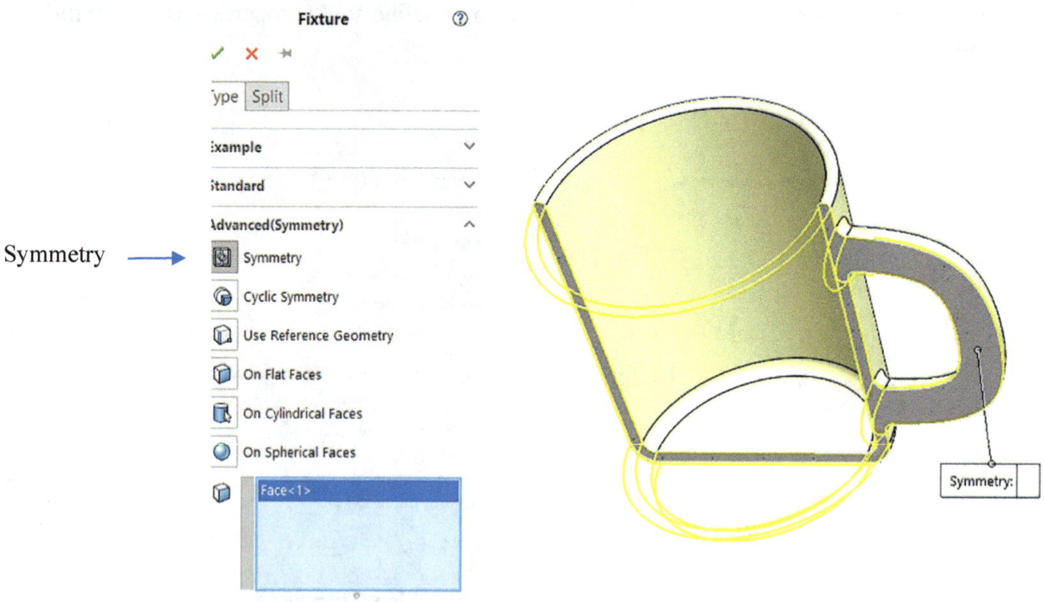

Figure 7-10: Symmetry boundary condition in study *03 stress step 1.*

Symmetry boundary conditions suppress translational degrees of freedom of nodes located on the plane of symmetry in the direction normal to the plane.

Symmetry boundary conditions will not restrain the model completely. Under the restraints shown in Figure 7-10, the model can slide in two directions along the plane of symmetry and rotate about the axis perpendicular to the plane of symmetry, meaning that the model has 3 rigid body motions (RBMs). We could add a **Fixed** restraint somewhere to the model but that would change stress results; remember that we want to see thermal stresses which are caused by uneven temperature distribution throughout the model. This is why we use the soft springs option (Figure 7-9) to eliminate these RBMs.

In a thermal stress analysis, nodal temperatures are imported from the thermal to structural (here static) study and that requires that the meshes in the thermal and structural studies are identical. The best way to make sure the meshes are identical is to copy the mesh from study *02 transient* to study *03 stress step 1.*

Run study *03 stress step 1*, ignore solver message about unstable model and display the stress results. Remember that von Mises stress must not be used when brittle material (ceramic porcelain) is analyzed. Instead, use the Maximum Principal stress (P1). Repeat the analysis of results using the next few time steps to see how stresses change while the mug is cooling down.

P1 stress results from step 1 are shown in Figure 7-11.

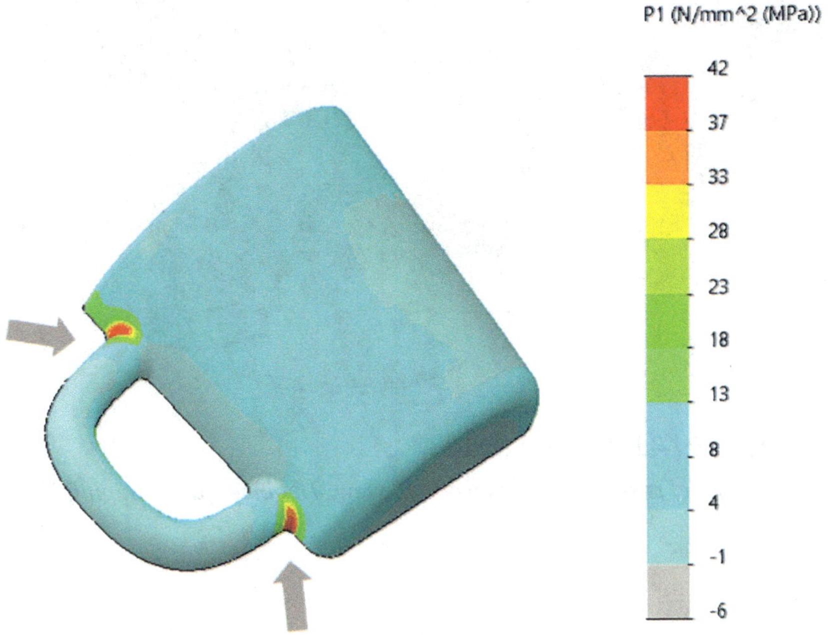

Figure 7-11: P1 stress results in step 1 of transient thermal analysis. Stress concentrations are indicated by arrows.

Display stress results with overlaid mesh to see that the mesh is at best marginal to model highly localized stress concentrations. Repeat this exercise with a more refined mesh.

Review the stress results from other steps to note that the highest stress of 41MPa is at the beginning of the cooling process. To calculate the factor of safety, the maximum P1 stress should be compared to the ultimate strength of the ceramic porcelain (173MPa). This calculation gives a factor of safety of 4.2.

To complete this exercise, animate displacement results from step 1 to see the pattern of thermal deformation. Next, construct a graph showing P1 stress as function of time (steps 1 through 10).

Deformations and stresses are caused by thermal effects only. Structural loads have not been used in this analysis.

Additional practice models

To reinforce the concepts presented in this chapter, repeat the analysis using the additional practice models. Define project input data following the approach used in the main exercise.

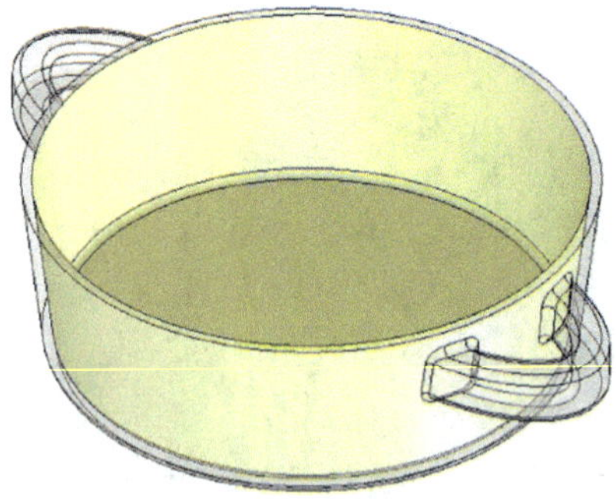

Figure 7-12: POT10 part model.

The model is shown in a transparent view. The inner face is highlighted in yellow.

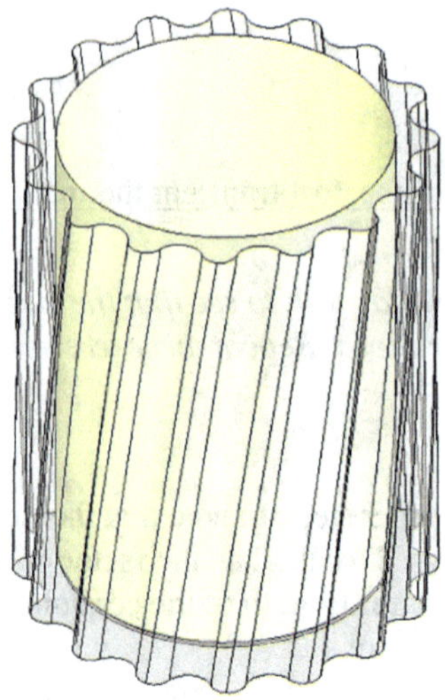

Figure 7-13: POT20 part model.

The model is shown in a transparent view. The inner face is highlighted in yellow.

Models in this chapter

Model	Configuration	Study Name	Study Type
MUG.sldprt	*02 half*	*01 steady state*	Thermal
		02 transient	Thermal
		03 stress step 1	Static
POT10.sldprt	Additional practice model		
POT20.sldprt	Additional practice model		

Notes:

8: Link

- Buckling caused by thermal expansion
- Interpretation of Buckling Load Factor

Project description

A steel Link is restrained by hinges on both ends. Its temperature is raised from the initial temperature of 298K to the final temperature 358K in six increments of 10K. We examine how the Buckling Load Factor (BLF) changes with the change of temperature.

Procedure

The analysis will be conducted using part LINK03. The temperature of Link at every step is uniform and that can be defined in Buckling analysis. There is no need for a pre-requisite thermal analysis. If the temperature was distributed non-uniformly, we would have to find temperature using a prerequisite thermal analysis.

Create a *Buckling* study called *b308* and verify that the study properties indicate 298K as the reference temperature at zero strain (Figure 8-1). Thermal options default to **Input temperature,** so no action is required.

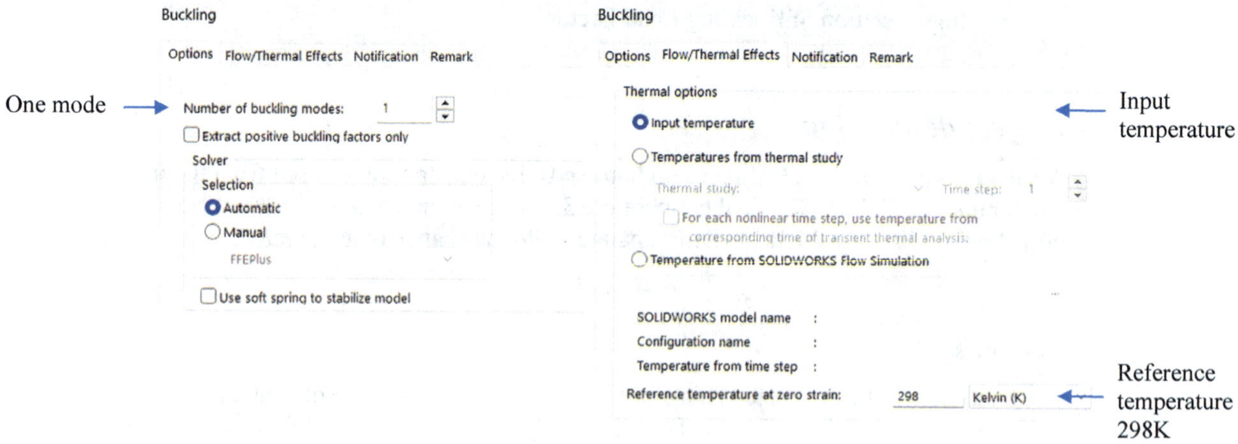

Options Flow/Thermal Effects

Figure 8-1: Properties of Buckling study.

One buckling mode is requested, the reference temperature at zero strain is 298K.

Define Fixed Hinge restraints to both ends (Figure 8-2).

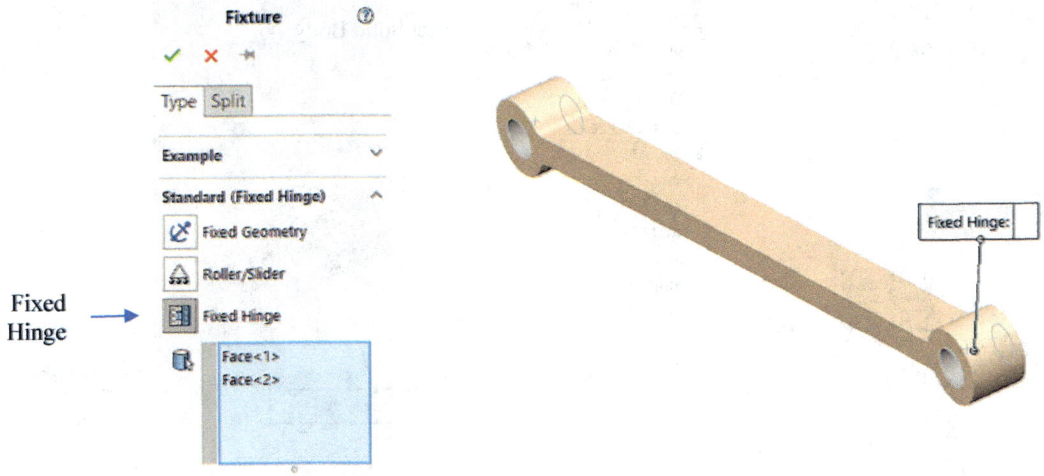

Figure 8-2: Link with hinge supports on both ends.

Fixed Hinge restraints are defined on both sides.

Apply Temperature of 308K to the solid body Link (Figure 8-3).

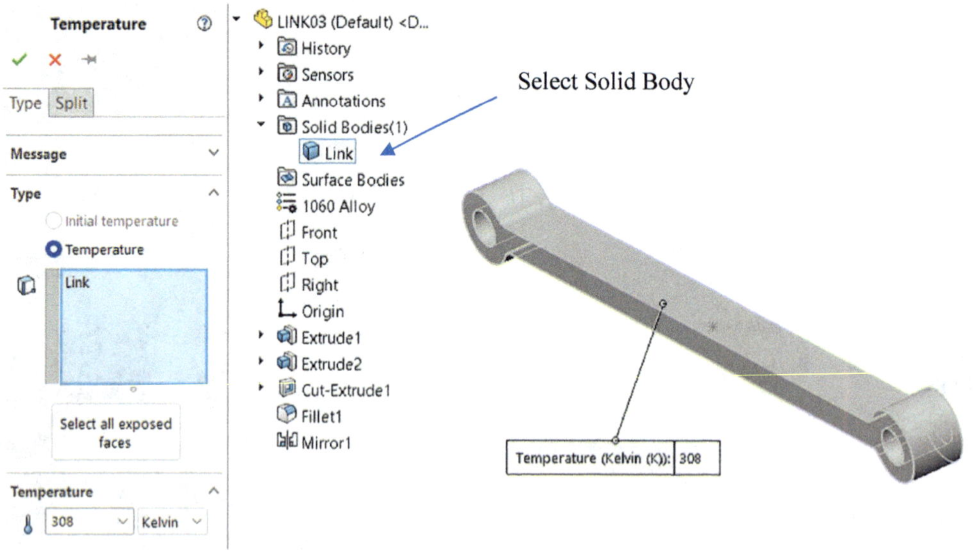

Figure 8-3: Temperature definition.

Temperature is applied to the solid body not to faces. Select the body Link from the fly-out menu.

Run *Buckling* study *b308* using Standard mesh with default element size and display the first buckling mode (Figure 8-4).

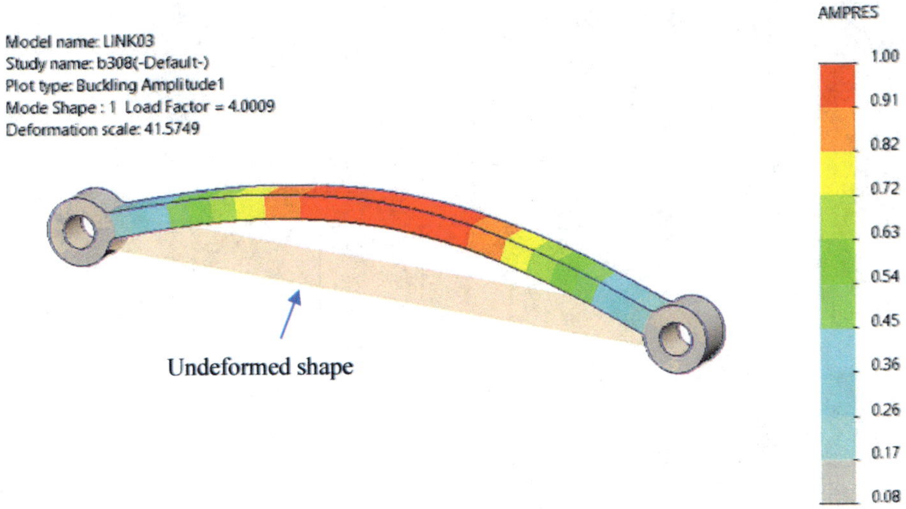

Figure 8-4: The first buckling mode, buckling load factor BLF=4.00.

Undeformed shape is shown; the numerical values are normalized to 1.

Numerical values shown in Figure 8-4 can be used only to find the ratio between displacement magnitudes in different locations. Absolute numbers are meaningless.

Animate results to see that the deformed shape can be either "up" or "down". A linear buckling analysis cannot determine which way the model buckles.

The first buckling mode shown in Figure 8-4 has a BLF of 4.00. The BLF is a ratio between the load causing buckling and the applied load:

$$BLF = \frac{Buckling\ load}{Applied\ load} = 4.00$$

The only loads on the model are the hinge reactions caused by the fact that hinges prevent thermal expansion of the Link. BLF=4.00 means that the reaction force would have to increase by a factor of 4.00 for buckling to take place. It does not refer directly to temperature.

To find those reactions, we need to run a *Static* study. Create static study *s308*; copy restraints, loads (**Temperature**), and mesh from the completed buckling study *b308* and obtain a static solution. Right-click the *Results* folder, select **List result force** and review the reaction forces in hinges (Figure 8-5).

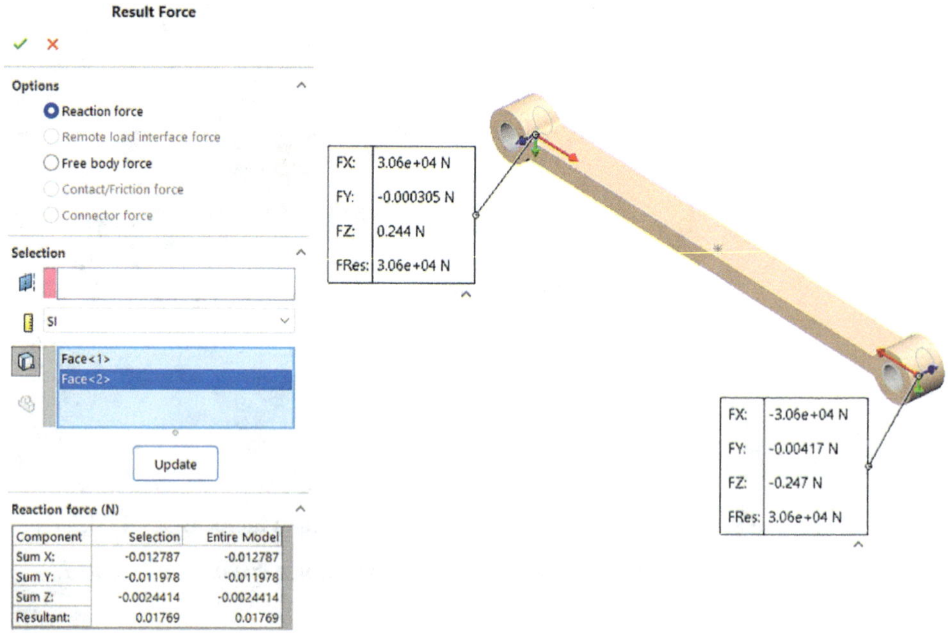

Figure 8-5: Reactions in hinges.

Reactions in y and z directions are caused by discretization errors.

Copy study *b308* and *s308* into *b318* and *s318* and make the Link temperature equal to 318K in these studies. Read the BLF from the buckling study and reaction force from the static study. Repeat the analysis in 10K increments creating studies *b328* and *s328, b338* and *s338, b348* and *s348, b358* and *s358*. Results are summarized in Figure 8-6.

Temperature [K]	**Buckling Load Factor**	**Reaction force** [N]
308	4.00	30627
318	2.00	61253
328	1.33	91880
338	1.00	122510
348	0.80	153130
358	0.67	183760

Figure 8-6: Summary of results of buckling and static studies.

BLF results come from buckling studies, reaction forces come from static studies.

As shown in Figure 8-6, the BLF at 338K is 1.00. It means that, according to the linear buckling analysis, the increase of temperature of the Link from initial 298K to 338K will cause buckling. The reaction force at temperature 338K is 122510N.

Figure 8-7 shows the BLF as a function of Link temperature.

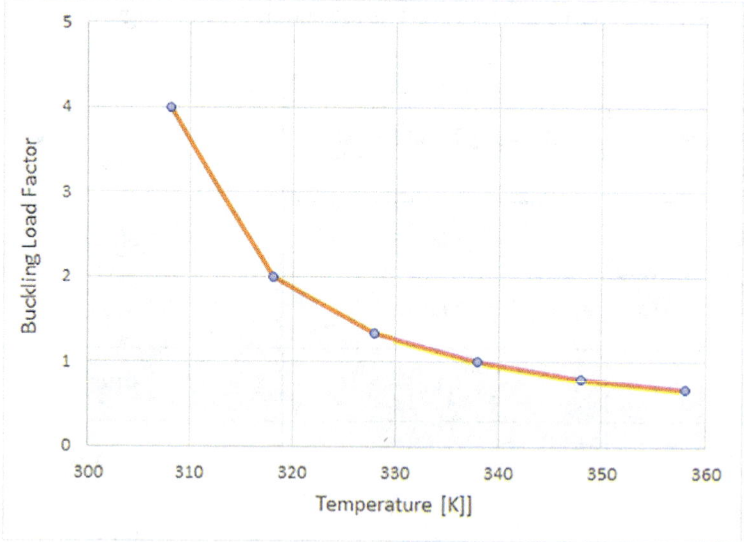

Figure 8-7: Buckling Load Factor as a function of Link temperature.

The BLF is inversely proportional to the increase of temperature ΔT (Figure 8-8).

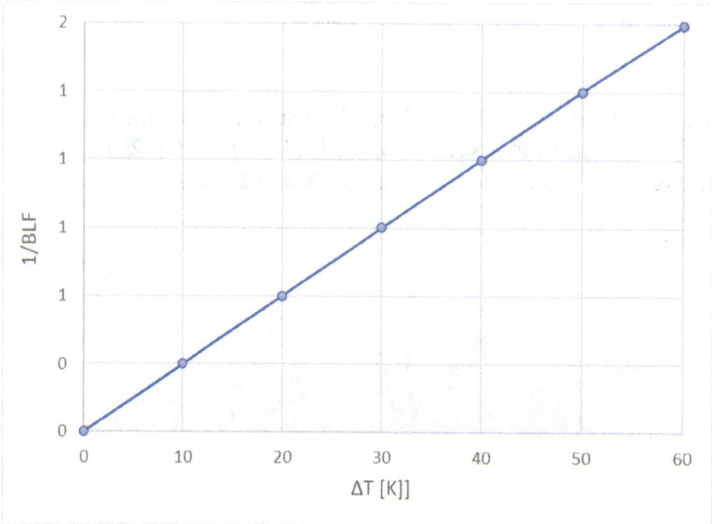

Figure 8-8: The inverse of BLF as a function of ΔT.

Additional practice models

To reinforce the concepts presented in this chapter, repeat the analysis using the additional practice models. Define project input data following the approach used in the main exercise.

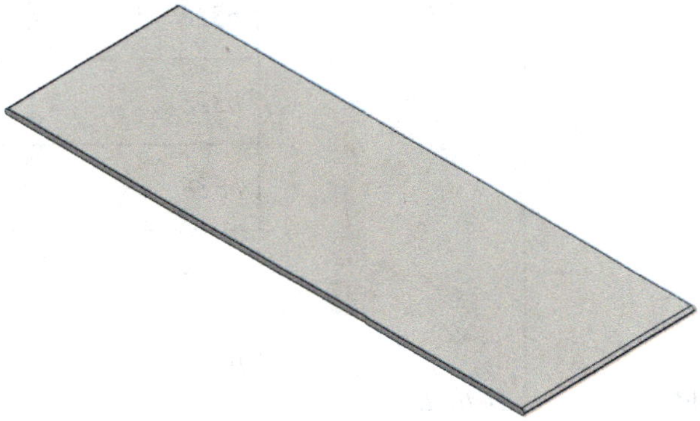

Figure 8-9: PLATE20 part model.

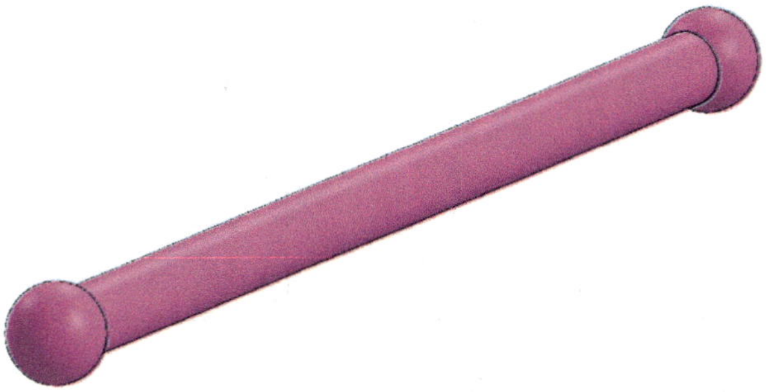

Figure 8-10: ROD20 part model.

Model	**Configuration**	**Study Name**	**Study Type**
LINK03.sldprt	*Default*	*b308*	Buckling
		b318	Buckling
		b328	Buckling
		b338	Buckling
		b348	Buckling
		b358	Buckling
		s308	Static
		s318	Static
		s328	Static
		s338	Static
		s348	Static
		s358	Static
PLATE20.sldprt	Additional practice model		
ROD20.sldprt	Additional practice model		

9: Heat sink

- Analysis of an assembly
- Thermal contact conditions
- Steady state thermal analysis
- Transient thermal analysis
- Thermal resistance layer
- Thermal symmetry boundary conditions

Project description

We need to find the relationship between the height of cooling fins of an aluminum radiator used to cool an electronic component and the temperature of radiator. We will demonstrate that fins that are too short do not provide adequate cooling while fins that are too long do not offer additional advantages in cooling.

HEAT SINK assembly model is shown in three configurations in Figure 9-1.

Configuration *01* Configuration *02* Configuration *03*

Figure 9-1: HEAT SINK assembly model.

The assembly has three configurations. The difference between the three configurations is the height of the cooling fins.

HEAT SINK assembly consists of two components: a ceramic microchip and an aluminum radiator. All heat generated by the microchip dissipates through the radiator. The two faces of the microchip: the cylindrical side face and the bottom flat face, are insulated.

The double mirror symmetry of the HEAT SINK assembly model offers an opportunity to simplify the analysis by using one half or one quarter of the model. We decide to use one half of the model and work with geometry shown in Figure 9-2.

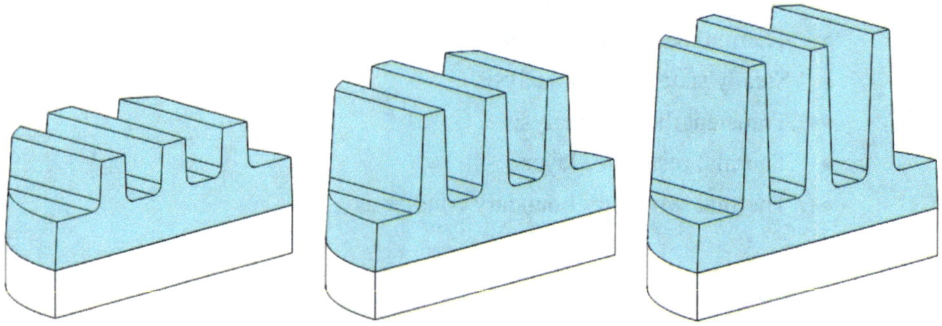

Configuration *01half* Configuration *02 half* Configuration *03 half*

Figure 9-2: *01 half, 02 half* and *03 half* configurations used for analysis.

We use half of the assembly to simplify analysis.

The ceramic microchip generates a heat power of 50W, and the aluminum radiator dissipates that heat. The ambient temperature is 27°C (300K). Heat is dissipated to the environment by convection through all exposed faces of the radiator. The microchip is insulated; it cannot dissipate heat directly to ambient air, but only through the face touching the radiator. The convection coefficient is 25 $W/m^2/K$ in this model; this value approximates a natural convection taking place without a cooling fan.

Heat flowing from the microchip to the radiator encounters thermal resistance on the boundary between the microchip and the radiator. Therefore, a thermal resistance layer must be defined on the interface between these two components.

To select the height of the cooling fins, we will determine the temperature and heat flux of the assembly in steady state conditions for the model in three configurations. This will require steady state thermal analysis.

Once we select the height of the cooling fins, we will study the temperature in the assembly as a function of time when the assembly is initially at room temperature and the power is cycled on and off every 10s. That will require transient thermal analysis.

Procedure

Switch to configuration *01 half* and create a *Thermal* study called *01 half*. Note that the *Solids* folder contains two bodies corresponding to the two assembly components with material properties already assigned: Ceramic Porcelain to the microchip and 1060Alloy to the radiator.

Before proceeding, we need to look at the *Connections* folder. By default, the Global Contact between parts in an assembly is Bonded. As the name implies, all parts in the assembly behave as one and heat encounters no resistance flowing from one part to another. We need to override the Global Contact condition by defining a Contact Set.

Right-click the *Connections* folder and select Contact Set to open the Contact Set window shown in Figure 9-3. Select Thermal Resistance with Node to surface as the contact type. This contact condition overrides the global Bonded contact condition. Use the exploded view to select the contacting faces and enter a **Distributed Thermal Resistance** of $0.001 Km^2/W$. The value of thermal resistance may be obtained by testing.

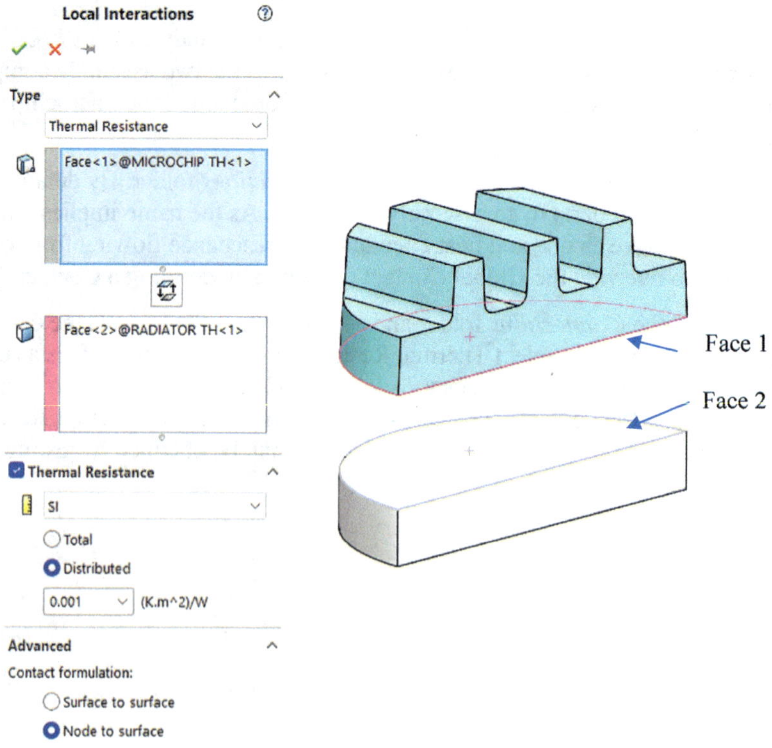

Figure 9-3: Definition of Thermal Resistance Contact Set.

Define a local Contact Set for contacting faces to introduce a layer of thermal resistance. Use an exploded model view to define the Contact Set. Use the Node to surface option in Advanced settings.

Next, specify the heat power generated in the microchip. To do this, right-click the *Thermal loads* folder to open the pop-up menu. Select **Heat Power…** to open the **Heat Power** window (Figure 9-4), and then from the fly-out menu select the *MICROCHIP TH* component and define 25W heat power, one half of the heat power generated in the microchip. This applies heat power to the volume of the selected component.

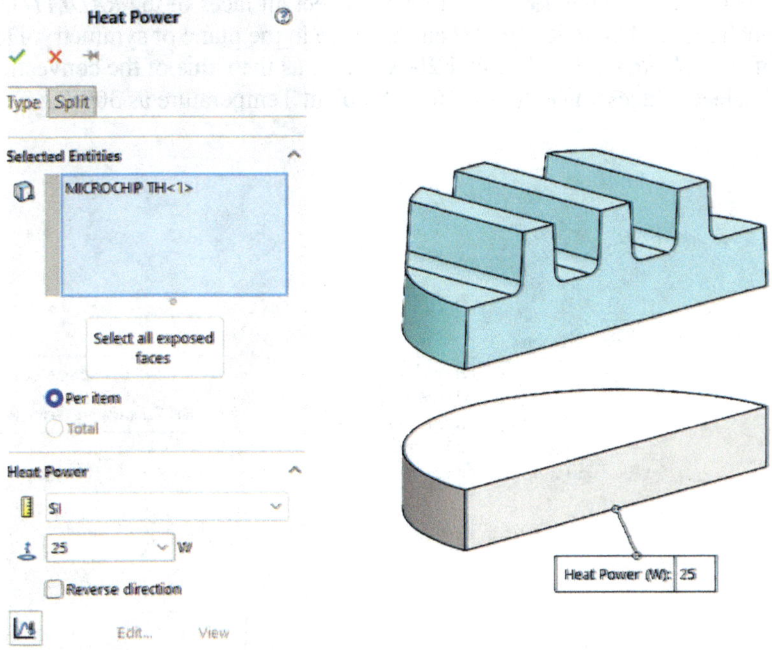

Figure 9-4: Heat Power is applied to the volume of the microchip.

Reversing the direction in Heat Power definition window would produce cooling.

So far, we have assigned material properties to each component, a heat source, and a thermal resistance layer. For heat to flow, we must also establish a mechanism for heat to escape the model. This is accomplished by defining convective boundary conditions.

Right-click the *Thermal Loads* folder to open a pop-up menu and select Convection… to open the Convection window (Figure 9-5). Select all faces of the *RADIATOR TH* except the one touching the *MICROCHIP TH* and the face in the plane of symmetry. Do not select any face of the *MICROCHIP TH*. Enter 200W/m^2/K as the value of the convection coefficient for all selected faces and enter the Bulk Ambient Temperature as 300K.

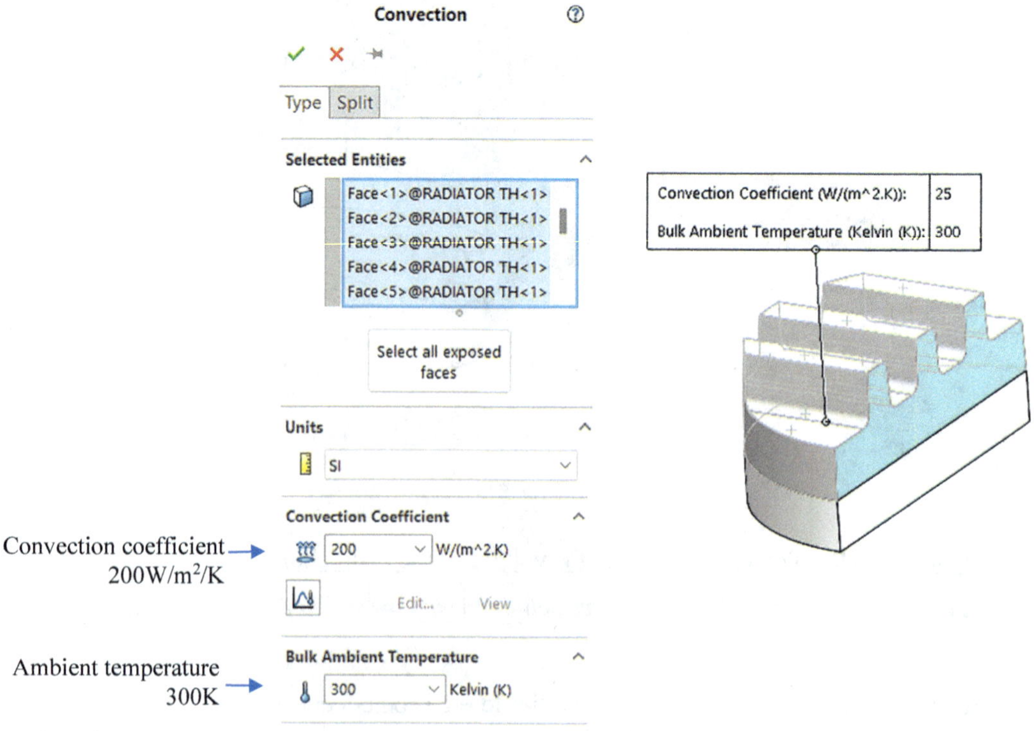

Figure 9-5: Definition of convective boundary conditions on the outer faces of the radiator.

Use this window to specify both the Convection Coefficient and the Ambient Temperature. Do not define convection on the face in the plane of symmetry, on the face in contact with the microchip, or to any faces of the microchip.

The last step before solution is creating the mesh. For accurate heat flux results, we need several elements modeling the fillet curvature. Use **Curvature based mesh** as shown in Figure 9-6.

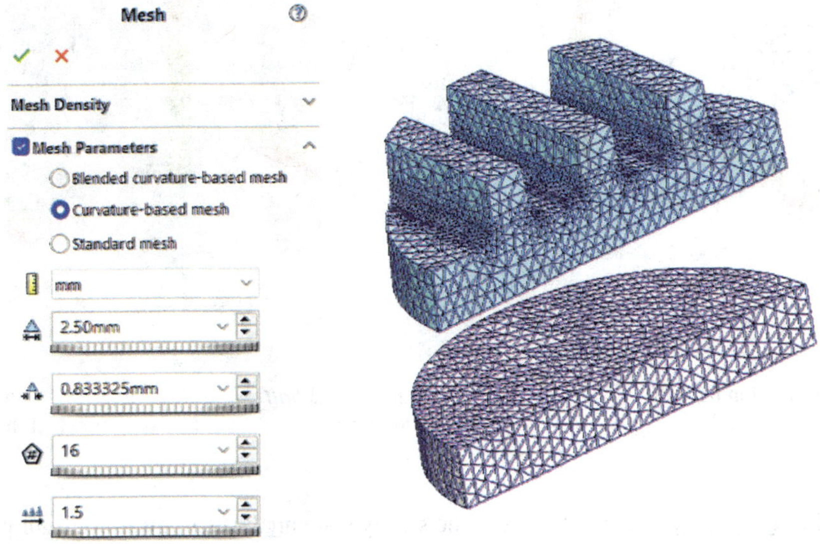

Figure 9-6: Curvature-based mesh assures correct meshing of fillets without the use of mesh controls: element size 2.5mm, 16 elements per circle.

Curvature-based mesh produces a low element turn angle at the base of each fin.

We use Curvature based mesh with settings shown in Figure 9-6 for all Steady State studies, even though the heat flux will not be analyzed. The Transient analysis will be performed with a default standard mesh.

Once the solution is ready, examine the temperature results. Repeat the analysis for *02 half* and *03 half* configurations; the summary is shown in Figure 9-7.

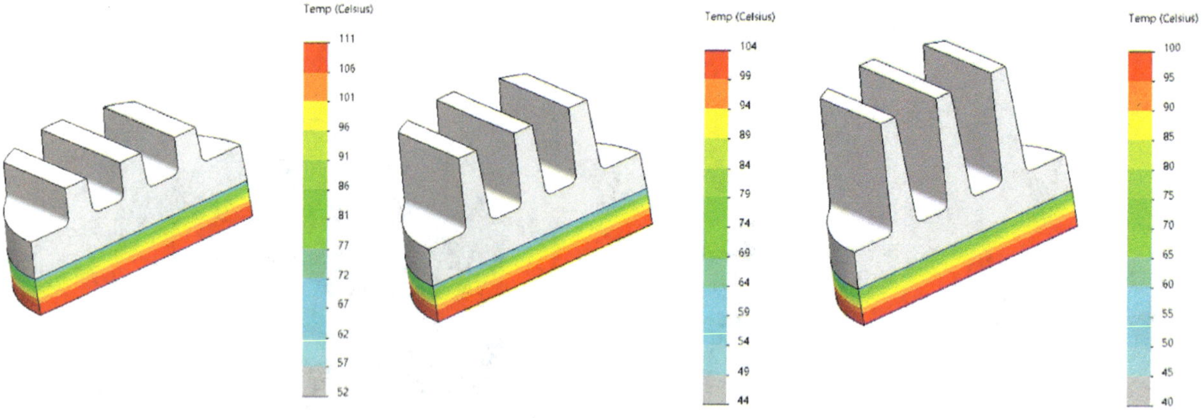

Configuration *01 half*
Fins 10mm high

Configuration *02 half*
Fins 20mm high

Configuration *03 half*
Fins 30mm high

Figure 9-7: Temperature plots in the steady state analyses in three configurations.

Note that the temperature of the radiator is practically uniform due to high thermal conductivity of aluminum. Temperature in the microchip is the highest on the bottom face.

We decide that 30mm high fins offer sufficient cooling and proceed with a transient analysis of the model in the *03 half* configuration.

Copy the study *03 half* into *03 half transient* and make it into a **Transient** study by defining properties as shown in Figure 9-8.

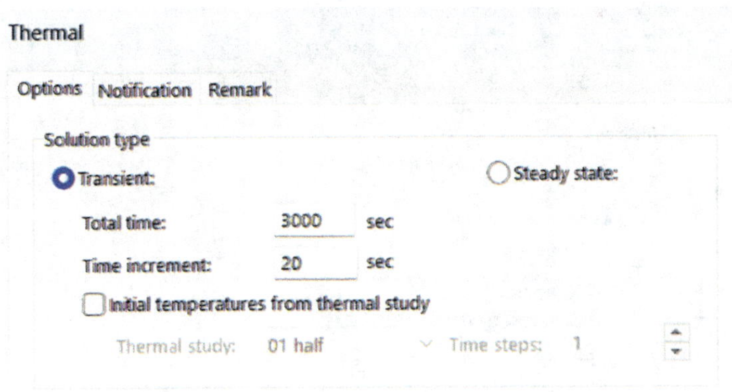

Figure 9-8: Properties of the transient thermal study.

Analysis will be conducted for 3000s in 20s intervals.

Overwrite the mesh copied from study *03 half* by meshing the assembly with a Standard mesh using a default global element size to reduce the number of elements. Large elements are used to reduce solution time in this analysis and are acceptable if we limit the analysis of results to temperatures. However, we would not be able to rely on heat flux results.

As in any transient thermal analysis, the **Initial temperature** must be defined for both components (Figure 9-9).

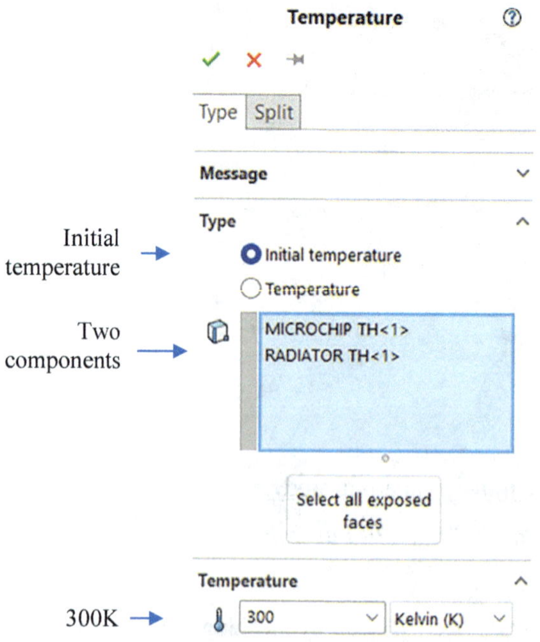

Figure 9-9: Initial temperature defined for two assembly components.

Select both components from the fly-out menu not shown in this illustration.

The definition of the convection coefficient remains unchanged, but the heat power definition must be modified to make it a function of time. In this analysis power cycles on and off every 100s.

Open the Excel file HEAT SINK TH and follow the steps shown in Figure 9-10.

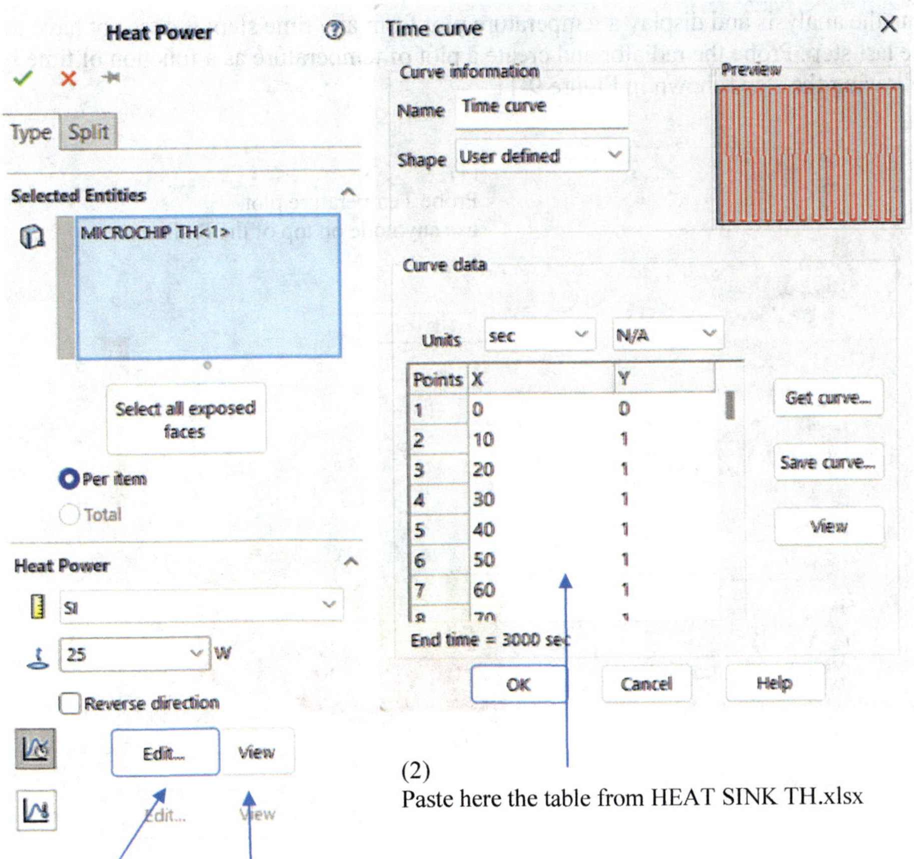

(2)
Paste here the table from HEAT SINK TH.xlsx

(1)
Click Edit to open Time curve definition window.

(3)
Click View to see the graph showing the heat power as a function of time.

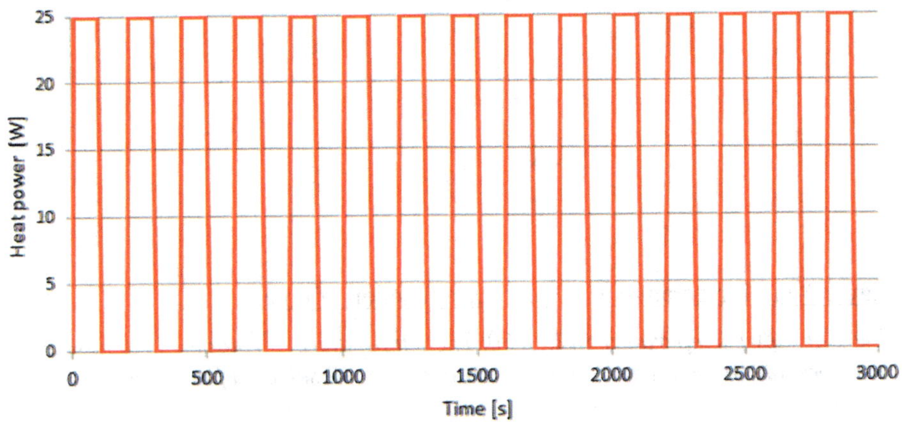

(4)
Review the graph

Figure 9-10: Definition of transient heat power.

Copy the table from HEAT SINK TH.xlsx.

Run the analysis and display a temperature plot from any time step; it does not have to be the last step. Probe the radiator and create a plot of temperature as a function of time by following the steps shown in Figure 9-11.

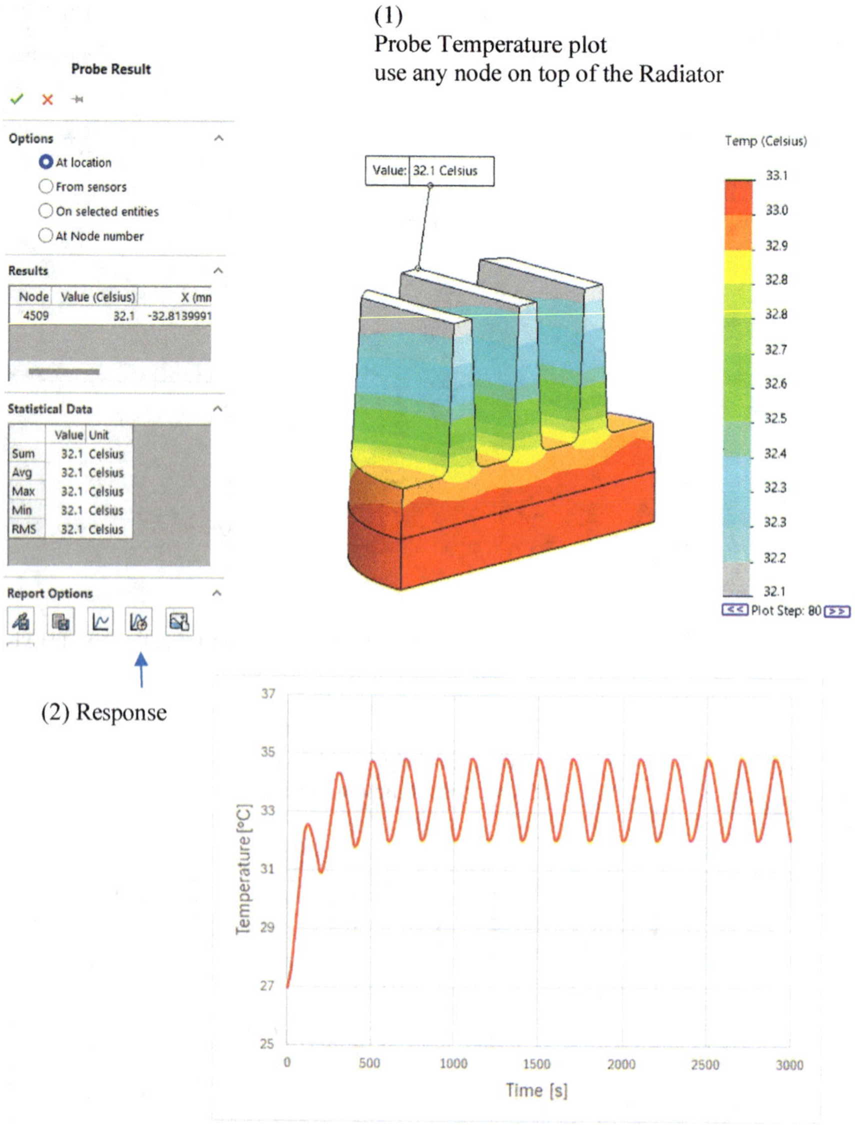

Figure 9-11: Temperature of Radiator as a function of time.

The plot shows temperature in step 80. The temperature of radiator is almost uniform; therefore, any point away from the microchip may be selected for probing temperature results.

The graph in Figure 9-11 shows that after 3000s, the temperature fluctuations stabilize in the range of 32-35°C.

All temperature plots defined so far have shown uniform temperature in the heat sink because the temperature gradient in the heat sink is very low as compared to the temperature gradient in the microchip.

Use plot Definition to select the time step and use Chart Options to adjust the range of temperature. Results for step 80 are shown in Figure 9-12.

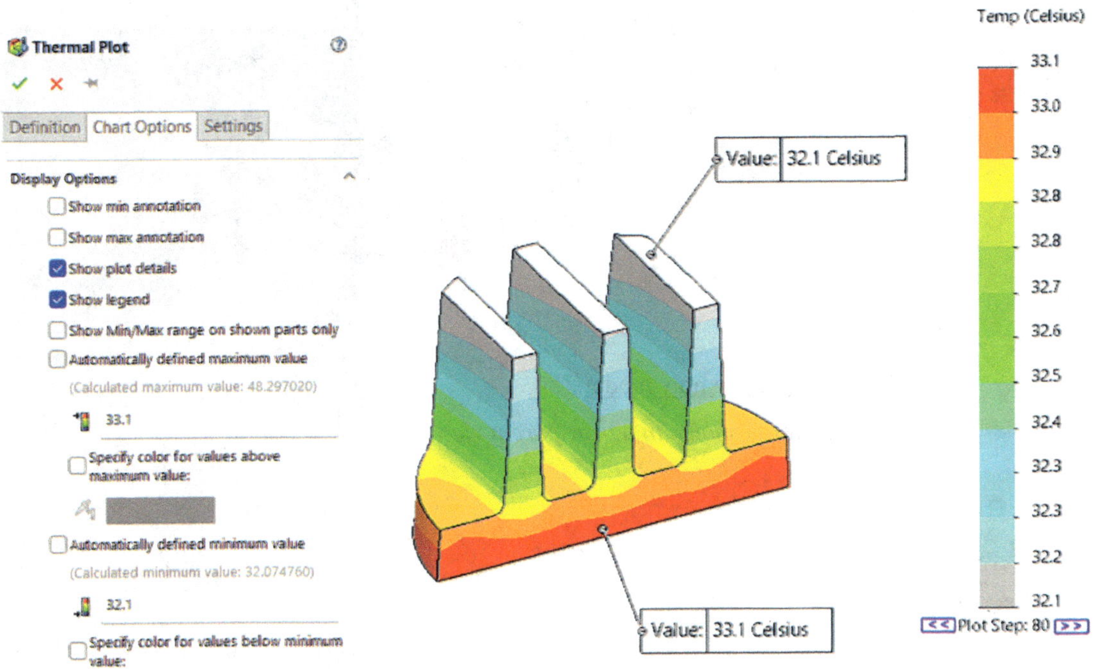

Figure 9-12: Temperature in Radiator in step 80 (time t=1600s).

The temperature plot shows step number 80. The temperature range defined in the plot is 32.1°C – 33.1°C, Microchip component is hidden.

Additional practice models

To reinforce the concepts presented in this chapter, repeat the analysis using the additional practice models. Define project input data following the approach used in the main exercise.

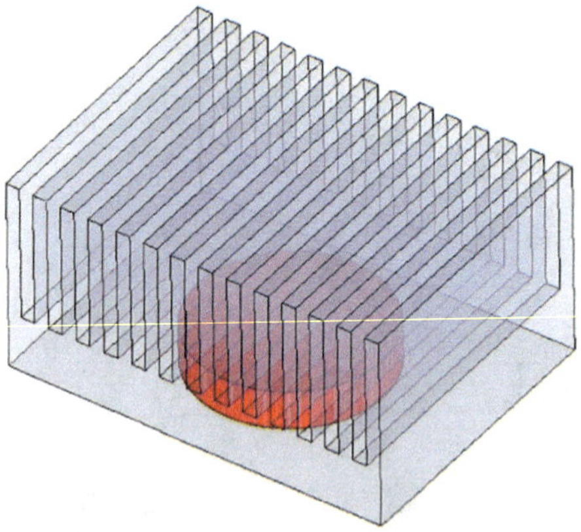

Figure 9-13: Assembly model Z80.

The radiator is shown in a transparent view.

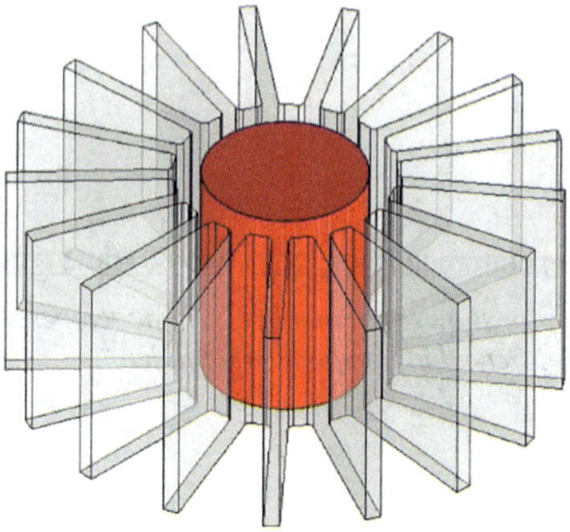

Figure 9-14: Part model Z85.

This is a multi-body part. The radiator is shown in a transparent view.

Summary of studies completed

Model	Configuration	Study Name	Study Type
HEAT SINK.sldasm	*01 half*	*01 half*	Thermal
	02 half	*02 half*	Thermal
	03 half	*03 half*	Thermal
	03 half	*03 half transient*	Thermal
Z80.sldasm	Additional practice model		
Z85.sldprt	Additional practice model		

Notes:

10: Furnace

- Steady state heat transfer
- Transient heat transfer
- Initial temperature
- Heat power
- Convective boundary conditions
- Symmetry boundary conditions

Project description

A large industrial furnace is powered by gas. The operating temperature of the furnace is defined by the temperature of the inner wall at 900°C. The outer faces transfer heat to the surrounding air at 25°C, a convection is coefficient $20Wm^{-2}K^{-1}$.

The furnace is a cube with 10m interior dimension and 0.5m thick walls. The wall material is Ceramic Porcelain.

We need to find:

- The heat power required to keep the furnace running with 900°C temperature of the inner wall.
- The time for the inner faces of the furnace to cool down to temperature of 35°C after gas heating has been turned off. The temperature of 35°C is considered a safe temperature to work inside the furnace.
- The time for the inner surface of the furnace to cool down to the temperature of 35°C with added cooling inside the furnace.

An idealized model geometry and the same convective boundary conditions on all outer walls make it possible to use a simplified model by taking advantage of a triple mirror symmetry using configuration *1_8* (Figure 10-1).

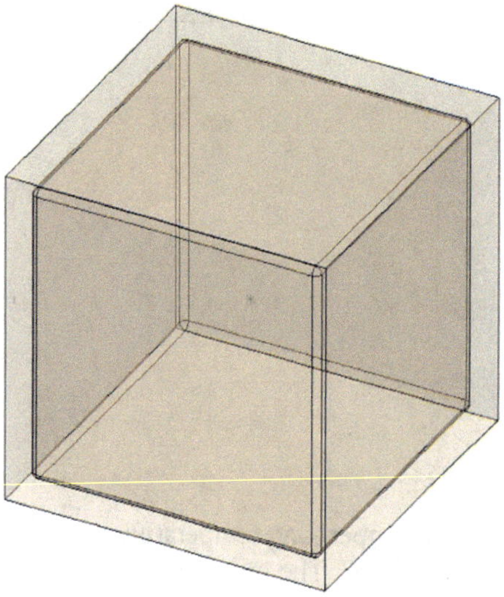

Configuration *Full*

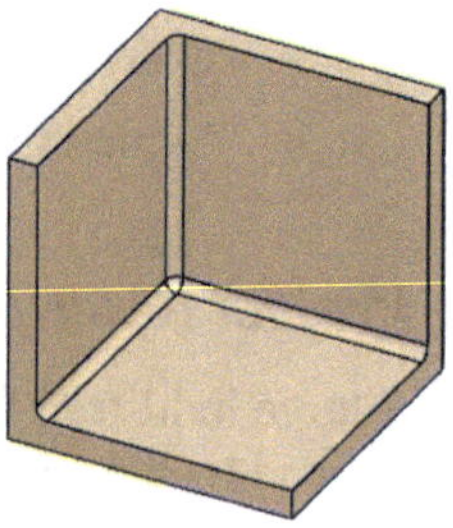

Configuration *1_8*

Figure 10-1: FURNACE part model in two configurations.

Configuration Full is shown in a transparent view. Configuration 1_8 is used for analysis.

We start with an analysis of a steady state heat transfer using configuration *1_8*.

Apply prescribed temperature 900°C to the inner faces, apply convective boundary conditions: ambient 25°C, convection coefficient $20Wm^{-2}K^{-1}$ to the outer faces. To satisfy thermal symmetry boundary conditions, do not apply any conditions to the faces in the planes of symmetry.

Mesh the model using mesh settings shown in Figure 10-2.

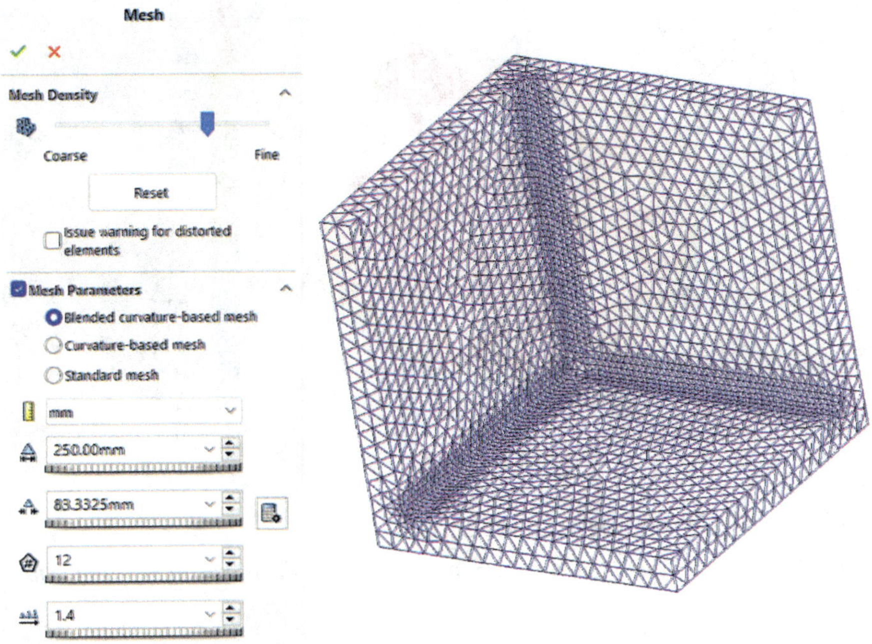

Figure 10-2: Mesh settings and mesh of 1/8 of the model.

Using element size 250mm places two elements across the wall thickness. Using Curvature based geometry with 12 elements in a circle produces correct mesh in fillets.

Run the solution and show the temperature plot (Figure 10-3).

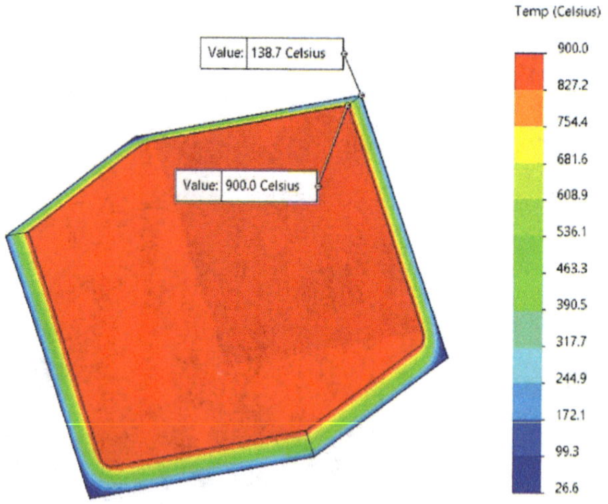

Figure 10-3: Steady state temperature plot.

Callouts show probed temperature in the center of the inner and the outer face.

Probe **Heat Power** on three outer faces or on seven inner faces (Figure 10-4).

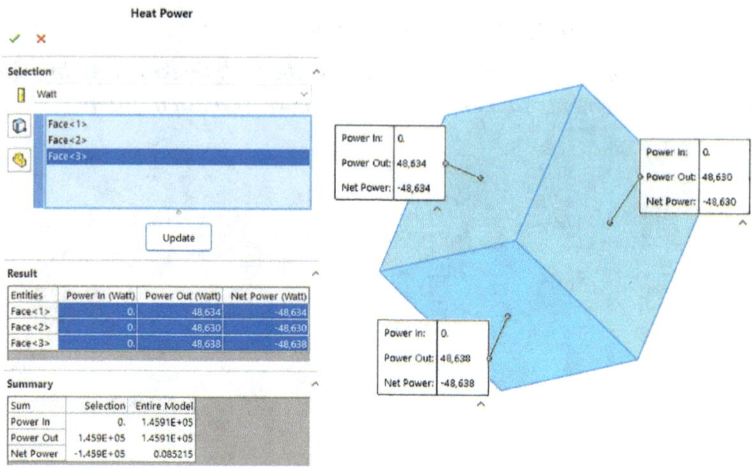

Figure 10-4: Heat power transferred to air by three outer faces is 145.9kW.

Small differences between heat power transferred by three faces are caused by discretization errors.

To calculate the heat power required to run the furnace at the operating temperature of 900°C of the inner faces, we multiply the results shown in Figure 10-4 by 8. The heat required to run the furnace is $145910 \times 8 \approx 1.17\text{MW}$.

Now we move to the next part: an analysis of furnace cooling after heat has been turned off. Copy study *Thermal1* into *Thermal2,* including the mesh. Edit study properties as shown in Figure 10-5.

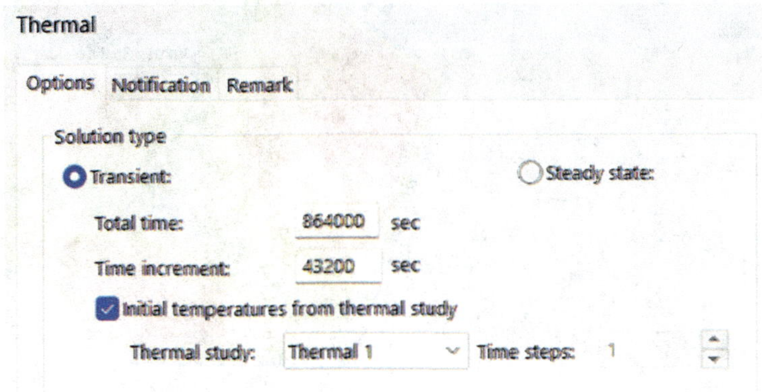

Figure 10-5: Settings of transient thermal study. The initial temperature is taken from the steady state study *Thermal1.*

Transient analysis will cover the period of 10 days with time increment of 12 hours.

The initial temperature in transient study is taken from steady state solution. Therefore, delete the initial temperature, which is a leftover from study *Thermal1*. Successful transfer of temperatures between steady state and transient studies requires that both studies use the same mesh, and that was assured by copying study, including mesh, from study *Thermal1* into *Thermal2.*

Leave convective boundary conditions unchanged on the outer faces. The inner faces don't have any boundary conditions defined meaning that they are insulated.

Obtain the solution, use temperature plot from any time step to probe locations shown in Figure 10-6. Select Response and export results to Excel.

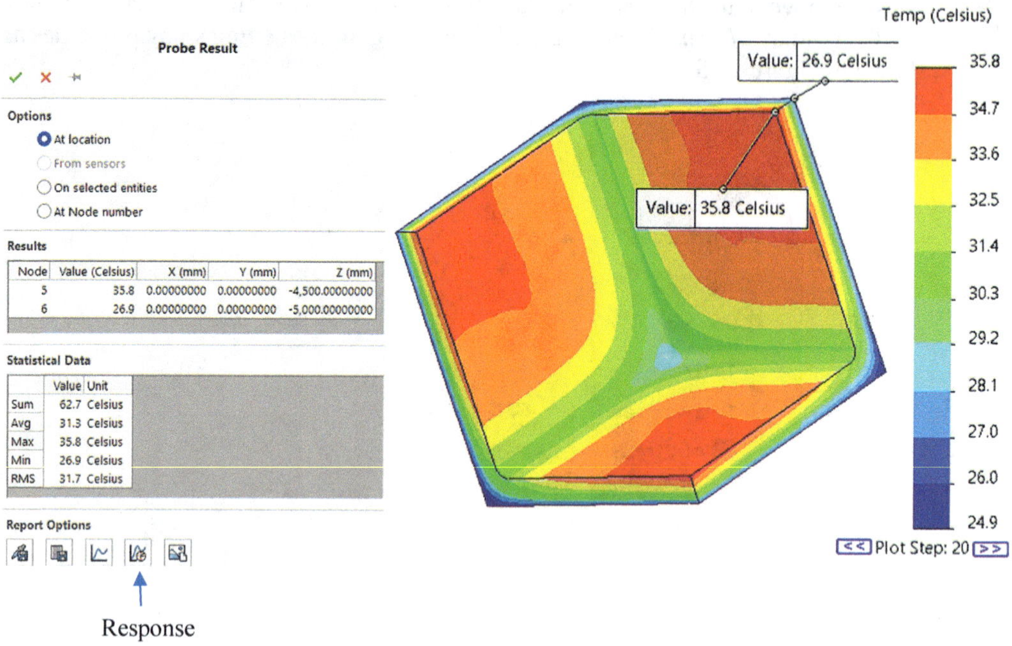

Figure 10-6: Temperature results from the last step of study *Thermal2.*

Compare the temperature in the probed locations to those shown in Figure 10-3.

In Excel, we see two curves: cooling of the inner and the outer face. Add to them points at t=0 using values from the steady state solution (Figure 10-3). As shown in Figure 10-7, temperature of the outer face after 10 days is approximately 35°C.

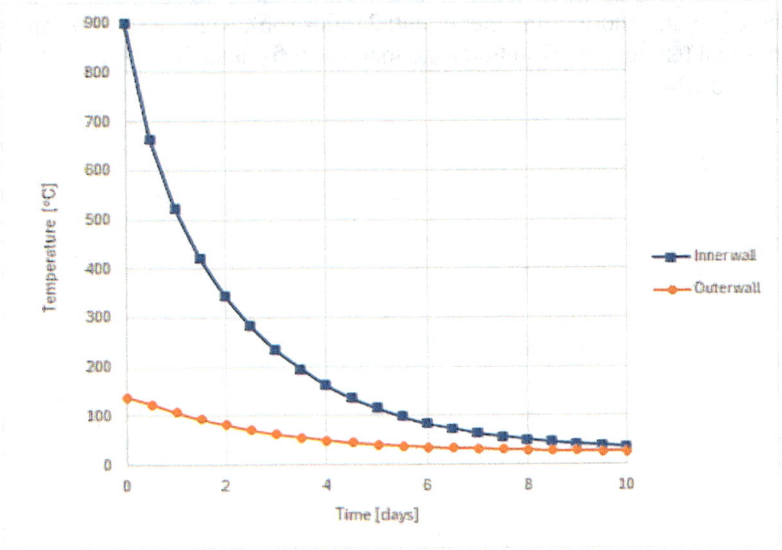

Figure 10-7: Temperature of the inner and the outer wall as a function of time.

Time is expressed in days, rather than in seconds used in the properties of transient study.

Transient temperature results show that it takes 10 days for inner face of the furnace to cool down to 35°C. To speed it up we add cooling inside the furnace, for example by opening the door and placing there an air blower.

Copy study *Transient2* to *Transient3.* To model the presence of a blower, add convection to the inner faces using the same values as on the outer faces. Cooling will be much faster; therefore, use shorter time increment: 21600s (6h). Run the solution and summarize transient temperature results for the inner wall from studies *Thermal2* and *Thermal3* (Figure 10-8).

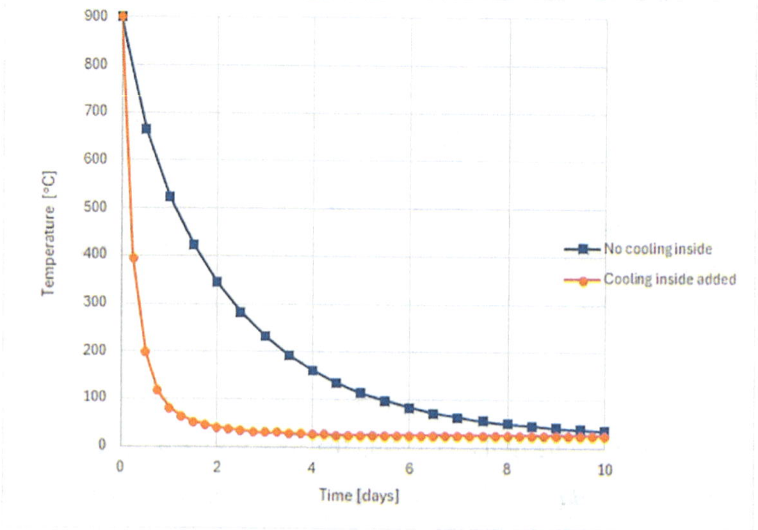

Figure 10-8: Temperature of the inner wall with and without added cooling as a function of time.

Adding convection to the inner faces reduces the cooling time to 35 °C from 10 days to 3 days.

Additional practice models

To reinforce the concepts presented in this chapter, repeat the analysis using the additional practice models. Define project input data following the approach used in the main exercise.

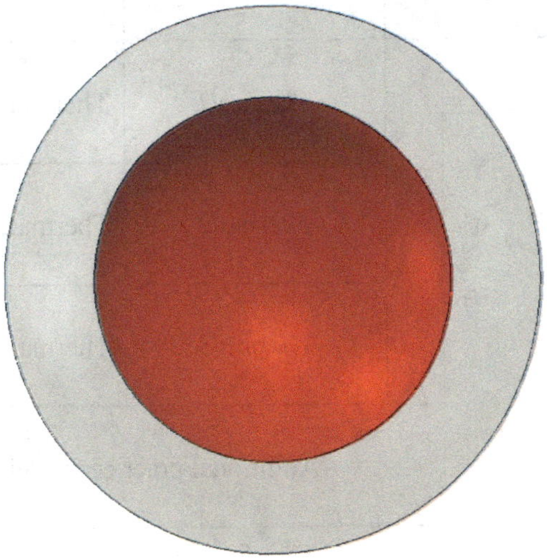

Figure 10-9: GLOBE part.

Face of the cavity is highlighted in red.

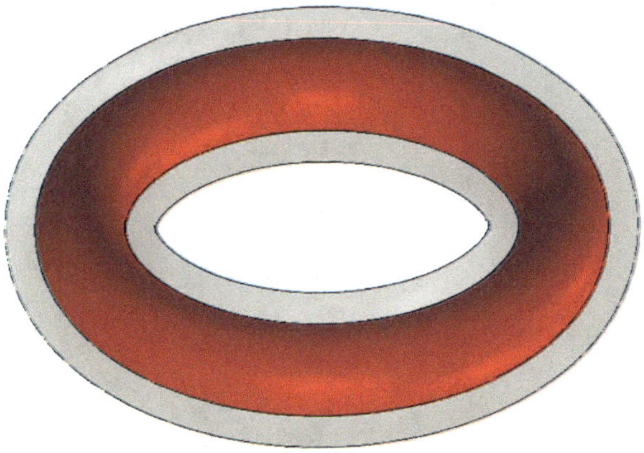

Figure 10-10: TORUS part.

Face of the cavity is highlighted in red.

Models in this chapter

Model	Configuration	Study Name	Study Type
FURNACE.sldprt	*1_8*	*Thermal1*	Thermal, Steady State
		Thermal2	Thermal, Transient
		Thermal3	Thermal, Transient
GLOBE.sldprt	Additional practice model		
TORUS.sldprt	Additional practice model		

Part 2

Radiative Heat Transfer

The analysis is extended to include radiative heat transfer using SOLIDWORKS Simulation. Radiation introduces additional modeling considerations, including surface emissivity, view factors, and the nonlinear nature of radiative heat exchange.

Conduction in solids continues to be modeled with the finite element method, while convection—when present—is still represented through boundary conditions. Adding radiation produces a more complete description of heat transfer while remaining within the framework of FEA-based thermal analysis.

Part 2 builds directly on the methods introduced earlier while expanding the range of physical phenomena that can be represented.

Notes:

11: Radiation of a black body

- Heat transfer by radiation
- Emissivity
- Black body
- Radiating heat out to space
- Transient thermal analysis
- Heat power
- Heat energy

Project description

A graphite Ball has a surface area of $1m^2$. It is surrounded by a vacuum, and its initial temperature is 0K. At time t=0s, a source of power activates such that 1000W is generated uniformly in the Ball volume. We want to know the steady state temperature of the Ball's face and the time required to reach that steady state assuming the Ball's face has the emissive properties of a black body.

The objective is to study a single body radiating heat out to space without any interference from other objects. This problem has a very simple analytical solution so we will be able to compare numerical and analytical results.

Procedure

Open GRAPHITE BALL and create a thermal study called *01 transient*. Define *Options* as shown in (Figure 11-1).

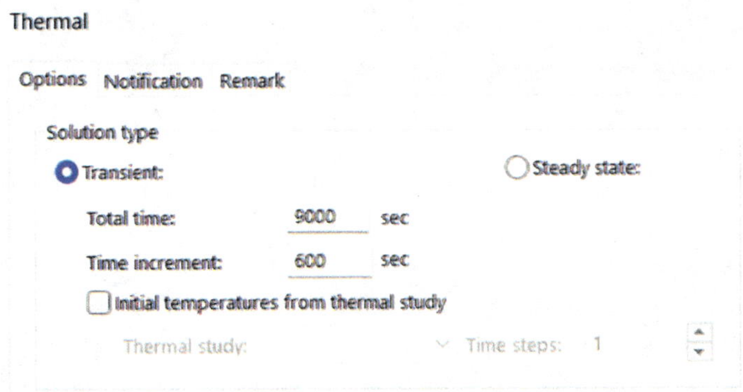

Figure 11-1: Properties of transient thermal study: total time 9000s, time increment 600s.

Most often, trial runs are required to define Total time and Time increment.

Define initial temperature of model as 2.7K, which is the background temperature of the Outer Space (Figure 11-2).

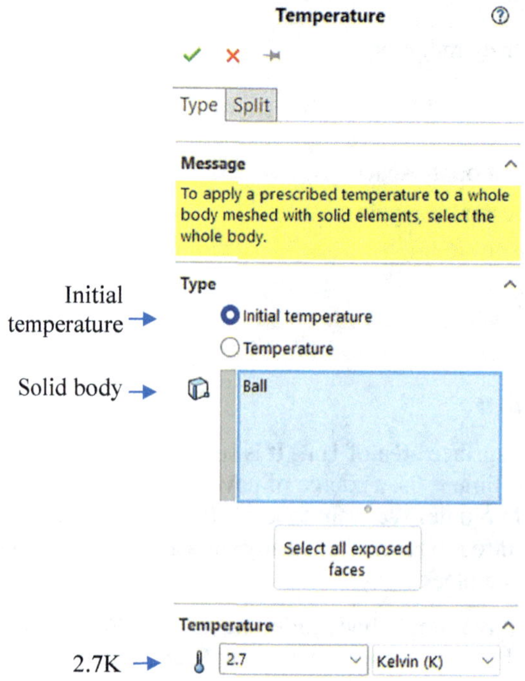

Figure 11-2: Definition of Initial temperature.

Select the Solid Body named Ball from the fly-out menu not shown here.

Define **Radiation** boundary conditions to the face of the ball (Figure 11-3).

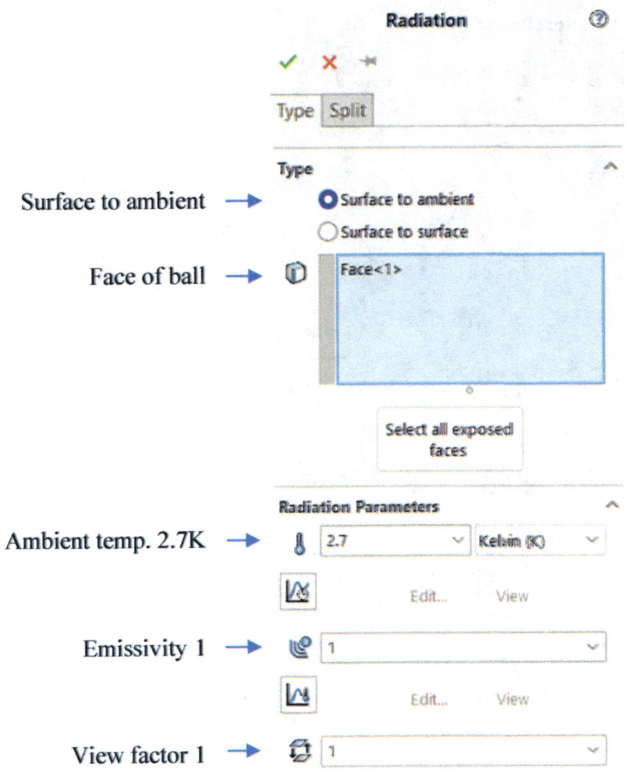

Figure 11-3: Radiation boundary conditions.

Radiation boundary conditions are applied to the face, not to the volume.

An **Emissivity** of 1 means that the face has the emissive properties of a black body. Nothing is better at emitting radiative heat than a black body. A **View Factor** of 1 in combination with a **Surface to ambient** type of radiative boundary condition means that all heat is radiated out to space without interfering with anything.

Define **Heat Power** as shown in Figure 11-4.

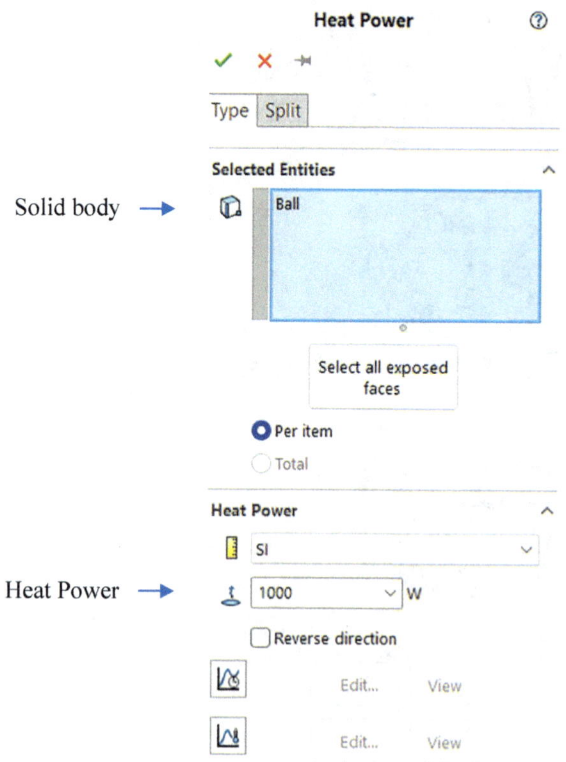

Figure 11-4: Definition of Heat Power.

From the fly-out menu, select the Solid Body to apply Heat Power to the volume of the ball.

Mesh the model with a default Standard mesh and run the solution. The solution is completed in 15 steps. Prepare Temperature plot in the last step using a section plot (Figure 11-5).

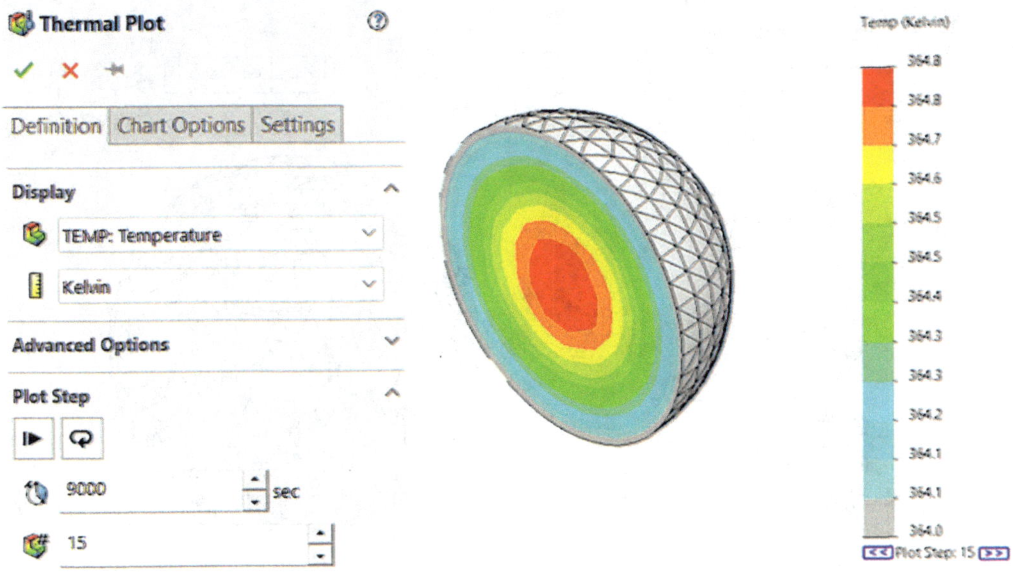

Figure 11-5: Temperature results in step 15 at time 9000s.

Mesh is shown on the uncut portion of the model.

The section plot indicates a low temperature gradient (0.8K). The temperature range is 364.0K to 364.8K.

To graph a temperature time history, display plot from any time step and probe any location on the face of the Ball (Figure 11-6).

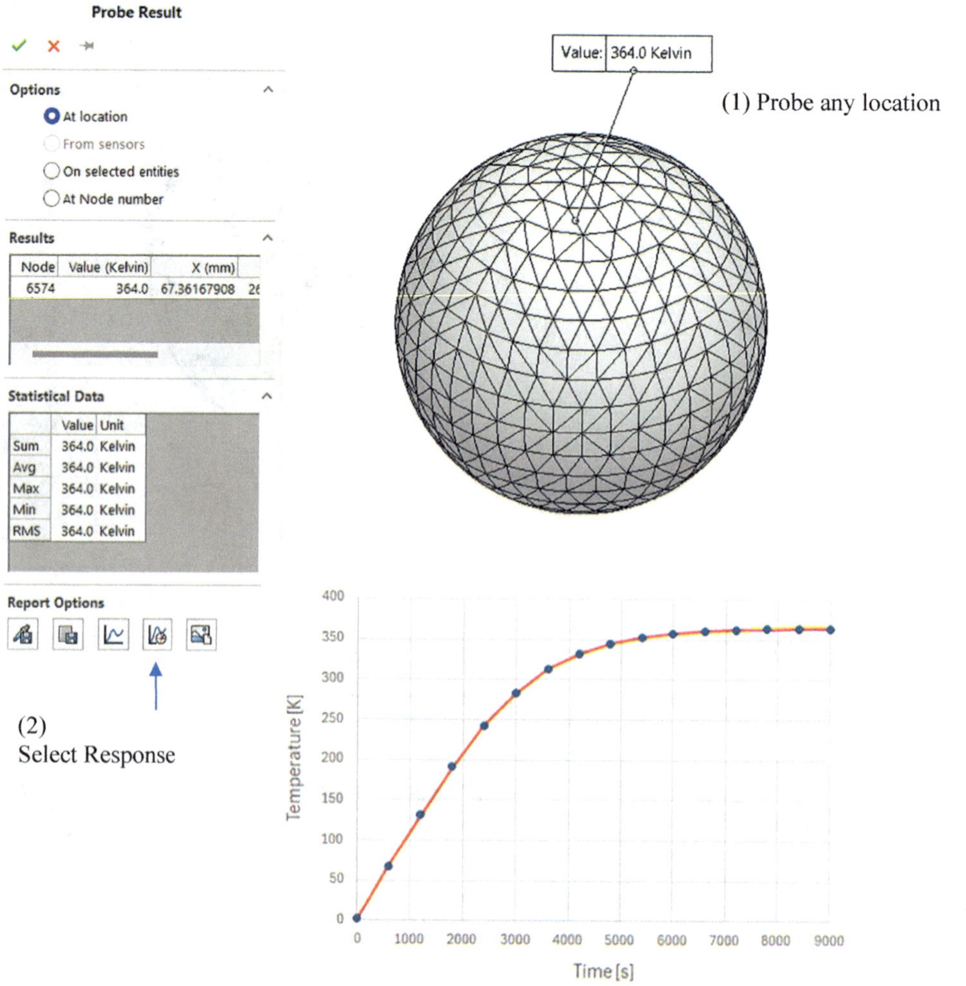

Figure 11-6: The temperature in step 15 and the temperature time history.

The Ball's face temperature is uniform, probe any location. Mesh is shown to demonstrate that the probed location snaps to the closest node; in this case, this is a mid-side node. The graph has been formatted in Excel, the first point (0s,2.7K) has been added.

As the graph in Figure 11-6 indicates, the steady state temperature has been practically reached after 9000s.

Review the **Heat Power** at step 15 and **Heat Energy** produced during the 9000s (Figure 11-7).

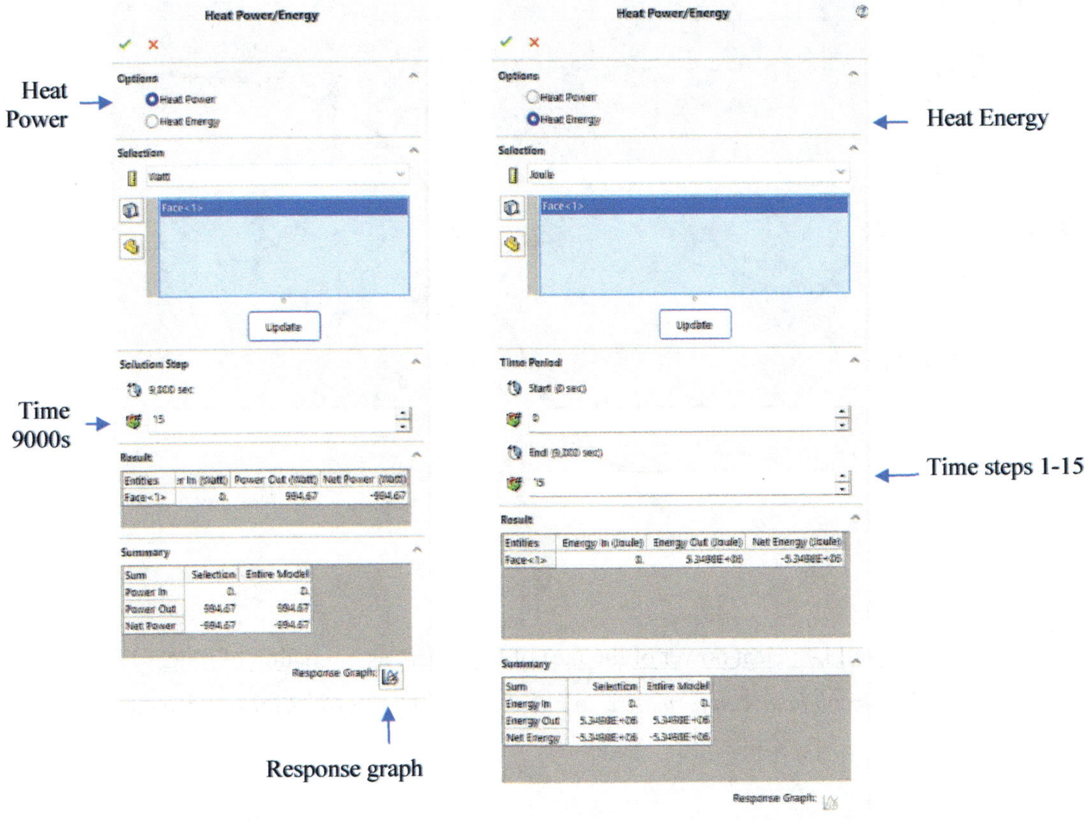

Heat Power emitted by the face in step 15 (9000s)

Heat Energy radiated out during 9000s

Figure 11-7: Heat Power at step 15 and the total Heat Energy during 9000s. Select the sphere face in both windows.

After 9000s the face is emitting 995W, the total energy emitted by radiation during 9000s is 5.325MJ. Review Response Graph in Heat Power window.

Construct Heat Power time history by selecting Response Graph in Heat Power window shown in Figure 11-7. The time history graph is shown in Figure 11-8.

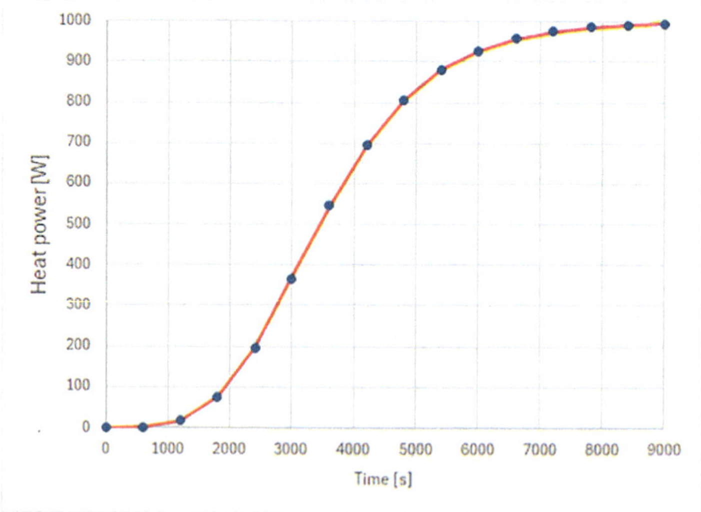

Figure 11-8: Heat power of the face of the sphere as a function of time.

The graph has been formatted in Excel, the first point (0s, 0W) has been added.

Very simple model makes it easy to compare the results of the numerical simulation with analytical results. Review model and results to note that:

The surface area of the Ball is 1m^2

The emissivity of the Ball face is $\varepsilon = 1$ (it is a black body)

Stefan-Boltzmann constant $\sigma = 5.67\text{x}10^{-8}$ $\text{W/m}^2\text{/K}^4$ (see chapter 1)

Heat flux $q = 995\text{W}/1\text{m}^2 = 995\text{W/m}^2$ (Figure 11-7)

Using the above, the surface temperature T_S can be found from the Stefan-Boltzmann law:

$$q = \varepsilon\sigma T_S^4$$

$$T_S = \left(\frac{q}{\varepsilon\sigma}\right)^{0.25} = \left(\frac{995}{1 \times 5.67 \times 10^{-8}}\right)^{0.25} = 364K$$

This result is the same as the numerical result $T_S = 364\text{K}$ shown in Figure 11-5. If results were truly steady state, we could use a heat flux of 1000W/m^2 from the input data.

We will now review energy balance.

Specific heat of graphite: $c = 44$ J/kg/K (read from material properties)

Mass of graphite Ball: 210.64kg (measure this)

Energy used to raise the temperature of the graphite ball from 2.7K to 364K:

$$E_C = mc\Delta T = 210.64 \times 44 \times 361.3 = 3349kJ$$

Energy radiated out from the Ball's face (Figure 11-7):

$$E_R = 5350kJ$$

Total energy:

$$E = E_C + E_R = 3349kJ + 5350kJ = 8699kJ$$

This result is within 3% of the total energy calculated as:

$$E = P \times t = 1000W \times 9000s = 9000kJ,$$

where P is the heat power and t is the duration of the analyzed process.

Additional practice models

To reinforce the concepts presented in this chapter, repeat the analysis using the additional practice models. Define project input data following the approach used in the main exercise.

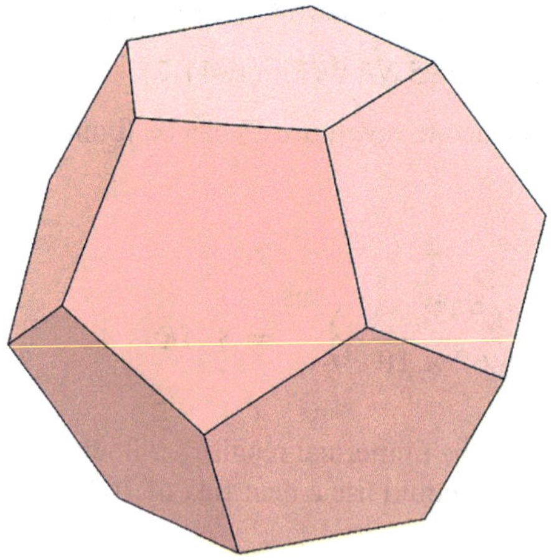

Figure 11-9: DODECAHEDRON part model.

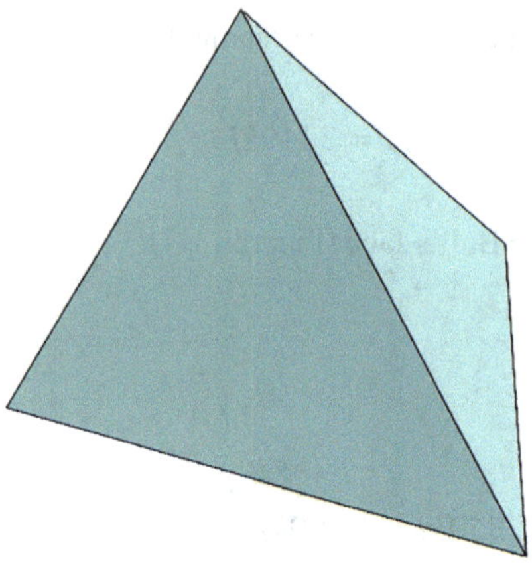

Figure 11-10: TETRAHEDRON part model.

Models in this chapter

Model	Configuration	Study Name	Study Type
GRAPHITE BALL.sldprt	*Default*	*01 transient*	Thermal
DODECAHEDRON.sldprt	Additional practice model		
TETRAHEDRON.sldprt	Additional practice model		

Notes:

12: Radiation of a hemisphere

- Heat transfer by radiation
- Emissivity
- Radiating heat out to space
- View factors
- Heat power

Project description

A nickel hemisphere produces heat power of 800W in its volume. All faces are insulated except for the concave face that exchanges heat by radiation with a distant enclosure at 30°C, the face emissivity is 0.4. The hemisphere is in vacuum. Heat is emitted by radiation only through the concave face. We need to find the steady state temperature of the hemisphere.

Procedure

Open HEMISPHERE part (Figure 12-1), create a thermal study called *01 steady state*.

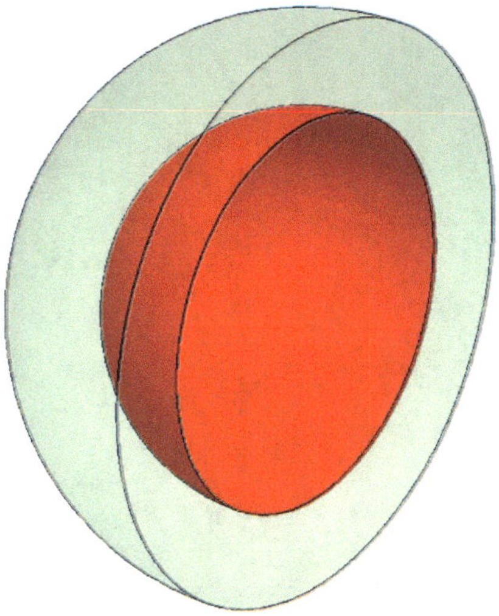

Figure 12-1: HEMISPHERE part model.

The model is shown in a transparent view. The concave face radiating heat is shown in red.

Define **Heat Power** as shown in Figure 12-2.

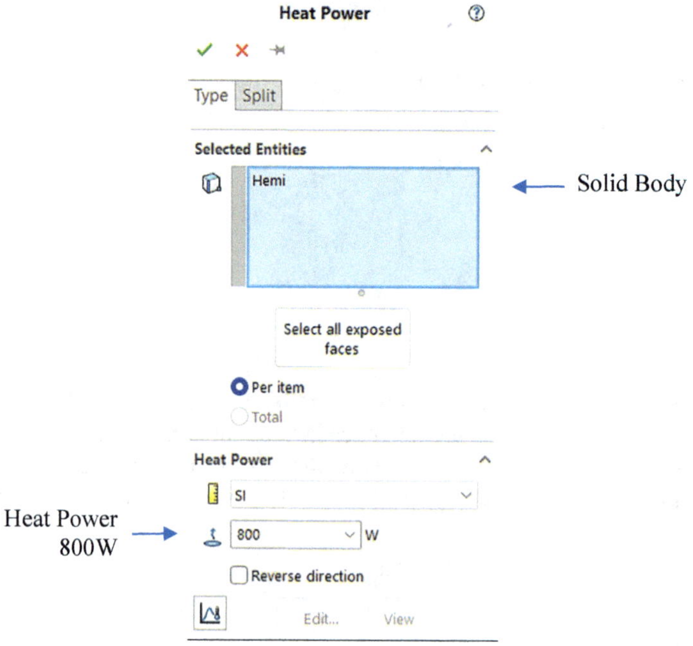

Figure 12-2: Heat Power is generated in the volume of HEMISPHERE.

Select Solid Body Hemi from the fly-out menu.

Define **Radiation** boundary conditions as shown in Figure 12-3.

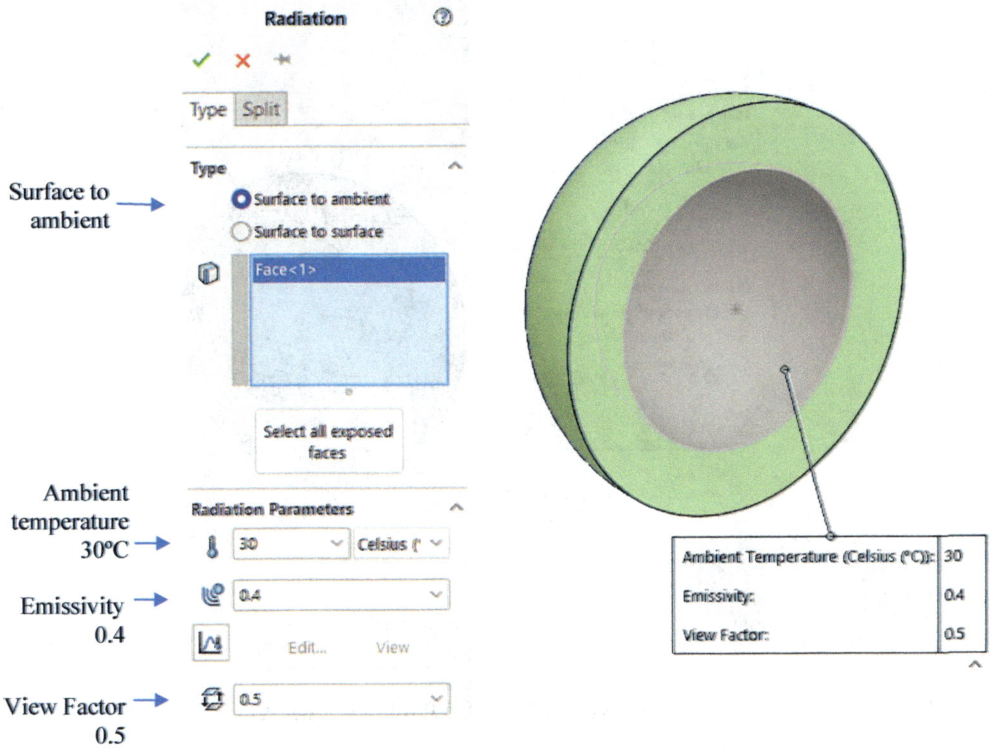

Figure 12-3: Radiative boundary conditions.

Radiative boundary conditions are defined on the concave face.

Ambient temperature is a part of radiative boundary conditions. You may conceptualize it as the temperature of a large enclosure in which the model is located. **Emissivity** is a measure of how well the face emits or receives radiation in comparison to a black body, which has the emissivity equal to 1. **View Factor** is a measure of what portion of radiation is radiated out directly to space. If radiative boundary conditions were **Surface to ambient** with a **View Factor** equal to 1, then all power would be radiated out directly to space as was the case with the GRAPHITE BALL in chapter 11. The **View Factor** of 0.5 used in the HEMISPHERE accounts for the fact that this concave face can "see itself" and some of the heat radiated out hits this face again before being radiated out.

Mesh the model using a Blended **curvature-based mesh**; use element size 15mm as shown in Figure 12-4.

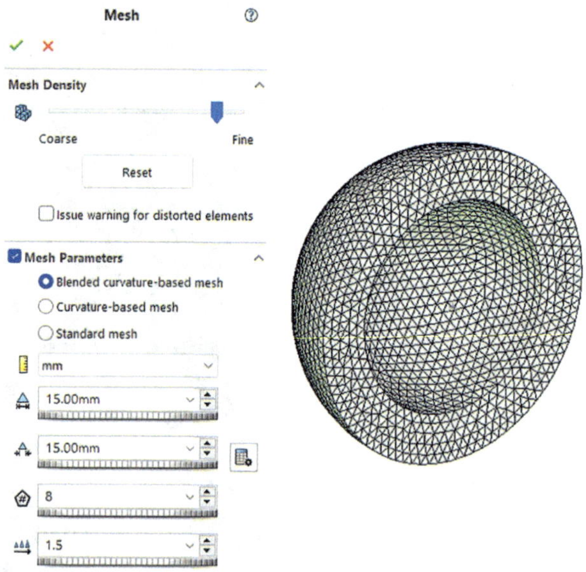

Figure 12-4: Blended curvature-based mesh is a natural choice for this type of geometry.

Set element size to 15mm.

Obtain a solution and show a **Temperature** plot (Figure 12-5).

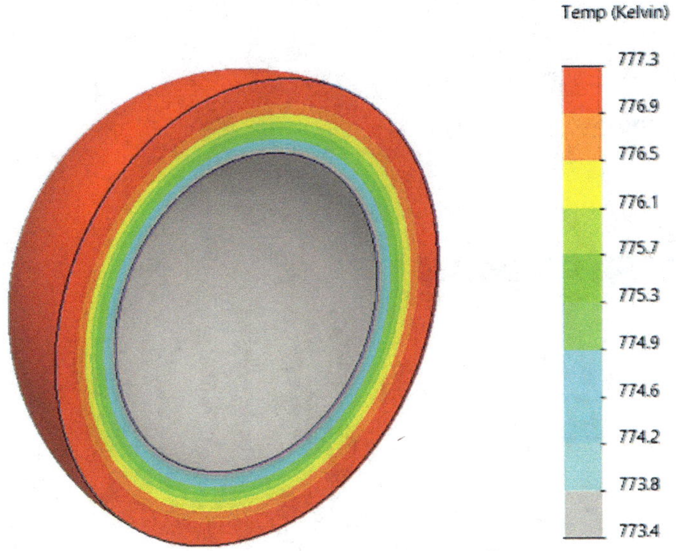

Figure 12-5: Temperature plot shows a low temperature gradient due to a high thermal conductivity of Nickel.

In radiation problems, temperature is often expressed in Kelvins.

Follow steps in Figure 12-6 to review **Heat Power** results and verify that all power generated in the volume to HEMISPHERE is radiated out by the concave face where the radiative boundary conditions have been defined.

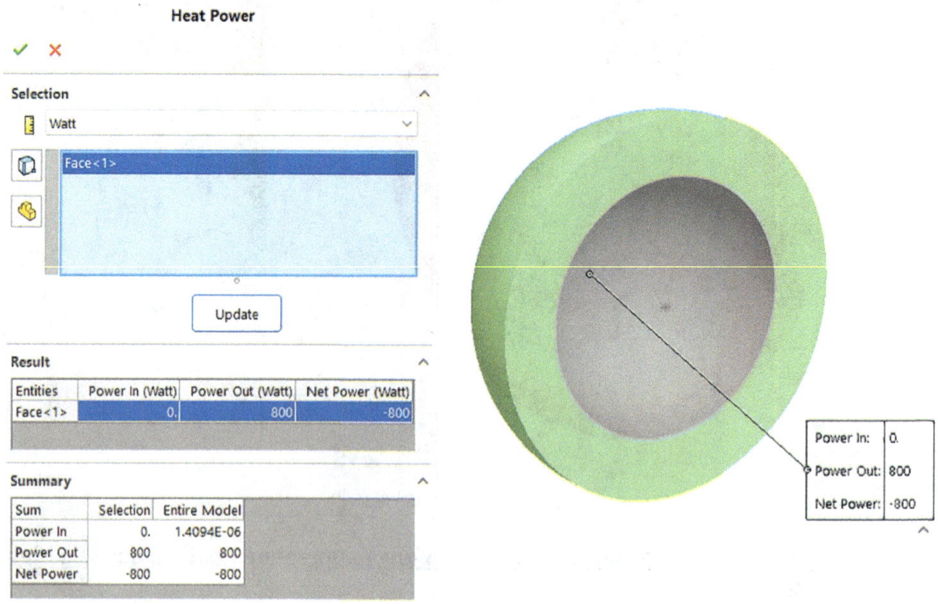

<u>Figure 12-6: Heat Power radiated out is 800W.</u>

The generated heat leaves the HEMISPHERE through the face where the radiative boundary conditions are defined. It is equal to the heat power generated in the volume of the model.

Additional practice models

To reinforce the concepts presented in this chapter, repeat the analysis using the additional practice models. Define project input data following the approach used in the main exercise.

Figure 12-7: TETRAHEDRON100 part model.

Figure 12-8: SPHERE100 part model.

Models in this chapter

Model	Configuration	Study Name	Study Type
HEMISPHERE.sldprt	*Default*	*01 steady state*	Thermal
TETRAHEDRON100.sldprt	Additional practice model		
SPHERE100.sldprt	Additional practice model		

13: Radiation between bodies

- Heat transfer by radiation
- Heat transfer by convection
- Emissivity
- Radiating heat out to space
- Heat power
- Open system
- Closed system
- Steady state heat transfer
- Transient heat transfer
- Initial temperature

Project description

Heat power is generated in the volume of a Ball placed in the focal point of a parabolic Reflector. Heat is radiated out towards a Plate, which dissipates the heat by convection. We are looking for temperature of the Reflector and Plate and the portion of heat that escapes to the environment without hitting the plate (Figure 13-1).

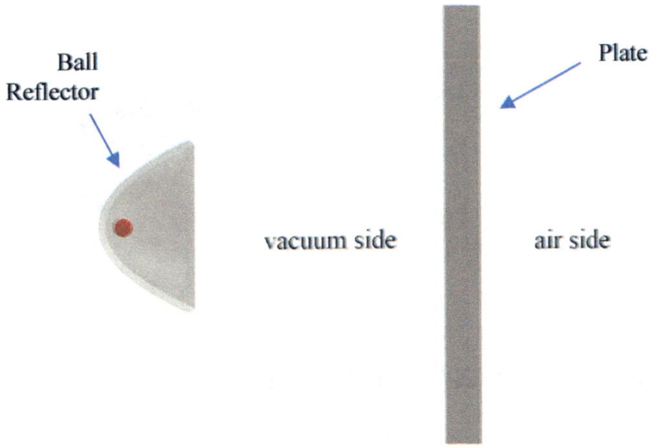

Figure 13-1: REFLECTOR assembly has three parts: Ball, Reflector, Plate.

Reflector is shown in a transparent view.

Ball, Reflector and the face of Plate facing the Reflector are in a vacuum. The opposite face of the Plate is exposed to air. Side faces of Plate are insulated; they do not exchange heat.

There are three mechanisms of heat transfer in this model: conduction, radiation, and convection. Heat moves by conduction inside the solid bodies. Heat is exchanged by radiation between all three bodies on the vacuum side. Some heat escapes to the environment because this is an open system. Heat received by the Plate travels by conduction to the air side where it is dissipated by convection.

Note that in Simulation, heat transfer between two or more detached bodies can only be exchanged by radiation. This is because convection models heat exchange between a face and surrounding fluid, not between two faces.

Procedure

Open REFLECTOR assembly. Note material assignment: Ball: Graphite, Reflector: Alloy Steel, Plate: Ceramic Porcelain. Create a steady state thermal study *Thermal1*.

Apply 800W **Heat Power** to the Ball (Figure 13-2).

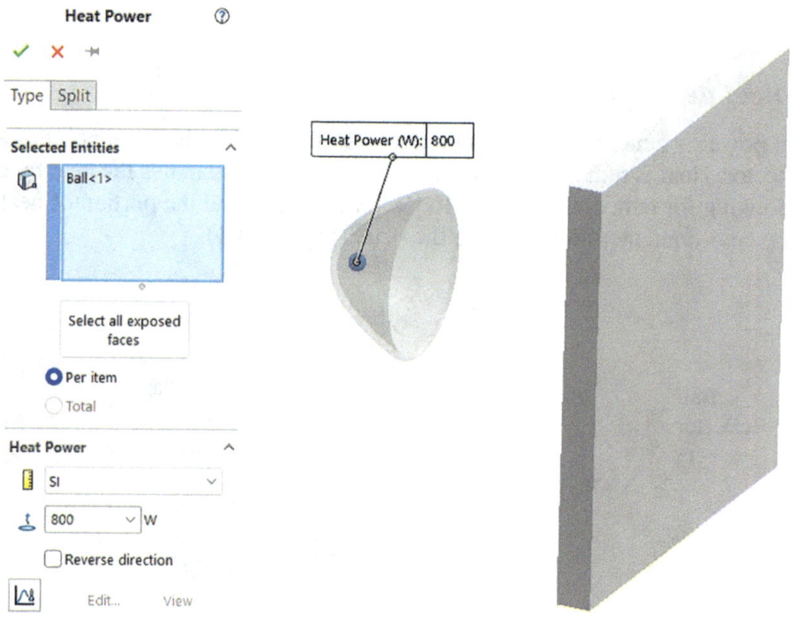

Figure 13-2: 800W Heat Power is applied to the volume of the Ball.

Apply **Radiative boundary conditions** to all faces exchanging heat by radiation (Figure 13-3).

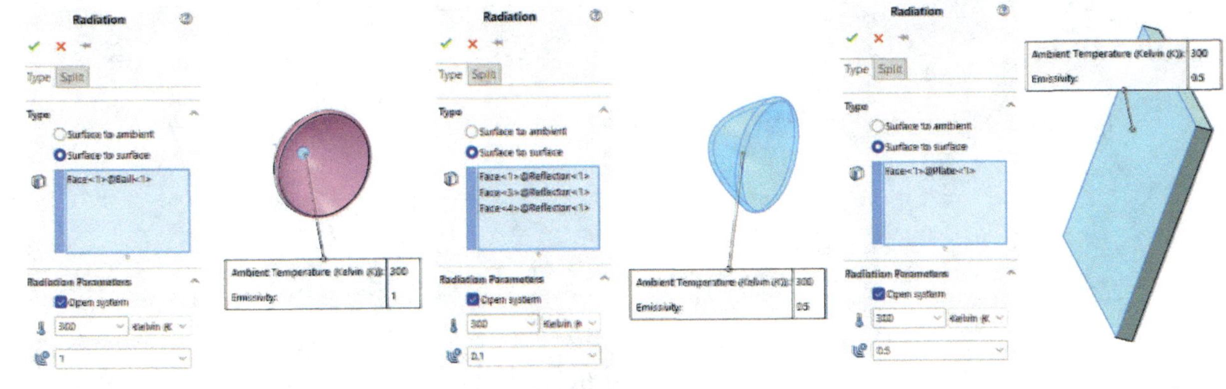

Face of Ball

- Surface to surface
- Open system
- Ambient 300K
- Emissivity 1

All faces of Reflector

- Surface to surface
- Open system
- Ambient 300K
- Emissivity 0.1

Front face of Plate

- Surface to surface
- Open system
- Ambient 300K
- Emissivity 0.5

Figure 13-3: Radiative boundary conditions in the model.

Radiative boundary conditions of Ball, Reflector and Plate differ only by the emissivity.

It is important to comment on the **Radiative boundary conditions** defined in Figure 13-3. Without selecting **Open system,** we would assume that all the heat radiated out travels without any loss to the face of Plate. That would be unrealistic; by selecting Open System we allow some heat to escape to environment. View factors are calculated by solver.

So far, we have established a mechanism of heat transfer by radiation between three bodies. Now we'll define how the heat leaves the system. Define **Convective boundary conditions** as shown in Figure 13-4.

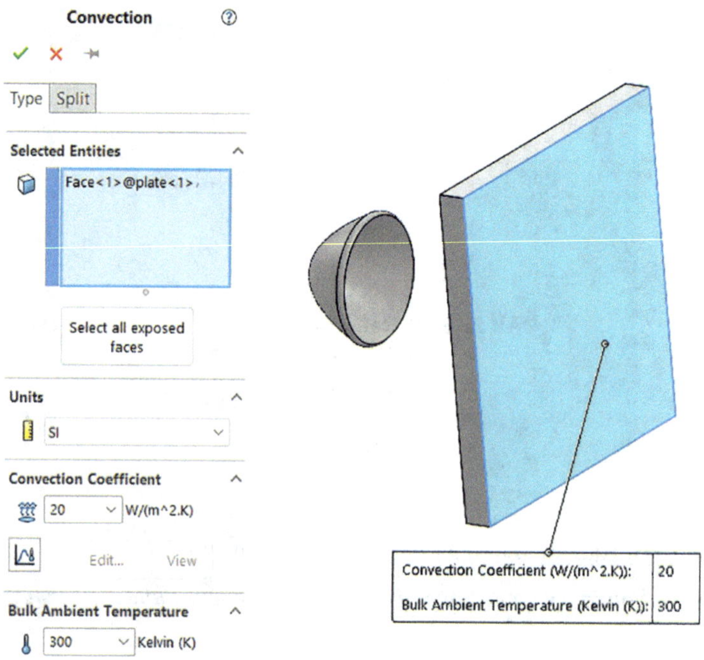

Figure 13-4: Convective boundary conditions in the model.

The back face exchanges heat with air by convection. It is assumed that the side faces of the Plate are insulated.

The ambient temperature in **Radiative boundary conditions** and Convective **boundary conditions** is numerically the same: 300K, but it has a very different meaning.

In radiative heat transfer, this is the temperature of a distant enclosure—often called the far-field temperature—that is the effective radiative temperature of the surroundings that "see" the surface. It represents the temperature of an imaginary large enclosure that surrounds the object and exchanges radiation with it. In convection heat transfer this is the temperature of the surrounding fluid, here: air.

Apply the following mesh control: Ball 10mm, Reflector 20mm and mesh the assembly with Blended curvature based mesh with element size 60mm. Obtain solution and prepare two temperature plots with ranges adjusted to the maximum and the minimum temperature of the Reflector and of the Plate (Figure 13-5).

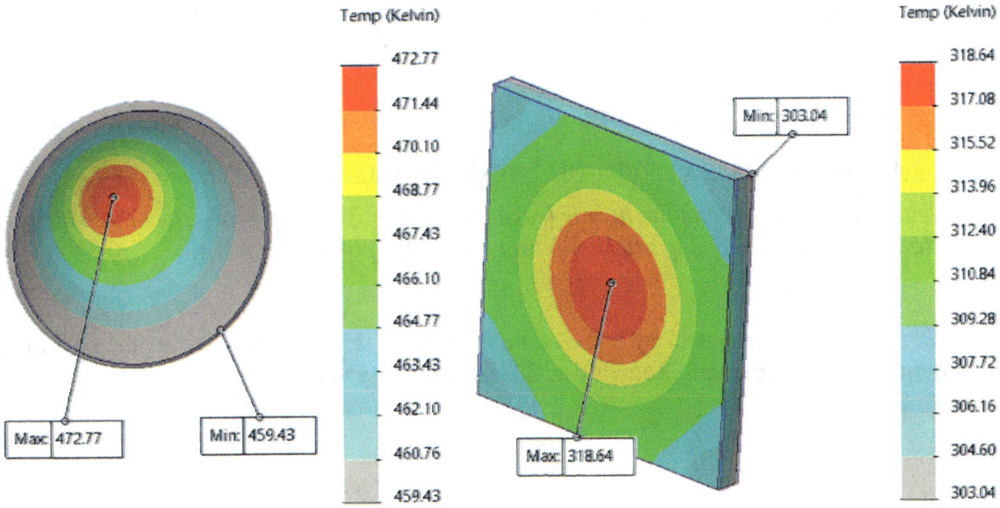

Figure 13-5: Temperature plots in Reflector and in Plate.

Temperature range is adjusted to the maximum and the minimum temperature in each plot. Reflector plot has Ball and Plate parts hidden. Plate plot has Ball and Reflector parts hidden.

Find **Heat Power** transferred to air (Figure 13-6).

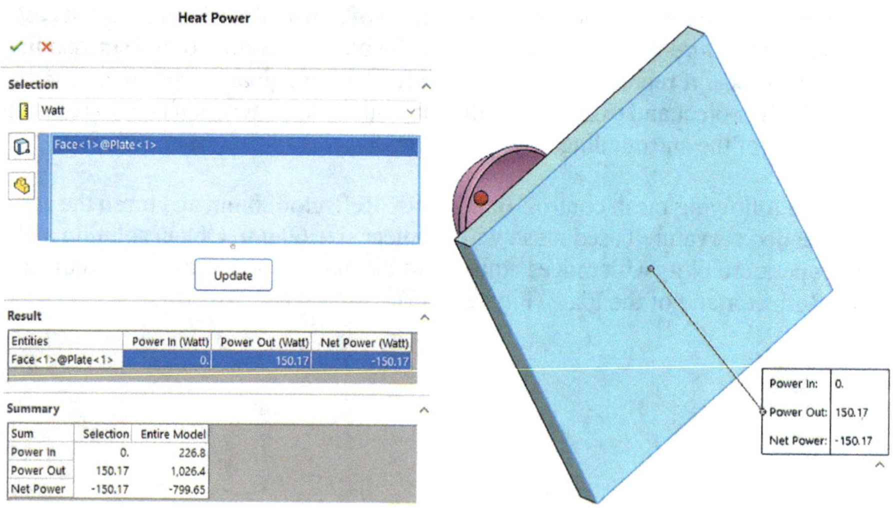

Figure 13-6: Heat Power transferred to air via convection is -150W.

Negative sign means that the heat is leaving the Plate. You may probe the other side of the Plate, to see the same magnitude of power but with a positive sign.

If 150W leaves the system by convection, then 800W-150W=650W leaves the system by radiation to environment. Remember, this is an open system.

Now, we will conduct a numerical experiment. It won't have any direct physical interpretation but will be useful to demonstrate properties of heat transfer in **Open System** and in **Closed System**.

Copy study *Thermal1* to *Thermal2.* Delete convective boundary condition and modify both radiative boundary condition to make them **Closed System** by deselecting **Open System**. This is not an engineering analysis, just a numerical experiment so it is OK to delete all mesh controls and use default element size for meshing to speed up the solution.

An attempt to solve study *Thermal2* produces an error message shown in Figure 13-7.

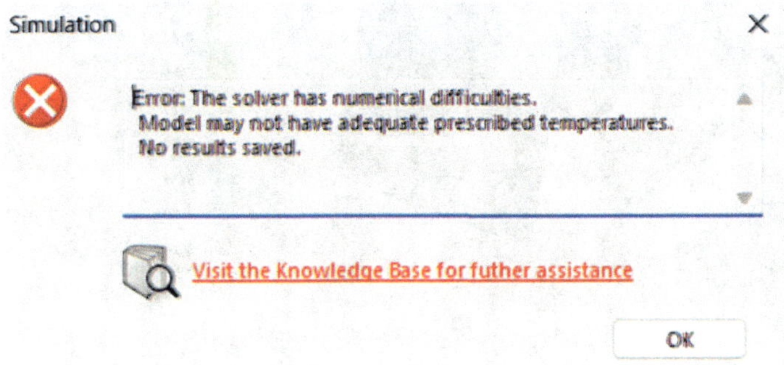

Figure 13-7: Solution of study with Closed System and no Convection fails.

Heat generated in the Ball has no way of escaping from the closed system where convection has been eliminated. This is analogous to applying a force to an unsupported model.

To explain the above error further, copy study *Thermal2* to *Thermal3*; make it Transient with settings shown in Figure 13-8.

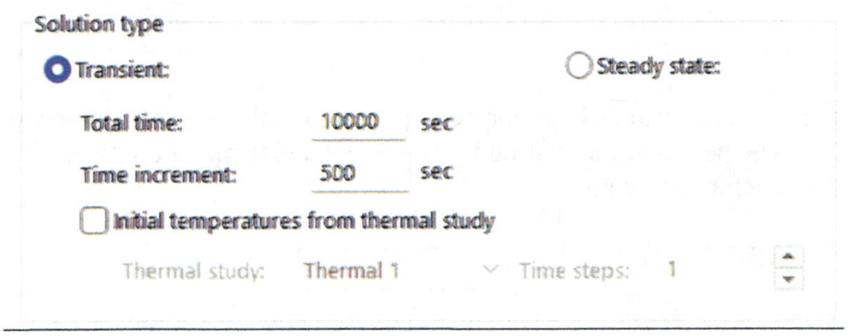

Figure 13-8: Settings of transient thermal study *Thermal3.*

Apply an initial temperature of 300K to all parts. Run the solution and observe that it does not fail. Probe temperature plots from any step and construct temperature time response graph (Figure 13-9).

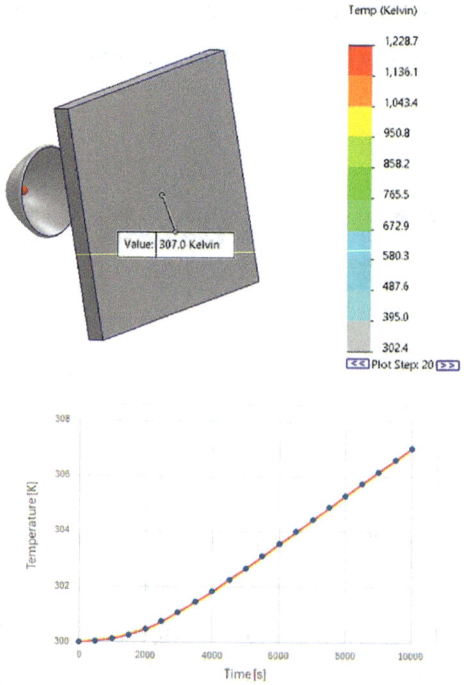

Figure 13-9: Temperature of the back of the Plate as a function of time.

Graph shows divergence of temperature in transient solution. You may probe any location in the model to see divergent results.

Figure 13-9 demonstrates that the heat generated in the Ball has no way of escaping the system. The heat is accumulating in the system and temperature time history graph shows divergent temperature results.

Additional practice models

To reinforce the concepts presented in this chapter, repeat the analysis using the additional practice models. Define project input data following the approach used in the main exercise.

Figure 13-10: BLOCKS part model.

This is a multi-body part.

Figure 13-11: ENCLOSURE part model.

This is a multi-body part.

Models in this chapter

Model	**Configuration**	**Study Name**	**Study Type**
REFLECTOR.sldasm	*Default*	*Thermal1*	Thermal, steady state
		Thermal2	Thermal, transient
		Thermal3	Thermal, transient
BLOCKS.sldprt	Additional practice model		
ENCLOSURE.sldprt	Additional practice model		

Part 3

Conjugate Heat Transfer with CFD

The previous parts considered convection as a prescribed boundary condition. Many engineering problems, however, require convection to be calculated from the fluid motion itself. Such analyses are performed using SOLIDWORKS Flow Simulation, sometimes in combination with SOLIDWORKS Simulation.

In these models the interaction between fluid flow and heat transfer is solved directly. This approach, known as conjugate heat transfer, simultaneously accounts for conduction in solids, convection in fluids, and—when required—radiation.

At this stage the analyses include all major heat-transfer mechanisms, providing a more complete representation of real engineering systems.

14: Internal fluid flow

- Introduction to Flow Simulation
- Using Flow Simulation for finding convective boundary conditions
- Interfacing between Flow Simulation and Thermal analysis
- Interfacing between Flow Simulation and Structural analysis

Project description

In the preceding chapters, we introduced thermal analysis as a tool of analysis of heat transfer in solids. On many occasions we pointed out that heat exchange between a solid body and a surrounding fluid is governed by convective boundary conditions. To define heat exchange between a face of a solid and the surrounding fluid, we defined a convection coefficient and a reference (ambient) temperature. The fluid itself was not modeled in Simulation.

In this chapter, we use a very different approach; we will find the convective boundary conditions (convection coefficient and ambient temperature) by simulating fluid flow. We will then use those convective boundary conditions to analyze heat transfer in a solid body.

Numerical simulation of fluid flow belongs to the discipline called **Computational Fluid Dynamics (CFD)**. In **SOLIDWORKS** it is implemented as an add-in called **Flow Simulation** which is different from **Simulation**.

Those similar and somewhat confusing names require some explanations. First, let us agree on the following name convention: **Simulation** means the add-in for finite element analysis. **Flow Simulation** means the add-in used for **CFD**.

Simulation is based on a numerical technique called **Finite Element Method** which we customarily call **FEA. Simulation** is used for structural and thermal analysis of solid bodies. **Flow Simulation** is based on a numerical technique called **Finite Volume Method (FVM)**. It is used for the analysis of fluid flow, which may, but does not have to include heat transfer in solids.

If heat transfer is not considered in an analyzed problem, then **Flow Simulation** is concerned only with the space where fluid flow occurs. This may be a cavity inside a solid and/or space around a solid.

If heat transfer is included in the analysis of fluid flow, then **Flow Simulation** models the heat transfer both in fluids and in solids. Convection conditions governing heat transfer between fluids and solids are found from fluid flow conditions. This is very different from **Thermal** analysis with **Simulation** where the convection conditions are introduced as boundary conditions.

Here is an important note on terminology. The terms **Finite Element Analysis (FEA)** and **Computational Fluid Dynamics** (CFD) are each consistent when used on their own, but they are not consistent when used together. FEA refers to a numerical technique (the finite element method), whereas CFD refers to a field of application rather than a specific numerical method. A more consistent pairing would be **Finite Element Method (FEM)** and **Finite Volume Method (FVM)** because CFD uses Finite Volume Method. Nevertheless, because the terms FEA and CFD are firmly established in engineering practice and commercial software, we'll use them throughout this book.

Flow Simulation can be interfaced in different ways with **Thermal** and structural (**Static**, **Nonlinear**) analyses available in **Simulation** (Figure 14-1).

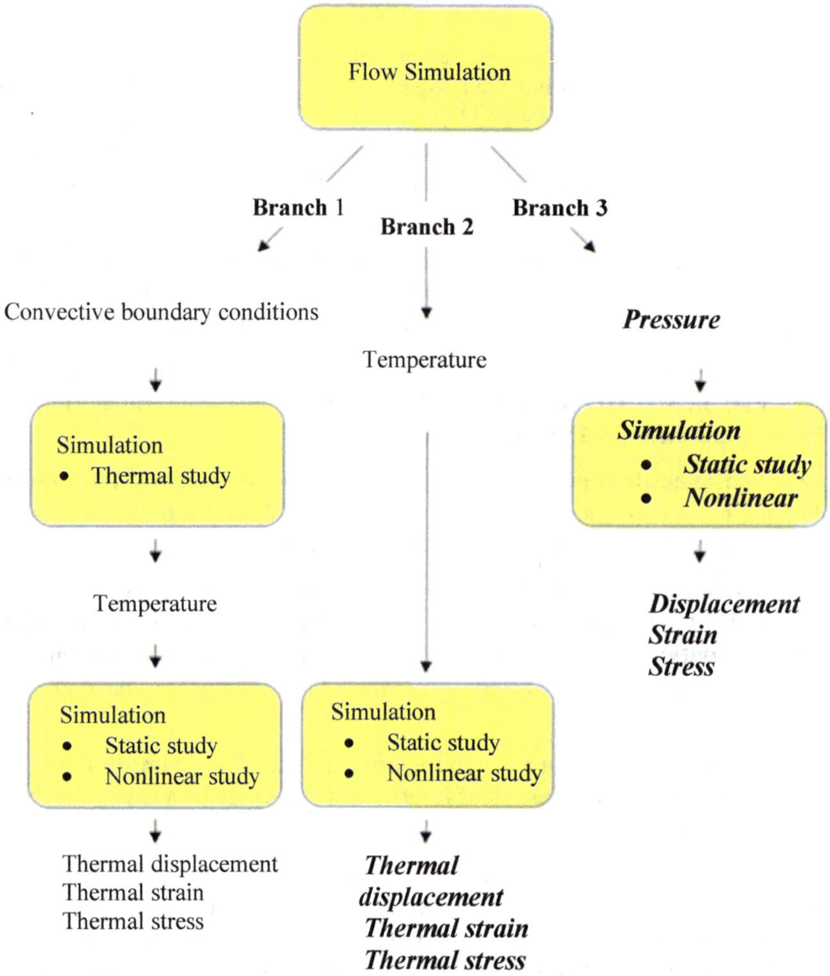

Figure 14-1: Interfacing between Flow Simulation and Simulation.

If only thermal displacements and stresses are required, it is easier to follow Branch 2. Branch 3 is out of the scope of this book.

Model ELBOW (Figure 14-2) will serve to introduce the Finite Volume Method used in Flow Simulation.

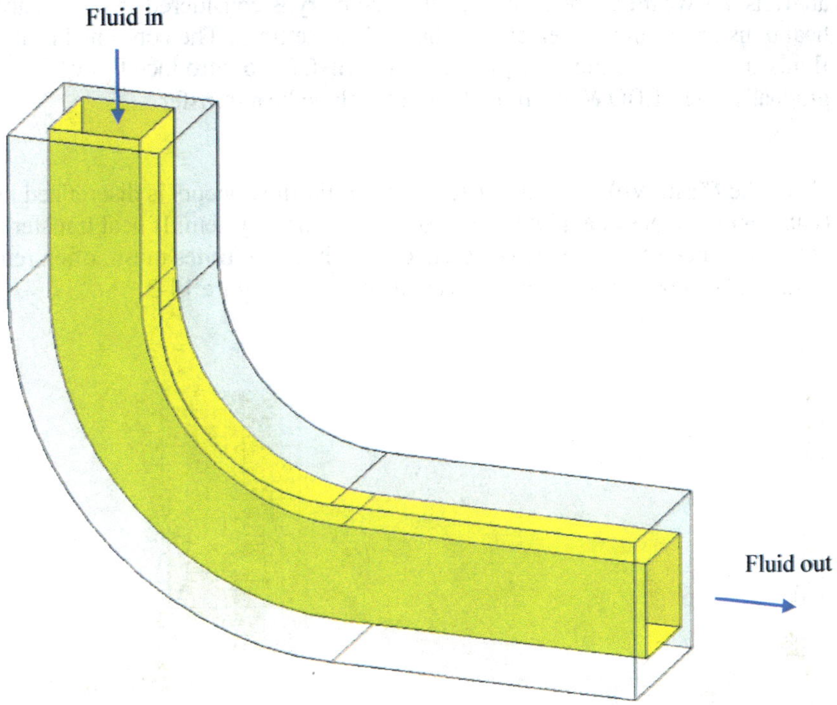

Figure 14-2: ELBOW part model shown in a transparent view. Faces of the cavity where the fluid flow occurs are highlighted in yellow.

This model as shown here is not yet watertight.

The flow of fluid happens here in the cavity inside the solid model, not in the solid model itself. Definition of the space when fluid flow occurs requires plugging up the model as shown in Figure 14-2. In this model, the solid geometry is used to define the space where fluid flow occurs. The flow is inside; therefore, only the inner faces of the cavity matter for analysis. As we mentioned earlier, solid geometry is considered in flow analysis only if heat transfer in solids is selected in the analysis settings. The combined heat transfer in fluids and solids is called **conjugate heat transfer**. To introduce Flow Simulation gradually, the ELBOW example does not include heat transfer.

Using the **Finite Volumes,** the space where fluid flow occurs is discretized into cubes (cuboids) with faces parallel to the global coordinate system. If heat transfer in solids is requested, then solids are also discretized. A **Finite Volumes** mesh, often referred to as a grid, can be shown in section views as illustrated in Figure 14-3.

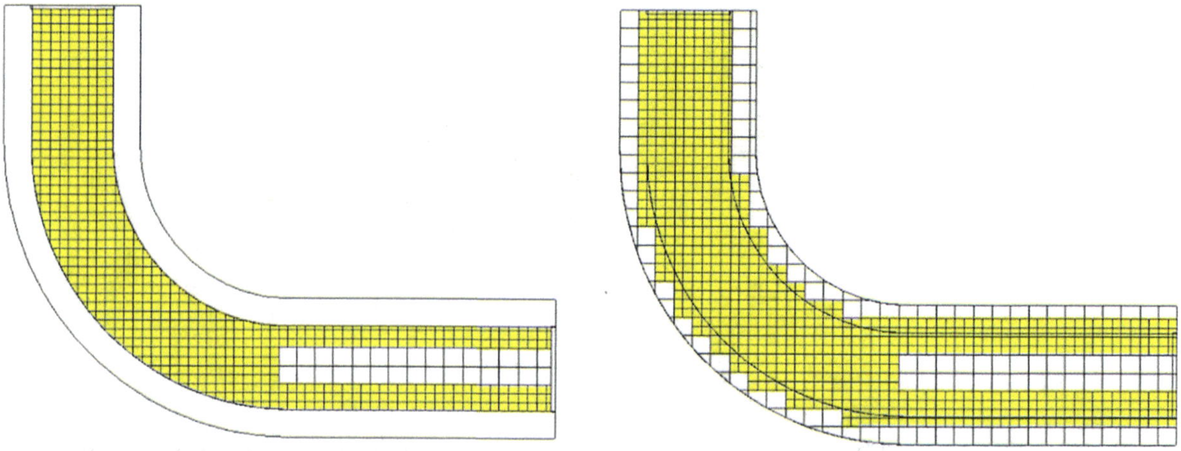

No conduction
Fluid is discretized
Solid walls are not discretized

Conduction present
Fluid is discretized
Solid walls are discretized

Figure 14-3: Section through the Finite Volume grid. ELBOW part is used to prepare this plot.

Solid model is discretized only if Conduction is considered in the model. Solid cells will not be present in the ELBOW project. The illustration on the right is not related to this project.

The grid cells may be classified into three types: fluid, solid and partial. Partial cells are located on boundaries between fluid and solid and include both solid and fluid volume. The size of the cubes depends on the geometry and on the requested level of solution accuracy. 3D grid refinement is conducted by splitting a cell into eight smaller cells.

As we said before, the ELBOW model is an introductory exercise in fluid flow analysis with no thermal conditions. First, make sure that Flow Simulation is an active Add-in (Figure 14-4).

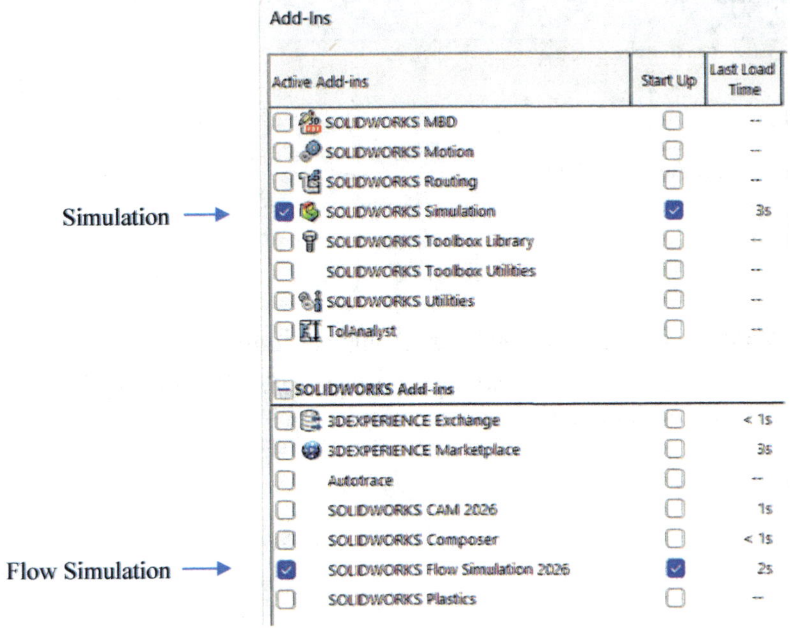

Figure 14-4: Activate Simulation and Flow Simulation add-ins.

Select Simulation and Flow Simulation Add-ins.

Once Flow Simulation has been added, it shows as a tab in the Command Manager (Figure 14-5).

Start a new Flow Simulation project using a **Wizard** (Figure 14-5). The **Wizard** will walk you through all steps necessary to set up a project.

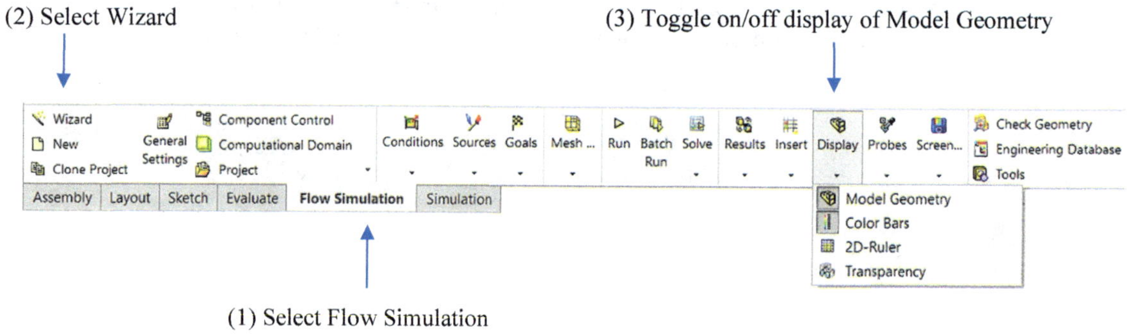

<u>Figure 14-5: Starting a Flow Simulation Project using a Wizard.</u>

The Wizard will walk you through the steps necessary to define Project, which is equivalent to a Study in Simulation. Try toggling geometry display.

Steps in the project definition are shown in Figures 14-6 through 14-12. Steps are described in captions of illustrations and indicated by the arrows in the **Navigator** window.

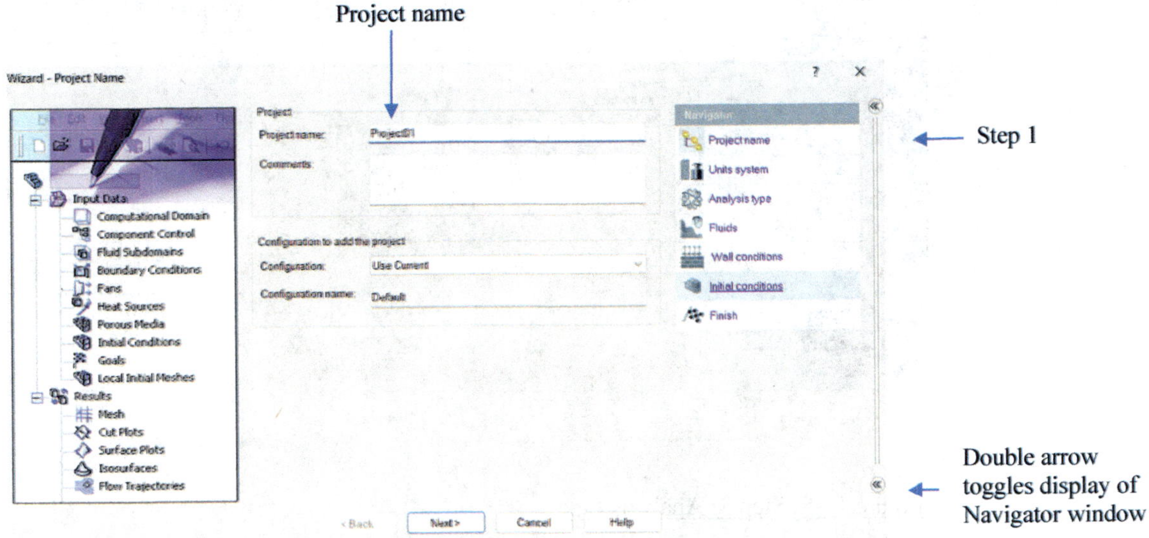

Figure 14-6: Step 1: Project name; enter project name *Project01.*

The project windows are more informative if you keep the Navigator window open. The window on the right lists all the steps performed during project definition. Click Next or Back to move through the steps.

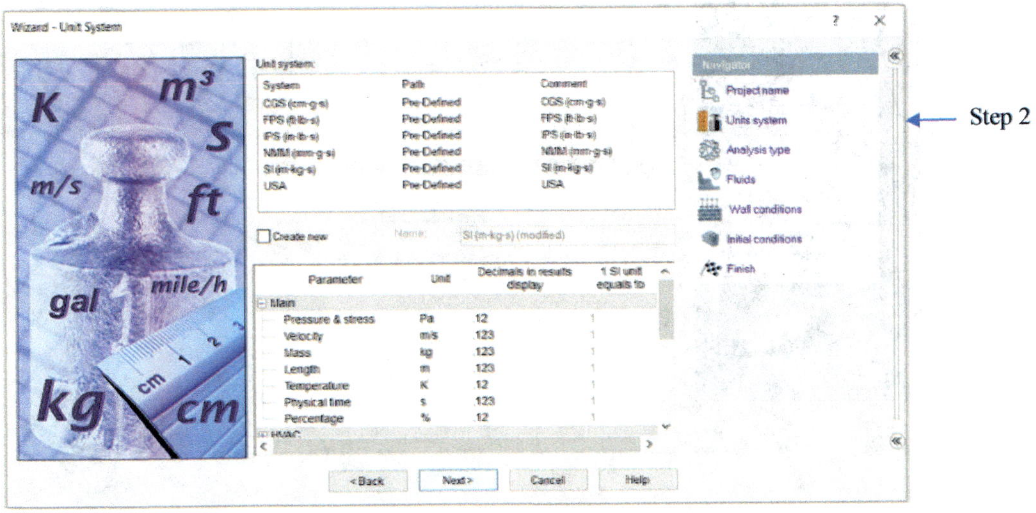

Figure 14-7: Step 2: Selection of units.

Accept the default SI system of units.

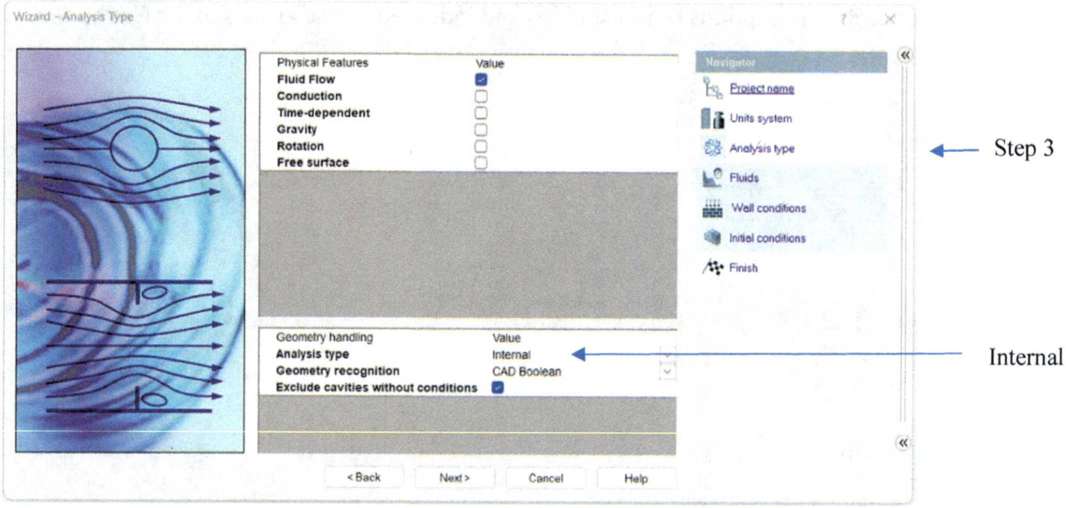

Figure 14-8: Step 3: Analysis type.

Select the Internal type of analysis; do not select Conduction.

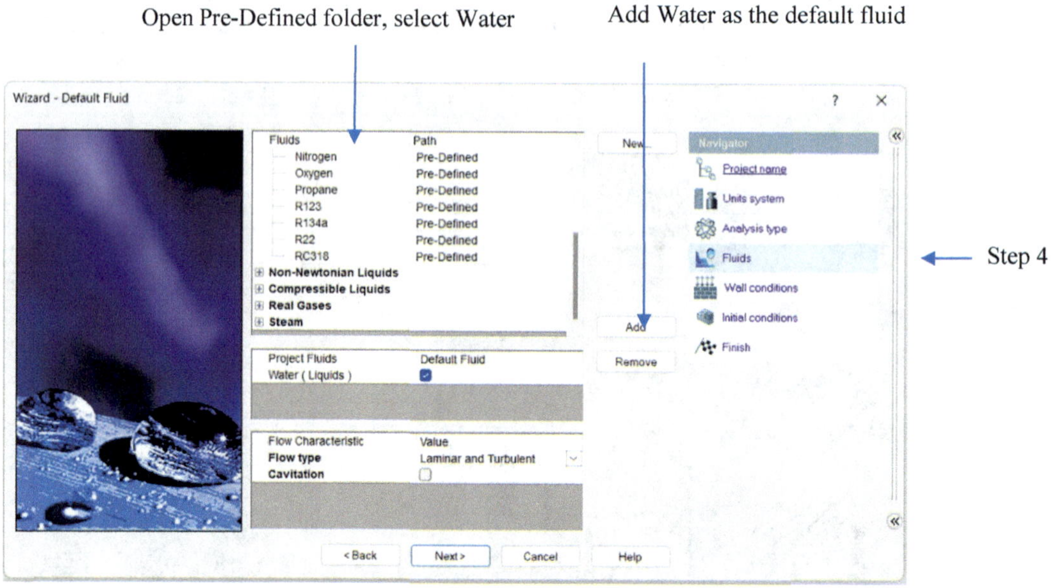

Figure 14-9: Step 4: Default Fluid.

Select Water from the list of pre-defined liquids.

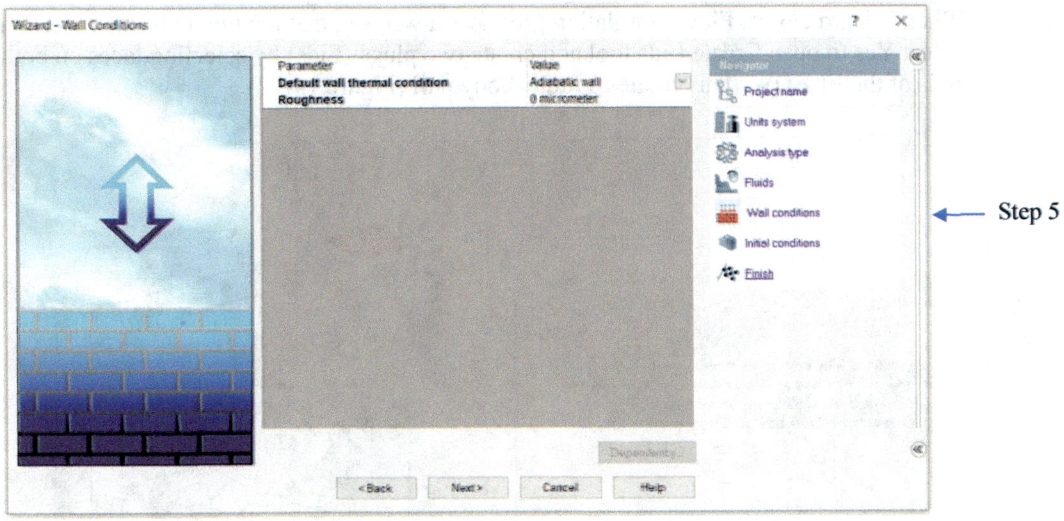

Figure 14-10: Step 5: Wall conditions.

Adiabatic wall means no heat exchange; do not change anything here.

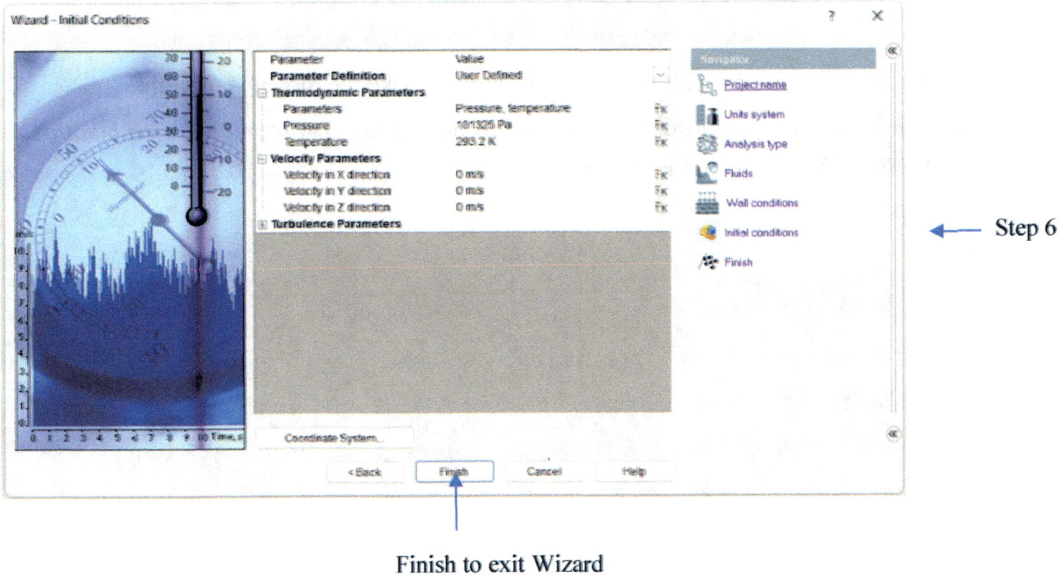

Figure 14-11: Step 6: Initial Conditions.

Do not change anything here. The example we are setting up is a steady state fluid flow; velocity parameters will be found by the solver.

When Wizard closes, Flow Simulation produces a warning that the model is not watertight. Select Yes to open Create Lids tool and create two plugs (Lids) by selecting faces on both ends of the ELBOW. This creates a multi-body part (Figure 14-12).

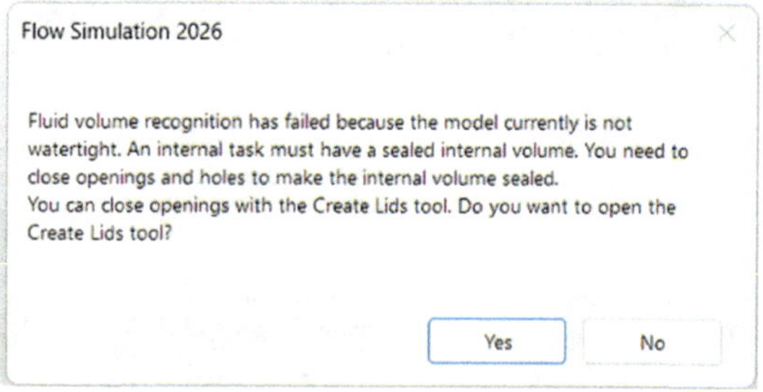

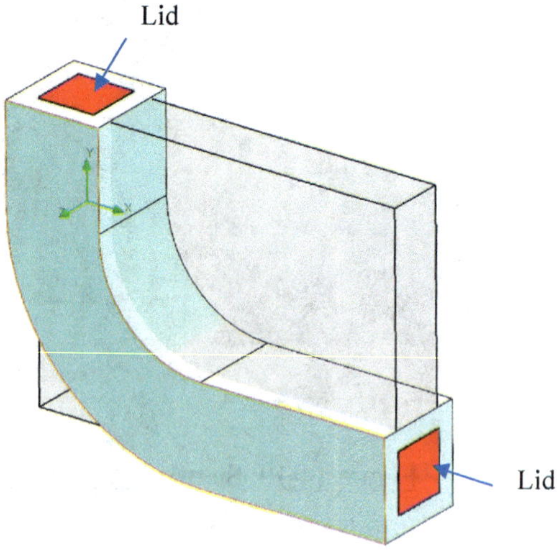

Figure 14-12: ELBOW with two plugs (Lids) that make the model watertight.

Lids are two bodies separate from ELBOW. A multi-body part is created. Computational Domain is shown in a transparent view.

When the **Wizard** is closed, Flow Simulation creates a Project window with several folders in it. Right-click on *Mesh* folder to open **Global Mesh Settings** window (Figure 14- 13).

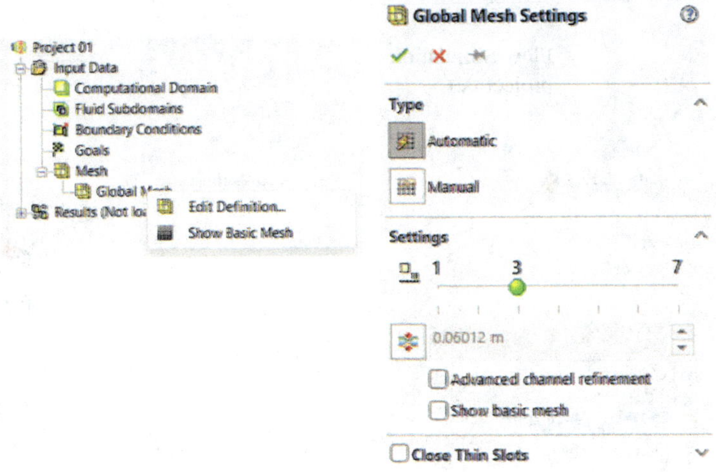

Figure 14-13: Global Mesh Settings window.

Accept default level 3. This controls the level of grid refinement. It is similar to mesh refinement in FEA.

A **Flow Simulation** project tab has been added, and the model view now shows the **Computational Domain**. Note that the Computational Domain does not include solid walls because we have not selected heat transfer in solids (Figure 14-14).

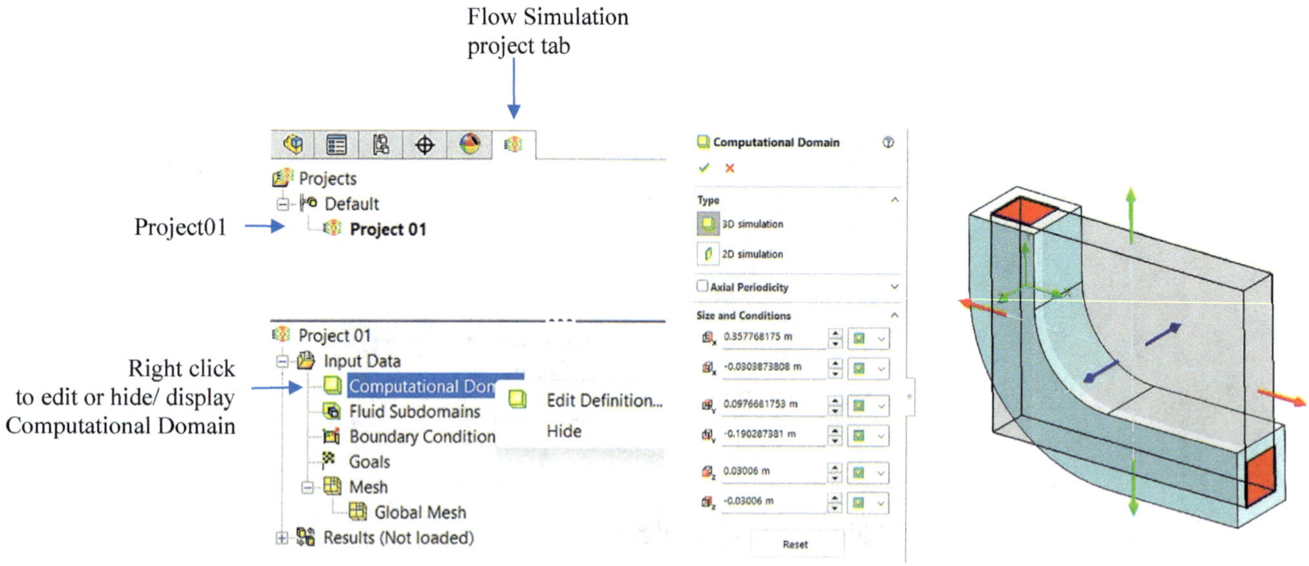

Figure 14-14: The computational domain is aligned with the global coordinate system.

Open Computational Domain window by right-click Computational Domain in Project folder. Practice hiding and showing the model, the Computational Domain and the Global Coordinate System. Right-click Project 01 to control the display of the Global Coordinate System.

To define the flow by setting up inlet and outlet boundary conditions, right-click **Boundary Conditions** and select **Insert Boundary Conditions**, follow steps in Figure 14-15.

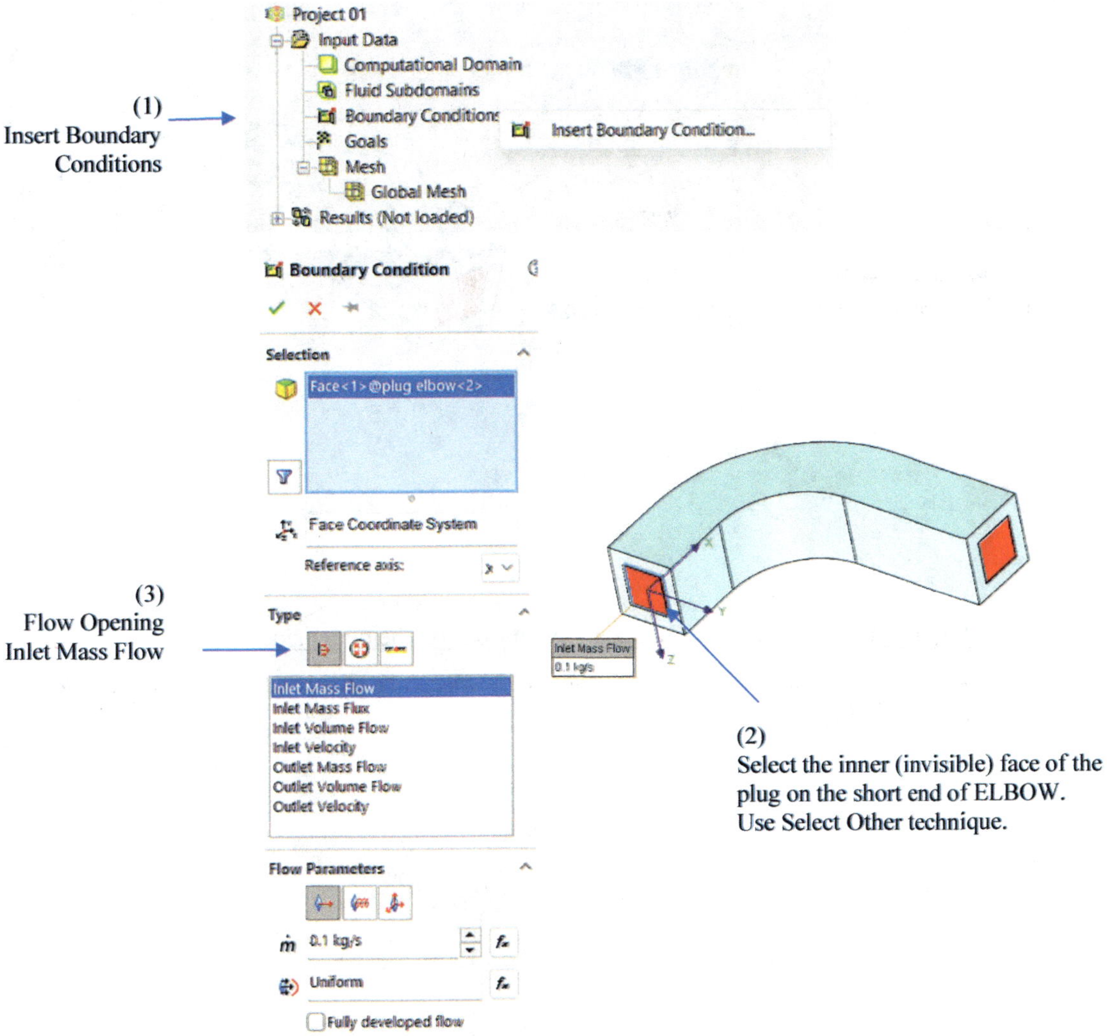

Figure 14-15: Definition of boundary conditions on the inlet side.

Note that a call-out is added to the face where the boundary condition has been defined. Instead of using Select Other technique, you may use a section view to select the inner face. The inner face of the plug touches water.

Follow the steps in Figure 14-16 to complete the fluid flow definition on the outlet side.

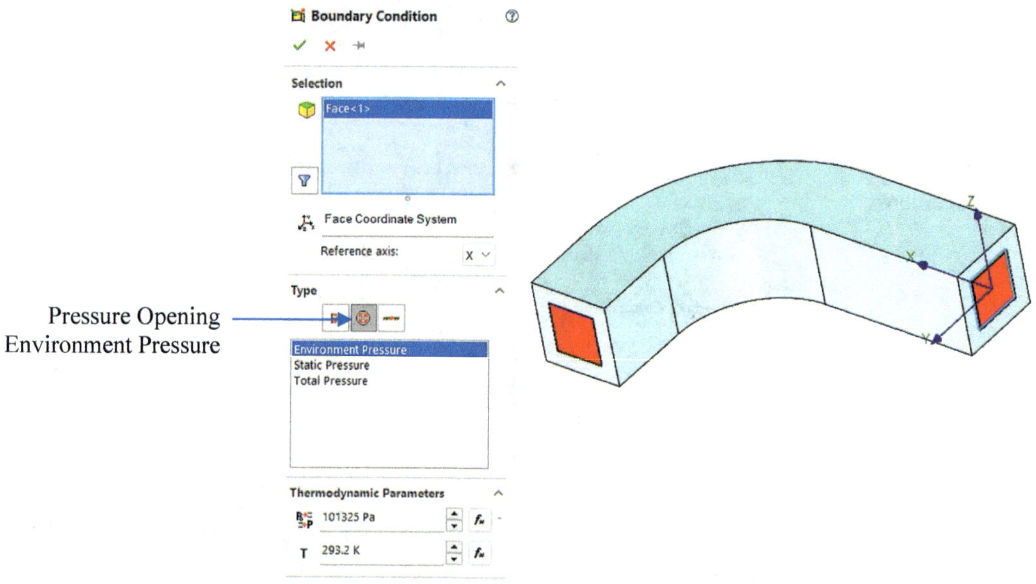

Figure 14-16: Definition of boundary conditions on the outlet side.

Accept the default pressure and the default temperature. Temperature has no importance in this analysis.

The last step before running the solution is the set up of **Goals** for the project. These are selected flow parameters. Selecting them as goals makes it possible to examine their convergence during solution (Figure 14-17).

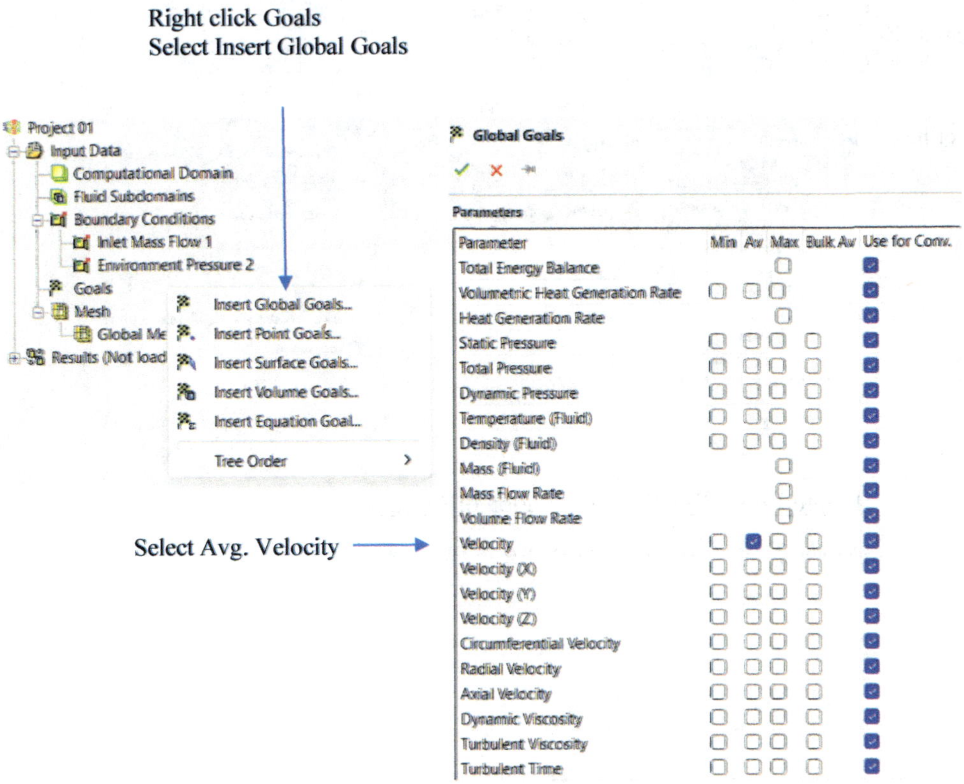

Figure 14-17: Definition of solution Goals.

Only one Global Goal is selected as a parameter of interest.

The flow analysis in ELBOW is for demonstration purpose only; therefore, we define only one **Goal**. This choice is arbitrary; you may choose different parameters.

Right-click **Project 01** in either place shown in Figure14-18 and select **Run**.

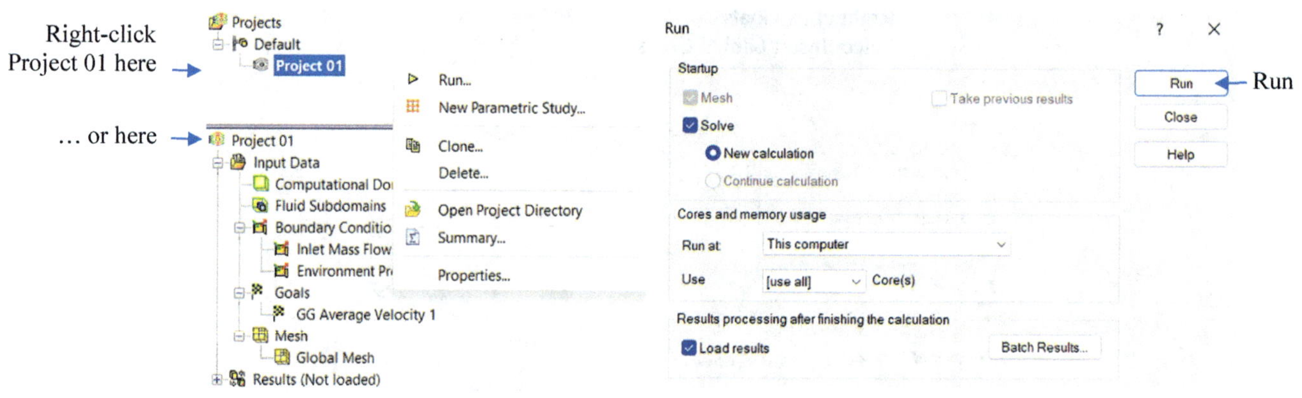

Figure 14-18: Running the solution of *Project01.*

Starting the solution requires two steps shown above.

Solution may be monitored during progress and reviewed after it completes using the **Solver** window (Figure 14-19).

Select windows to display

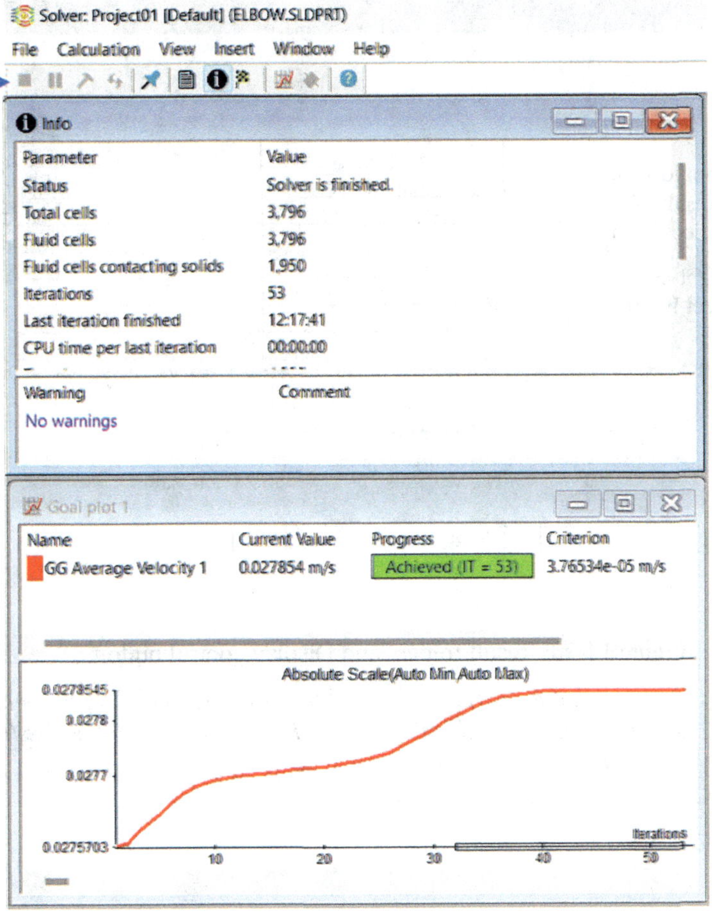

Figure 14-19: Solver window with Info and Goal Plot.

Info window and Goal Plot window are shown. Display other windows using the buttons on the top. Rearrange window positions as needed.

Closing the **Solver** window allows you to access the results (Figure 14-20).

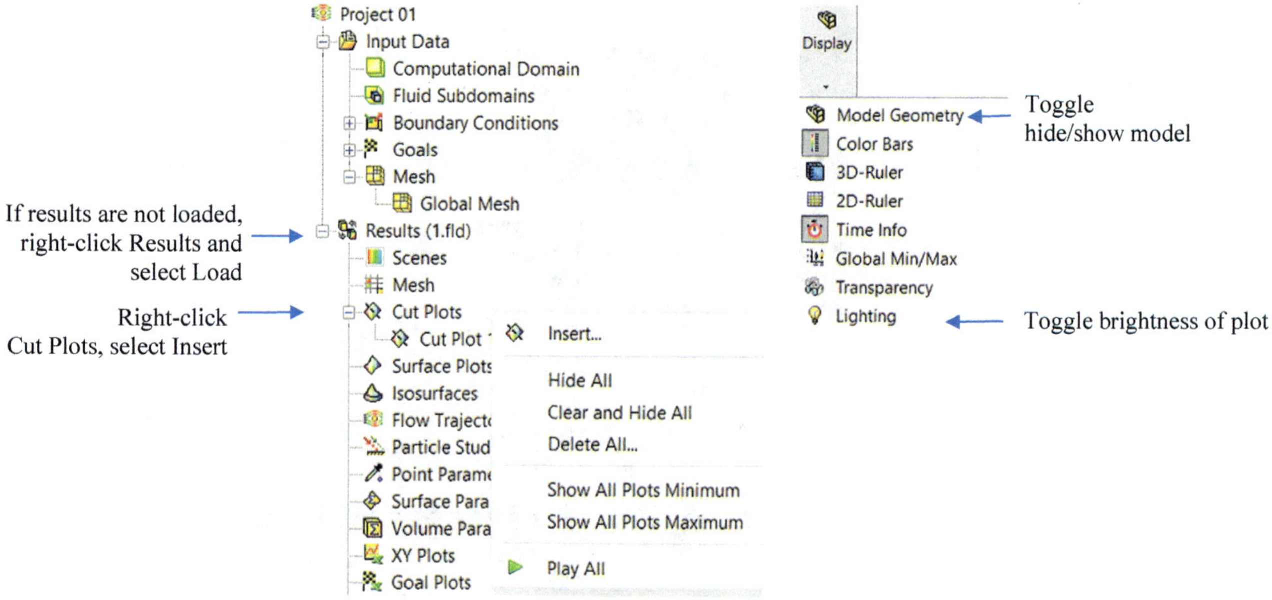

Figure 14-20: Result folders and Display control button.

Right-click the desired folder and select Insert to add a plot of the desired type. Model geometry must be hidden to see Cut Plots. Cut Plots folder is shown with one plot already inserted.

In this introductory exercise, we limit the analysis of results to a review of pressure (Figure 14-21) and velocity (Figure 14-22).

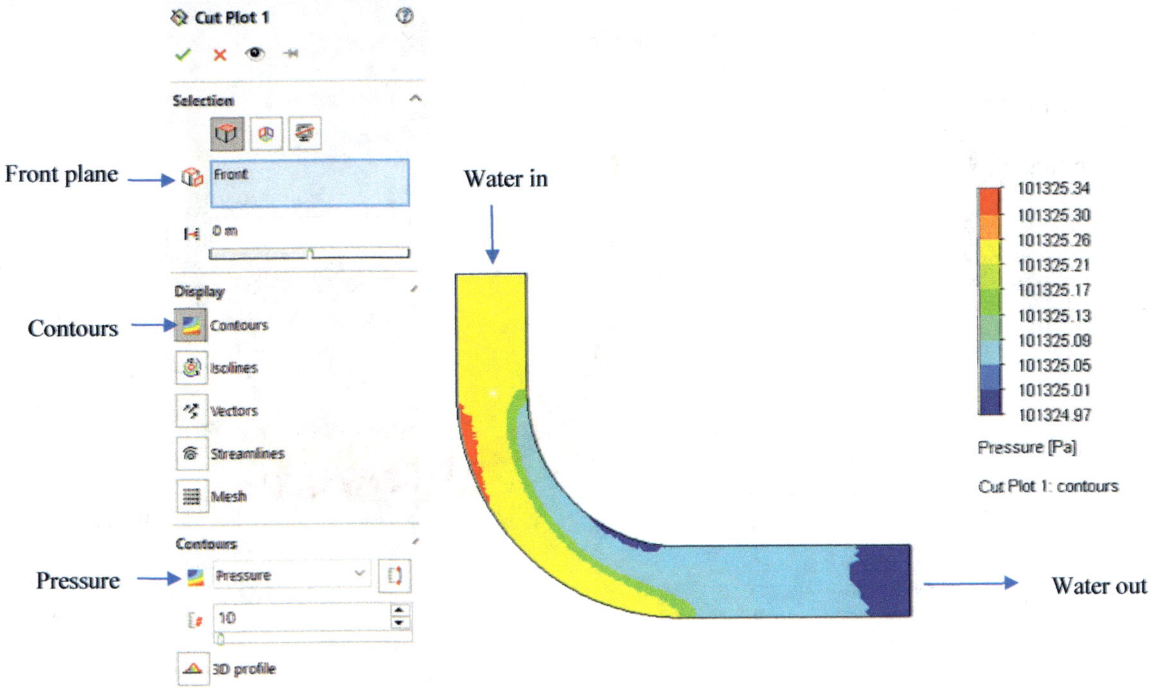

Figure 14-21: Pressure plot; a very low pressure drop can be seen.

To construct this plot, make the indicated selections.

Hide the above plot before constructing the next one.

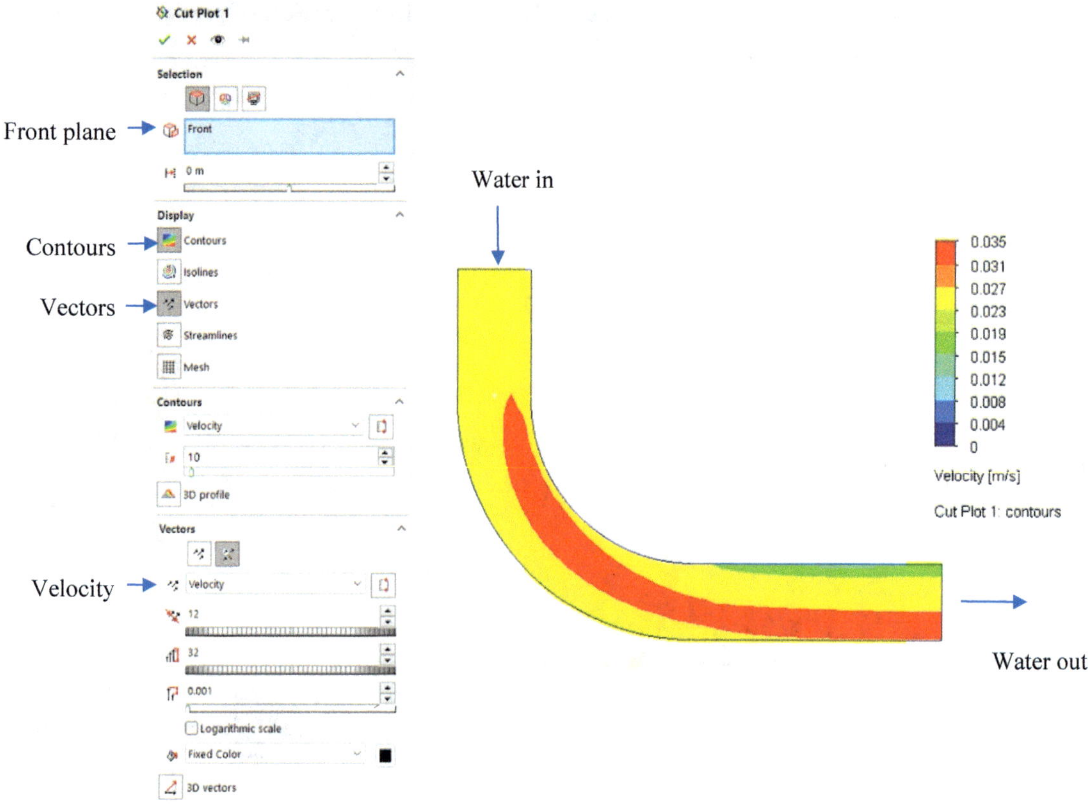

Figure 14-22: A velocity plot illustrates a non-uniform velocity distribution caused by the curvature of ELBOW.

To construct this plot, make selections as indicated, try different vector settings.

To complete this exercise, construct a mesh plot (Figure 14-23).

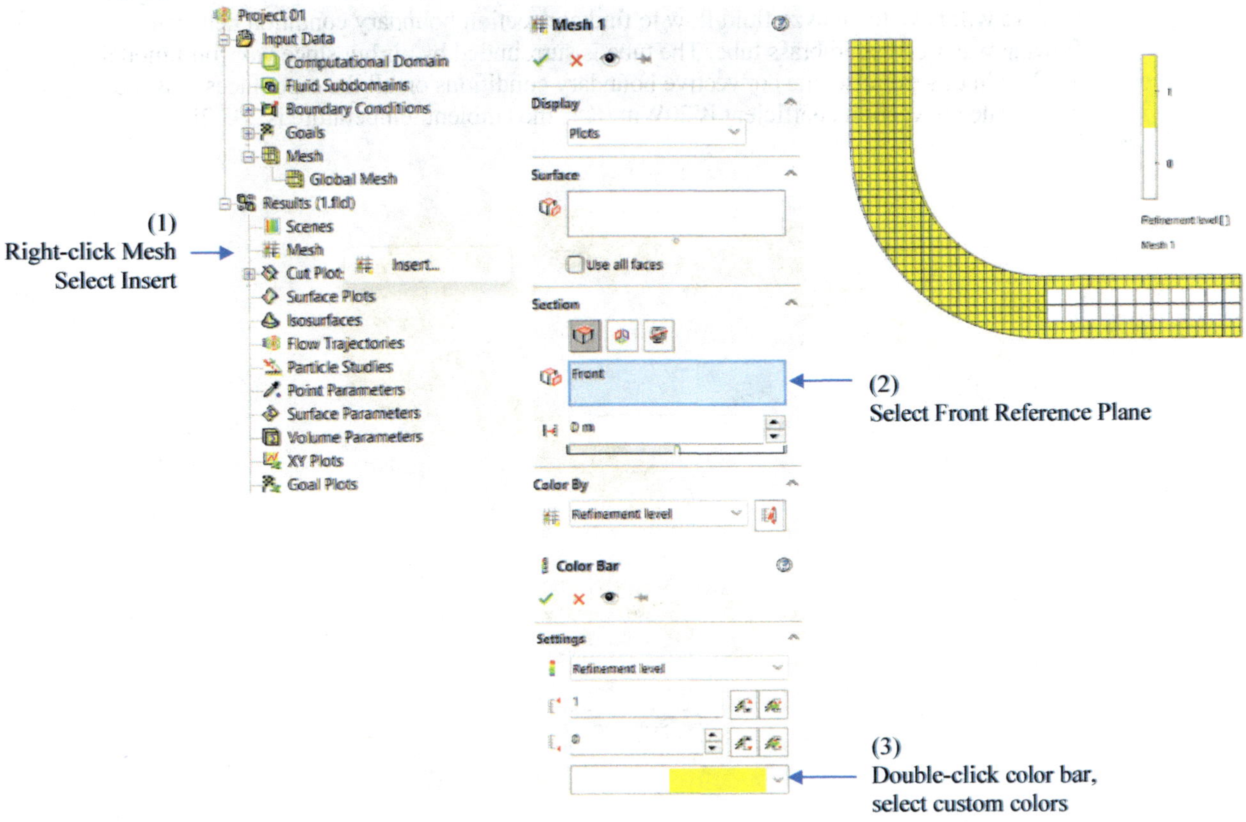

Figure 14-23: Mesh plot.

To construct this plot, make selections as indicated. Change colors if desired. Hide model using the Display button in the Flow Simulation Command Manager (Figure 14-20).

Display only one plot at a time or else plots will be overlaid. Note that the cavity where flow occurs is meshed while the solid walls are not meshed. This is because Conduction has not been requested and there was no need to mesh the solid geometry.

We now move to a **Conjugate** heat transfer problem where fluid flow is accompanied by a heat flow. Open part model COOLING TUBE shown in Figure 14-24. Our objective is to find the amount of heat exchanged between water and air and thermal expansion. Along the way we will have to analyze fluid flow to find convection boundary condition between flowing water and solid brass tube. The tube is surrounded by air but since we won't model air flow in this exercise, the convective boundary conditions on all the outer faces must be given. The convection coefficient is $20Wm^{-2}K^{-1}$, the ambient temperature is 293.2K.

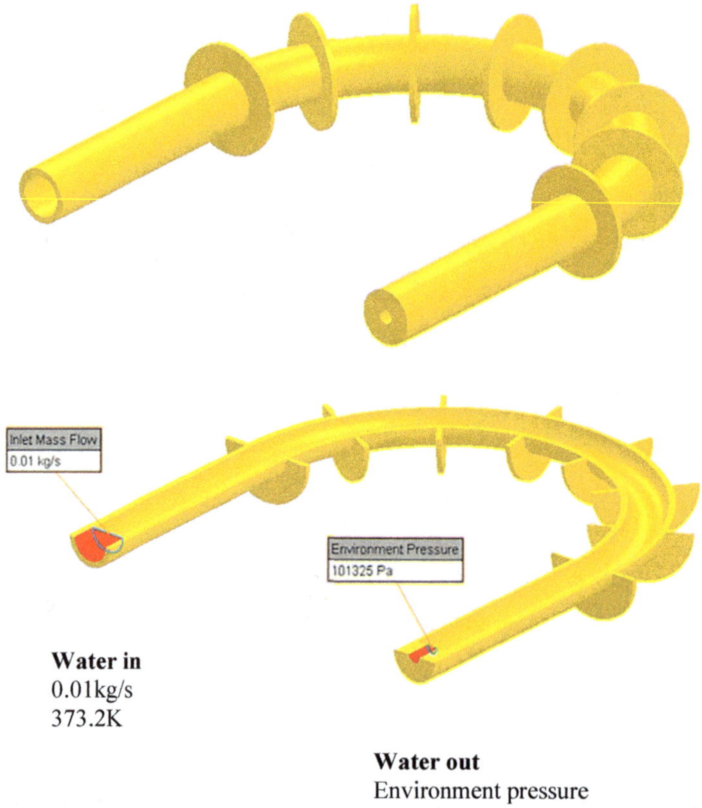

Figure 14-24: COOLING TUBE model.

The model is made watertight by plugging up the inlet and outlet. The plugs are shown in a section view. This is a multi-body part; the plugs are separate bodies. Note an orifice at the outlet. Lids (plugs) were modeled prior to analysis. Lid creation tool was not used.

The following parameters define conjugate heat flow analyzed with Flow Simulation:

Flow in	0.01kg/s, temperature 373.2K
Flow out	Ambient pressure 101325Pa Temperature 293.2K
Convection BC on outer faces	Convection coefficient 20W/(m^2K) Ambient temperature 293.2K
Material	Brass

The following parameters define structural analysis analyzed with Simulation:

One end face is restrained
Case 1 Temperatures imported from the **Thermal** study in **Simulation** Branch 1 in Figure 14-1
Case 2 Temperatures imported from **Flow Simulation** Branch 2 in Figure 14-1

Use the **Wizard** to create a **Flow Simulation** project called *Project 01*. We show only those windows that are different from the ELBOW project.

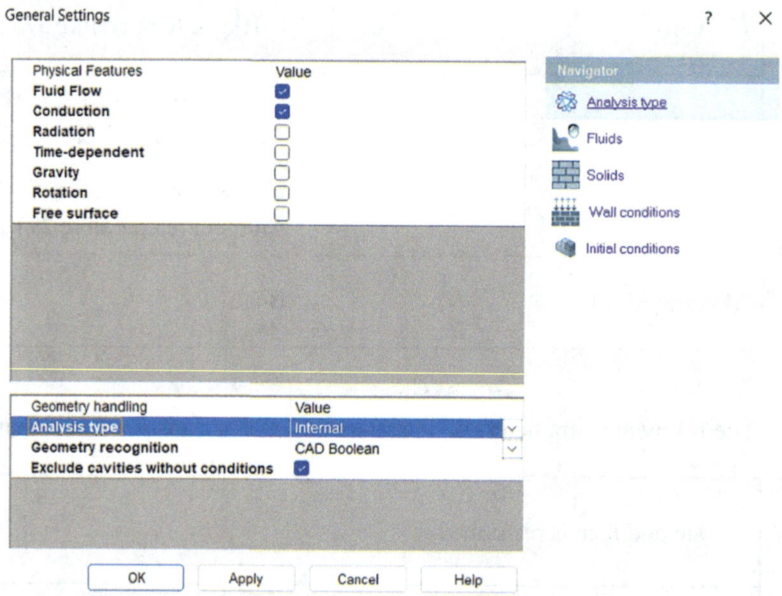

Figure 14-25: Analysis type: select Internal flow with Conduction.

Select Conduction; this way heat transfer in the fluid and in the solid will be modeled.

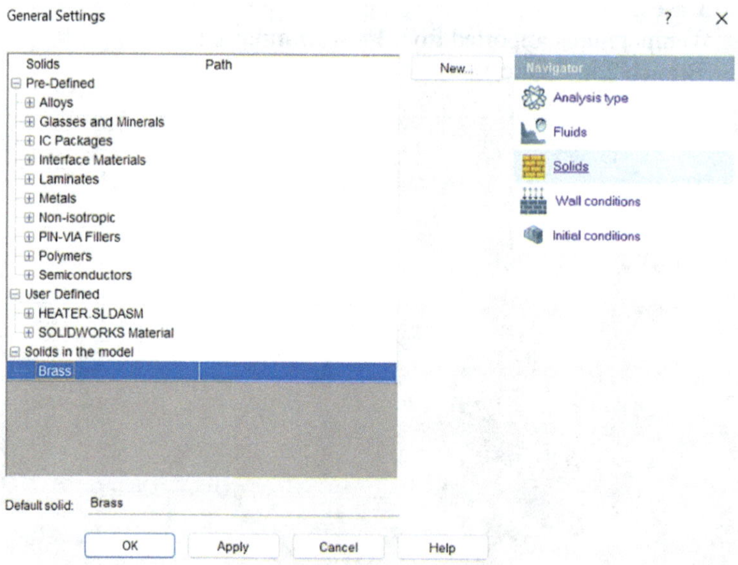

Figure 14-26: Default Solid: Brass.

Select Brass from the Solids in the model list.

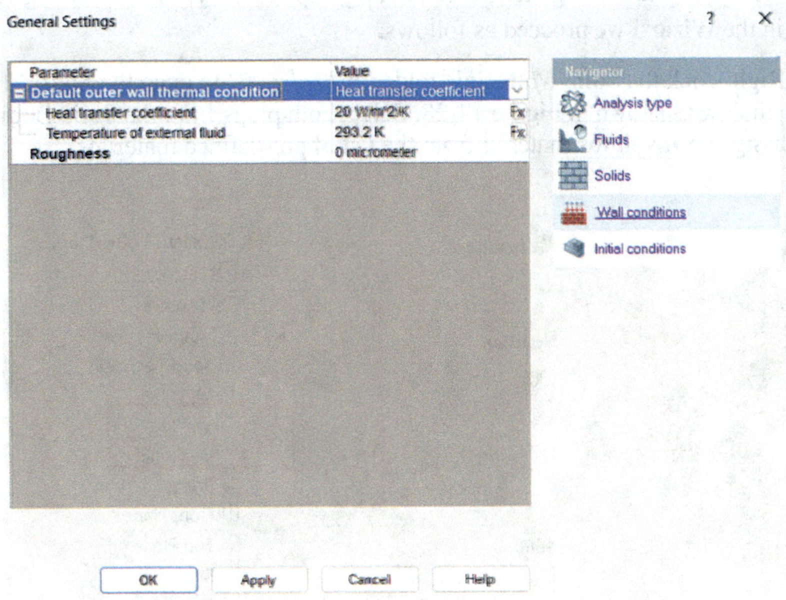

Figure 14-27: Wall Conditions: convection coefficient 20W/(m^{2}K), ambient temperature 293.2K.

These are default convection conditions on the outer wall.

Convective boundary condition on the outer faces must be known because fluid flow on the outer wall of the tube is not modeled.

Accept default settings for the remaining steps of the **Wizard**. Having completed the steps in the **Wizard** we proceed as follows:

Right-click the **Solid Materials** folder in *Project 01* to open the **Solid Material** definition window as shown in Figure 14-28. Select both plugs from the Solid Bodies folder and assign an **Insulator** material from the list of pre-defined materials.

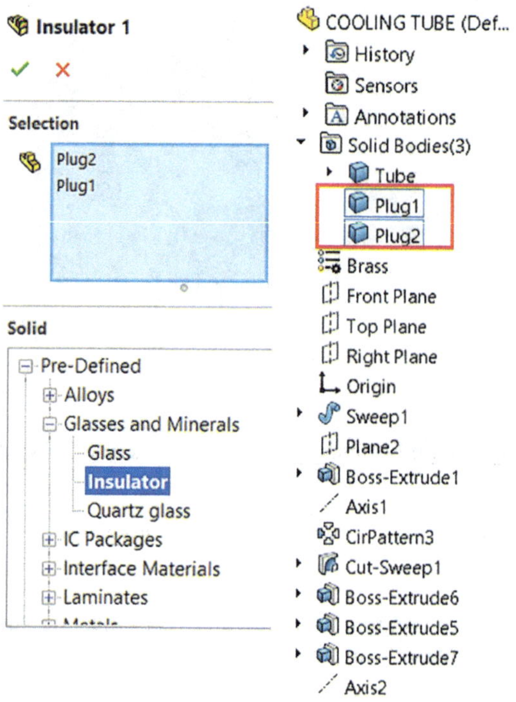

Figure 14-28: Insulator material assigned to plugs.

Material is defined as Insulator to prevent plugs from participating in heat transfer.

Plugs do not exist as real parts. They are added to the model to make it watertight. By defining their material as **Insulator**, we exclude plugs from heat transfer analysis with **Flow Simulation**. Later, we will exclude them from **Thermal** and **Structural** analyses with **Simulation**.

Define flow boundary conditions on the inlet: flow is 0.01kg/s; water is at 373.2K (Figure 14-29).

Figure 14-29: Flow boundary conditions in the inlet. This is a slow flow of 0.01kg/s.

Plug is shown in a section view. Use a section view or Select other command to select the back face of the plug.

Define flow boundary conditions on the outlet as shown in Figure 14-30.

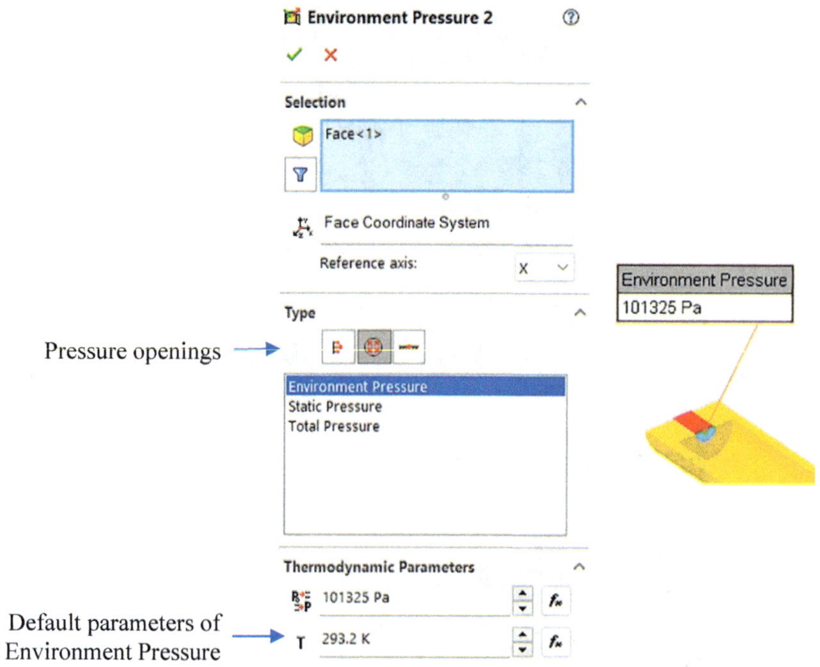

Figure 14-30: Flow boundary conditions in the outlet.

Accept default parameters of Environment Pressure; waterflows out to the environment.

To mesh the model, use Global Mesh Settings shown in Figure 14-31.

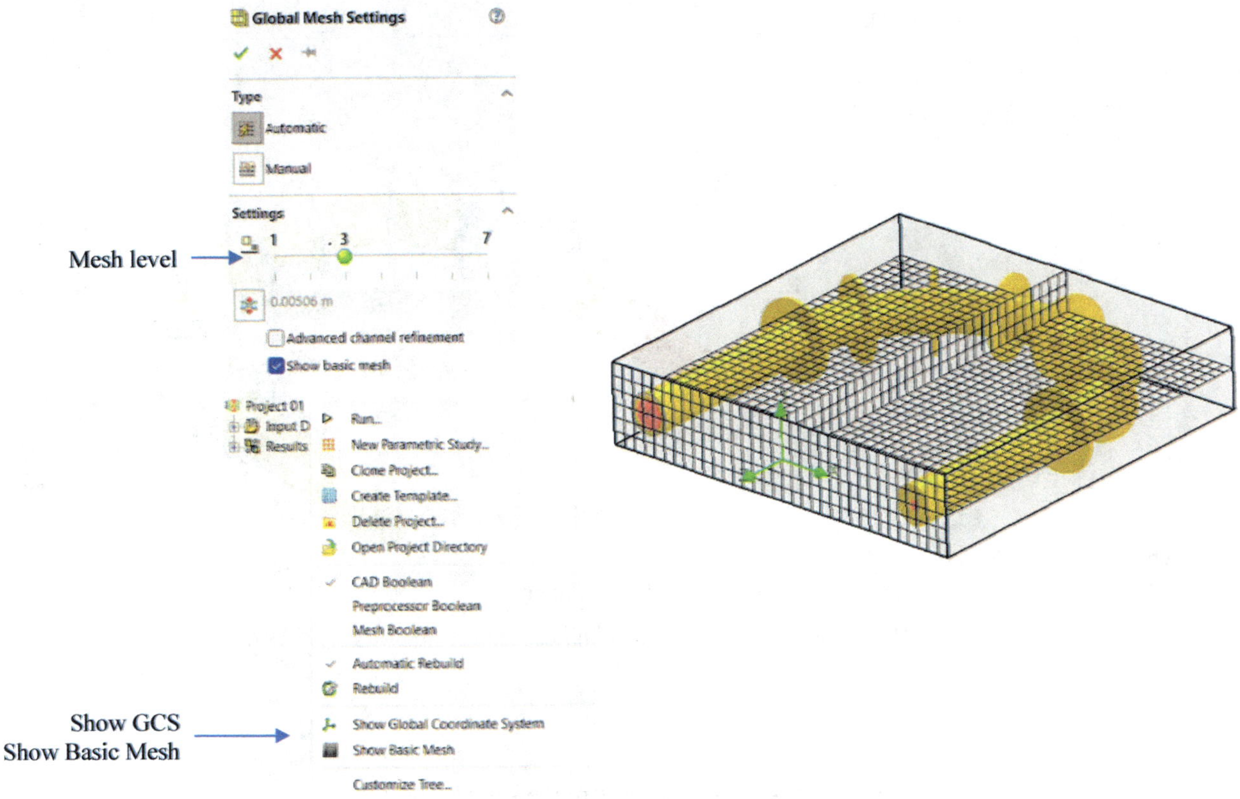

<u>Figure 14-31: Global Mesh Settings set to level 3. Basic mesh and Global Coordinate System are shown.</u>

Right-click Project 01 to display menu where you can control the display of Basic Mesh and Global Coordinate System (GCS).

You may now run the solution; later you may repeat it with different levels of mesh refinement; observe longer solution times when more refined meshes are used.

Review the results of the **Flow Simulation**, especially those that are related to subsequent analysis with **Simulation**.

Temperature of faces of solid body are shown in plot in Figure 14-32.

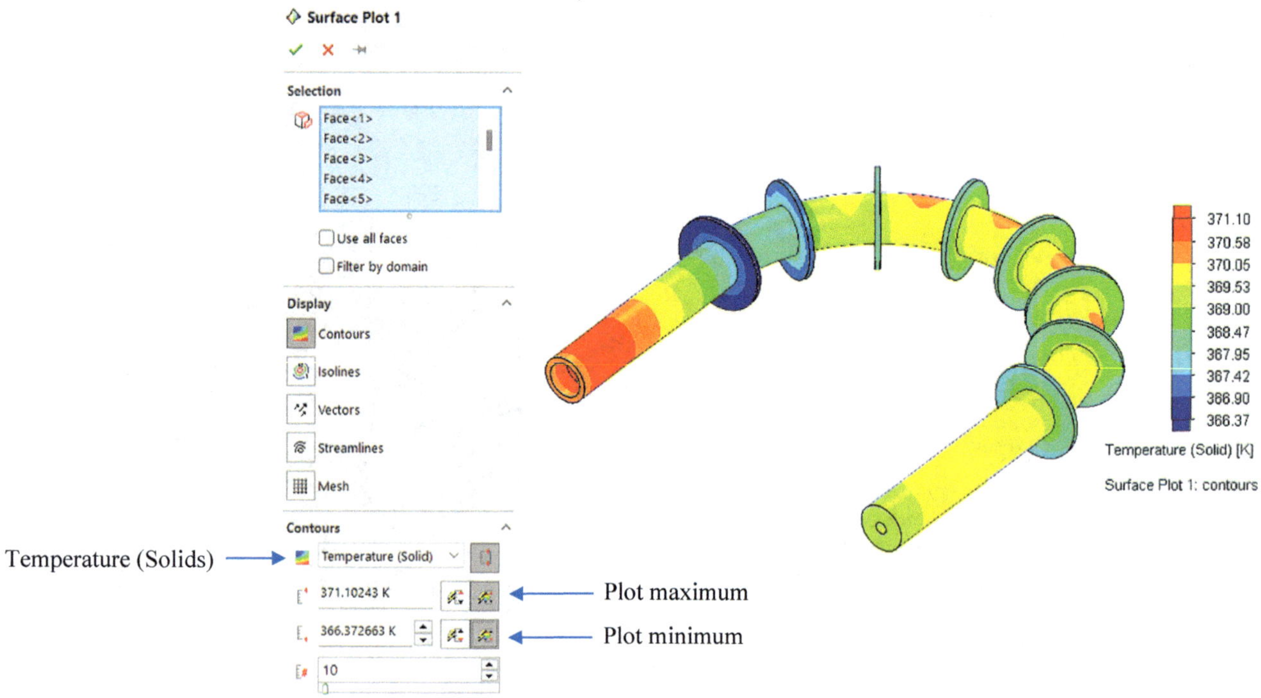

Figure 14-32: Plot of temperature the walls of the solid body.

Model geometry is hidden.

Having solved the fluid flow problem, we transfer results from **Flow Simulation** to **Thermal** study and to **Static** study in **Simulation** but first we need to know where the results of **Flow Simulation** are stored.

Management of results in Flow Simulation is different from Simulation. Results files are named by numbers, which are not derived from the project name. They are in folders with the same numerical names as result file names. Results may be loaded or unloaded using the Load/Unload command in the Flow Simulation Command Manager window or through the Flow Simulation Feature Manager as shown in Figure 14-33. Look at Results folder to see that Flow Simulation solution is stored in file **3.fld**. The name in your project will be different.

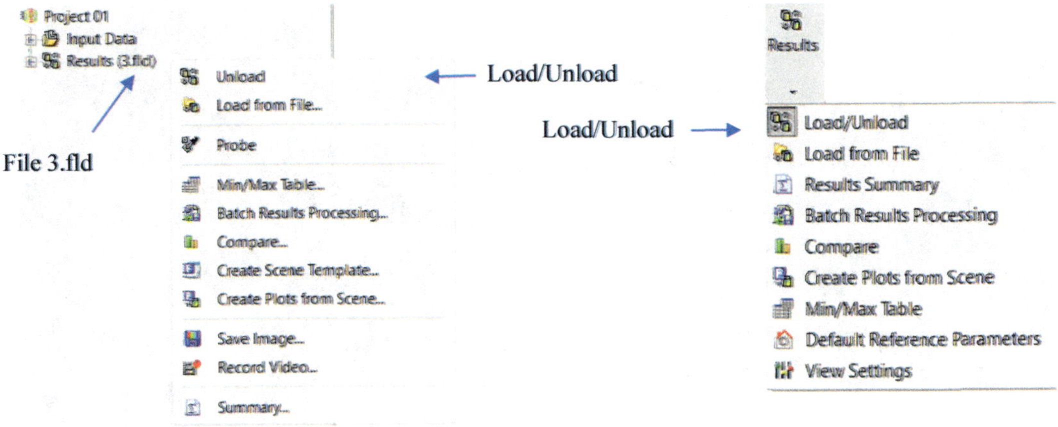

Figure 14-33: Load/Unload can be executed through the pop-up menu invoked by right-clicking on the Results folder or through the Flow Simulation Feature Manager window.

The load command will load default results associated with the project. You may also load other results selecting Load from File. Your file will have a different name.

Refer to Figure 14-34 for information on how to find the **Flow Simulation** project results.

Figure 14-34: Example of Flow Simulation solution folders.

Folders 1, 2, 3, ... are created by Flow Simulation. Your result files will be numbered differently depending on the order in which you have completed the exercises. Summary of projects related to each model is stored in html files. You may open them with apps such as Edge or Chrome.

Results of **Flow Simulation** must be transferred to **Simulation** as shown in Figure 14-35. Save the model before and after exporting the results.

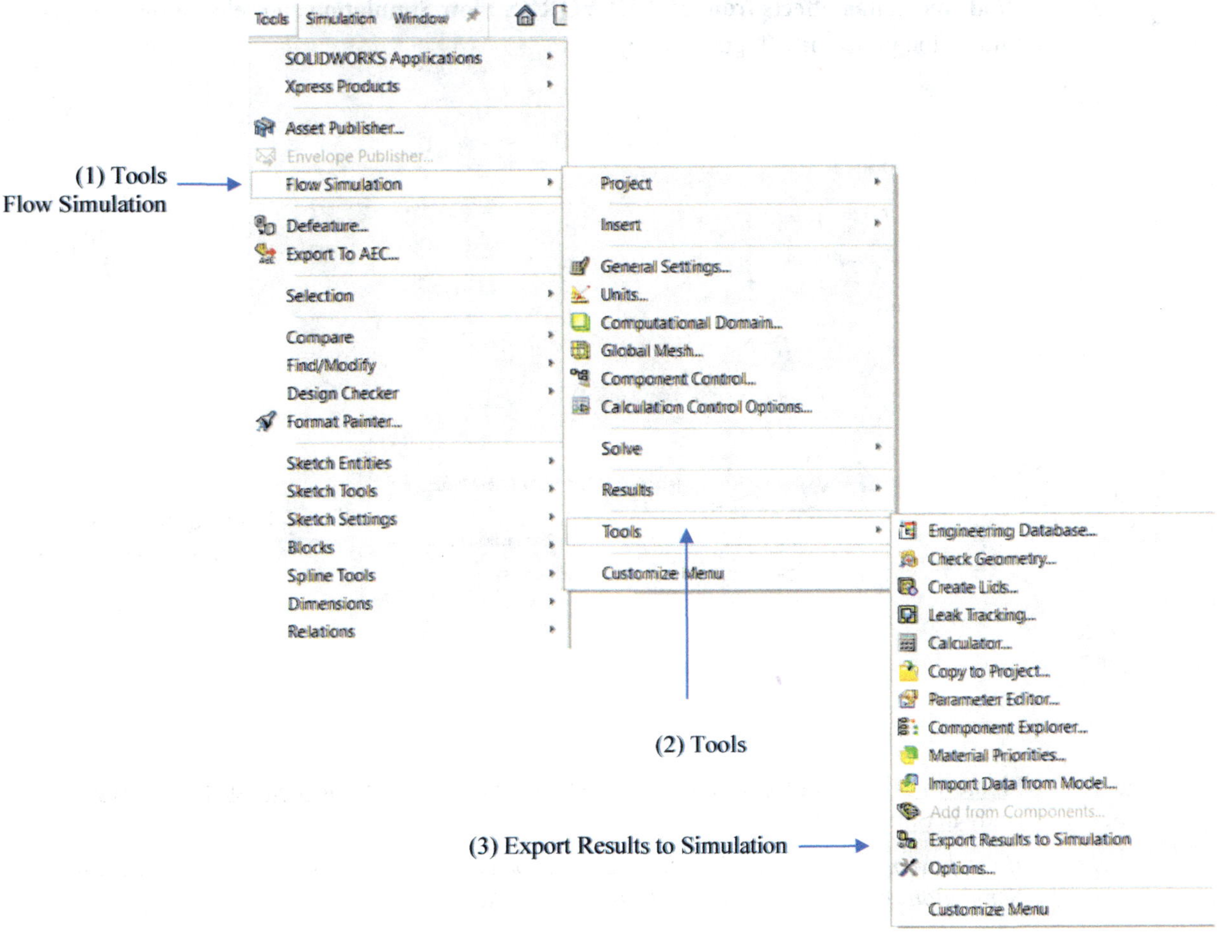

Figure 14-35: Transferring results from Flow Simulation to Simulation.

Save the model before and after exporting results to Simulation.

Note that when you move to Simulation, the model display and its visibility as well as display of Flow Simulation results plots are still affected by visibility settings in Flow Simulation. Learn how to move between windows of Feature Manager, Simulation studies and Flow Simulation projects.

Hide the plugs (Lids) from view (but do not suppress them) in SOLIDWORKS Feature manager and create a Thermal study *01 Thermal*.

We will now follow Branch 1 in Figure 14-1. In *01 Thermal* study properties select **Include fluid convection effects from SOLIDWORKS Flow Simulation** and select Flow Simulation project file (Figure 14-36).

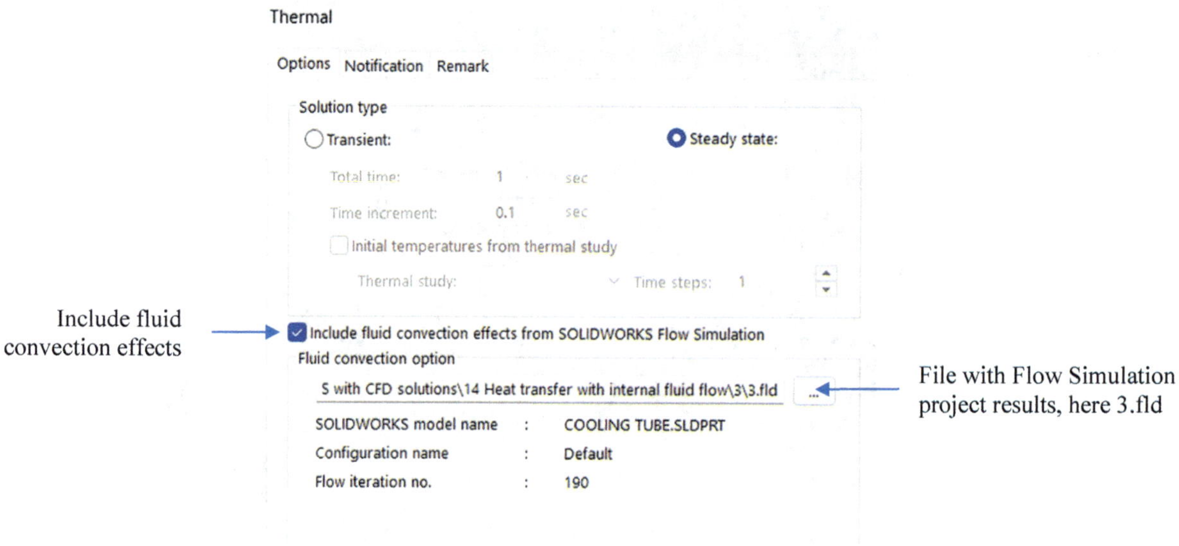

Figure 14-36: Importing convective boundary conditions from Flow Simulation to Thermal study in Simulation.

If you have more than one Flow Simulation project, make sure to select the correct Flow Simulation results file. In this illustration, file 3.fld is selected.

Importing **Flow Simulation** results as shown in Figure 14-36, only brings into the **Thermal** study the convective boundary conditions that have been calculated in **Flow Simulation**. Convection coefficients and the ambient temperatures that have been defined as Wall conditions (Figure 14-27) must be defined again in the **Thermal** study.

Exclude both plugs from the analysis and define a convection coefficient of 20W/(m^{2}K) with an ambient temperature of 293.2K on all external faces. This corresponds to the **Wall Conditions** defined in Flow Simulation (Figure 14-27).

01 Thermal study window is shown in Figure 14-37.

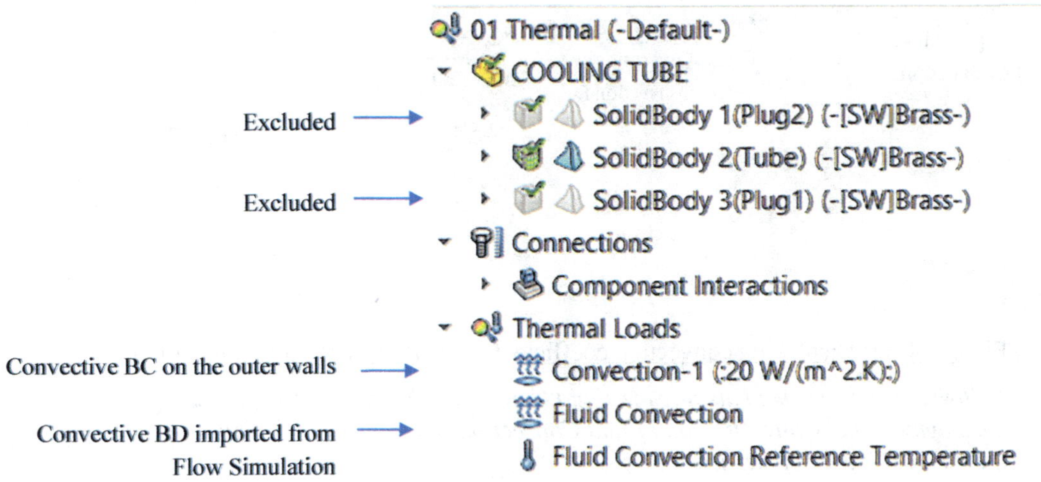

Figure 14-37: Study *01 Thermal* ready to mesh and run.

Plugs are hidden in SOLIDWORKS and excluded from analysis in 01 Thermal study. Convective boundary conditions imported from Flow Simulation are Fluid Convection coefficients and Fluid Convection Reference Temperature.

Mesh the model using a **Curvature Controlled Mesh** with 3mm element size; leave other mesh parameters on defaults.

Thermal conditions imported from **Flow Simulation** can be reviewed in Simulation study (Figure 14-38).

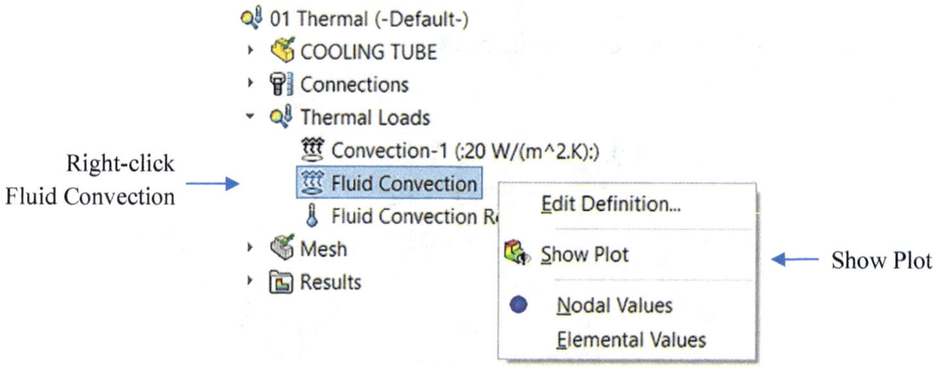

Figure 14-38: Displaying convection coefficients imported from Flow Simulation.

Follow the same steps to display the Fluid Convection Reference Temperature plot. Displaying Fluid Convection and Fluid Convection Reference Temperature will work only if the model has been meshed.

In this project, the imported Fluid Convection coefficients and Fluid Convection Reference Temperatures are defined on the inner faces of the tube. Since section plots are not available for these types of plots, the review of plots is limited to openings on the side of inlets and outlet. Because of these limitations the plots are not shown here.

Run *01 Thermal* study, display a Temperature plot and compare results with Temperature results from Flow Simulation project (Figure 14-39).

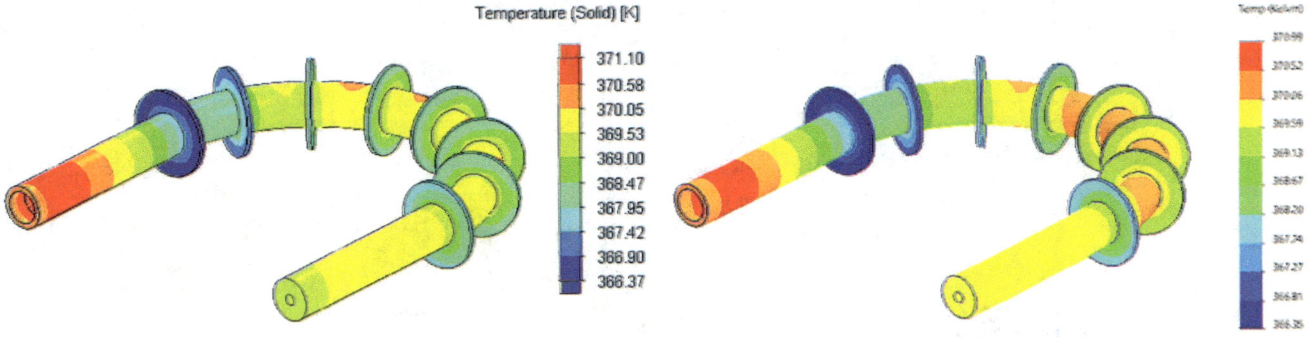

Flow Simulation project

Simulation study

Figure 14-39: Temperature results in Flow Simulation project and in Simulation study.

The left plot is a repetition of Figure 14-31. These plots show very similar results.

The difference between temperature results for solids reported by **Flow Simulation** and **Thermal** analysis in **Simulation** is caused by the error of translation of fluid convection effects from **Flow Simulation** to **Simulation** and by discretization errors in both applications.

If temperature in solids was our only objective, we could have used Flow Simulation only and review results without a need to transfer them to thermal FEA study. But, having solved Simulation study, we will review thermal conditions on the "FEA side" instead of the "CFD side".

Heat Power results are shown in Figure 14-40.

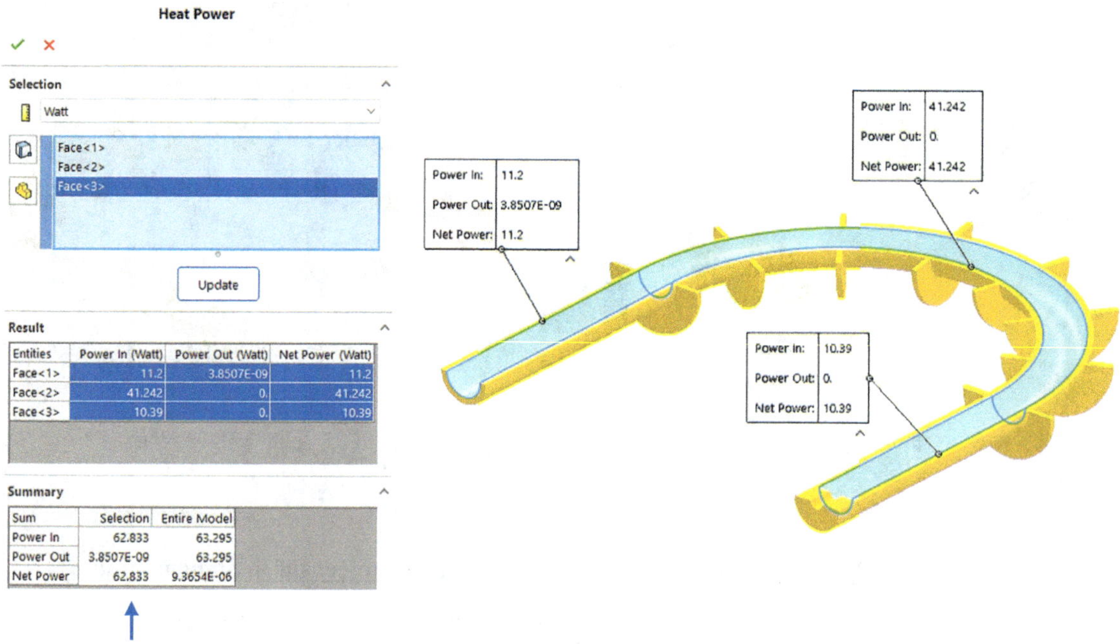

Total heat power 62.8W

Figure 14-40: Heat Power results in Thermal analysis.

Use section view for easy selection of the inner walls. Alternatively, select all outer walls and observe that heat power will be reported with negative sign (heat leaving the selected faces).

We will now perform an analysis of thermal expansion. We may proceed in two ways: temperature results may be imported either from Thermal study (branch 1 in Figure 14-1) or from Flow Simulation (branch 2 in Figure 14-1). We use the second method. Create a static study called *02 Thermal Expansion.*

In the properties of this study specify **Temperature from SOLIDWORKS Flow Simulation**, select the result file (Figure 14-41).

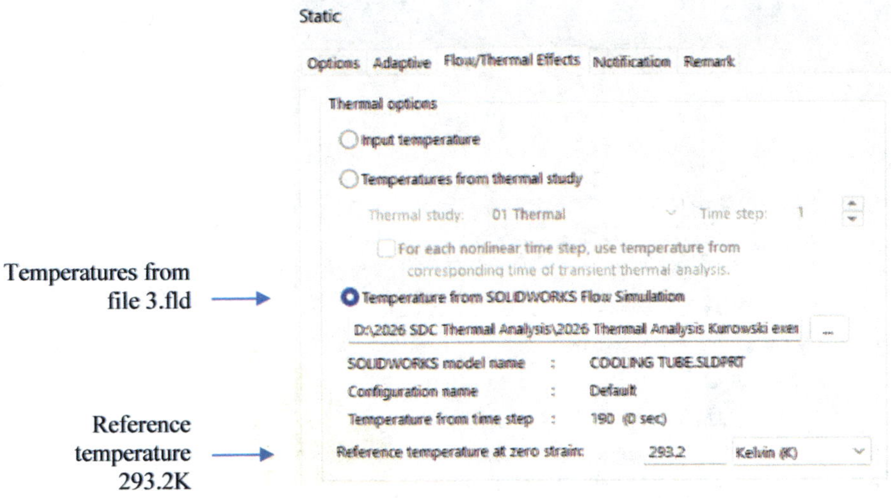

Figure 14-41: Properties of *02 Thermal Expansion* study.

The reference temperature at zero strain corresponds to the temperature of fluid. The result file in your project will have a different name.

Verify that Brass material is assigned to the model. Exclude plugs from analysis and copy the mesh from *01 Thermal* study. However, since we are not transferring results between Thermal and Static studies, the meshes don't have to be the same in these studies.

As in any structural analysis, the model must have restraints that eliminate Rigid Body Motions. We will define restraints that fully restrain the model but avoid interfering with thermal expansion (Figure 14-42).

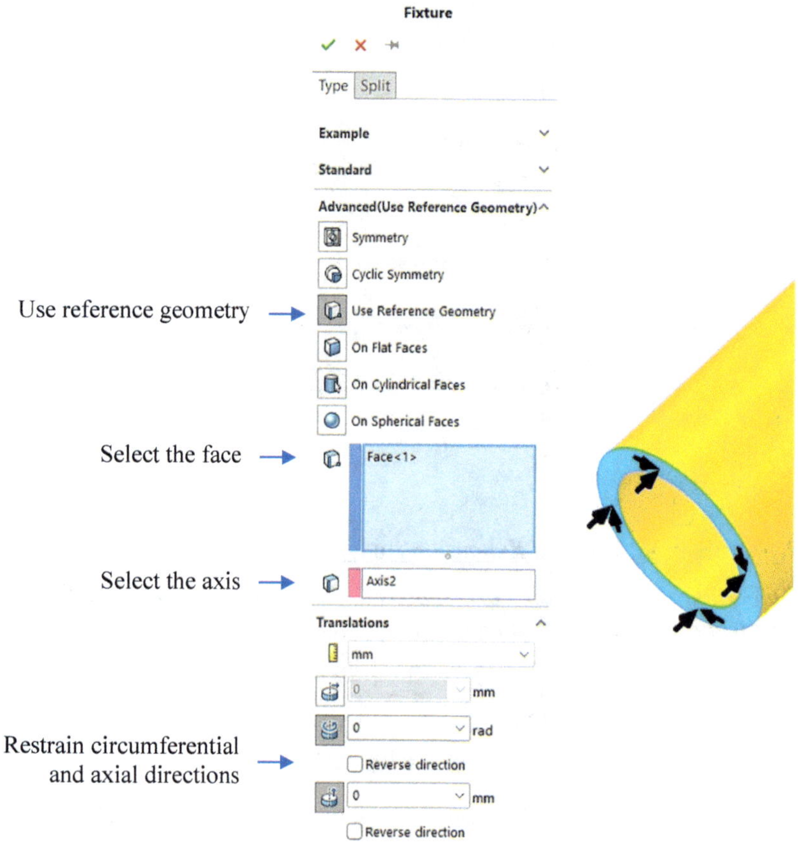

Figure 14-42: Restraints in *02 Thermal Expansion* study defined on the end face. This restraint may be defined on either end.

This restraint eliminates rigid body motions but does not interfere with thermal expansion except that it keeps the face flat.

Run the solution and review displacement results (Figure 14-43).

Figure 14-43: Resultant displacement results in *02 Thermal Expansion study.*

Displacements are measured from the restrained end.

In COOLING TUBE exercise, we demonstrated two ways of interfacing between **Flow Simulation** project, **Thermal** study and **Static** study (Figure 14-1). If thermal analysis in solids is required, you may stay in **Flow Simulation** or follow Branch 1 to **Thermal** study. If thermal stresses are required, you may interface directly following Branch 2.

You may want to extend this exercise to include pressure effects from **Flow Simulation** in a **Static** analysis. To obtain meaningfully high stress, increase the water flow.

Additional practice models

To reinforce the concepts presented in this chapter, repeat the analysis using the additional practice models. Define project input data following the approach used in the main exercise.

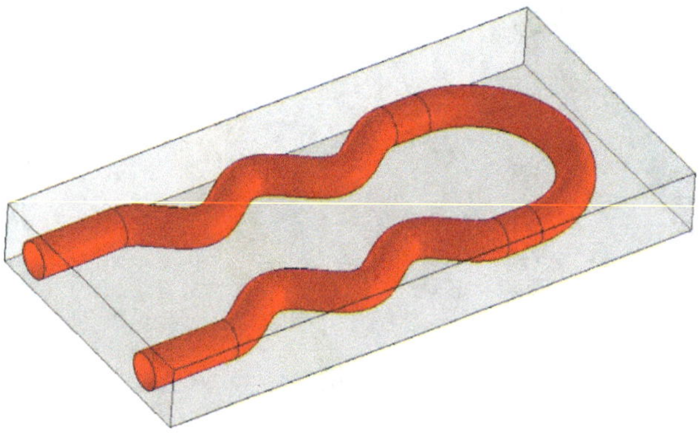

Figure 14-44: CHANNEL part model.

Model is shown in a transparent view. The faces of channel are shown in red color.

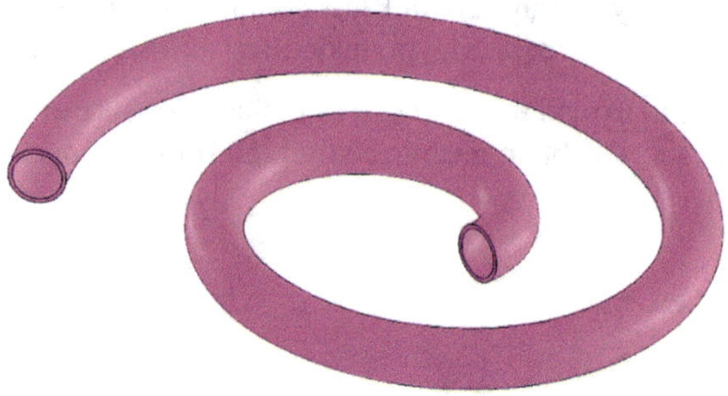

Figure 14-45: SPIRAL part model.

Models in this chapter

Model	Status
ELBOW.sldprt	*Solved with Flow Simulation* *Project01*
COOLING TUBE.sldprt	*Solved with Flow Simulation* *Project01* *Solved with Simulation* *01 Thermal* *02 Thermal expansion*
CHANNEL.sldprt	*Additional practice models*
SPIRAL.sldprt	*Additional practice models*

Notes:

15: External fluid flow

- External fluid flow
- Using Flow Simulation for finding convection coefficients in external fluid flow
- Interfacing between Flow Simulation and Thermal analysis in Simulation
- Types of result plots in Flow Simulation
- Computational Domain

Project description

An External fluid flow is best explained by comparing it to an Internal fluid flow (Figure 15-1).

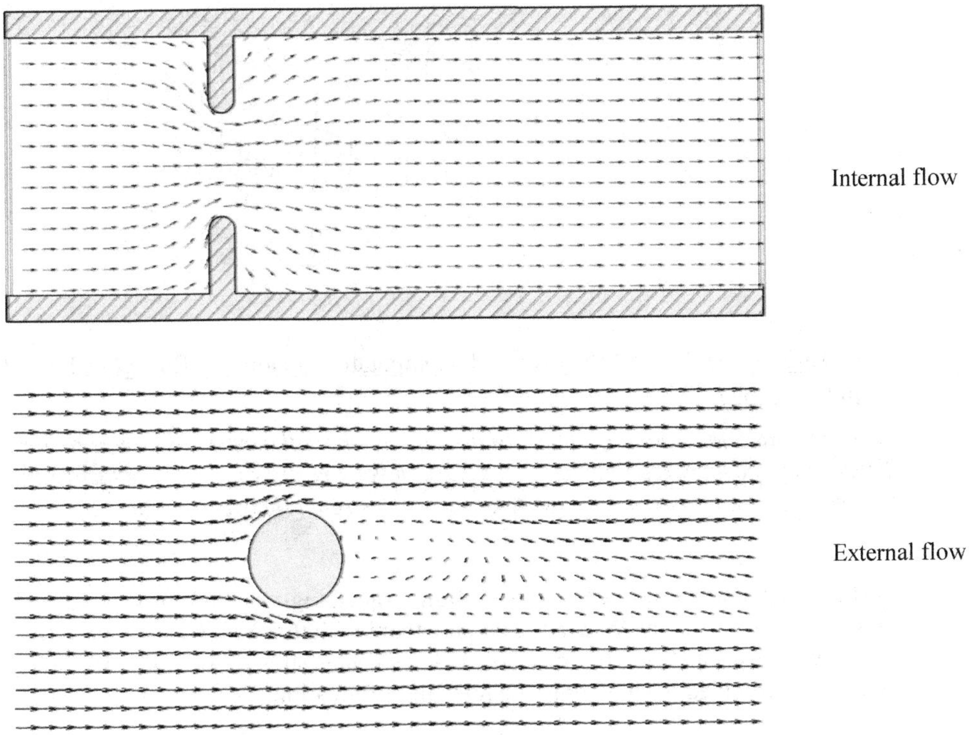

Figure 15-1: Internal and external fluid flow.

Velocity vectors are shown. The channel in Internal flow is shown in a section view.

To study heat transfer in the presence of external fluid flow we will analyze a brass ball submerged in a slow flowing water. The heat power generated in the volume of the ball is 1000W. The temperature of the cooling water is 293.2K; water is under atmospheric pressure, and the flow velocity is 0.01m/s.

Open part model BALL15 shown in Figure 15-2. The same figure also shows the **Computational Domain** automatically defined by the **Flow Simulation** wizard.

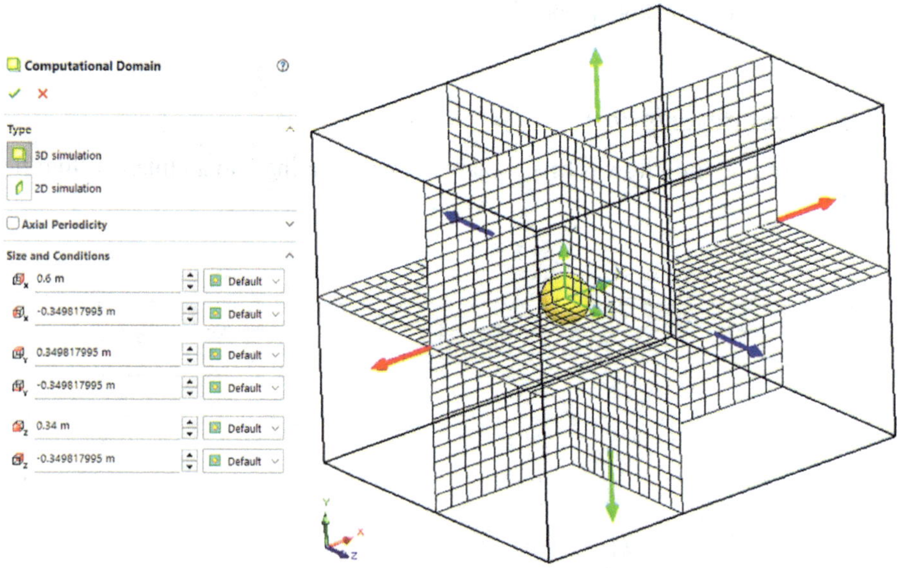

Figure 15-2: Model BALL15 shown with Computational Domain, Basic Mesh and Global Coordinate System.

The Computational Domain extends to the region where the external flow is no longer disturbed by the immersed object. Basic Mesh level 2 is shown. Note the larger extent of the computational domain in the x-direction downstream (leeward) of the ball.

Use the **Wizard** to define a **Flow Simulation** project. Figures 15-3 through 15-9 show steps performed using the **Wizard**. Compare them with the **Wizard** steps from the previous chapter where we analyzed Internal flows. Screen shots shown in Figures 15-3 through 15-9 have been trimmed to show only the relevant information.

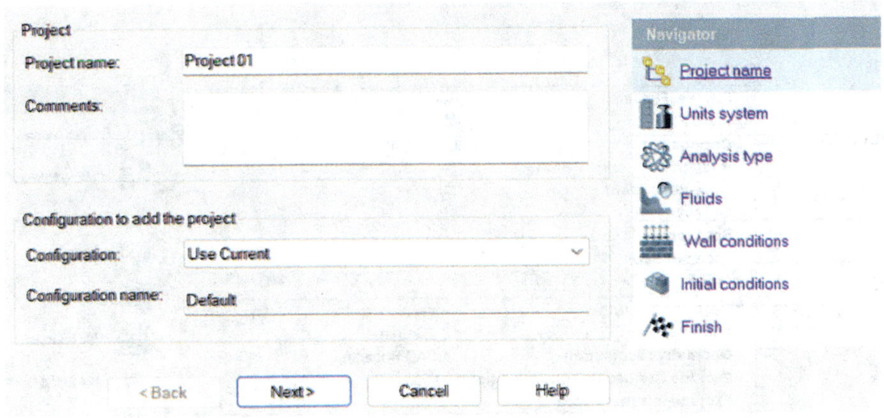

Figure 15-3: Step 1: Project name.

Move through windows using the Next button or by selecting steps from the Navigator menu on the right.

SI →

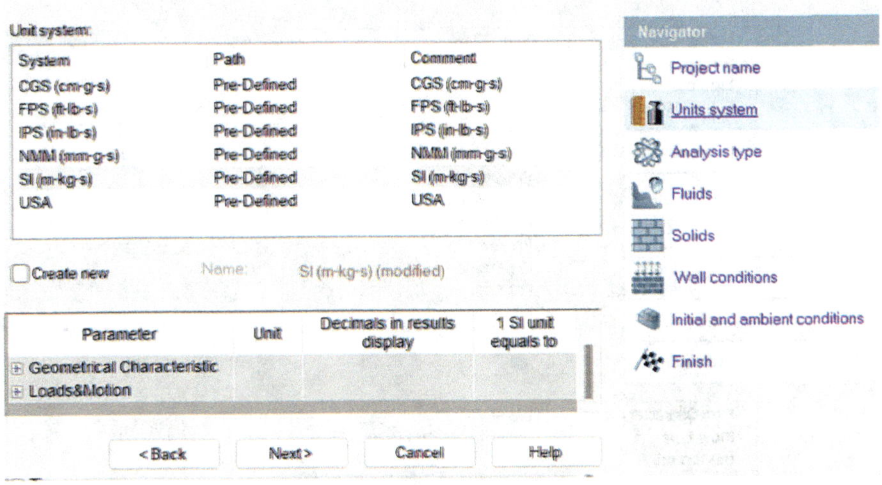

Figure 15-4: Step 2: Unit system.

Accept the default SI system of units.

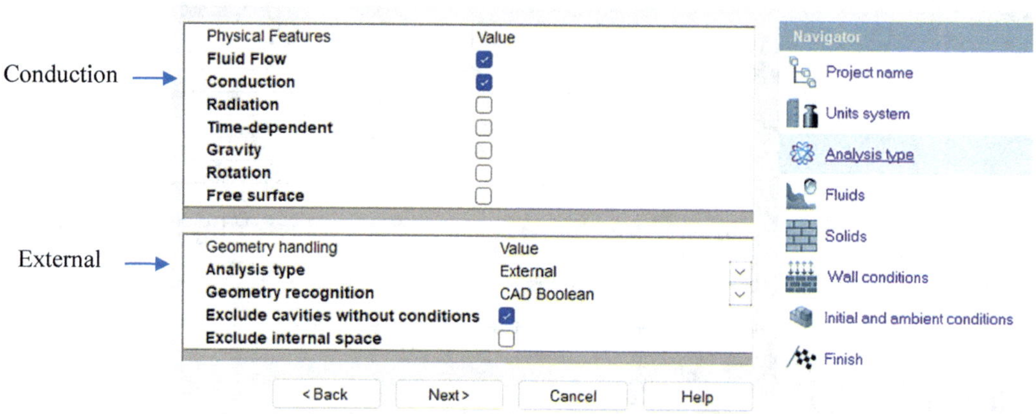

Figure 15-5: Step 3: Analysis type.

Select the External type of analysis; select Conduction and External.

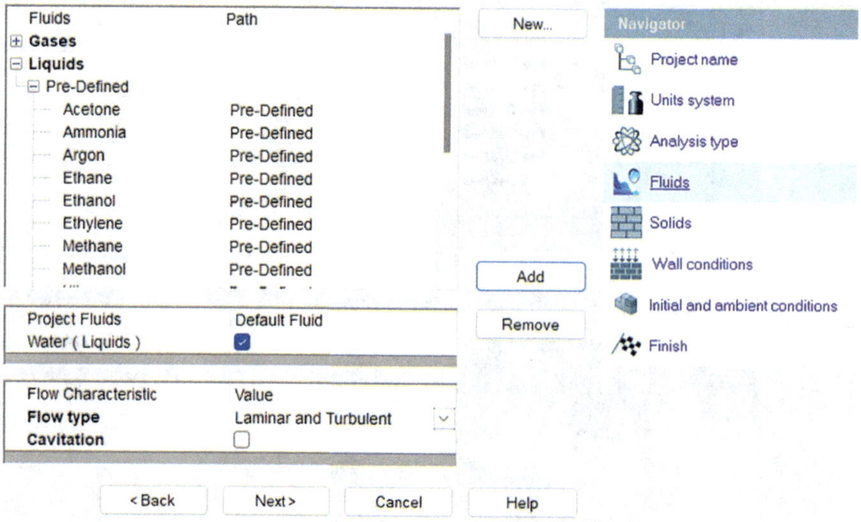

Figure 15-6: Step 4: Default fluid.

Select water from the list of pre-defined liquids and add it to the project database.

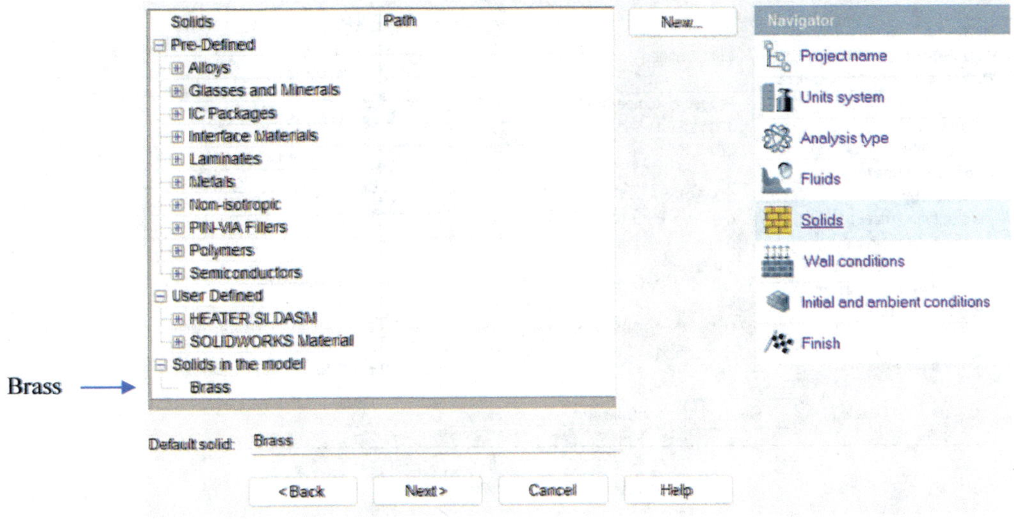

Figure 15-7: Step 5: Default Solid.

Select Brass from Solids in the model.

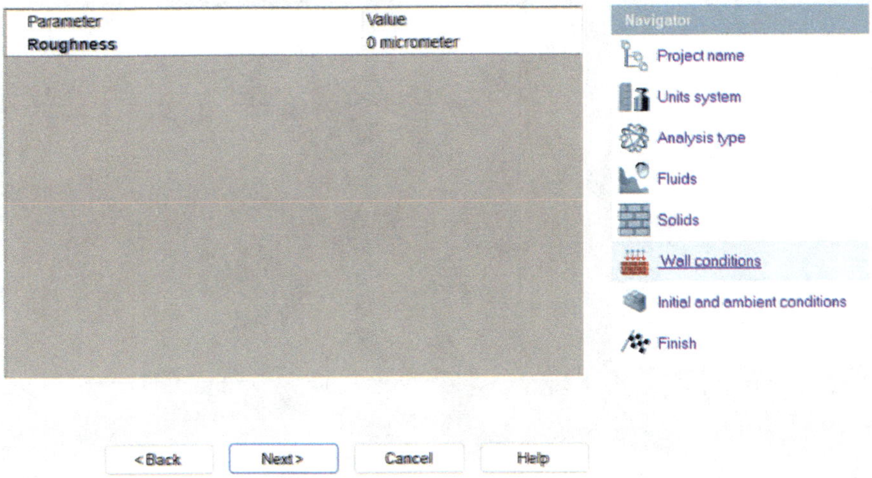

Figure 15-8: Step 6: Wall Conditions.

Do not change anything here; the Ball15 face is assumed to be perfectly smooth.

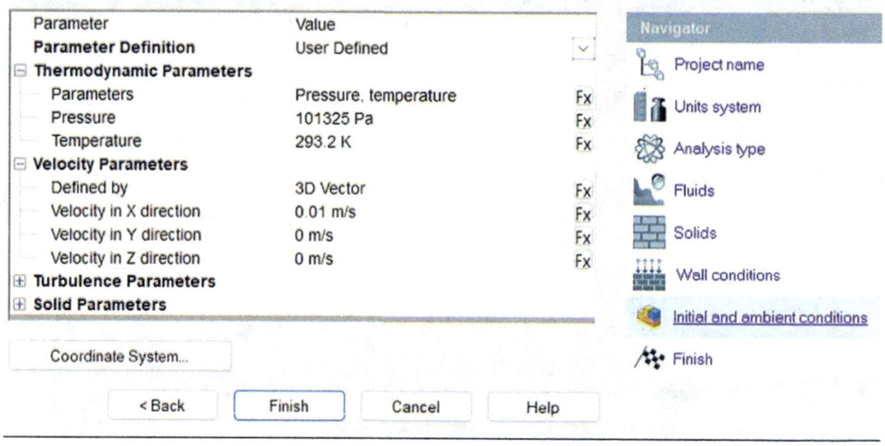

Figure 15-9: Step 7: Initial and Ambient Conditions

Flow velocity in X direction 0.01m/s, Pressure 101325Pa, Temperature 293.2K.

Click Finish to exit the Wizard.

Set Level 5 in **Global Mesh Settings** and Level 3 in **Local Mesh** on the face of the Ball (Figure 15-10).

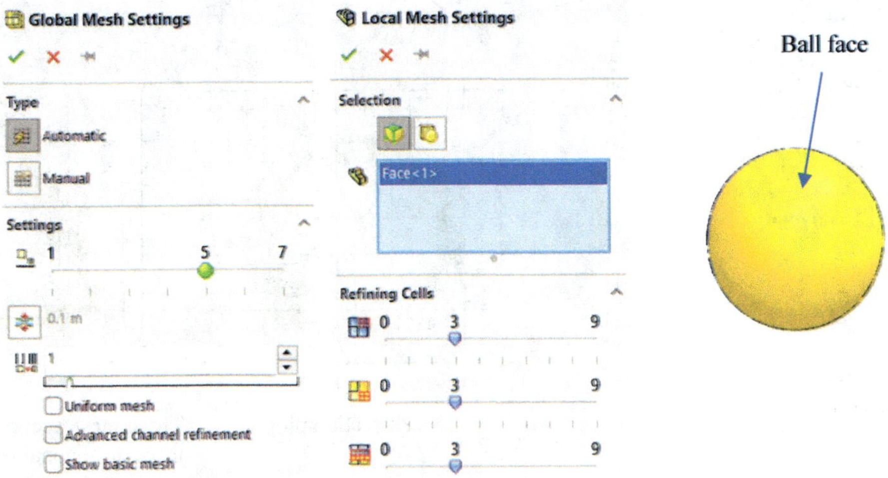

(1) Right –click Mesh
Open Global Mesh Settings
Select Level 5

(2) Right –click Mesh
Open Insert Local Mesh

(3) Select Ball face
Select level 3 in all categories

Figure 15-10: Global Mesh settings and Local Mesh settings.

Local Mesh is in a close analogy to Mesh Control in Simulation.

The finite volume mesh is created at the beginning of Flow Simulation solution. It can also be created without solving a problem if Run box is not selected in the Run window.

Figure 15-11 uses two different methods of mesh visualization: mesh sections and mesh on a face.

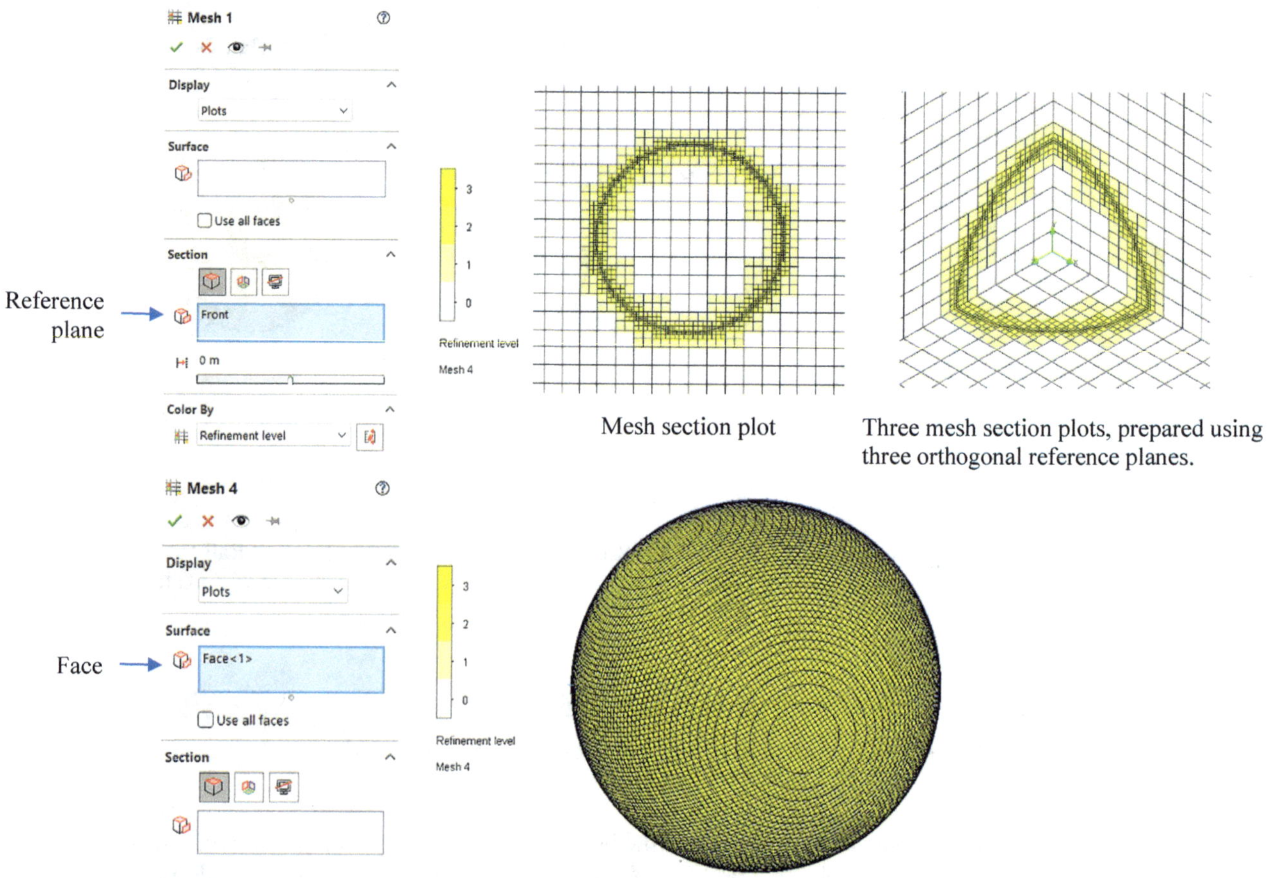

Figure 15-11: Finite Volume mesh in the vicinity of the ball. Three levels of refinement are defined by the Local Mesh.

A small fragment of the mesh is shown in the top two illustrations. More than one mesh plot may be displayed at the same time to help a 3D visualization of the mesh.

In the lower illustration, Mesh is shown on the face of the Ball. Double click the color bar to change the display colors to custom colors.

Define the 1000W heat power generated in the volume of the model. Select **Volume Source** either from **Sources** in Flow Simulation Command Manager or from **Tools** in the top menu (Figure 15-12).

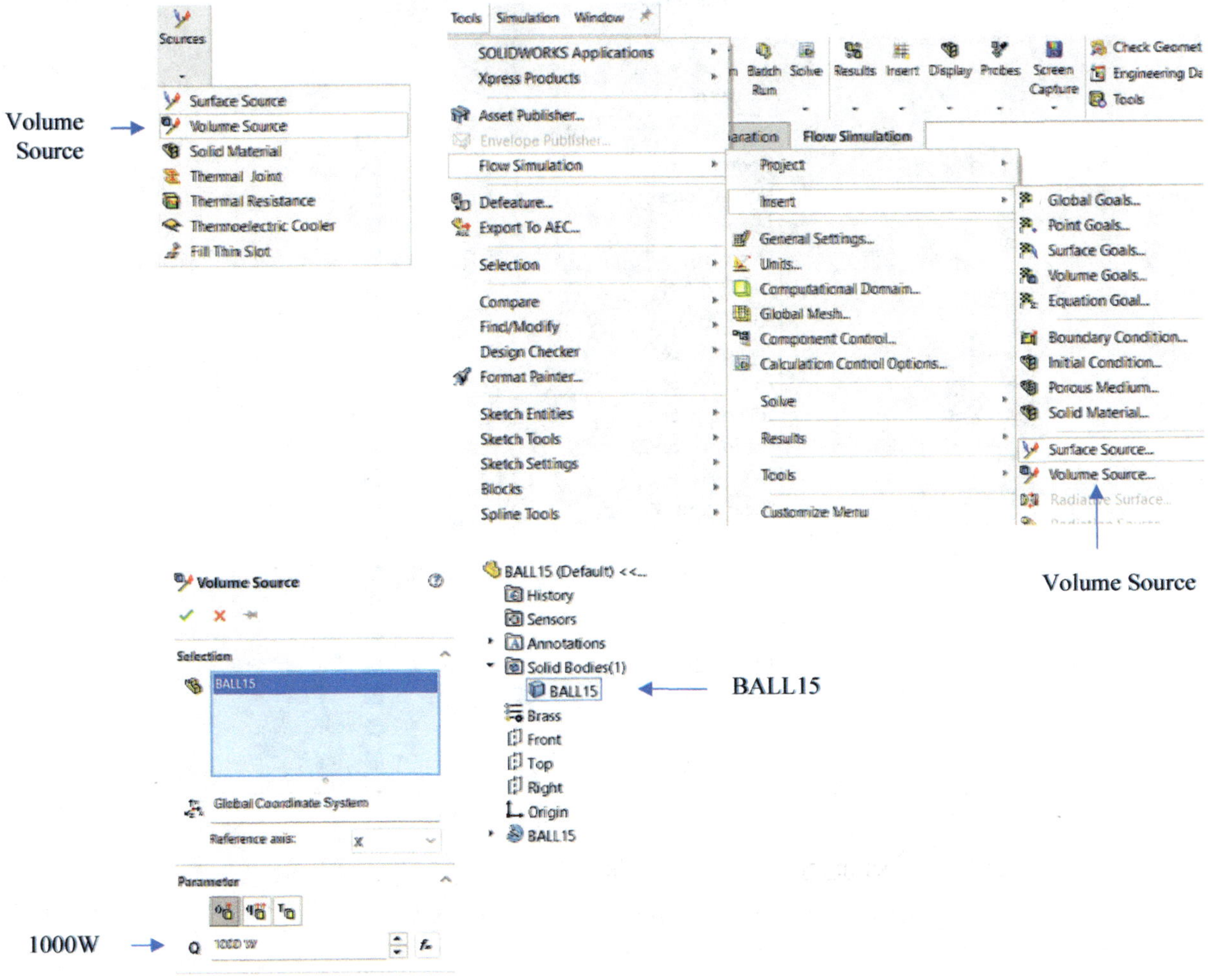

Figure 15-12: Definition of Heat Power.

Heat Generation Rate applies heat power to the volume of the Ball.

The objective of this analysis is to find a steady state temperature of the Ball15 cooled by water. Create **Global Goal** as shown in Figure 15-13.

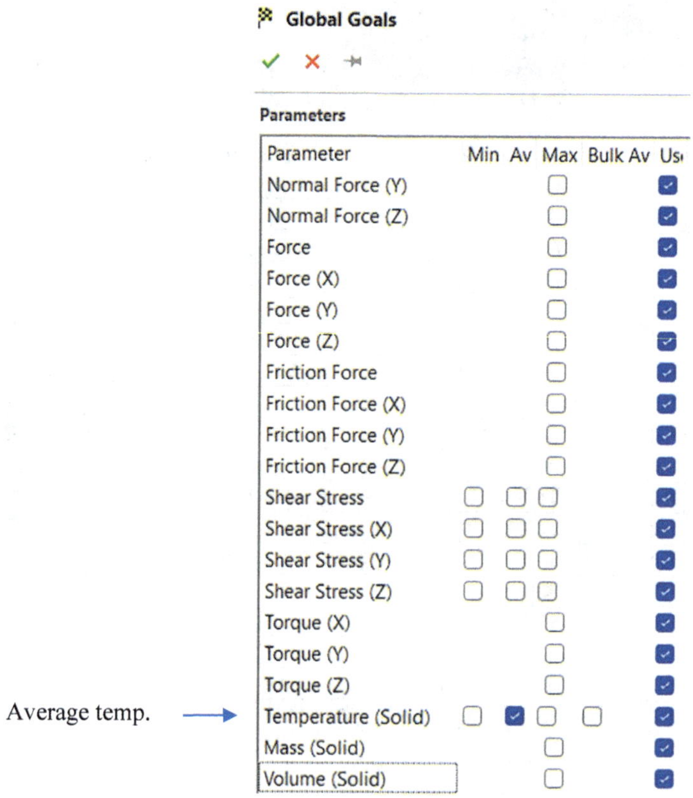

Figure 15-13: Definition of analysis goals.

The average temperature will be used in convergence graph.

Run the solution and monitor the convergence curve in the Solver window (Figure 15-14).

Insert Goal Plot

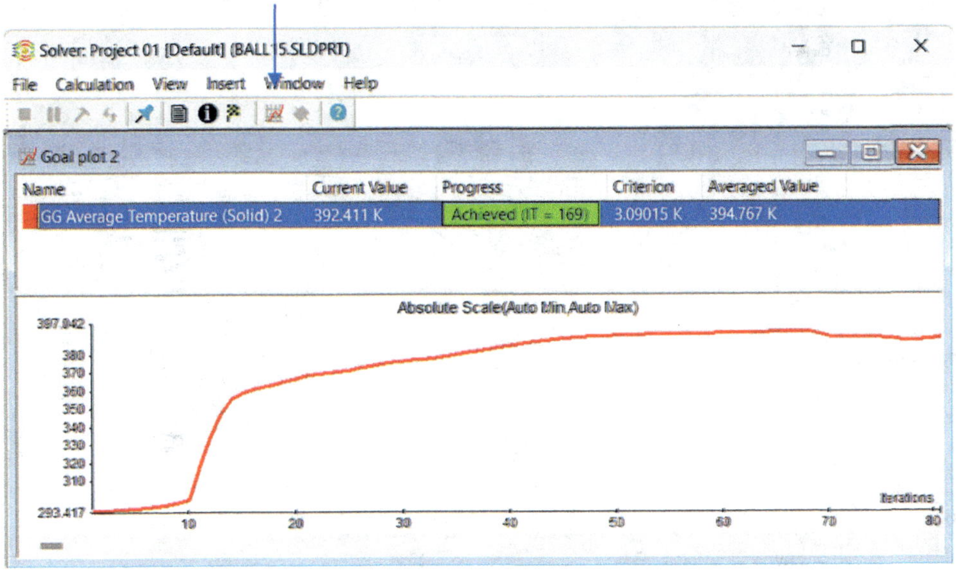

Figure 15-14: Monitoring solution progress in the Solver window.

The graph shows completed solution. Review other options available in the Solver window.

Analysis of water flow is not the main objective of this analysis. Still, you may want to look at results pertaining to the water flow. For example, create a **Cut Plot** of velocity as shown in Figure 15-15.

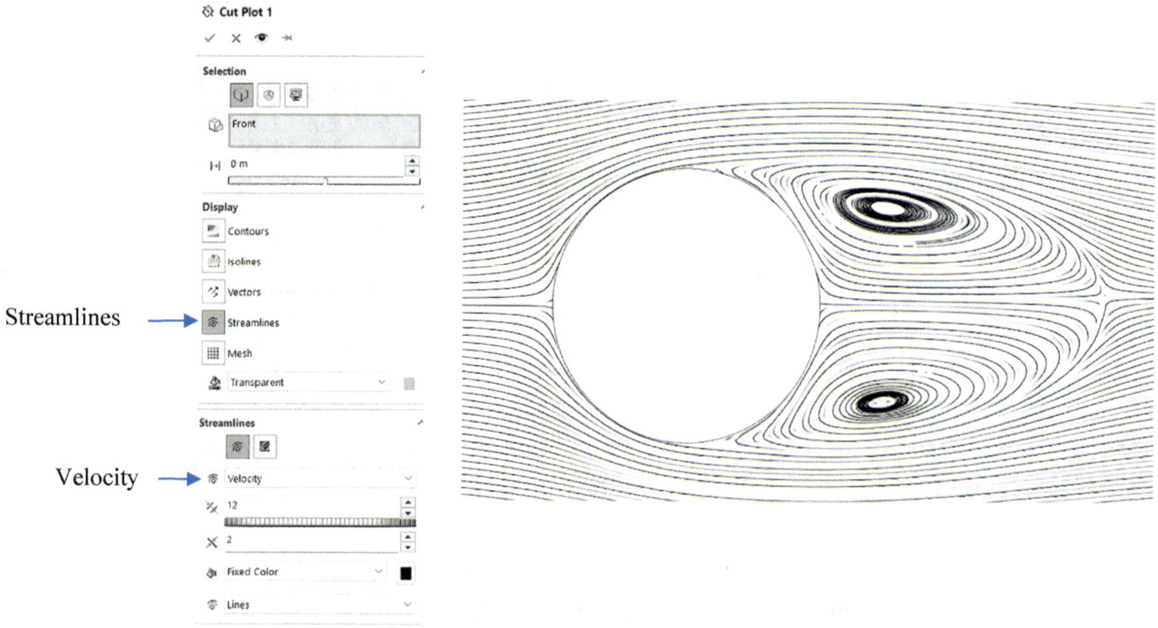

Figure 15-15: Velocity streamlines in the vicinity of the Ball.

The plot has been cropped. Explore other types of display and available options.

Define a **Cut Plot** showing temperature in the solid (Figure 15-16).

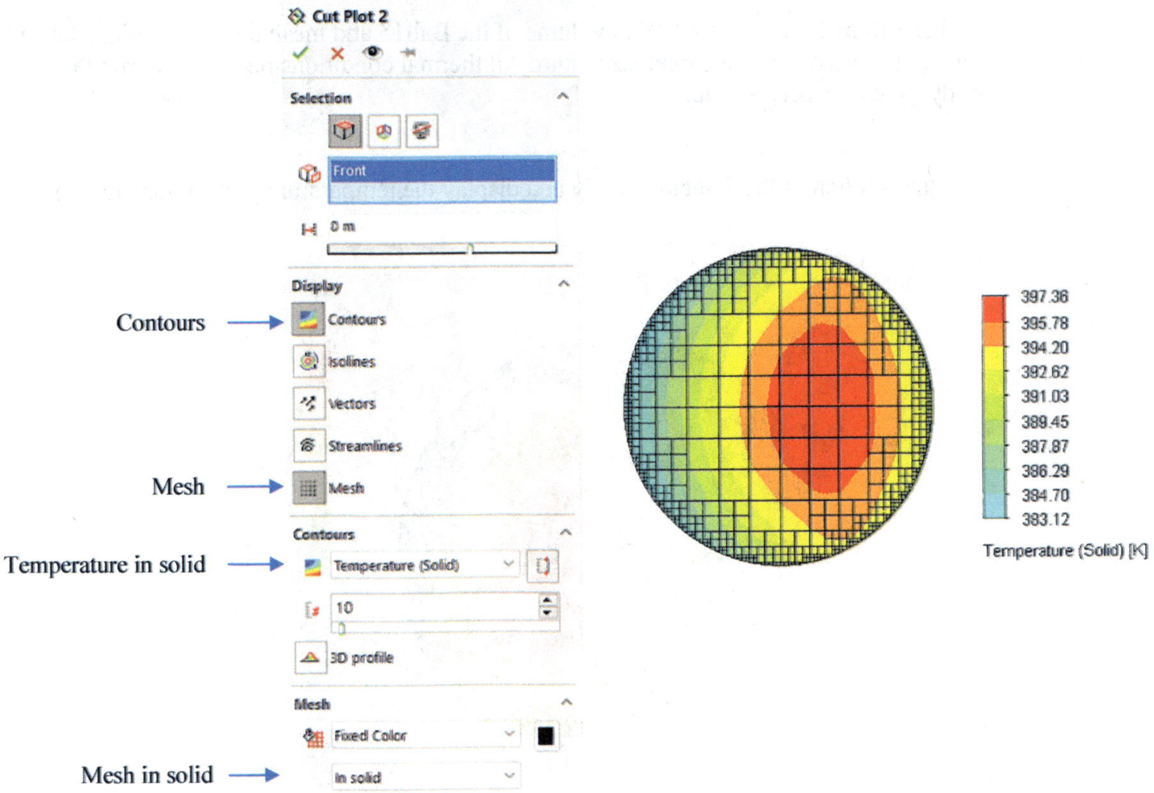

Figure 15-16: Temperature across the Ball.

The mesh in the solid includes solid cells and partial cells.

Hide all **Flow Simulation** plots and display the model geometry. Save the model before and export the results from **Flow Simulation** to **Simulation** as explained in Figure 14-35.

In Simulation, create Thermal study *Ball Thermal*. In Thermal study properties, select **Include fluid convection effects from SOLIDWORKS Flow Simulation**. Select the correct *.fld file as shown in Figure 14-33.

Define a **Heat Power** of 1000W in volume of the Ball15 and mesh the model with Blended Curvature Based mesh, element size 5mm. All thermal conditions necessary to run the study have now been set-up.

Run the solution of the **Thermal** study and display the temperature plot (Figure 15-17).

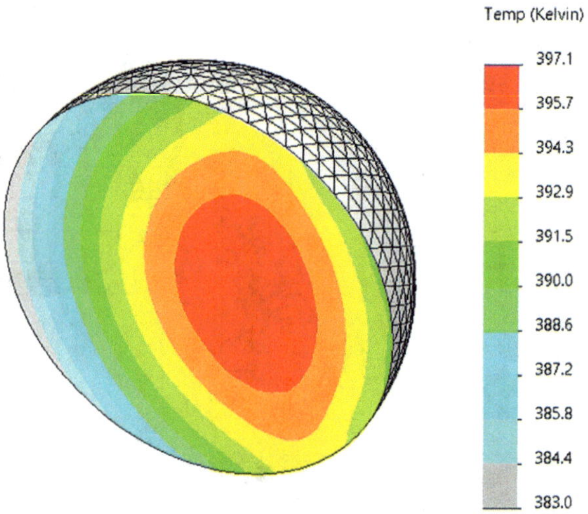

Figure 15-17: Temperature in the cross section of Ball.

This plot is directly comparable to the plot in Figure 15-16. Section Clipping and Custom colors are used.

Having obtained results of Thermal study, you may analyze thermal stresses. Create a Static study *Ball Structural* and copy mesh from *Ball Thermal* study. Open study properties window: in Options tab select **Use soft springs to stabilize model**. Next open **Flow/Thermal Effects** tab (Figure 15-18).

To follow Branch 1 in Figure 14-1, select **Temperatures from thermal study** and indicate the name of thermal study, here *Ball Thermal*. Mesh in *Ball Structural* and *Ball Thermal* must be the same.

To follow Branch 2 in Figure 14-1, select **Temperature from SOLIDWORKS Flow Simulation.**

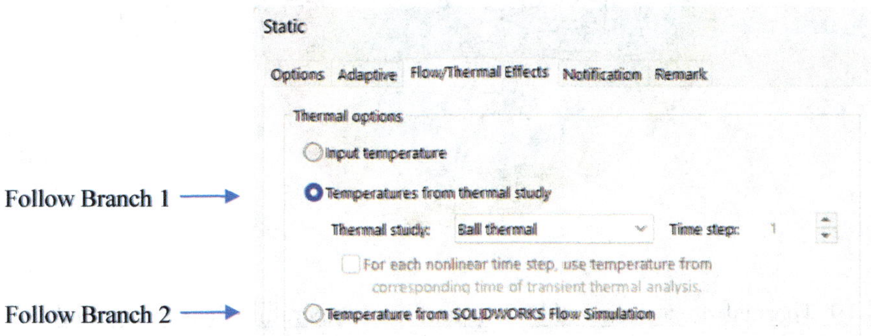

Figure 15-18: Two ways of importing temperature results into structural study.

Refer to Figure 14-1 for description of Branch 1 and Branch 2.

Thermal stress plot is shown in Figure 15-19.

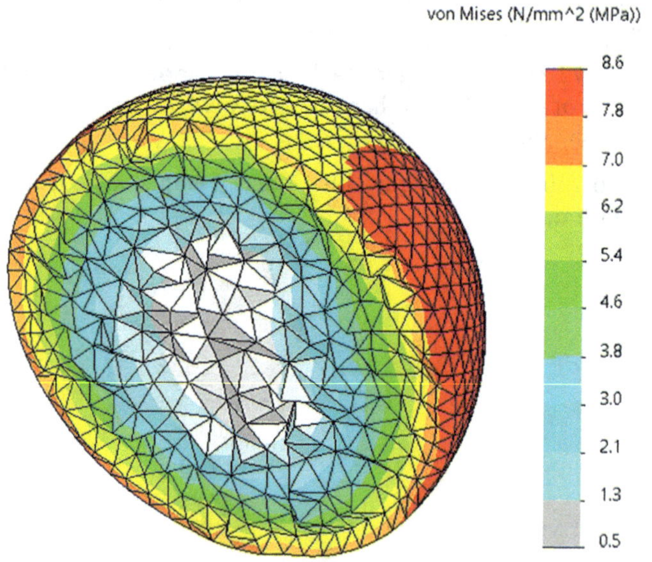

Figure 15-19: Thermal stresses caused by non-uniform temperature distribution in the model.

Mesh sectioning and Custom colors are used.

Repeat this exercise with different settings of the finite volume mesh and finite element mesh. Examine Fluid Convection and Fluid Reference Temperature plots showing convective boundary conditions transferred from Flow Simulation to Thermal study in Simulation.

Repeat the exercise with **Radiation** enabled in General Settings (Figure 15-5). A slight decrease in the temperature of Ball will be observed once Radiation is included. In the following chapters, we will illustrate a more pronounced influence of radiation when the temperatures are higher.

Additional practice models

To reinforce the concepts presented in this chapter, repeat the analysis using the additional practice models. Define project input data following the approach used in the main exercise.

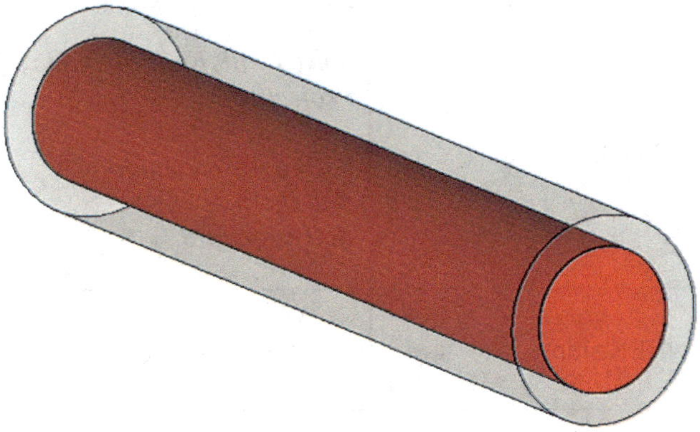

Figure 15-20: CYLINDER part.

This is a multi-body part.

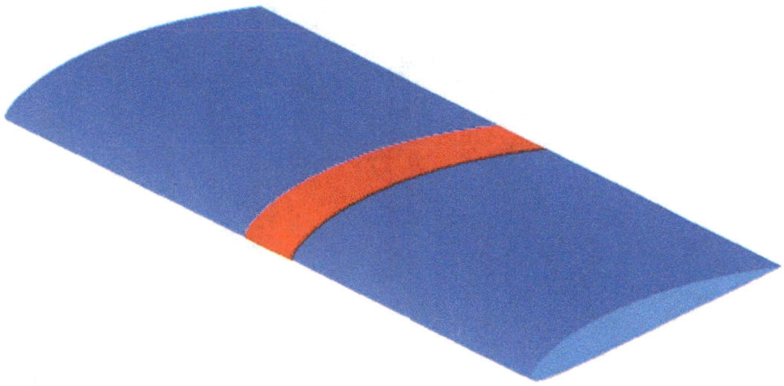

Figure 15-21: WING part.

This is a multi-body part.

Models in this chapter

Model	**Status**
BALL15.sldprt	*Solved with Flow Simulation* *Project01* *Solved with Simulation* *Ball thermal* *Ball structural*
CYLINDER.sldprt	*Additional practice model*
WING.sldprt	*Additional practice model*

16: Microchip cooling

- Conjugate Heat Transfer with External Flow
- Thermal Resistance
- Ideal wall
- Component control

Project description

We analyze thermal conditions in an assembly of a microchip and a radiator cooled by air. It may look like a repetition of the exercise in Chapter 9, but the air flow was not modeled there. To model the presence of air, convective boundary conditions were assumed on the faces of the radiator. In this exercise, we will conduct a conjugate heat transfer analysis with Flow Simulation to find temperatures in solid components. By modeling fluid flow around solids, we won't have to make any assumptions on convection.

MICROCHIP assembly is shown in Figure 16-1.

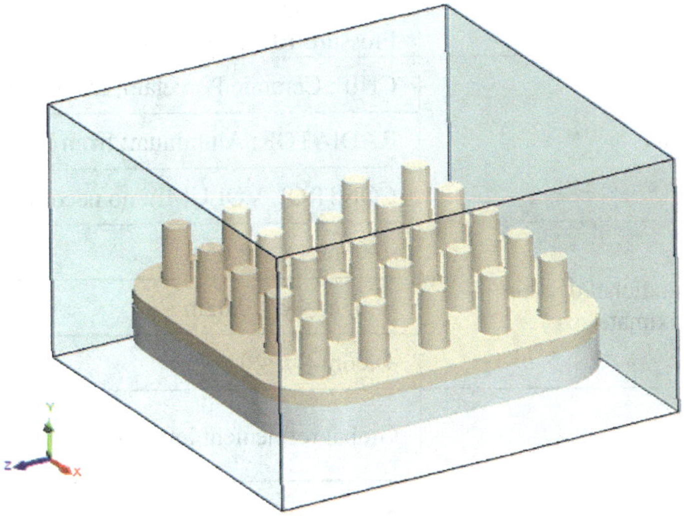

Figure 16-1: Aluminum Radiator (with pegs), porcelain Chip and Control Volume are components of the assembly.

The Chip is the heat source. Radiator disperses heat into air. The bottom face of Chip is insulated. A cuboid Control Volume encases the Radiator and Chip assembly. Control Volume is used to define the local mesh refinement.

Procedure

Open assembly MICROCHIP. Material properties (Ceramic Porcelain) are assigned only to CHIP part.

The assembly sits in the flow of air, velocity 5m/s, pressure 101325 Pa and temperature 293.2K. The CHIP generates 20W heat. The bottom face of Chip is insulated. Parts RADIATOR and CHIP are glued together with a layer of silicon. This connection will be modeled as Thermal Resistance.

This is a conjugate heat transfer problem with external flow, and radiation. Project settings are summarized below. You may use smaller Computational Domain to reduce the time of the solution. In this exercise we skip the analysis of the effect of domain size on the results.

Thermal Power	20W applied to volume of CHIP
Thermal resistance layer	Silicon, 0.5mm thick
Thermal BC	Bottom face insulated (Ideal Wall)
Flow	Air, 5m/s resultant velocity Components v_x: 1.77, v_y= - 4.33, v_z= - 1.77 Temp. 293.2K Pressure 101325Pa (environment)
Materials	CHIP: Ceramic Porcelain; from part
	RADIATOR: Aluminum; from Flow Simulation Data Base
	CONTROL VOLUME: no need for material
Computational domain (Approximate size)	-0.06m $\leq$ x $\leq$ 0.06m
	-0.05m $\leq$ y $\leq$ 0.08m
	-0.06m $\leq$ z $\leq$ 0.06m
Global Mesh	Global refinement level: 3
Local Mesh	Applied to CONTROL VOLUME Refinement level for fluid and solid cells: 2 Refinement for fluid cells containing solid: 3
Component Control	CONTROL VOLUME is excluded

Follow steps in Figures 16-2, ...16-4.

Select **Fluid Flow, Conduction** and **External** flow in Analysis type window. Select Air as the default fluid.

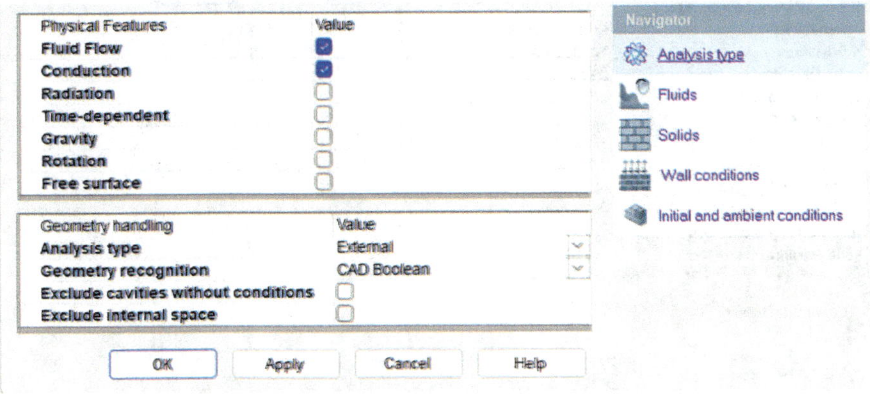

Figure 16-2: Analysis type: External Fluid Flow

Conduction and Radiation are selected. Select Air as the default fluid.

Select **Ceramic Porcelain** from **Solids in the model** as the default solid (Figure 16-3). Accept default Wall condition (window not shown).

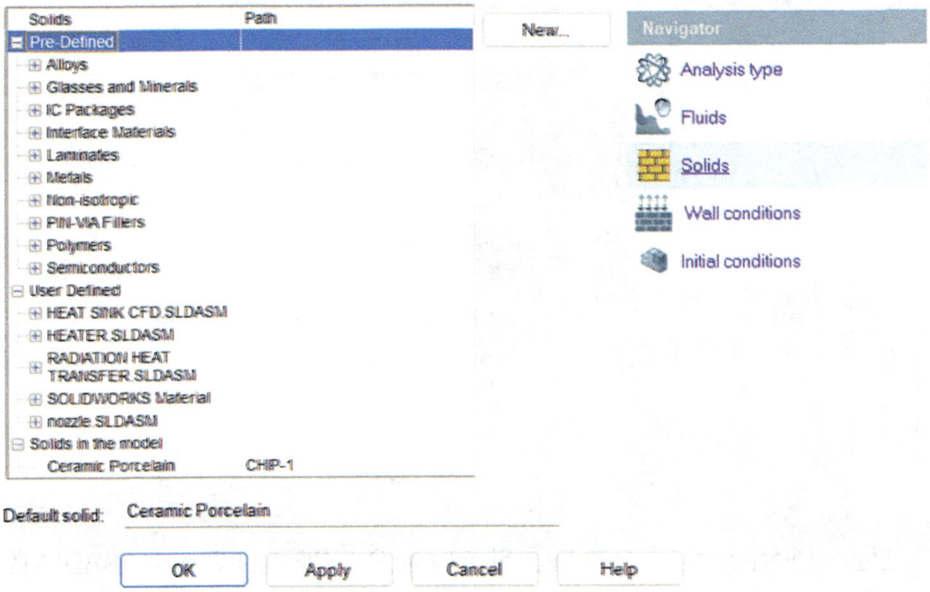

Figure 16-3: Default solid: Ceramic Porcelain.

Material properties are taken from CHIP part.

Define air flow velocity, temperature, and pressure in Initial and ambient conditions window as shown in Figure 16-4.

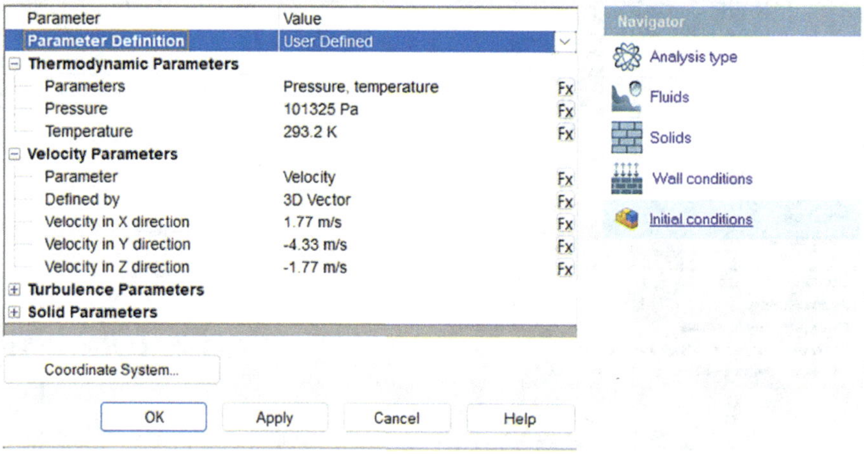

Figure 16-4: Air flow direction, temperature and pressure are all defined in Initial and ambient conditions window.

Once done with **General Settings**, right click **Solid Materials** folder and assign **Aluminum** from Flow Simulation Data Base to RADIATOR part (Figure 16-5).

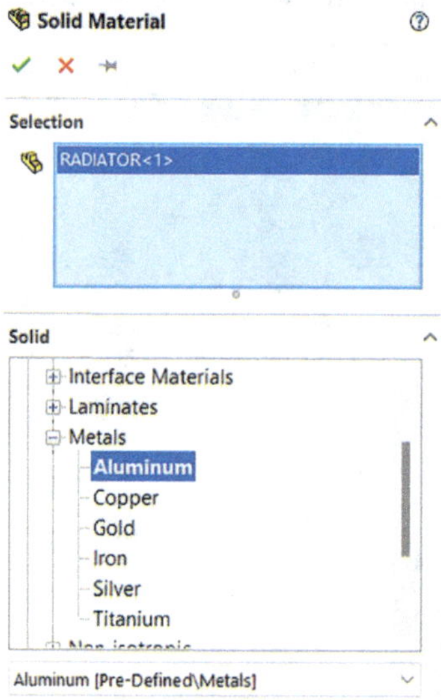

Figure 16-5: Aluminum from Flow Simulation Data Base is assigned to RADIATOR.

This assignment overwrites the previously defined Default Solid.

Assign Blackwall Radiative properties to the outer faces of CHIP (Figure 16-6).

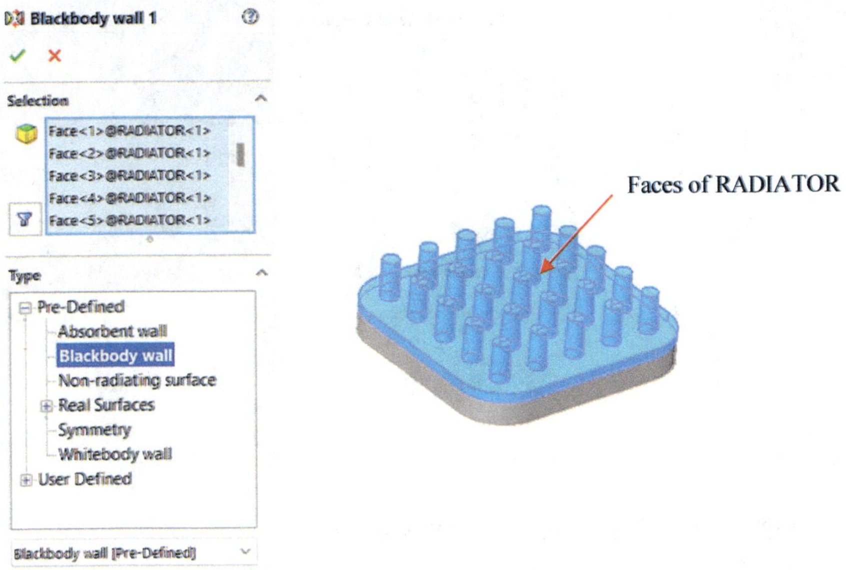

Figure 16-6: Blackwall radiative properties are assigned to the outer faces of RADIATOR.

Assume that faces of CHIP do not participate in heat transfer by radiation.

Exclude CONTROL VOLUME from analysis (Figure 16-7).

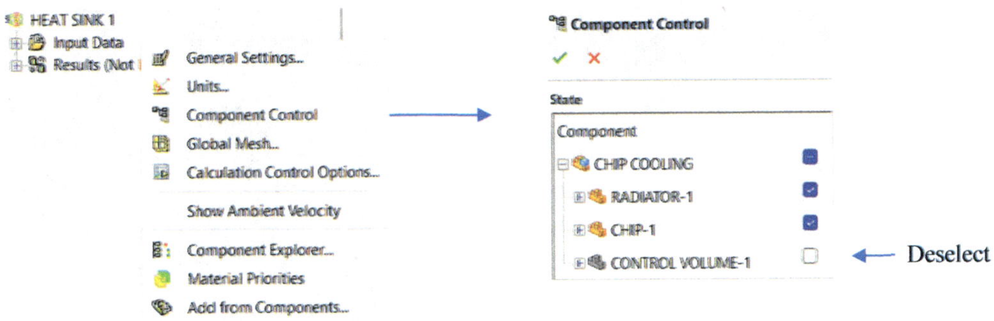

Figure 16-7: CONTROL VOLUME is excluded from the analysis, but it will be used to define Local Mesh refinement.

Deselect CONTROL VOLUME.

Assign Heat Generation Rate 20W to CHIP (Figure 16-8).

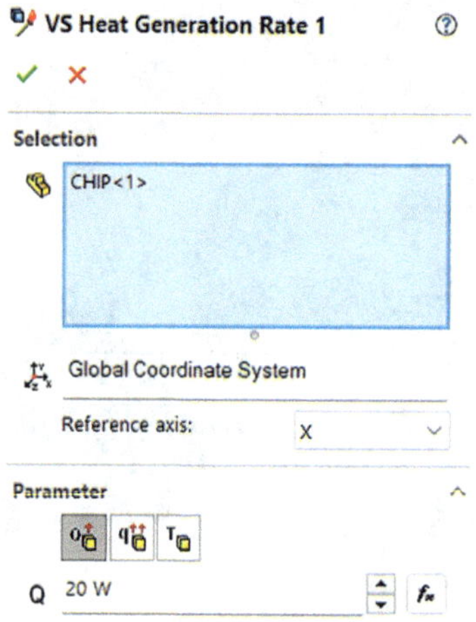

Figure 16-8: Definition of Heat Generation rate.

Heat power 20W is assigned to the volume of CHIP part.

Define the **Layer of Thermal Resistance** as shown in Figure 16-9. Make sure that in the pair of contacting faces only one face is selected, or else the contact resistance will be applied twice. Enter the layer thickness as 0.0005m.

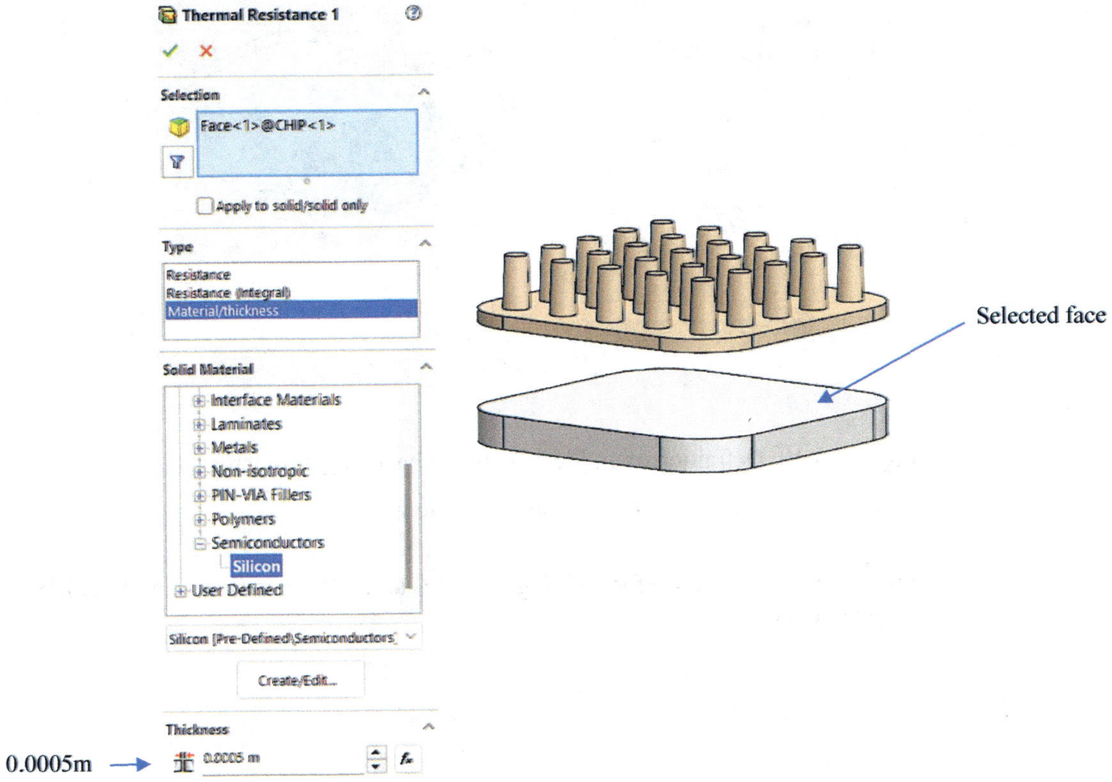

Figure 16-9: Definition of a Layer of Thermal Resistance.

Use Exploded View to select one of the two contacting faces.

To insulate the bottom face of CHIP, define it as **Ideal Wall**. This boundary condition sets the selected face as adiabatic (Figure 16-10).

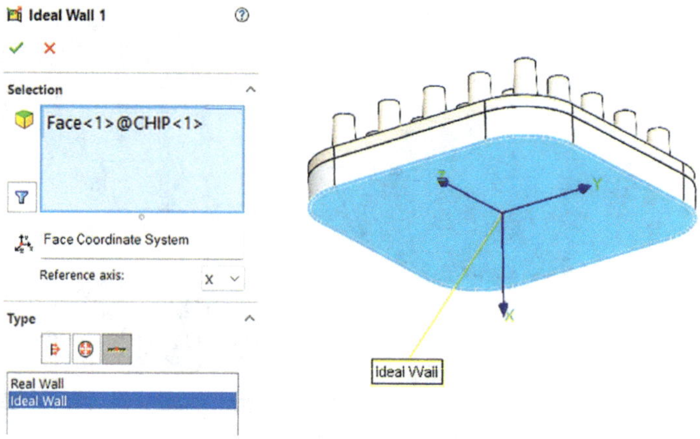

Figure 16-10: Definition of an Ideal Wall. No heat will flow across this face.

CONTROL VOLUME part is hidden in this view.

Finally, in the last step before solving, define **Global Mesh Settings** and **Local Mesh** (Figure 16-11).

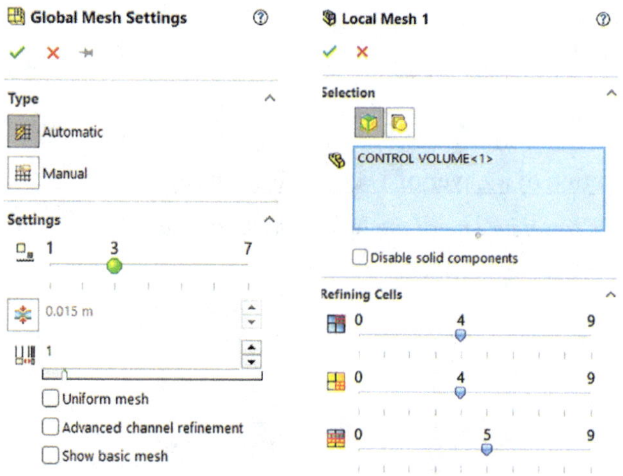

Figure 16-11: Global Mesh Settings and Local Mesh.

Local Mesh refinement is specified for all cell categories and applies to the volume occupied by CONTROL VOLUME.

We'll not define any **Goals** in this exercise.

The project is ready for solution. If you experience long solution time you may reduce the size of Computational Domain or use less refined Global Mesh and Local Mesh. However, it is important to note, that producing quality results requires runs with different size of Computational Domain and different mesh refinement to study the effect of different choices of discretization on the results.

Create Surface Plot of surface temperature of RADIATOR. Select all faces of RADIATOR except the one touching CHIP (Figure 16-12).

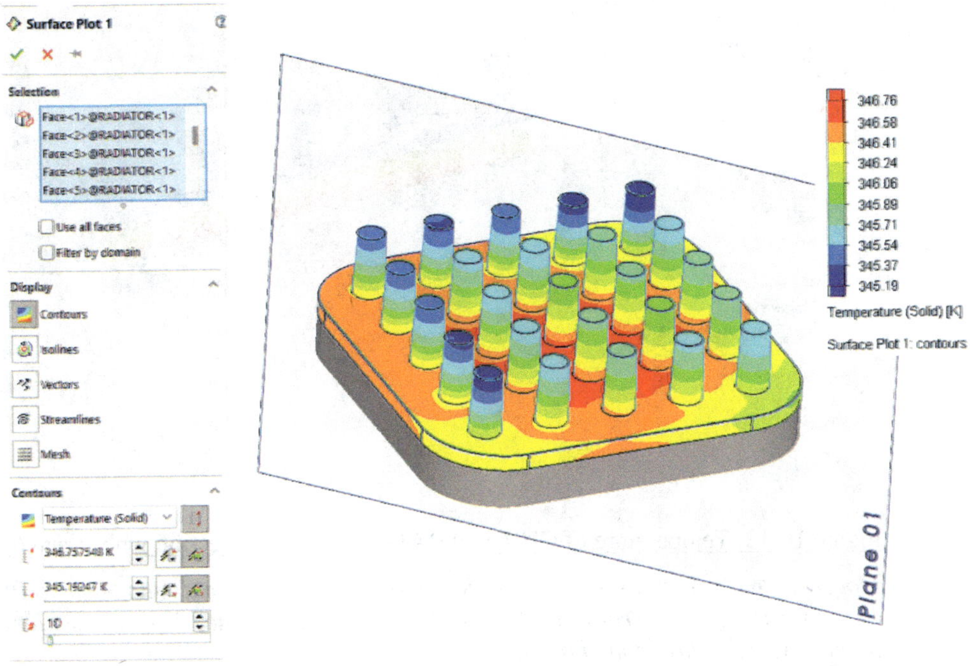

Figure 16-12: Surface temperature of RADIATOR.

Auto Scale to Plot minimum and Plot Maximum.

Temperature gradient seen in Figure 16-12 demonstrates the cooling effect of the air flowing along the reference plane *Plane 01*.

Create Cut Plot showing temperature in CHIP and in RADIATOR. To see this plot, the model geometry must be hidden or transparent (Figure 16-13).

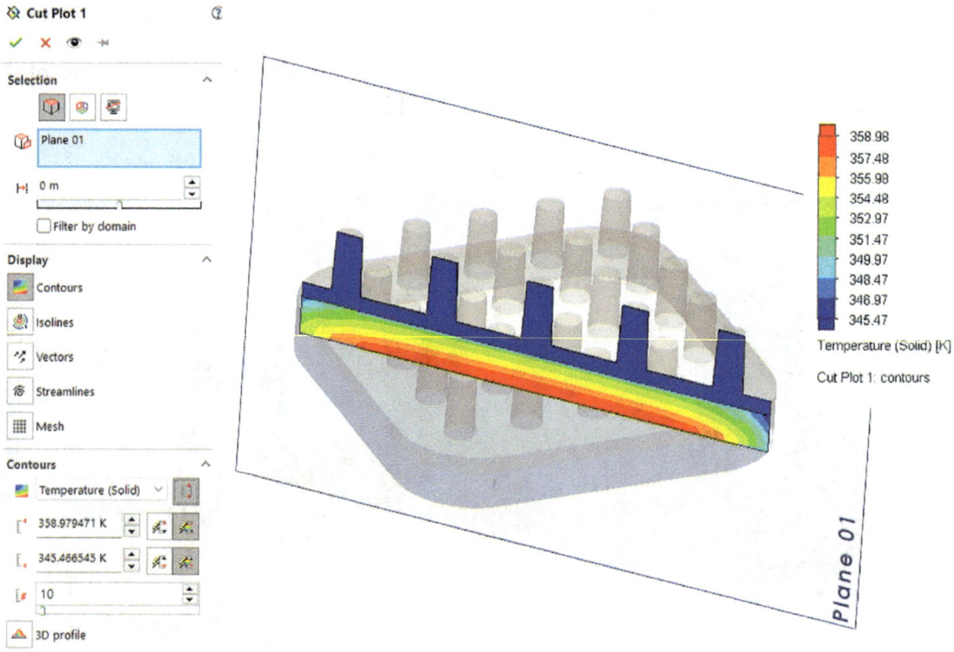

Figure 16-13: Temperature of CHIP and RADIATOR along section with *Plane 01.*

Model Geometry is transparent. Auto Scale to Plot minimum and Auto Scale to Plot Maximum to define the range of displayed temperatures. Plane 01 reference plane is aligned with the direction of air flow.

- Hot spot at the bottom of CHIP is caused by the insulation provided by the **Ideal Wall** boundary condition.

Create **Cut Plot** showing velocity of air flowing around the model (Figure 16-14).

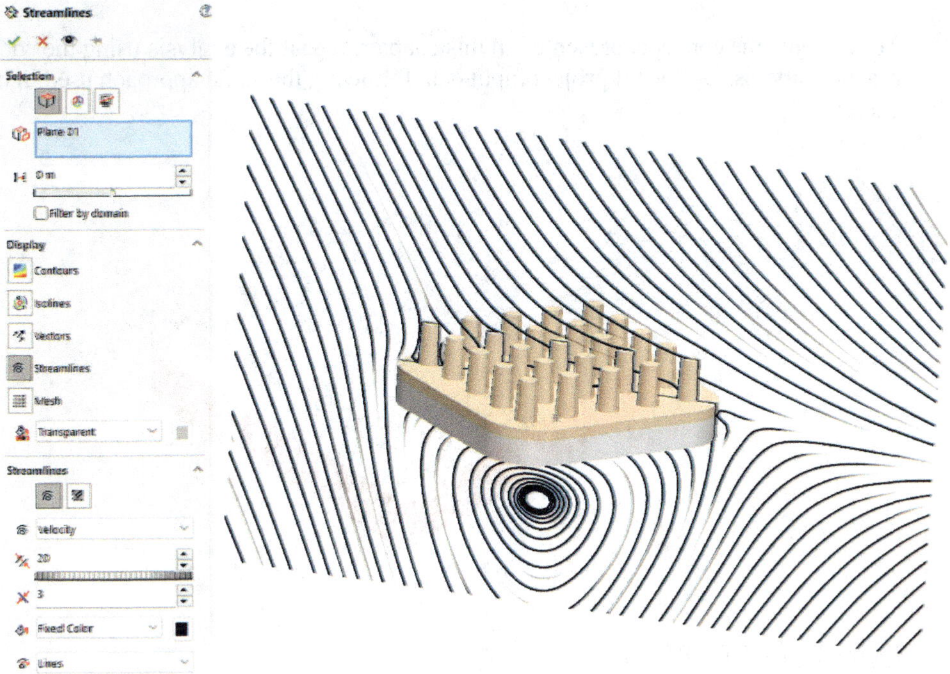

Figure 16-14: Streamlines of air along *Plane 01.*

Streamlines offer an easy way of flow visualization.

Repeat this exercise with different mesh setting to study the effect of mesh refinement on results. Note, that due to sharp re-entrant edges, the model is not suitable for analysis of heat flux.

Repeat the exercise with **Radiation** enabled in General Settings.

Additional Practice Models

To reinforce the concepts presented in this chapter, repeat the analysis using the additional practice models. Define all project input data following the same approach used in the main exercise.

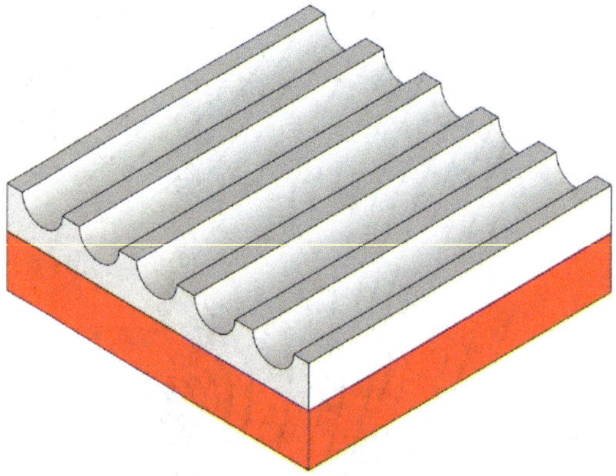

Figure 16-15: HEAT SINK 01 assembly.

Control Volume is not a part of this assembly.

Figure 16-16: DOME assembly.

Dome part is shown in a transparent view. Control Volume is not a part of this assembly.

Models in this chapter

Model	**Status**
MICROCHIP.sldasm	*Solved with Flow Simulation* *HEAT SINK*
HEAT SINK 01.sldasm	Additional practice model
DOME.sldasm	Additional practice model

Notes:

17: Radiative heat transfer

- Conjugate heat transfer
- Radiative heat transfer
- Emissivity
- Flow Simulation material library
- Simulation material library
- Thermal stresses

Project description

A light bulb producing 200W of heat sits inside a glass sleeve. The glass sleeve is heated by radiation and convection. Heat produces a buoyancy flow of air. We are looking for thermal stresses in the sleeve. LIGHT FIXTURE assembly shown in Figure 17-1.

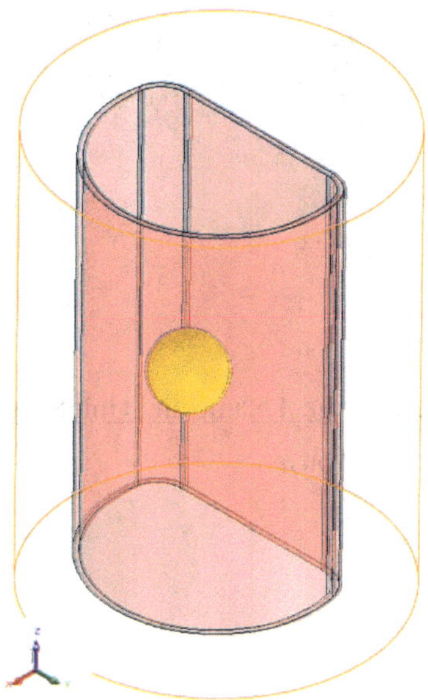

Figure 17-1: The Bulb is surrounded by a glass Sleeve. Bulb and Sleeve are encased in a cylindrical Control Volume. Gravity acts in the negative Z direction.

Sleeve is shown in a transparent view, Control Volume is shown in a wireframe view.

Procedure

Use the Flow Simulation Wizard to set up project *SLEEVE 1* (Figures 17-2 through 17-7).

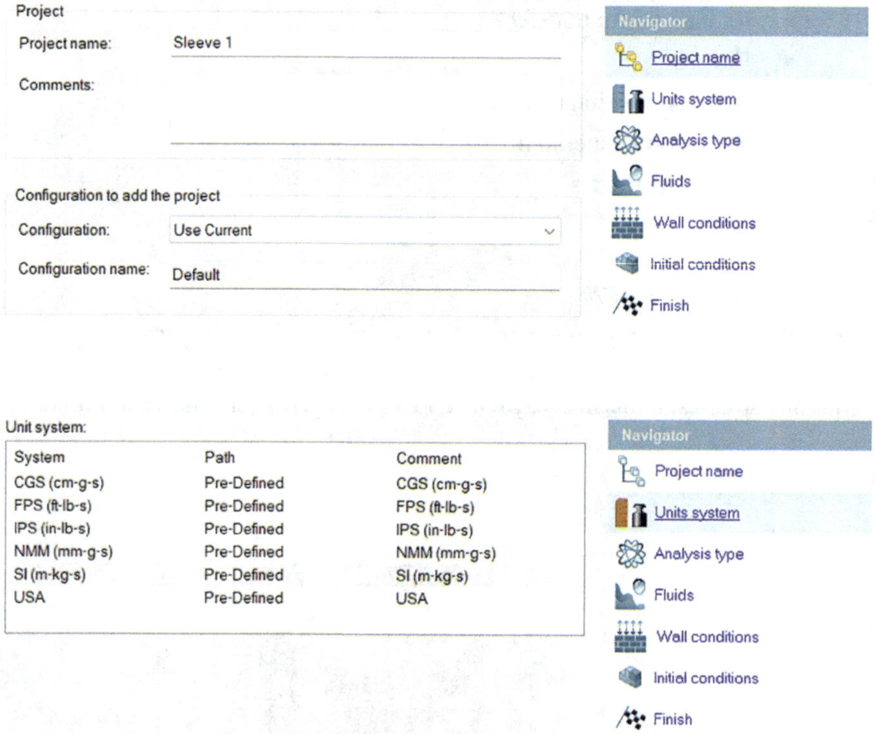

Figure 17-2: Step 1 and 2: Project Name and Unit System.

Navigation buttons are not shown.

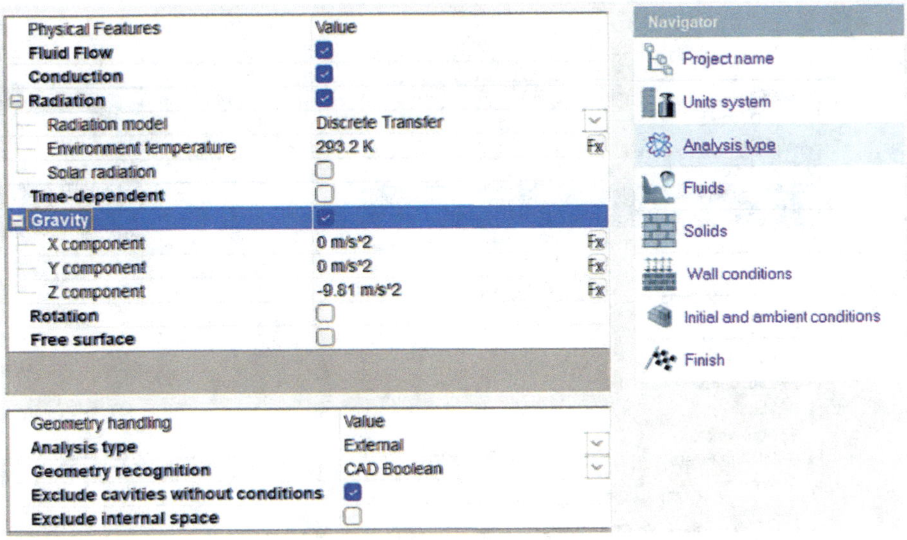

Figure 17-3: Step 3: Analysis Type.

Select: Fluid Flow, Conduction, Radiation, Gravity, Environment temp. 293.2K, analysis type: External.

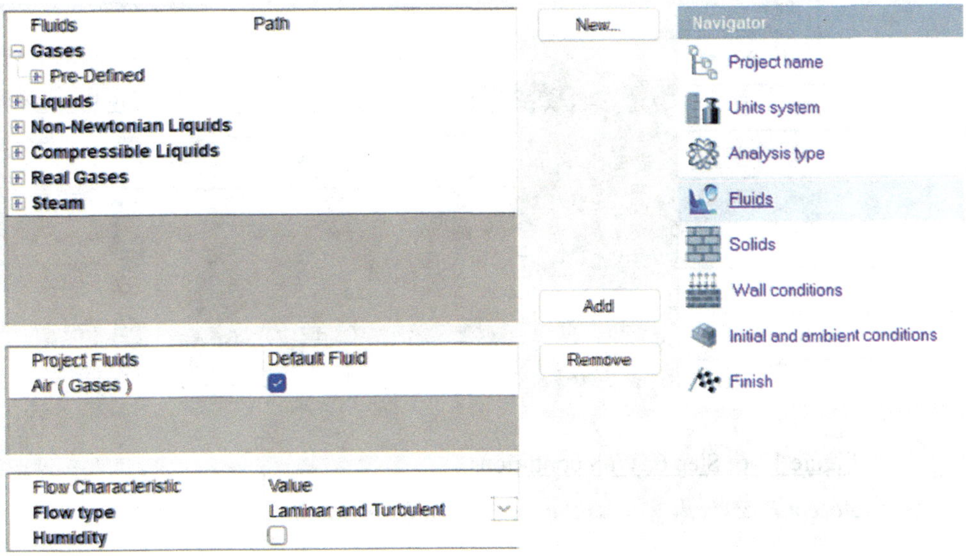

Figure 17-4: Step 4: Default fluid: Air.

Air is the default fluid.

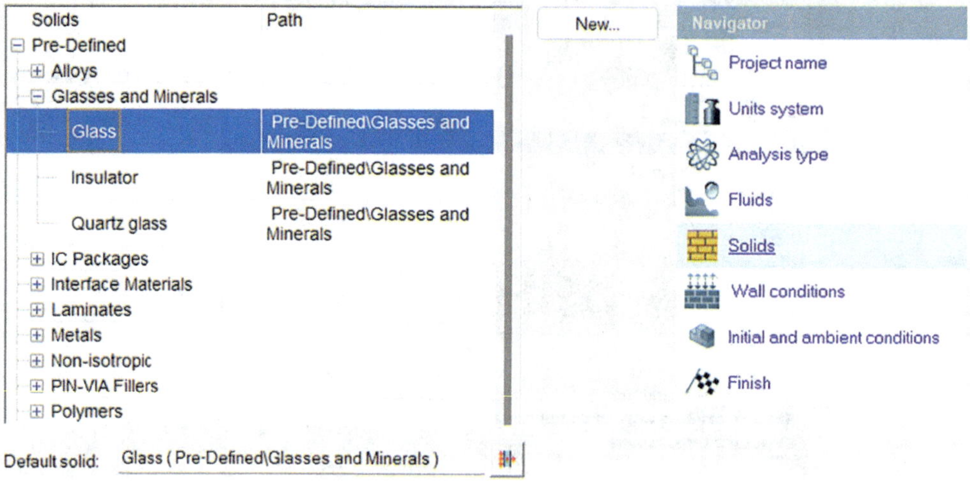

Figure 17-5: Step 5: Default solid: Glass.

Select Glass from Flow Simulation material library.

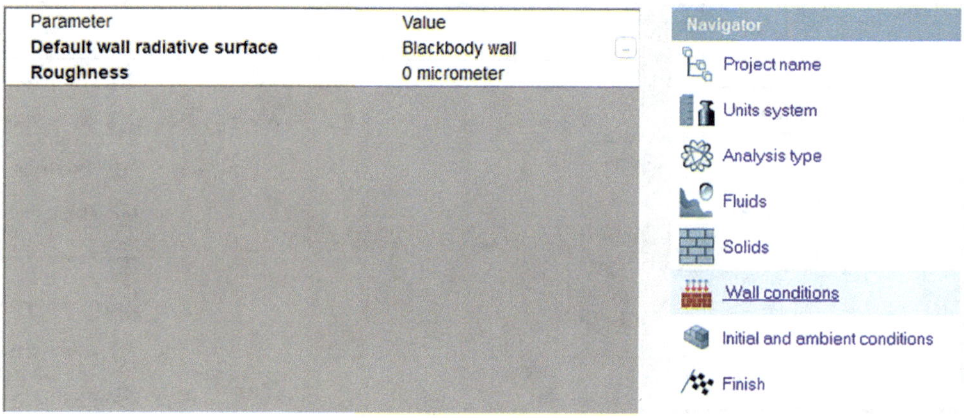

Figure 17-6: Step 6: Wall conditions.

Accept Blackbody wall as the default Wall condition.

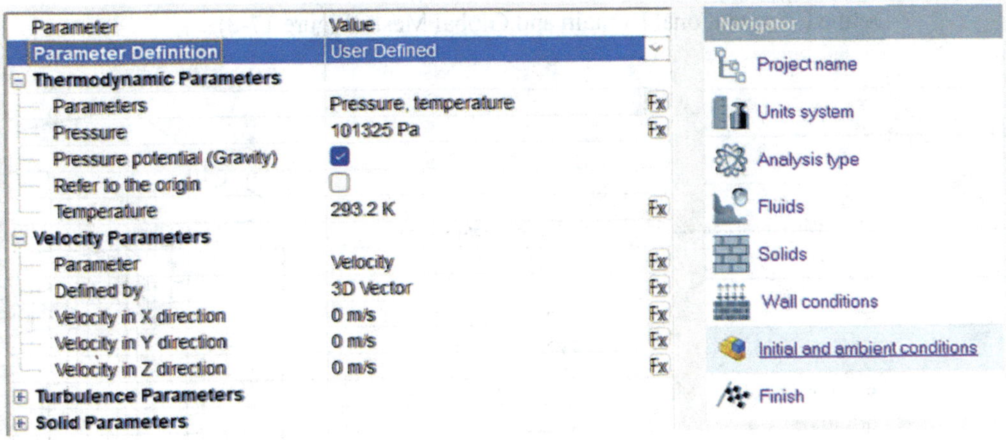

Figure 17-7: Step 7: Initial and ambient conditions.

This is a buoyancy induced flow; no air velocity is defined.

Define Computational Domain and Global Mesh (Figure 17-8).

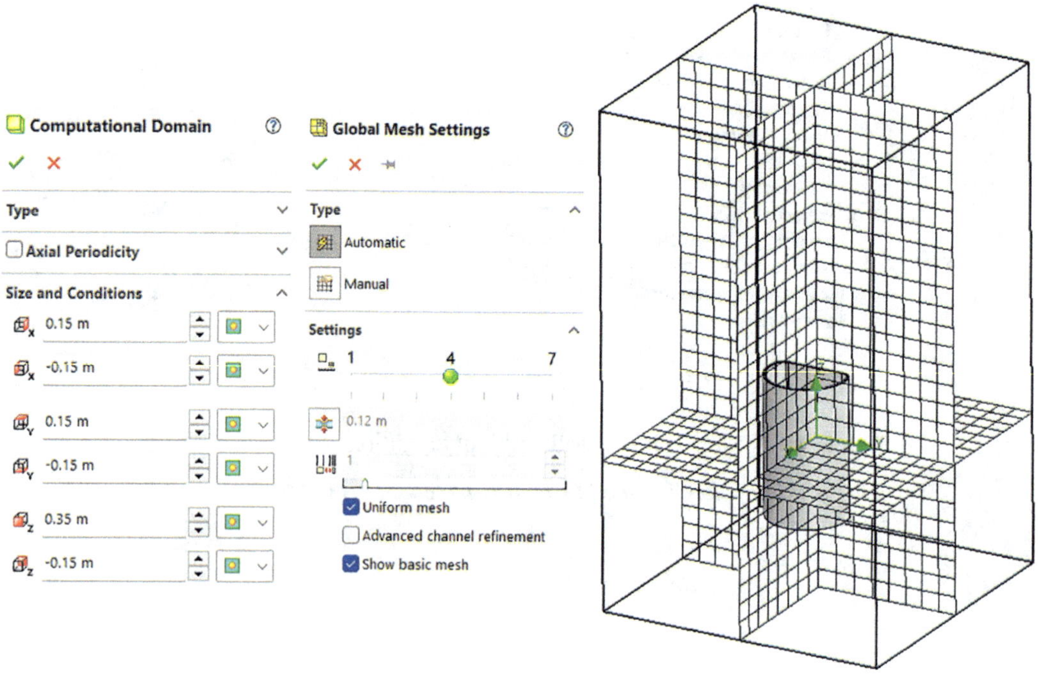

Figure 17-8: Solution Domain and Global Mesh settings.

Computational Domain is shown in wireframe view, Global Mesh is shown in three sections.

Define Local Mesh using Control Volume (Figure 17-9).

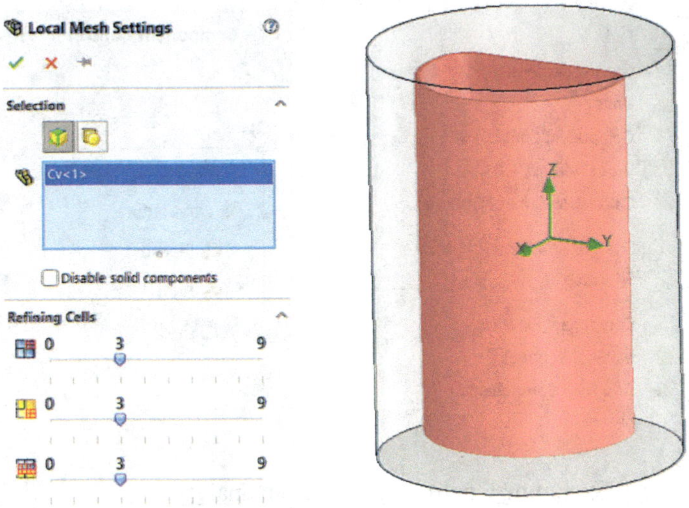

Figure 17-9: Local Mesh Settings.

The refinement in the Control Volume is measured relatively to Global Mesh settings.

The size of the Computational Domain and the settings of Global Mesh and Local Mesh used in this exercise are arbitrary. Repeat this exercise with different settings to examine the effect of discretization choices on the results.

Exclude Control Volume *Cv* from analysis (Figure 17-10).

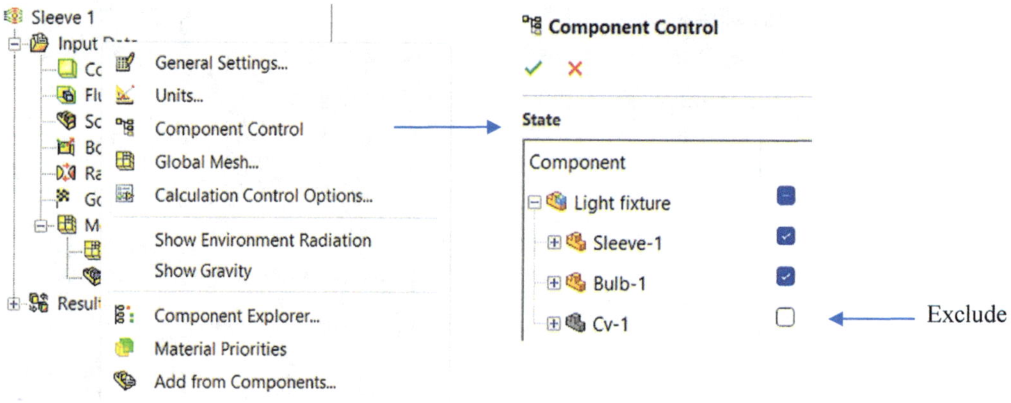

Figure 17-10: Excluding Control Volume from analysis.

The Control volume Cv is used only in definition of Local Mesh. It does not participate in analysis.

Review the mesh before running solution. Run **Mesh only** and create a section view of the mesh (Figure 17-11).

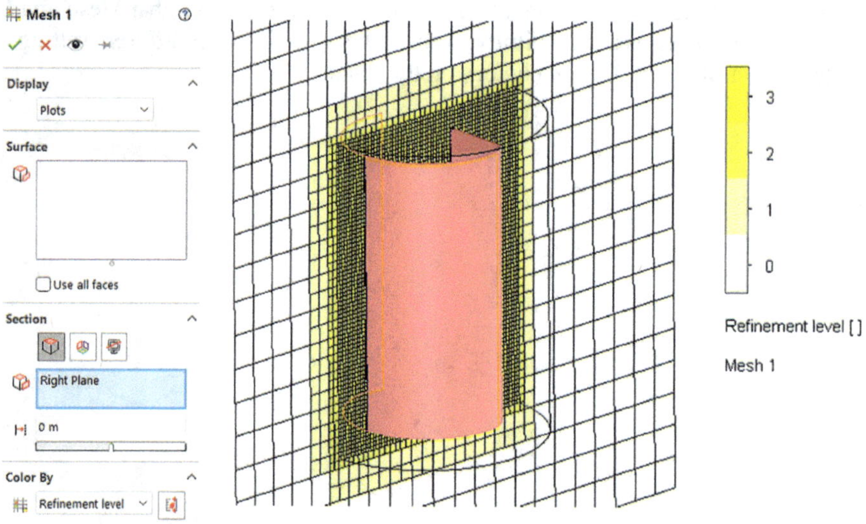

Figure 17-11: Section view of the finite volume mesh. Note three levels of the Local Mesh refinement relative to the Global Mesh.

Custom colors are used to enhance the readability of this illustration.

Assign radiative properties of **Glass, Pyrex** to all faces of Sleeve (Figure 17-12). That overwrites the default emissivity defined in Figure 17-6.

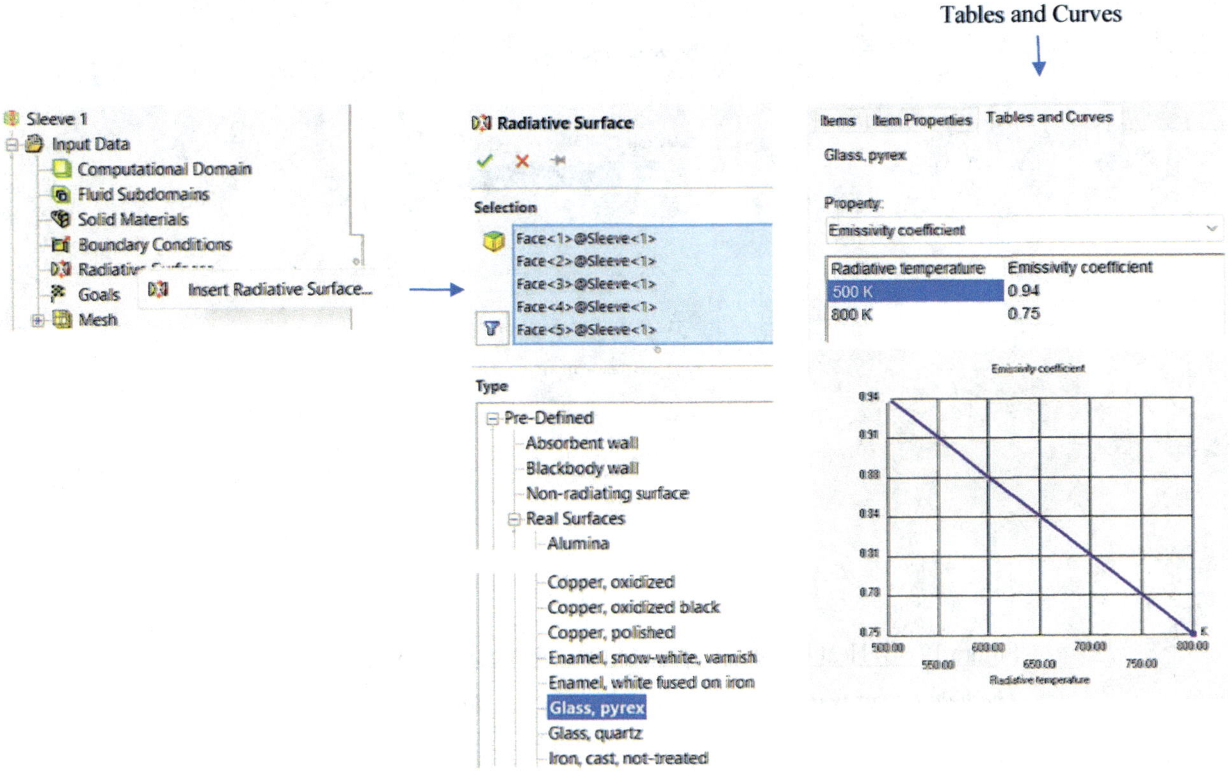

<u>Figure 17-12: Radiative properties of Glass, Pyrex assigned to all faces of Sleeve.</u>

Emissivity as function of temperature as defined in Tables and Curves tab.

The face of Bulb has the default emissivity of a Blackbody wall (Figure 17-6).

Define heat power 100W to the volume of the Bulb (Figure 17-13).

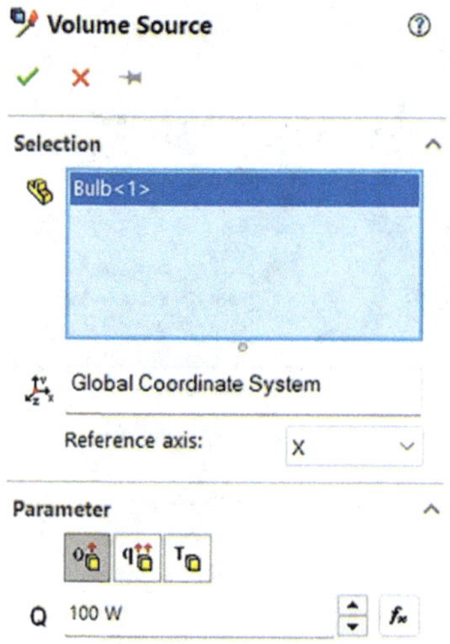

Figure 17-13: Heat Power assigned to the volume of the Bulb.

The heat power is generated in the volume of the Bulb.

In this exercise the Bulb is modeled in a simplified way, as a solid block of glass. It is a source of heat. Thermal analysis and thermal stress analysis will be limited to Sleeve.

Run the analysis and construct a plot of temperature on faces of Sleeve (Figure 17-14).

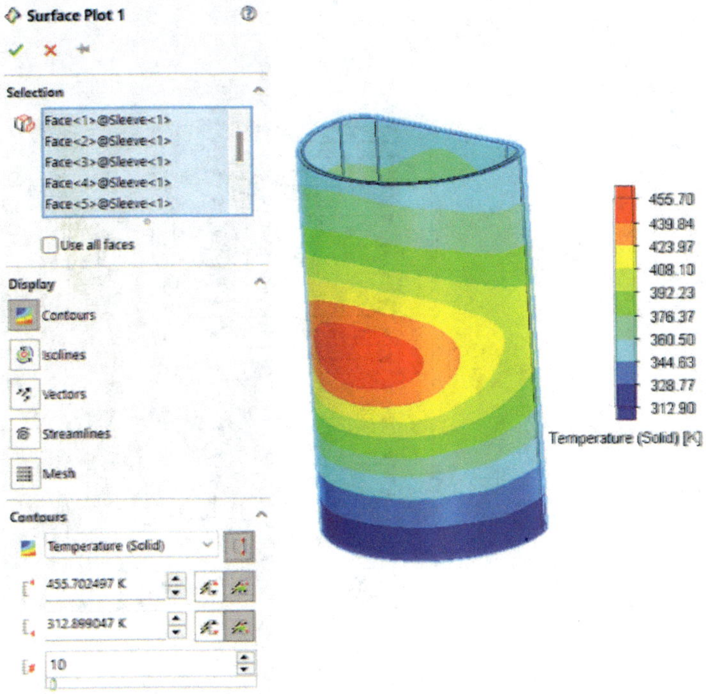

Figure 17-14: Plot of temperature on faces of Sleeve.

Values are adjusted to plot maximum and minimum.

Construct a section plot of air velocity using *PLANE1* (Figure 17-15).

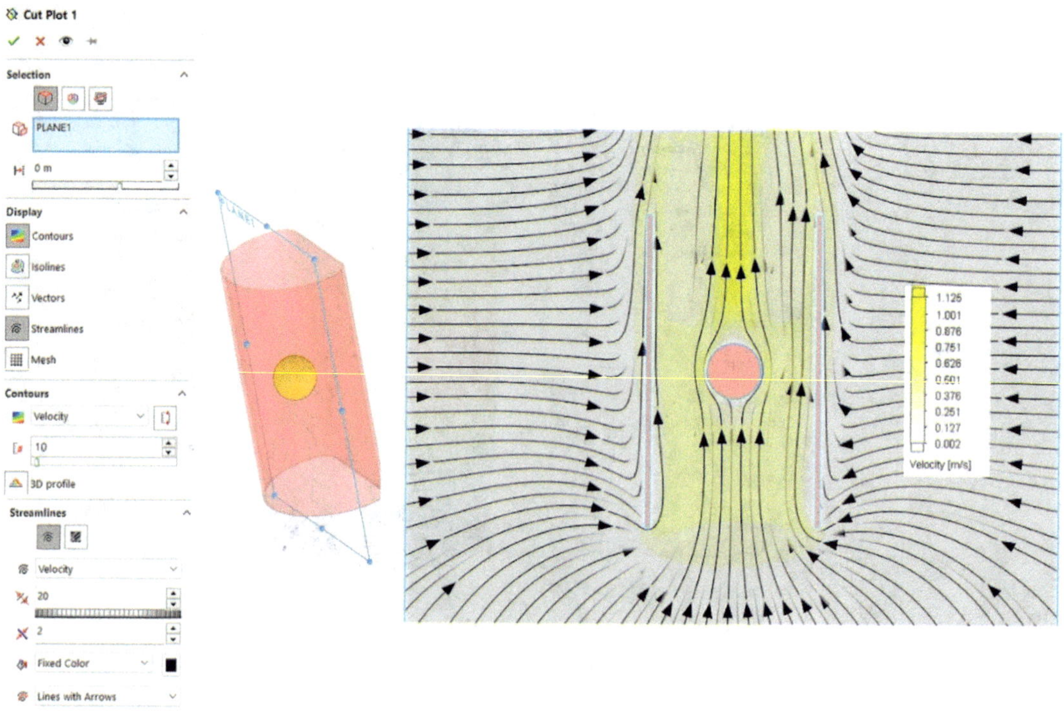

Figure 17-15: Air flow around Sleeve and Bulb.

Custom colors are used to enhance the readability of this illustration.

This completes the analysis with Flow Simulation. To analyze thermal stresses the results must be exported to Simulation (Figure 17-16).

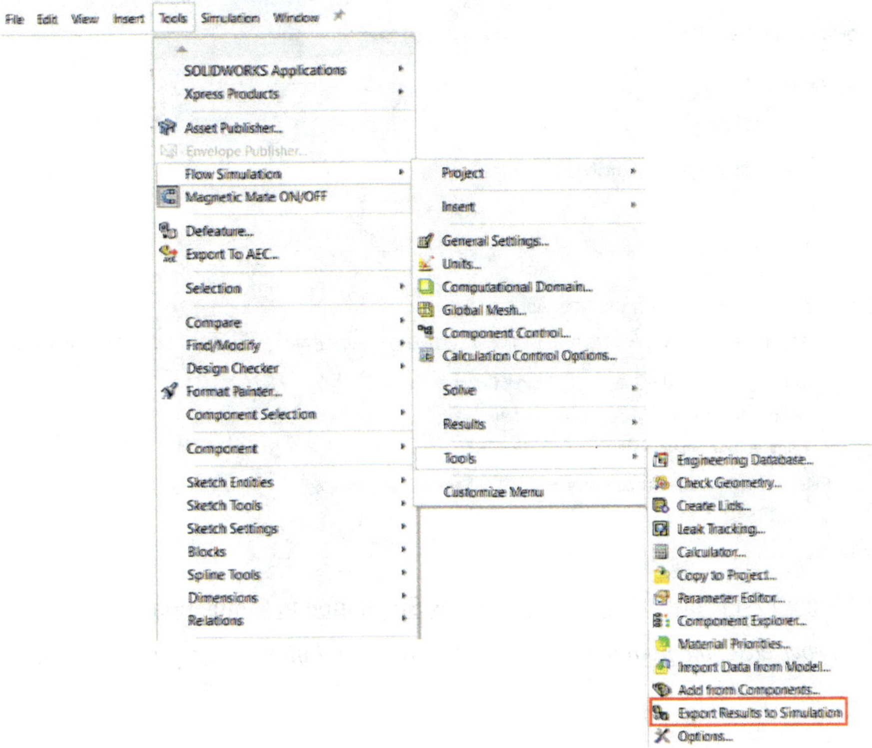

Figure 17-16: Exporting Temperature results to Simulation.

Flow Simulation results are exported to Simulation for analysis of thermal stress.

In Simulation, open Static **Study 1** and connect it to Flow Simulation results (Figure 17-17).

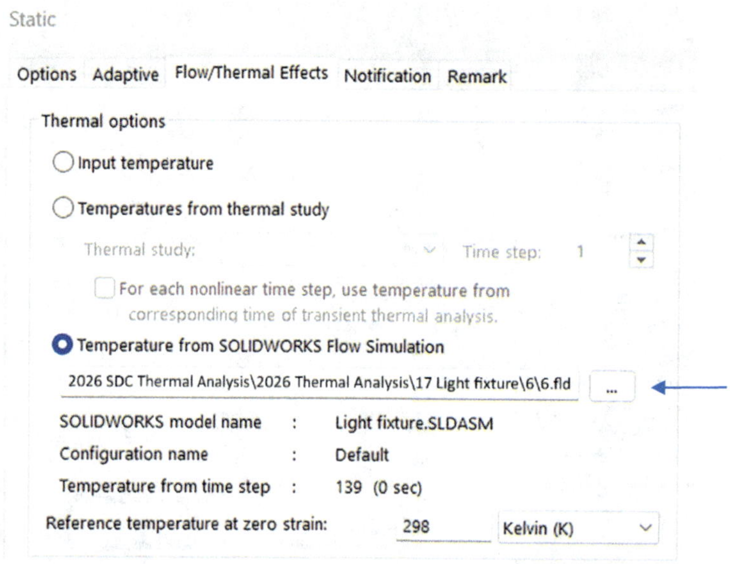

Path to Flow Simulation results

Figure 17-17: Importing results of Flow Simulation to Simulation.

In your case, the path and the name of Flow Simulation results file will be different.

Exclude *Bulb* and *Cv* parts from analysis (Figure 17-18).

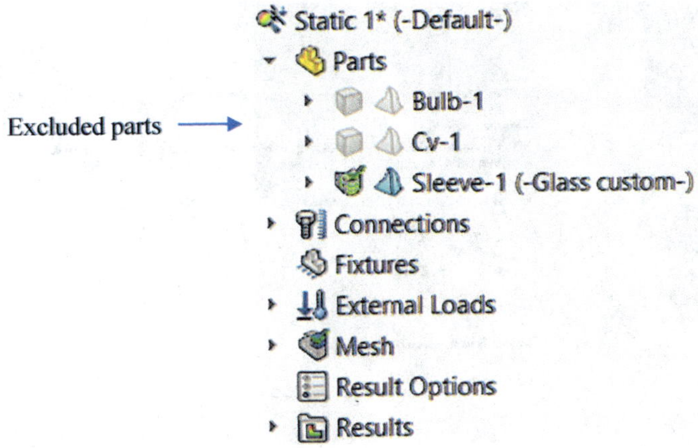

Figure 17-18: Bulb and Cv (Control Volume) parts are excluded from analysis.

The only active part is Sleeve.

Create custom material by modifying **Glass** material from Simulation library and assign it to Sleeve (Figure 17-19).

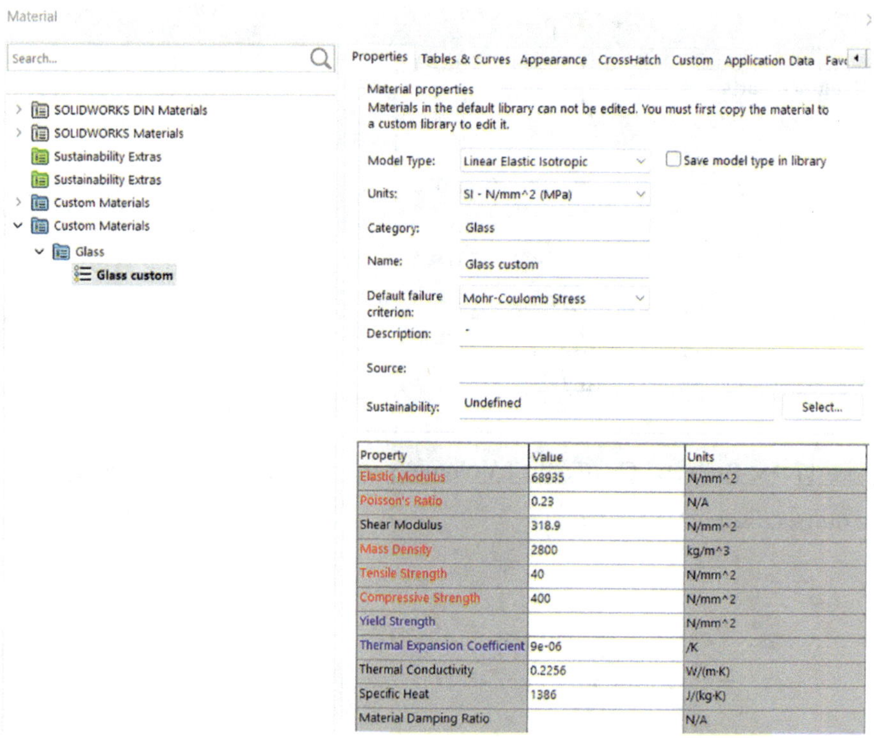

Figure 17-19: Custom material is created by adding Tensile Strength and Compressive Strength to material properties of Glass.

The added properties are needed to calculate the factor of safety based on Mohr-Coulomb criterion.

In properties of study **Static 1** select the option **Use Soft springs to stabilize model**. This will eliminate Rigid Body Motions in the model that has no supports. Mesh the model with Blended curvature base mesh using element size 2mm and solve the study.

Construct plot of the Maximum Principal Stress P1 (Figure 17-20).

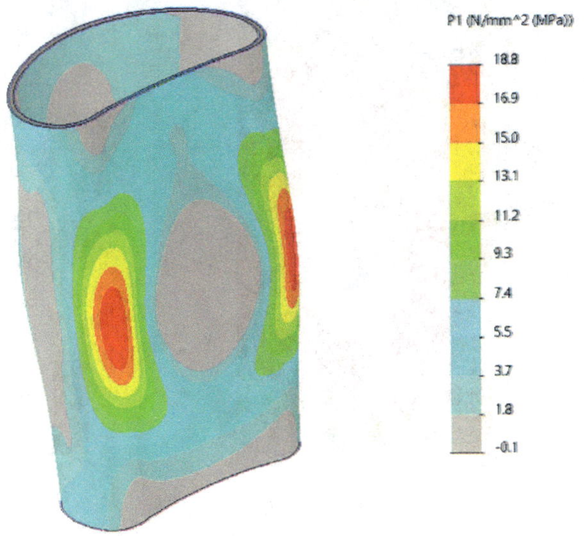

Figure 17-20: Maximum Principal Stress P1 stress in Sleeve.

Custom colors are used.

Complete the exercise by reviewing the Factor of Safety (FOS) based on Mohr-Coulomb criterion (Figure 17-21).

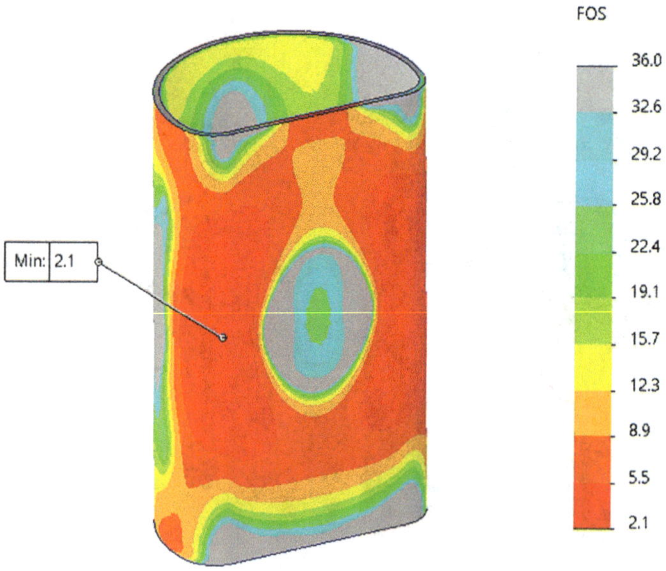

Figure 17-21: Plot of the Factor of Safety based on Mohr-Coulomb criterion.

The lowest FOS is 2.1. The range of values on the color scale has been limited to 36. Custom colors are used.

Based on the results shown in Figure 17-21, we may conclude that thermal stresses will not cause the failure of Sleeve.

Additional Practice Models

To reinforce the concepts presented in this chapter, repeat the analysis using the additional practice models. Define all project input data following the same approach used in the main exercise.

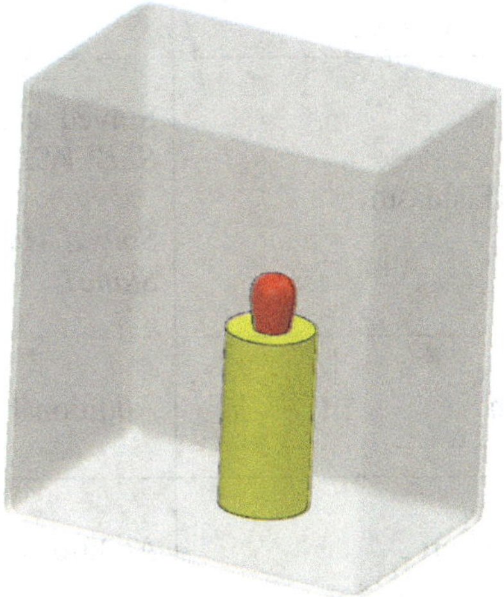

Figure 17-22: CANDLE assembly model.

CANDLE assembly consists of Flame, Candle and Glass Box. Glass Box is shown in a transparent view. Control volume is not modeled in this assembly.

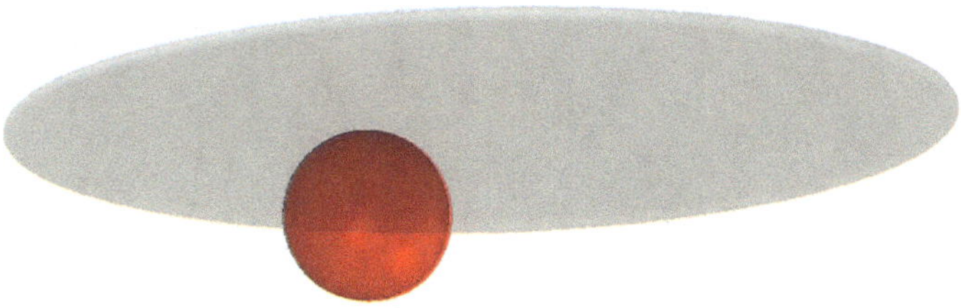

Figure 17-23: GLASS PLATE part model.

Plate and Ball are modeled as a multi-body part. The Plate is shown in a transparent view. Control volume is not modeled.

Models in this chapter

Model	**Status**
LIGHT FIXTURE.sldasm	Solved with Flow Simulation *SLEEVE1* *Solved with Simulation* *Static1*
CANDLE.sldasm	Additional practice model
GLASS PLATE.sldprt	Additional practice model

18: Pellets

- External flow
- Forced convection
- Heat transfer by convection
- Heat transfer by radiation

Project description

Three porcelain pellets generate a total of 40W heat. The pellets are encased in an aluminum block. The block is cooled by air at 293.2 K supplied through a nozzle at a pressure of 1kPa above ambient. The air jet discharges to ambient at 0 gauge pressure. We will analyze the effect of cooling by the air blown from the nozzle. The PELLETS assembly is shown in Figure 18-1.

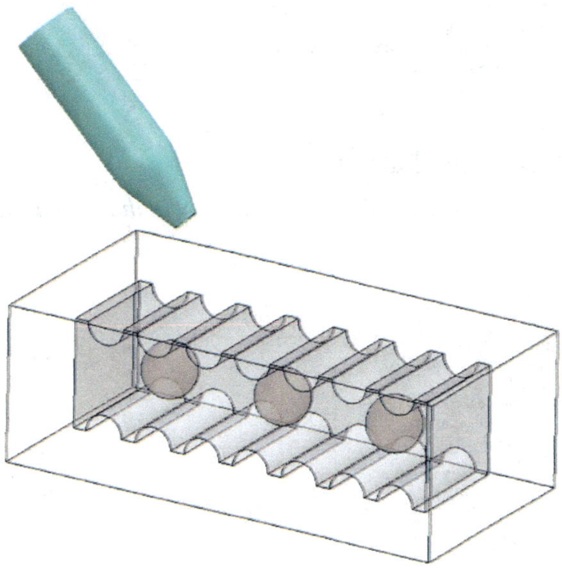

Figure 18-1: PELLETS assembly: three Porcelain Balls, Aluminum Block, Nozzle and Control Volume.

The Block is shown in a transparent view; the Control Volume is shown in a wireframe view.

Procedure

Open PELLETS assembly. Parts Block and Nozzle have 1060 Alloy material assigned. Porcelain Balls have Porcelain material assigned. In Flow Simulation, create a new project *01 nozzle*.

Right-click Input Data and open General Settings. In General Settings define Analysis Type, Fluids, Solids, Wall conditions and Initial conditions. You may use Wizard to guide you through steps shown in Figure 18-2, …18-6.

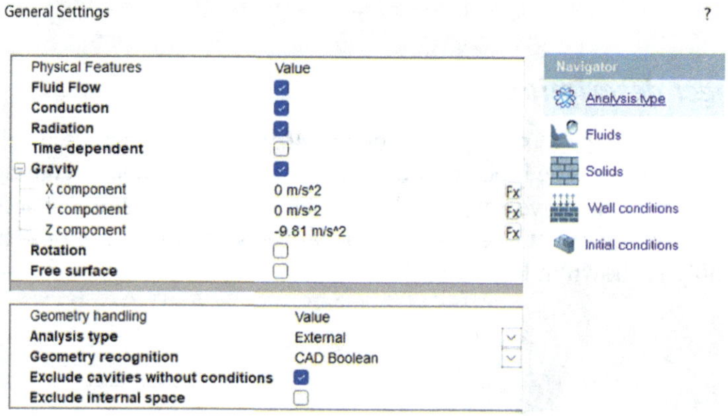

Figure 18-2: Analysis type: External.

Select Fluid Flow, Conduction, Radiation, Gravity in the default (negative Z) direction.

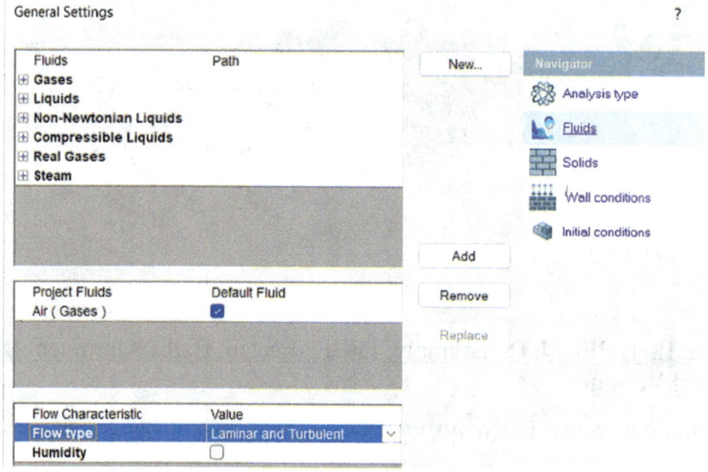

Figure 18-3: Fluids: Air.

Select Air as the fluid.

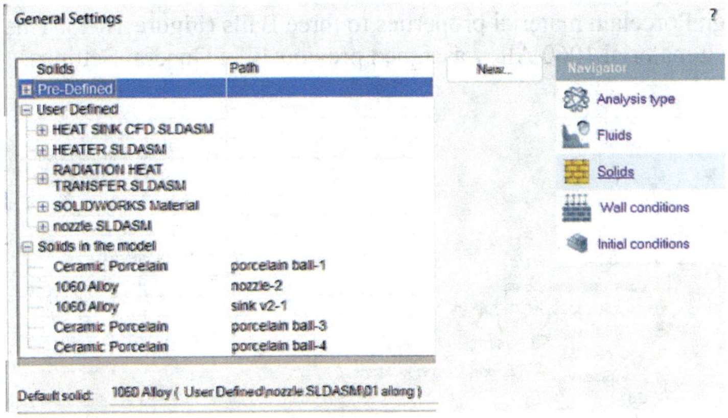

Figure 18-4: Solids: 1060 Alloy.

Select 1060 Alloy from Solids in the model.

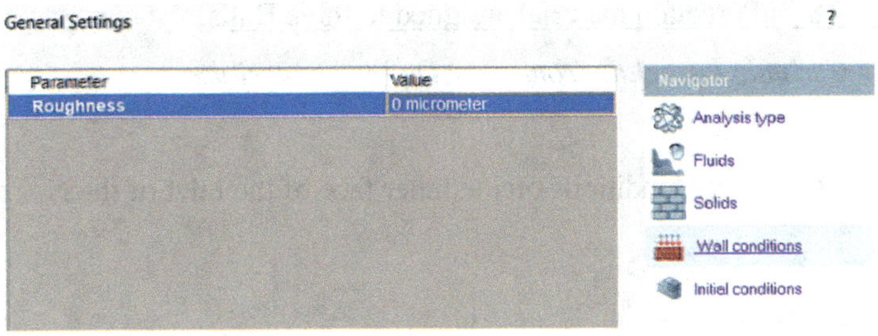

Figure 18-5: Wall conditions.

Accept defaults, no need to change anything here.

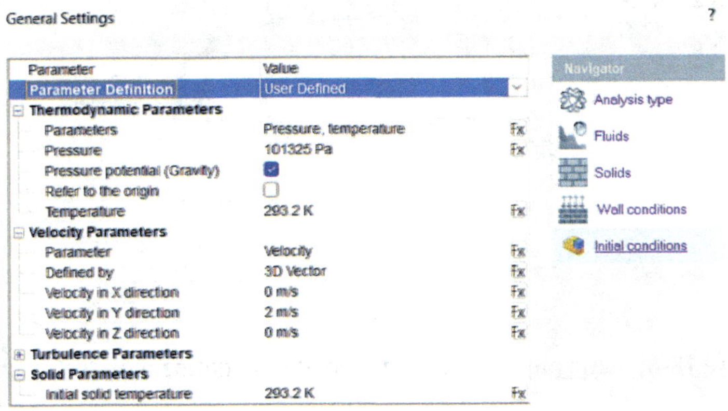

Figure 18-6: Initial conditions.

Define air flow 2m/s in Y direction, accept defaults for everything else.

Assign Porcelain material properties to three Balls (Figure 18-7). This will overwrite default material 1060 Alloy assigned previously in General Settings.

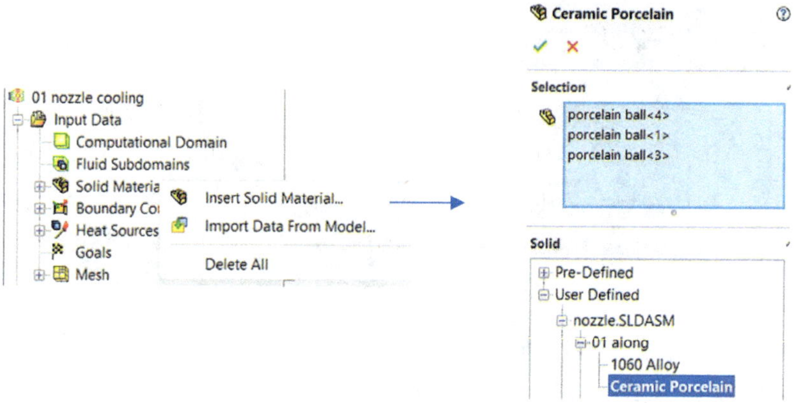

Figure 18-7: Porcelain material assigned to three Balls.

Select Ceramic Porcelain from User Defined materials.

Define Boundary Conditions on the inner face of the inlet of the Nozzle (Figure 18-8).

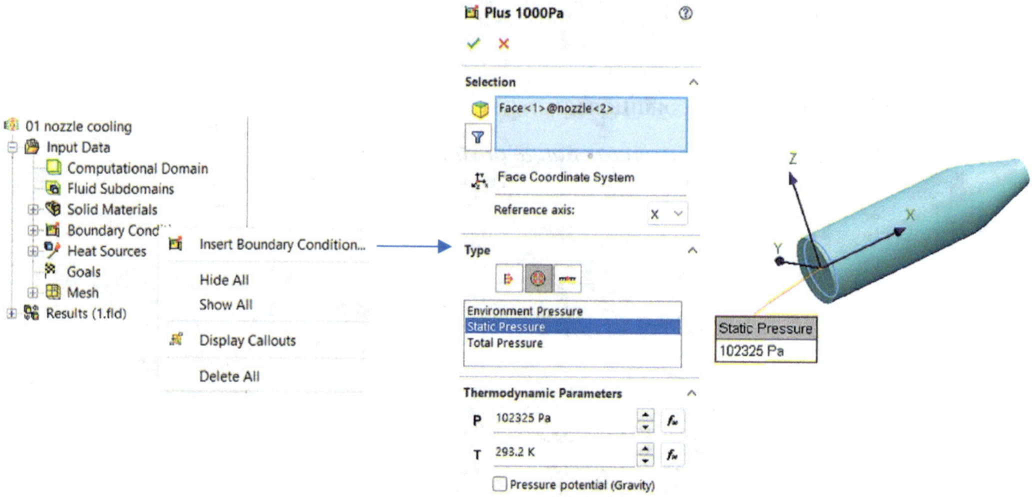

Figure 18-8: Static pressure boundary condition, define it on the inner face of the Nozzle.

Pressure 102325Pa is 1000Pa about the environment pressure 101325MPa. The window has been renamed as Plus 1000Pa. Use Click-inside to rename it.

Define heat sources as shown in Figure 18-9.

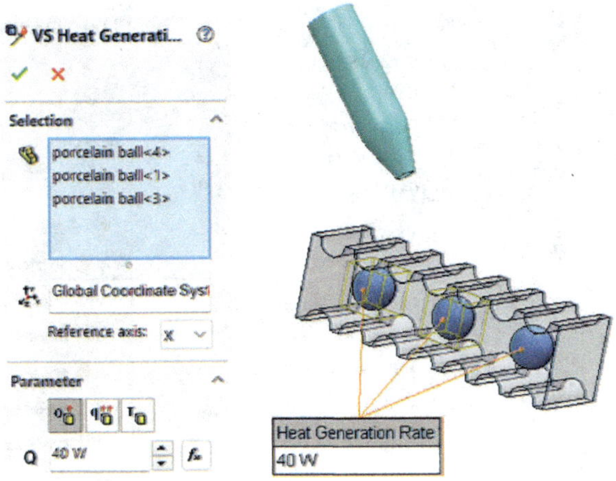

Figure 18-9: Heat Source assigned to three Porcelain Ball.

The total of 40W heat is generated in the volume of three Balls. This is 13.3W per Ball.

Assign Blackwall radiative properties to the outer faces of Block (Figure 18-10).

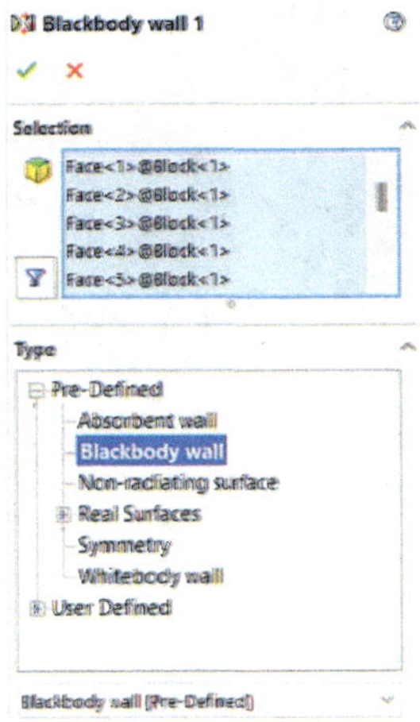

Figure 18-10: Blackbody wall properties are assigned to all outer faces of Block.

Blackbody wall properties are selected from the pre-defined list.

Control Volume is here to apply mesh controls; deselect it from analysis (Figure 18-11).

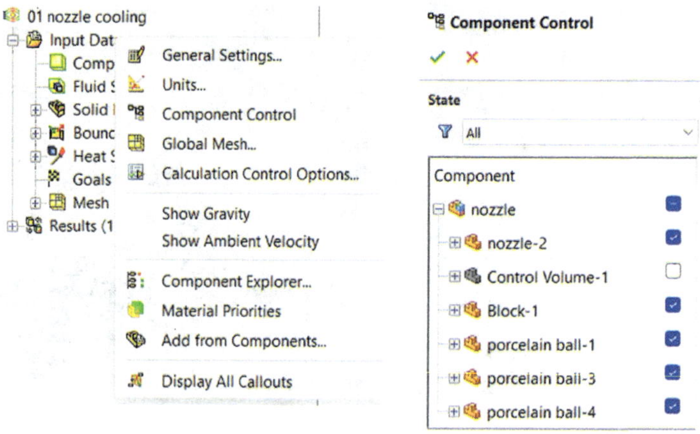

Figure 18-11: Control Volume is deselected from analysis.

Review Component Control window to see the active and removed components.

Follow Figure 18-12 to define the size of the Computational Domain.

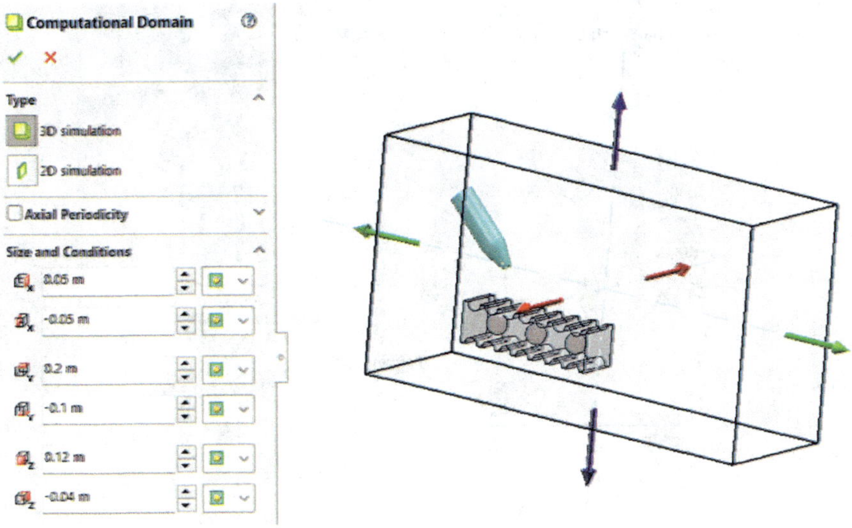

Figure 18-12: The size of Computational Domain.

Different settings may be used to investigate the influence of the size of Computational-Domaine on the results of analysis.

Use Global Mesh and Local Mesh settings shown in Figure 18-13.

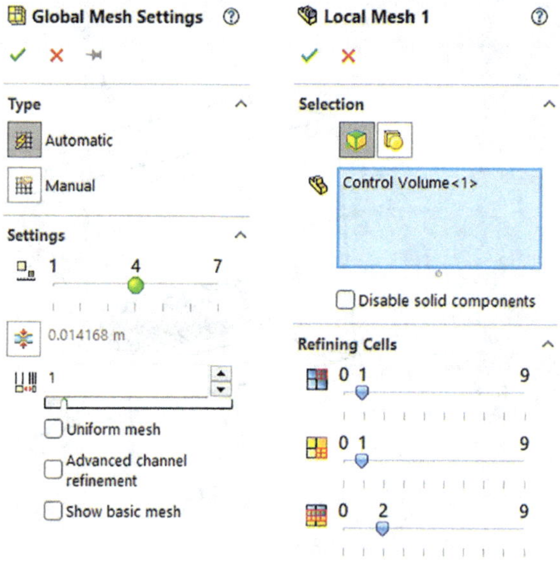

Figure 18-13: Local Mesh is defined using the Control Volume.

You may use different settings to study the effect of mesh settings on the results of analysis.

To review the mesh before committing time to solution, run **Mesh Only** solution and display mesh plot shown in Figure 18-14.

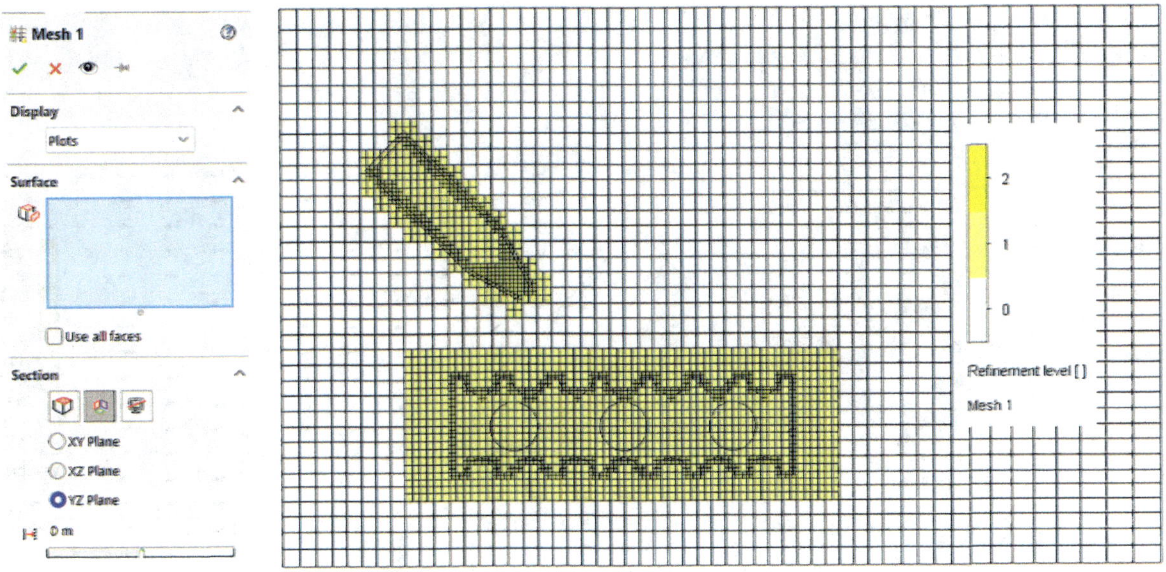

Figure 18-14: Finite Volume mesh shown in YZ section plane.

Custom colors are used to enhance the readability of this illustration.

Run the solution and construct a Cut Plot of velocity (Figure 18-15).

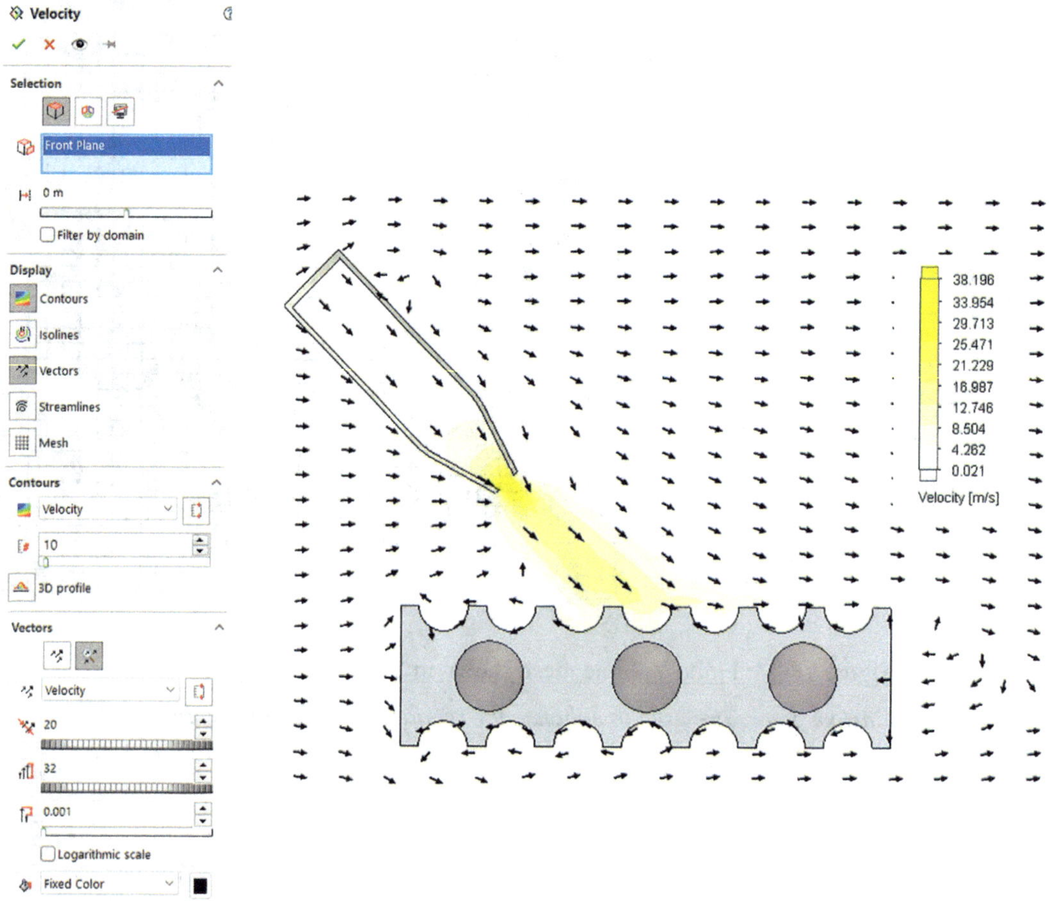

Figure 18-15: Plot of velocity in YZ section.

Scale values to plot maximum and plot minimum. Add vector display. The window has been renamed to Velocity. Custom colors are used to enhance the readability of this illustration.

To study the effect of cooling by the nozzle, copy this project to *02 no nozzle*. Delete pressure boundary conditions, exclude Nozzle from analysis and run the solution.

Construct plots of surface temperature of Block in two projects: *01 nozzle* and *02 no nozzle* (Figure 18-16).

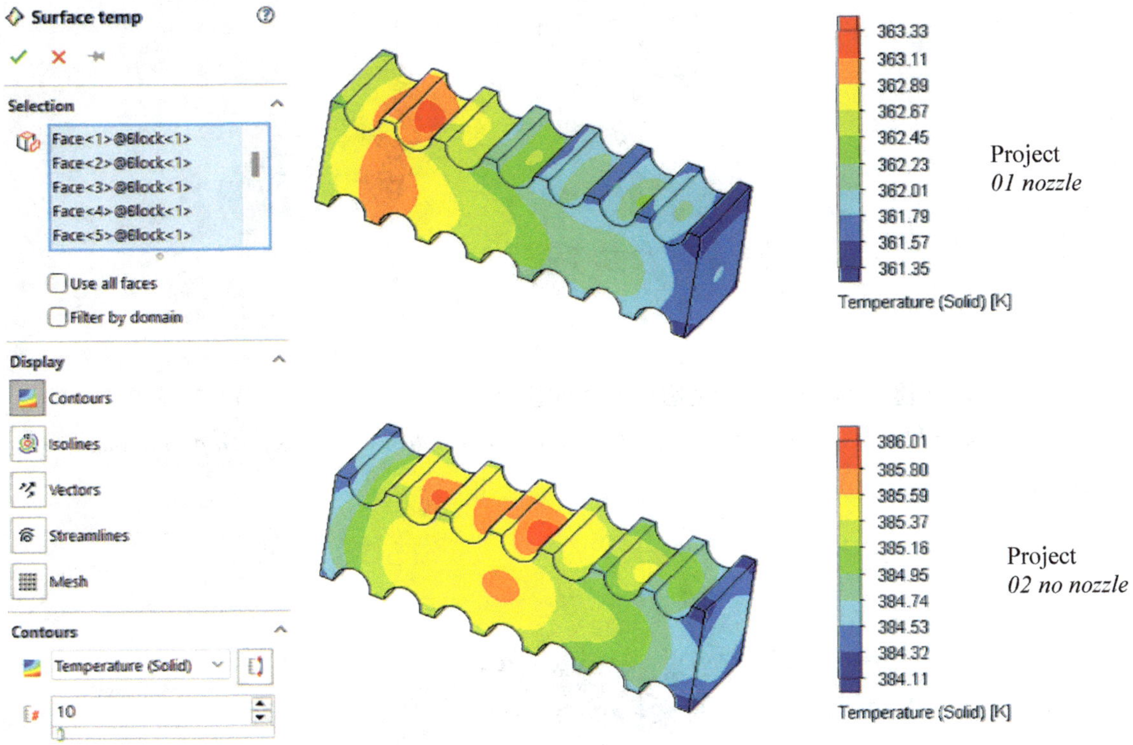

Figure 18-16: Plot of surface temperature of Block in two projects.

These results show the cooling effect of air flowing out of nozzle. Both plots use auto scale to plot maximum and minimum. The window has been renamed to Surface temp. The settings are the same for both plots.

Additional Practice Models

To reinforce the concepts presented in this chapter, repeat the analysis using the additional practice models. Define project input data following the approach used in the main exercise.

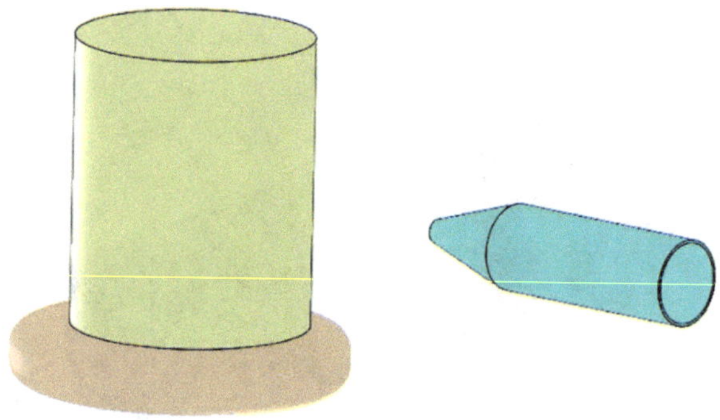

Figure 18-17: CYLINDER assembly model.

Assembly of Cylinder, Heating plate and Nozzle. Control volume is not a part of this assembly.

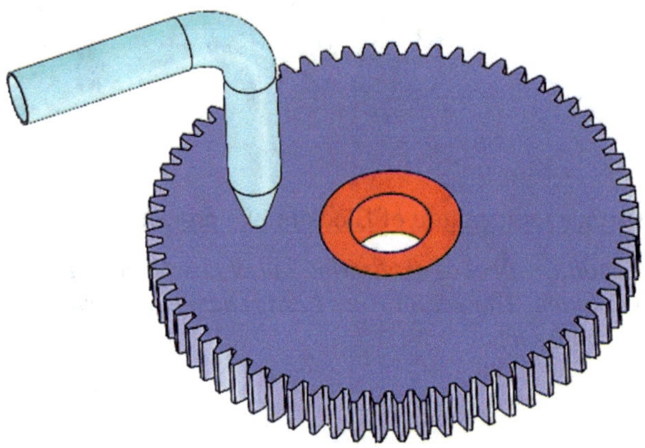

Figure 18-18: GEAR assembly model.

Assembly of Gear, Bearing and Nozzle. Control volume is not a part of this assembly.

Models in this chapter

Model	**Status**
PELLETS.sldasm	*Solved with Flow Simulation* *01 nozzle* *02 no nozzle*
CYLINDER.sldasm	*Additional practice model*
GEAR.sldasm	*Additional practice model*

Notes:

19: Loop

- Heat transfer by convection
- Heat transfer by radiation
- Size of Computational Domain

Project description

A steel Loop, a Graphite Core and a Control volume form an assembly (Figure 19-1). The Graphite Core produces 500W heat in its volume. The assembly is cooled by air flow in Y direction. We will study the importance of heat transfer by convection and by radiation.

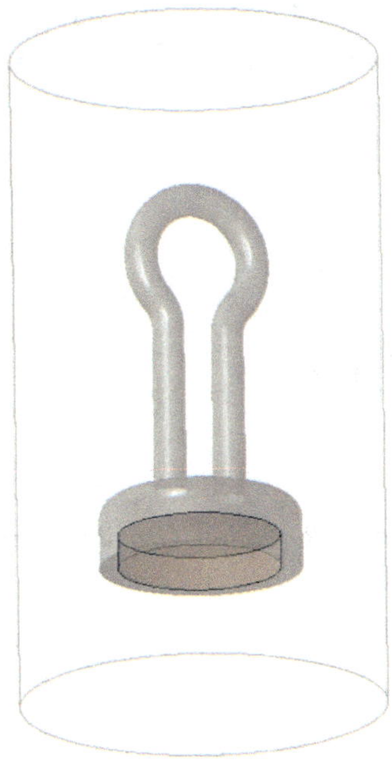

Figure 19-1: LOOP assembly model consists of Loop, Core, and Control Volume.

Loop is shown in a transparent view; Control Volume is shown in a wireframe view.

Procedure

To study the importance of Convection and Radiation in heat transfer, we will solve three projects:

- Project *01CR* *models Convection and Radiation*
- Project *02C* *models Convection only*
- Project *03R* *models Radiation only*

Create Flow Simulation project *01CR*, using following settings shown in Figures 19-2, ..., 19-6.

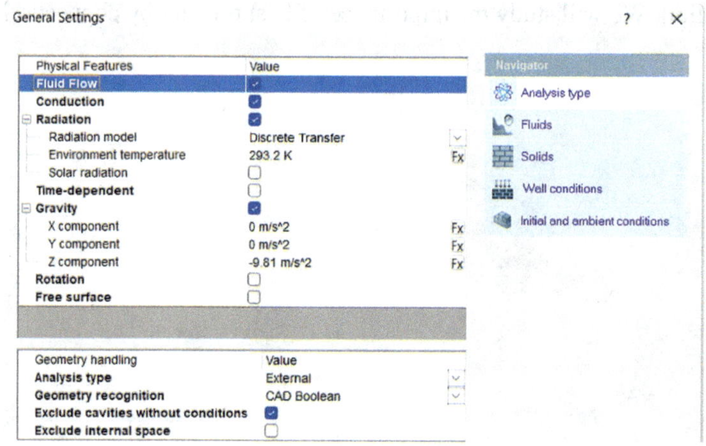

Figure 19-2: Analysis type.

Select Fluid Flow, Conduction, Radiation, Gravity, External flow.

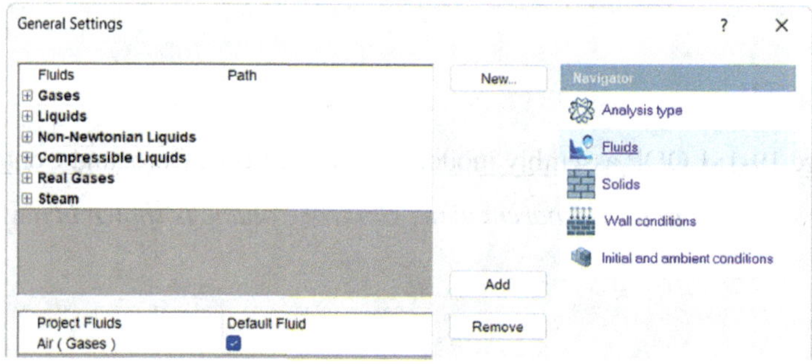

Figure 19-3: Fluids: Air.

Select Air.

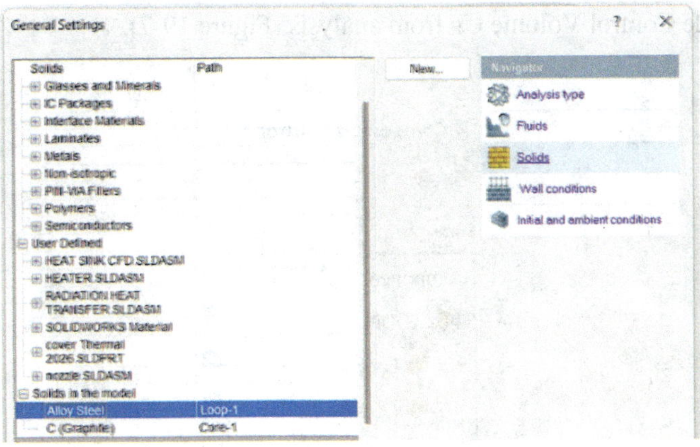

Figure 19-4: Solids: Alloy Steel from the model.

Select Alloy Steel from Solids in the model as the default solid.

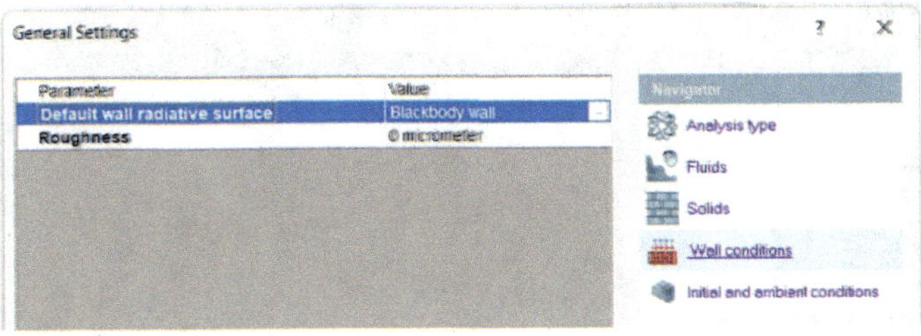

Figure 19-5: Wall conditions.

Accept the default Wall conditions.

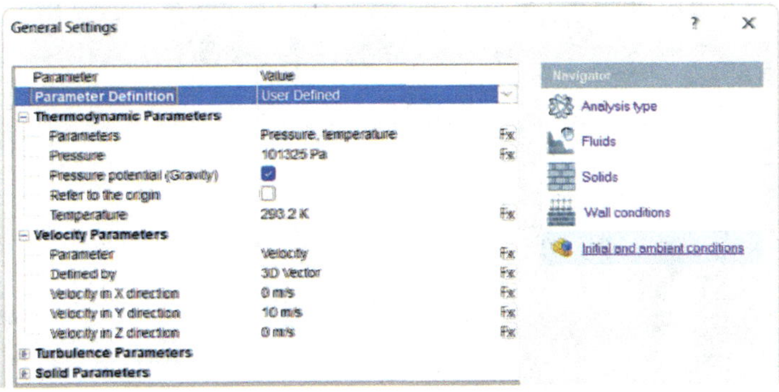

Figure 19-6: Initial and ambient conditions.

Define air flow velocity 10m/s in Y direction.

Exclude Control Volume *Cv* from analysis (Figure 19-7).

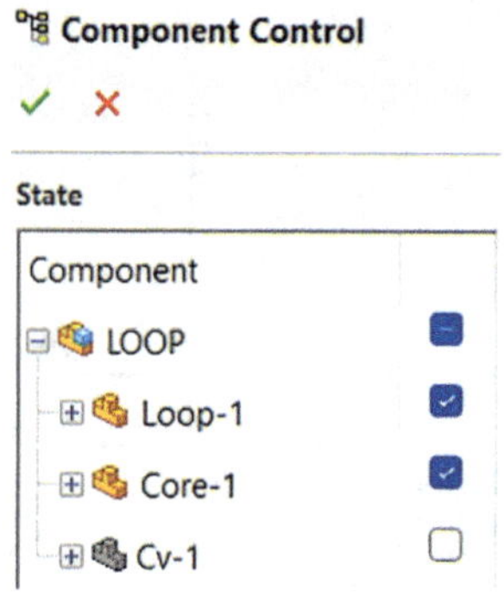

Figure 19-7: Component control; exclude the control volume Cv.

Component Cv is excluded from analysis. It will be used only to control the mesh refinement.

Define Computational Domain (Figure 19-8).

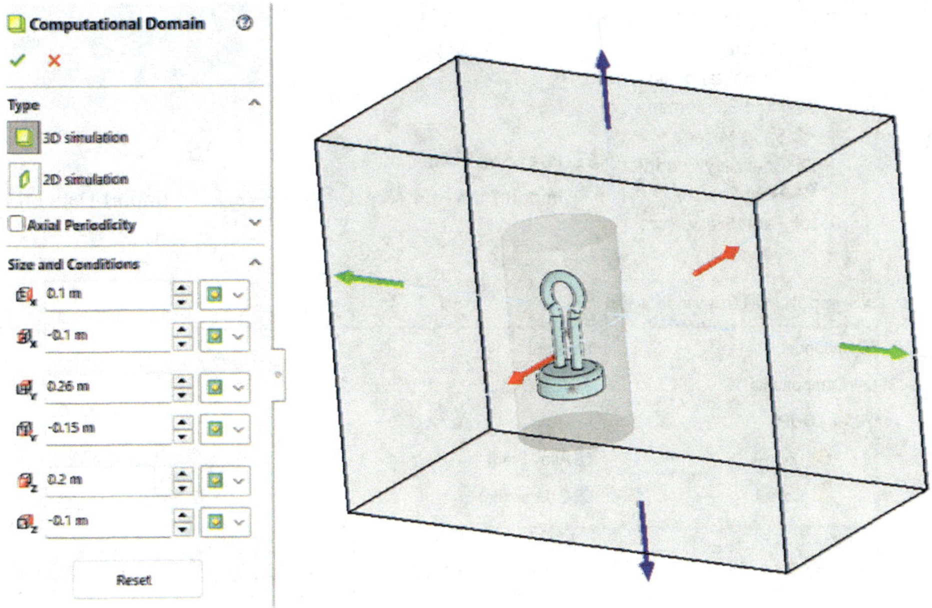

Figure 19-8: Definition of the Computational Domain.

The computational domain should be large enough for the fluid flow at the boundaries to remain undisturbed by the model. This will be verified once the results become available.

Define solid materials using **Import Data From Model** (Figure 19-9).

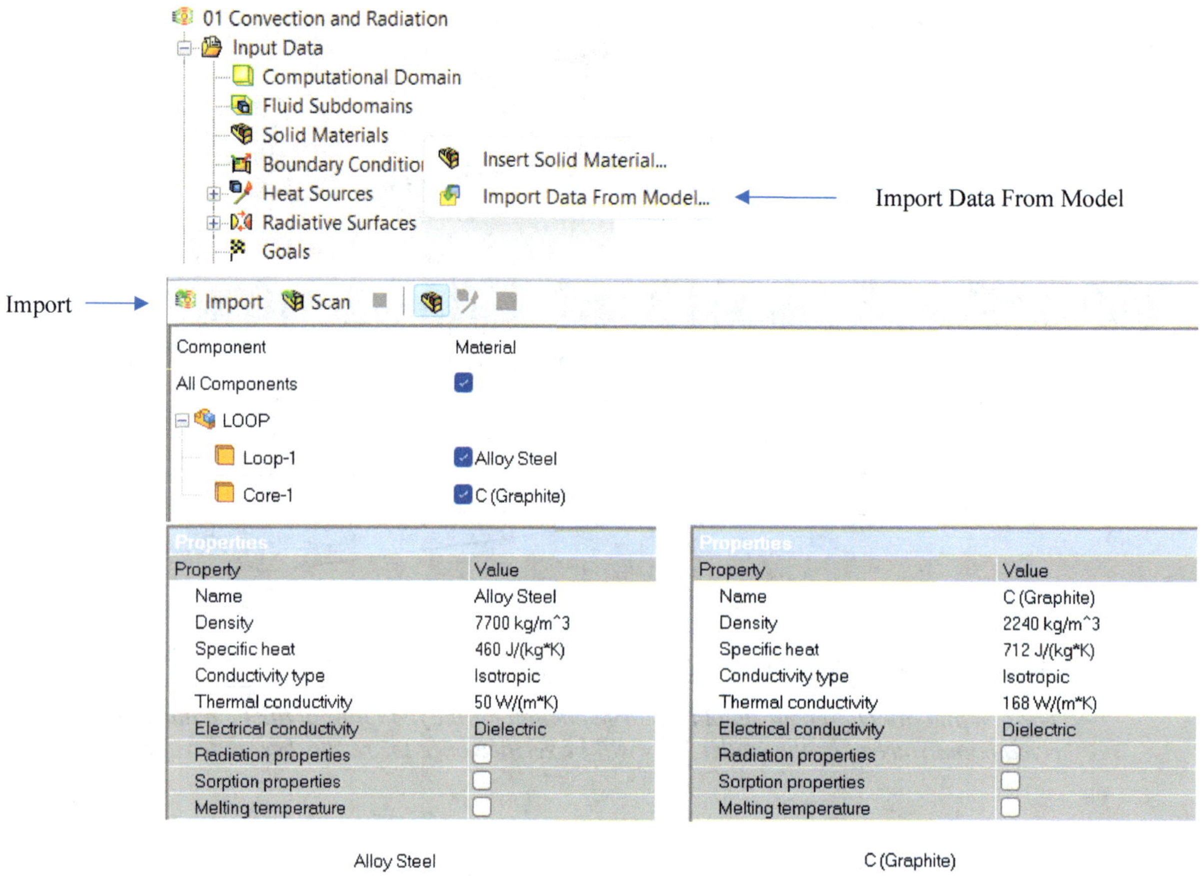

Figure 19-9: Assignment of solid materials using Import Data From Model.

Material properties are imported from LOOP assembly model.

Define 500W heat power generated in the volume of the Core (Figure 19-10).

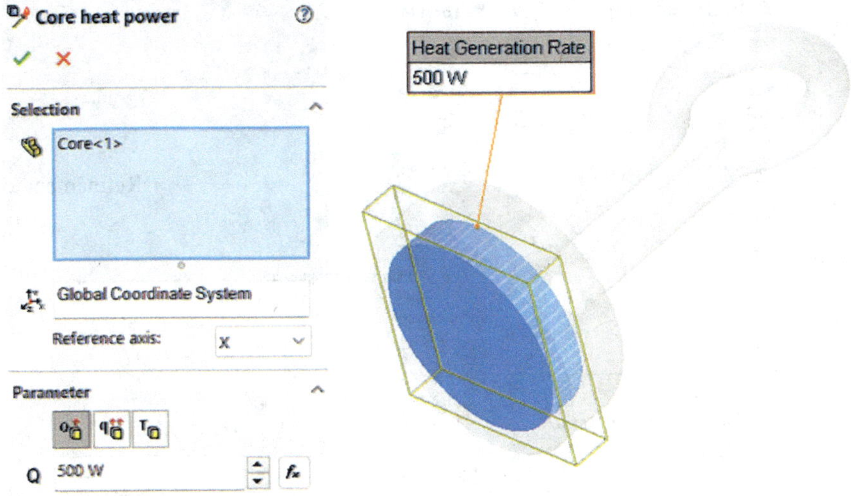

Figure 19-10: Definition of heat power.

Heat power 500W is assigned to the volume of Core.

Define Blackbody emissivity to all outer faces of the assembly (Figure 19-11).

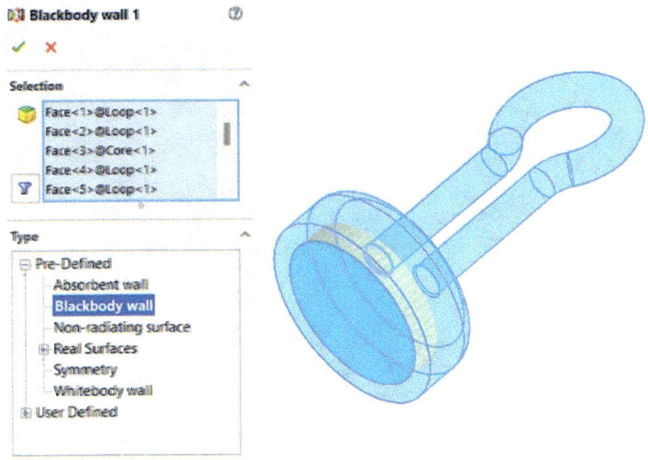

Figure 19-11: Definition of Radiative Surfaces.

Blackbody properties are assigned to outer faces of the assembly.

Define Global Mesh and Local Mesh as shown in Figure 19-12.

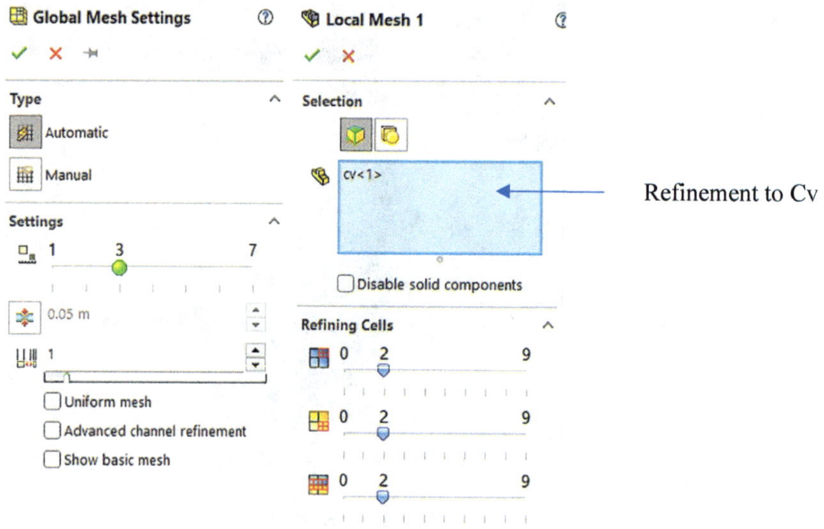

Figure 19-12: Definition of Global Mesh and Local Mesh.

Settings of the Local Mesh are relative to the setting of the Global Mesh.

The above mesh settings have been determined with several trial runs. They combine acceptable accuracy with not too long solution time. In your practice, remember to try different meshes to evaluate the effect of different choices of discretization on the results of analysis.

Run Mesh Only solution and review the mesh before solving the project.

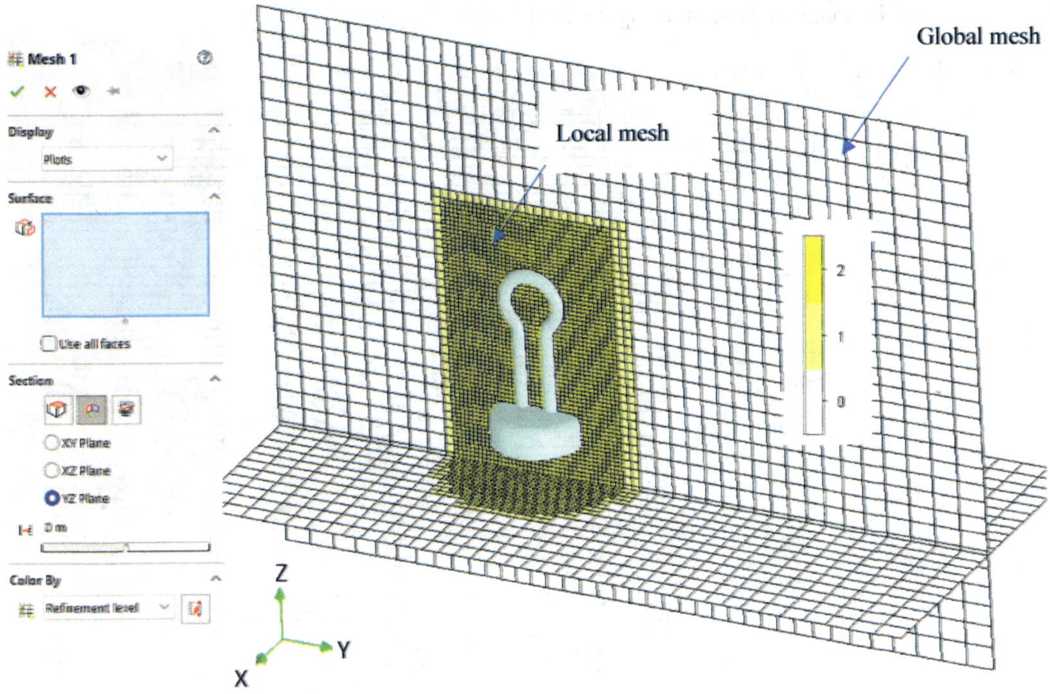

Figure 19-13: Global and Local Mesh seen in two sections.

The illustration shows two Mesh plots displayed simultaneously: section in XY and YZ planes. Note two levels of refinement of the local mesh relative to the Global mesh. Custom colors are used in the color legend.

Run the solution and prepare plots of Streamlines to check if the Computational Domain is large enough. The Computational Domain should produce an undisturbed air flow at the boundaries as seen in Figure 19-14.

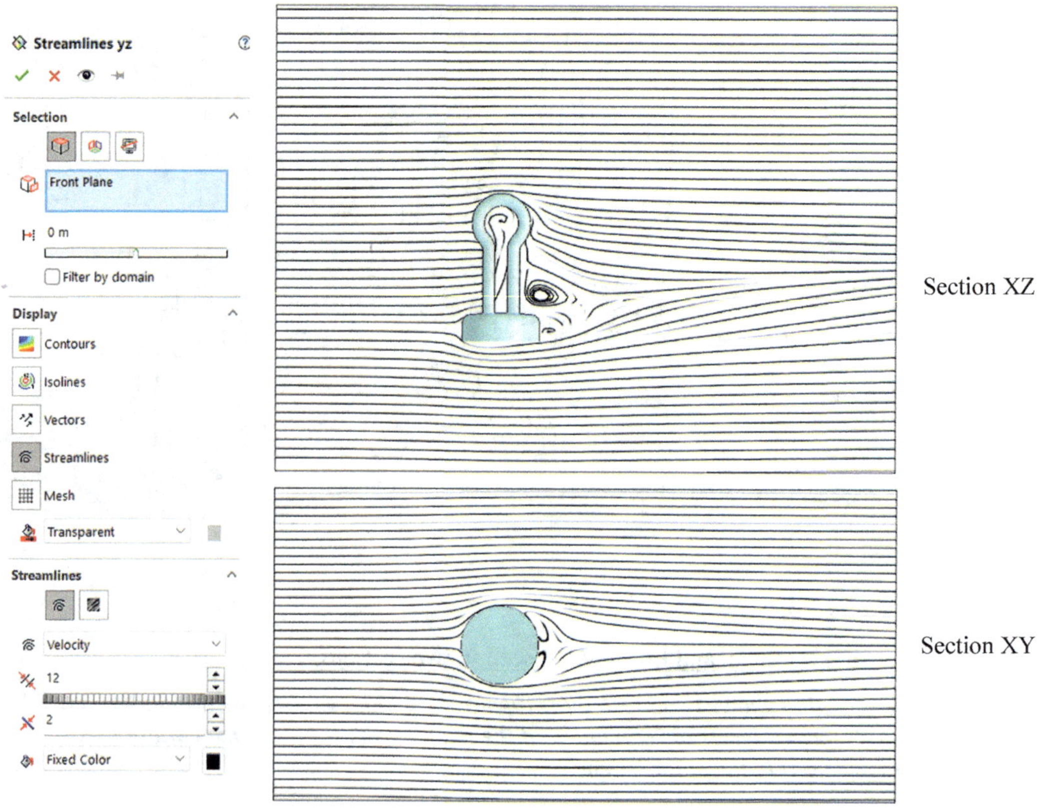

Figure 19-14: Plots of Streamlines in sections XZ and XY.

Undisturbed streamlines visible in both sections demonstrate that the Computational Domain is sufficiently large for this project.

Clone project *01CR* into *02C* and into *03R*. Edit projects *02C* and *03R* as shown in Figure 19-15.

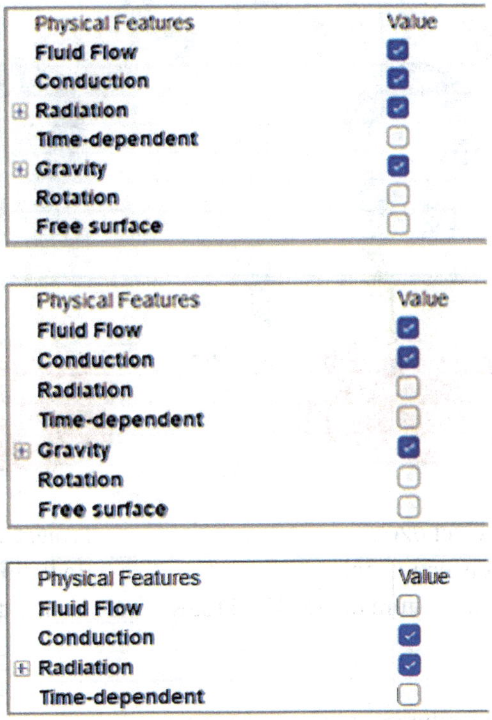

Project *01CR*

Fluid flow and Radiation selected

Project *02C*

Radiation deselected

Project *03R*

Fluid Flow deselected

Figure 19-15: Settings in projects: *01CR, 02C, 03R.*

In project 02C, Radiation is eliminated by deselecting it. In project 03R, Convection is eliminated by deselecting Fluid Flow. Conduction is selected in all projects.

Project *01CR* considers all three modes of heat transfer. The other two projects are used to examine the relative importance of Convection and Radiation; they do not provide a correct representation of the complete heat-transfer problem.

In addition to the already solved project *01CR*, solve projects *02C* and *03R*. In all projects prepare plots of temperature on the surface of solids. Figure 19-16 shows all three plots.

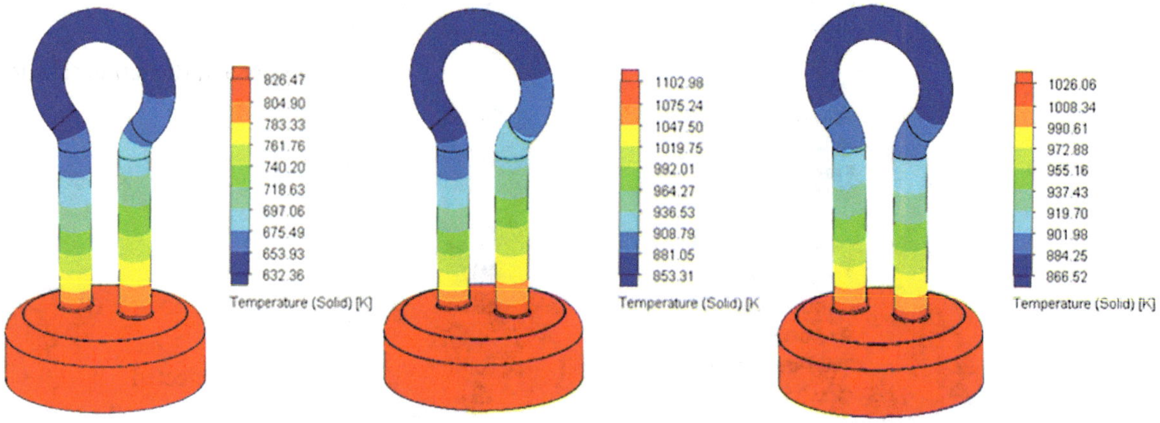

Project *01CR*
Convection and Radiation
Temperature range: 632-826K

Project *02C*
Convection only
Temperature range: 853-1103K

Project *03R*
Radiation only
Temperature range: 866-1026K

Figure 19-16: Summary of temperature results of three projects.

Relative importance of Convection and Radiation can be analyzed by comparing the above results.

Comparison of results (Figure 19-16) illustrates the importance of Radiation in heat transfer problems and demonstrates that neglecting Radiation may lead to erroneous results.

Additional Practice Models

To reinforce the concepts presented in this chapter, repeat the analysis using the additional practice models. Define all project input data following the same approach used in the main exercise.

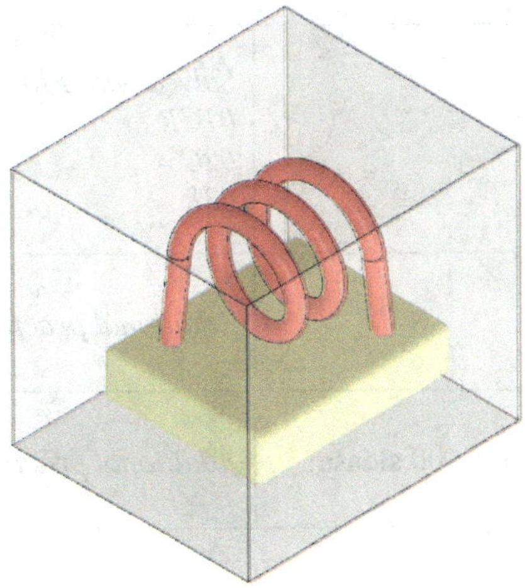

Figure 19-17: HELIX assembly model.

Control volume is shown in a transparent view. Helix and Base are separate parts.

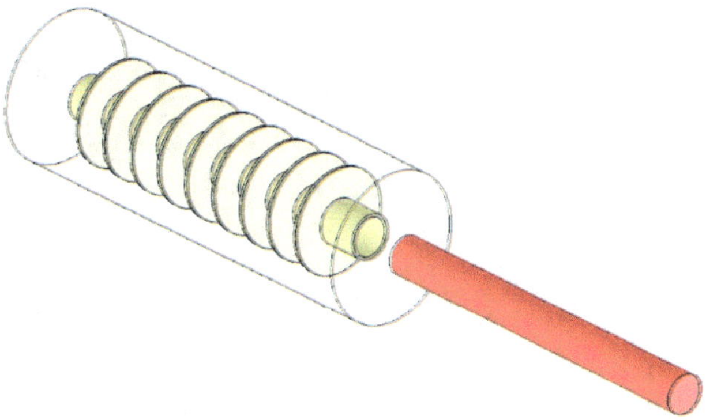

Figure 19-18: COOLING TUBE assembly model.

Cooling tube and core parts are shown in an exploded view. Control volume is shown in a wireframe view.

Models in this chapter

Model	Status
LOOP.sldasm	*Solved with Flow Simulation* *01CR* *02C* *03R*
HELIX.sldasm	*Additional practice model*
COOLING TUBE 100.sldasm	*Additional practice model*

Part 4

Benchmark Problems

The final part of the book applies the modeling techniques developed in earlier chapters to a set of benchmark problems published by NAFEMS. Benchmark problems provide well-defined reference solutions that allow numerical simulation methods to be verified.

These examples demonstrate how the methods introduced throughout the book can be used to solve problems with known solutions and documented results. Comparing simulation results with benchmark data helps develop confidence in the analysis process and highlights the importance of careful model setup, mesh selection, and interpretation of results.

Notes:

20: NAFEMS Benchmarks

- Importance of benchmarks
- One dimensional heat transfer with radiation
- One dimensional transient heat transfer
- Two dimensional heat transfer with convection

Project description

Benchmarks are standard tests, which can be applied to any Finite Element system. They are intended for users who are interested in the performance of specific codes. The classic set of benchmarks was first published in 1986 by the National Agency for Finite Element Methods and Standards (NAFEMS – see chapter 21). NAFEMS benchmarks were designed to be a little more "searching" than those typically published by software developers since these naturally intended to demonstrate the favorable performance of a system rather than deficiencies.

In this chapter, we will test the performance of SOLIDWORKS Simulation in three NAFEMS thermal benchmarks with known analytical solutions. Performance will be evaluated by comparing SOLIDWORKS Simulation results with targets (expected results) as specified in each test.

Very simple geometries used in these tests lend themselves to more than one representation. Therefore, these exercises will also serve as a review of finite element modeling techniques available in thermal analysis with SOLIDWORKS Simulation.

Procedure

Test T2 is used to study program performance in the steady state thermal analysis. A 1D bar has a constant prescribed temperature of 1000K applied to end A, and radiation to an ambient temperature of 300K to end B. There are no other boundary conditions present, meaning that the bar is insulated and there is no heat source. The section is uniform (Figure 20-1).

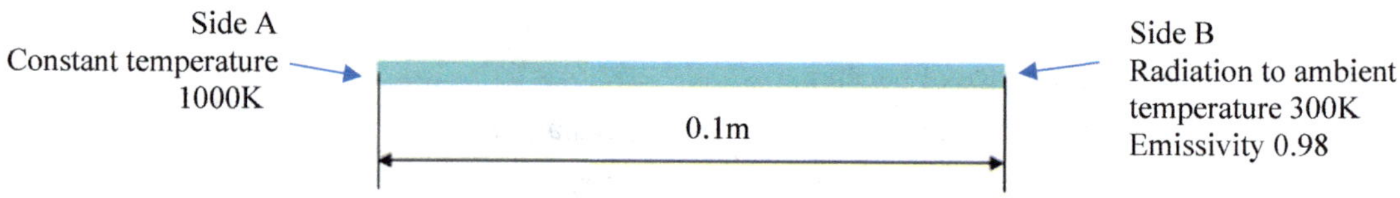

Figure 20-1: Geometry and boundary conditions in Test T2.

Since this is a 1D model, only length needs to be specified.

Benchmark Test T2 specifies material properties as follows:

Conductivity = 55.6W/m/K

Specific heat = 460J/kg/K

Density = 7850kg/m^3

Emissivity at boundary B = 0.98

Part model TEST T2 comes with these material properties defined.

Specific heat and density are not required for a steady state thermal analysis.

The target in Test T2 is temperature at end B. To pass the test, an FEA program should find this temperature to be equal to 927K.

This very simple geometry can be modeled in several ways, either as 3D or a 2D problem. 1D elements are not available in SOLIDWORKS Simulation. Therefore, our choice is between 3D and 2D representations.

Should we decide to model this as a 3D problem, any prismatic bar with a uniform cross section along the length could be used (Figure 20-2).

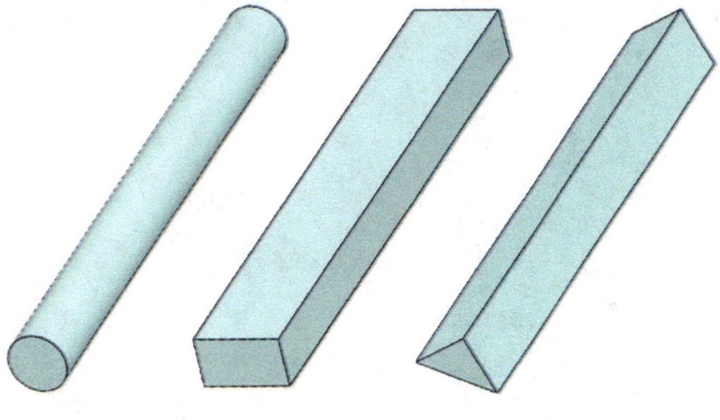

Figure 20-2: Examples of geometry that could be used in Test T2.

The shape and the area of the cross section are irrelevant in this 1D problem. Any of the above bars can be used as long its length is 0.1m.

Should we decide to model this as a 2D problem, there is again more than one way to accomplish it. First, a bar with a round section could be used to create a 2D axisymmetric model. Second, a bar with a rectangular cross section could be used to create a 2D extruded model (Figure 20-3). Alternatively, a surface geometry could be prepared in SOLIDWORKS and treated as an axisymmetric or extruded model in a 2D study.

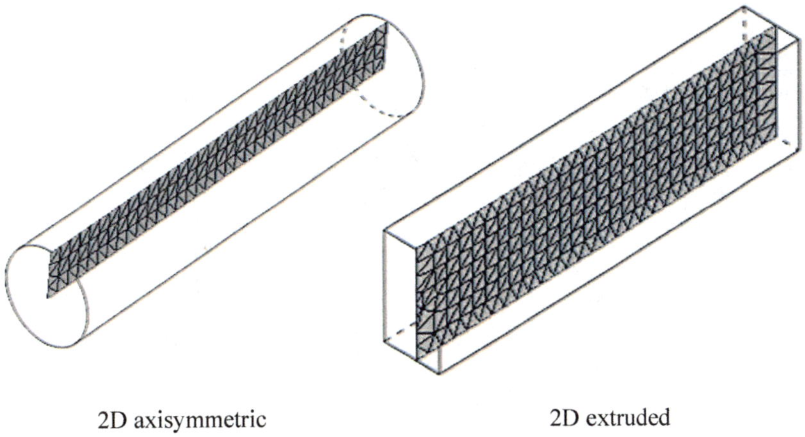

Figure 20-3: Geometry that can be used in the T2 test if 2D simplification is desired.

Large elements are shown for the clarity of this illustration. We will use much smaller elements for analysis.

For the T2 test, we will use a round bar and treat the problem as 3D. In test T3 which uses identical 1D geometry, we will use a square bar treating that problem as 2D extruded.

Open part model TEST T2 and review a custom material assigned to the model. Create a steady state thermal study and apply boundary conditions as shown in Figure 20-4 and Figure 20-5.

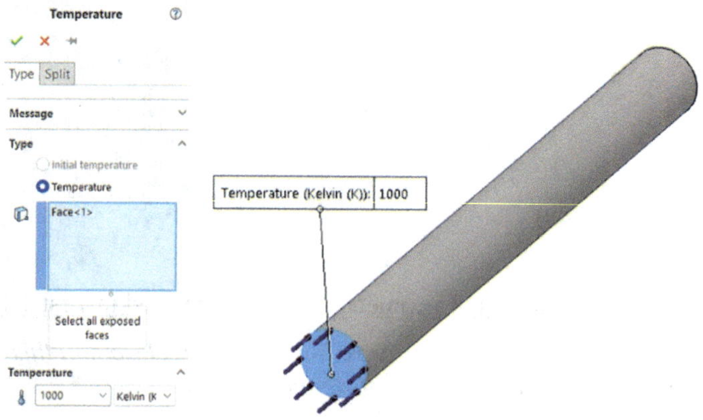

Figure 20-4: The Boundary Condition on side A is a prescribed temperature of 1000K.

A prescribed temperature is applied to side A. Prescribed temperature symbols are shown.

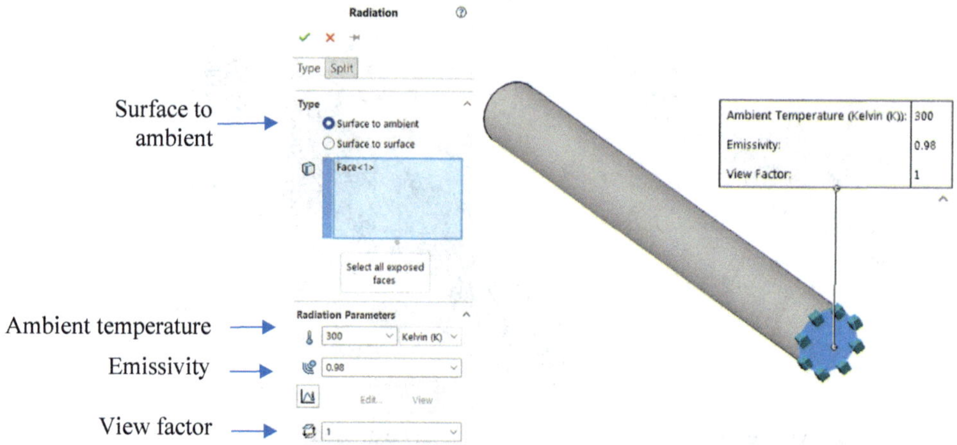

Figure 20-5: The Boundary Condition on side B is a Radiation Surface to ambient.

A radiative boundary condition is applied to side B.

An Ambient temperature of 300K is the temperature of a distant enclosure, which receives heat radiated out from side B. An Emissivity of 0.98 is very close to the emissivity of black body, so the model is very good at radiating out heat. To understand the meaning of a View factor of 1, take into consideration that Surface to ambient radiation is specified and that there is only one radiating face in the model. A View factor equal to 1 means that the heat radiated out does not reach that face again.

Mesh the model with a default mesh and obtain a solution. Show the Temperature plot and probe it as shown in Figure 20-6.

Figure 20-6: Probing shows the Temperature on the side where the Radiative Boundary Condition has been defined.

The probed temperature is 927K.

Probing shows a temperature of 927K, the same as specified as the benchmark target. This demonstrates the correct performance of Simulation in this radiation problem. Try running the same problem with a view factor of less than 1, which makes it more difficult to radiate the heat out. The temperature will be higher than 927K.

Benchmark Test T3 requires transient thermal analysis.

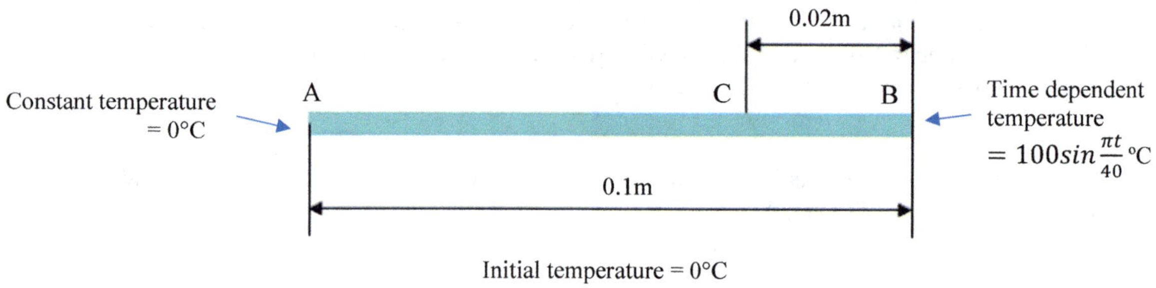

Figure 20-7: Geometry and Boundary Conditions of TEST T3.

The initial temperature = 0°C.

Benchmark Test T3 specifies material properties as follows:

Conductivity = 35.0W/m/K

Specific heat = 440.5J/kg/K

Density = 7200kg/m^3

Part model TEST T3 comes with these material properties defined.

Temperature on side B is a function of time; therefore, this is a transient thermal problem. Specific heat and density are the required material properties.

The target is a temperature at point C, at time t=32s. To pass this benchmark test, Simulation should find this temperature to be 36.6°C.

Open part model TEST T3 and define a thermal study with 2D simplification (Figure 20-8).

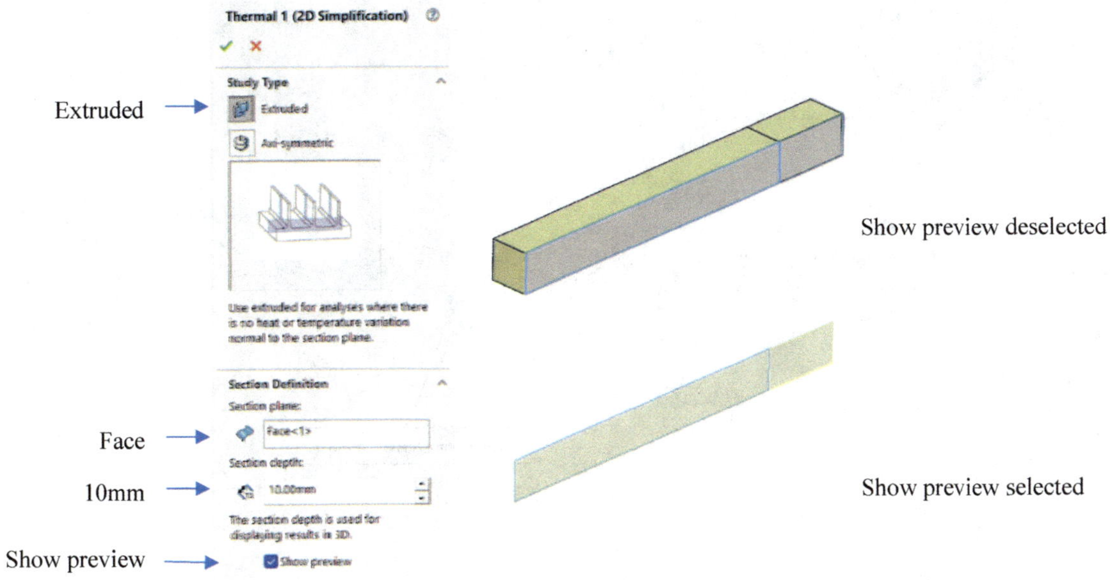

Figure 20-8: The 2D Simplification uses an Extruded 2D representation; thickness used here is 10mm, but any thickness will satisfy benchmark test requirements.

Switch between two views by selecting/deselecting Show preview. Split line marks the location where temperature results will be probed.

Define transient study properties as shown in Figure 20-9.

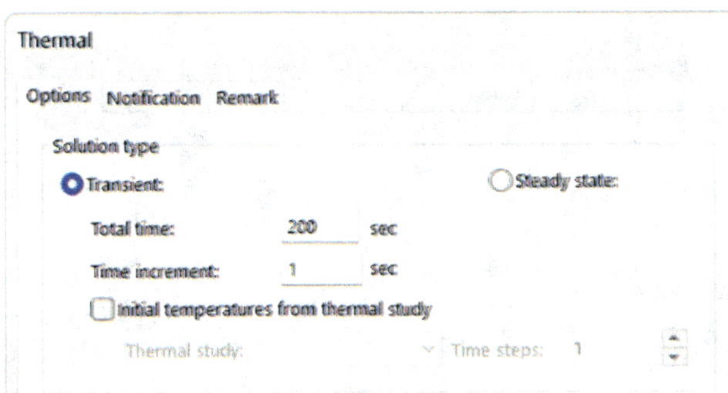

Figure 20-9: Properties of the transient thermal study.

The transient thermal study will be conducted for 200s with time increment of 1s. 200 steps will be executed.

Apply an Initial Temperature to two faces (Figure 20-10).

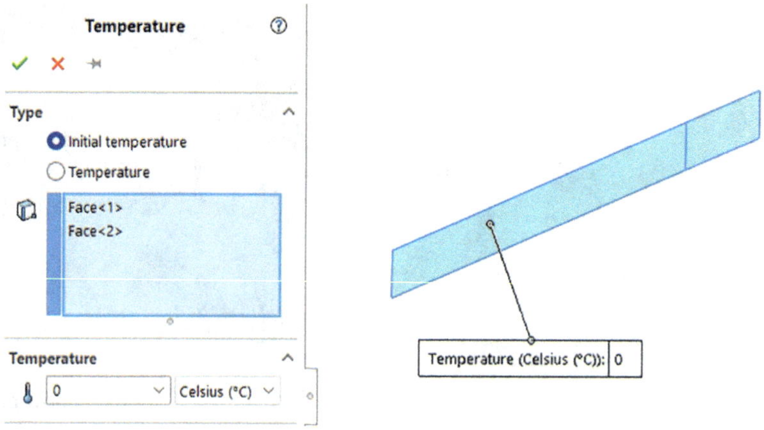

Figure 20-10: Definition of the Initial Temperature.

Initial temperature is applied to two faces; there are two faces in the 2D model because of the split line.

Apply Prescribed Temperature to side A (Figure 20-11).

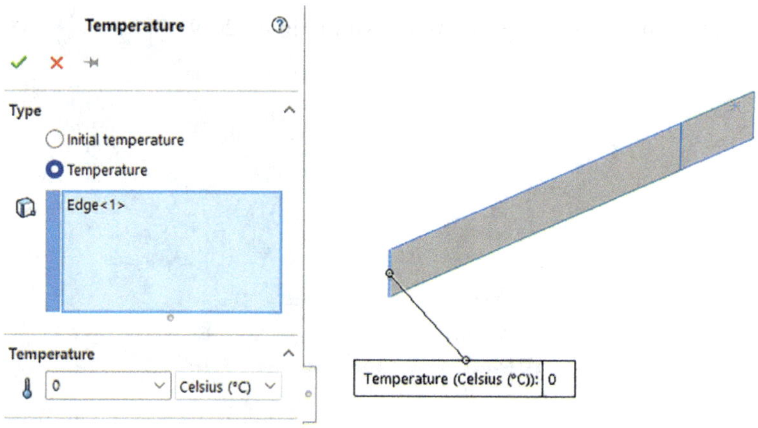

Figure 20-11: Definition of the Prescribed Temperature on side A.

Temperature is applied to the edge of 2D model that represents a face in a 3D model.

Follow the steps in Figure 20-12 to define a time dependent temperature on side B.

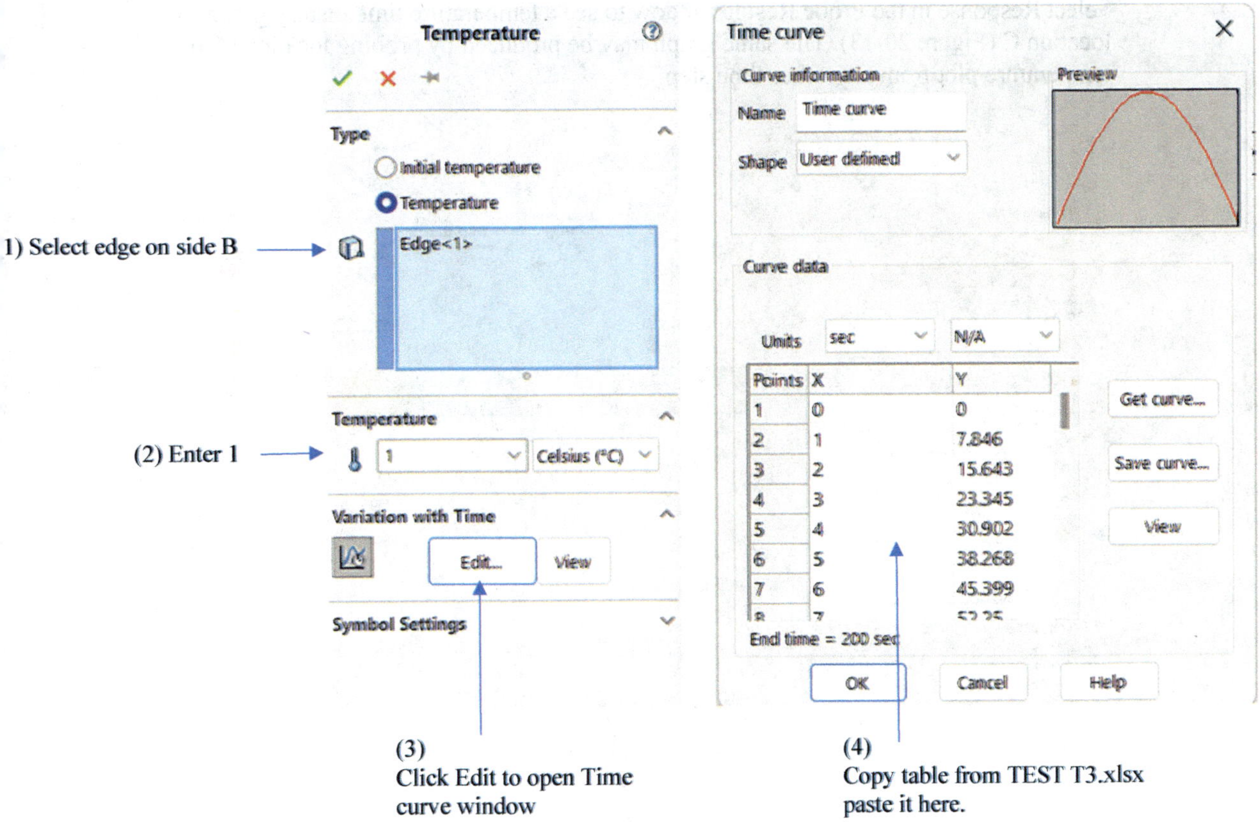

Figure 20-12: Definition of the time dependent temperature on side B.

The time dependency is illustrated by a curve shown in the Preview image. Value 1 is a multiplier of values in the Time curve table.

The table in spreadsheet TEST T3.xlsx has been created by tabling the equation shown in Figure 20-7 in the range 0-40s. Analysis runs for 200s; after 40s temperature of Side B remains constant at 0°C.

Mesh the model with default element size and run the solution. To check the target, probe Temperature plot at 32s as shown in Figure 20-13.

Select Response in the Probe Result window to see a temperature time history graph in location C (Figure 20-13). The same graph may be produced by probing location C in temperature plot from any other time step.

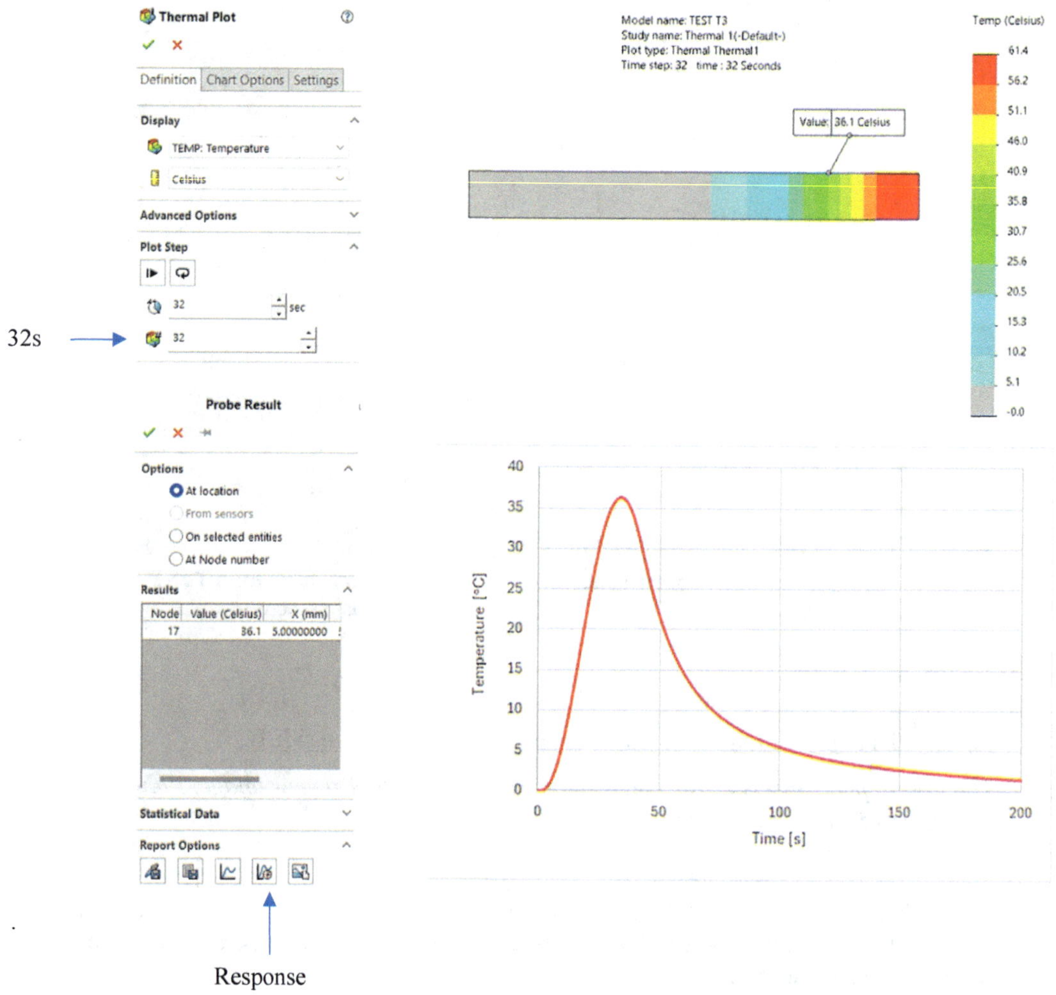

Figure 20-13: Selecting time step and probing temperature plot in location C shown in Figure 20-7.

Probe time step 32s where split line separates two faces. Probing shows a temperature of 36.1°C; this is close to the benchmark Test T3 target of 36.6°C. The graph has been formatted in Excel.

Benchmark Test T4 focuses on conductive heat transfer induced by prescribed temperatures and convection to ambient fluid (Figure 20-14).

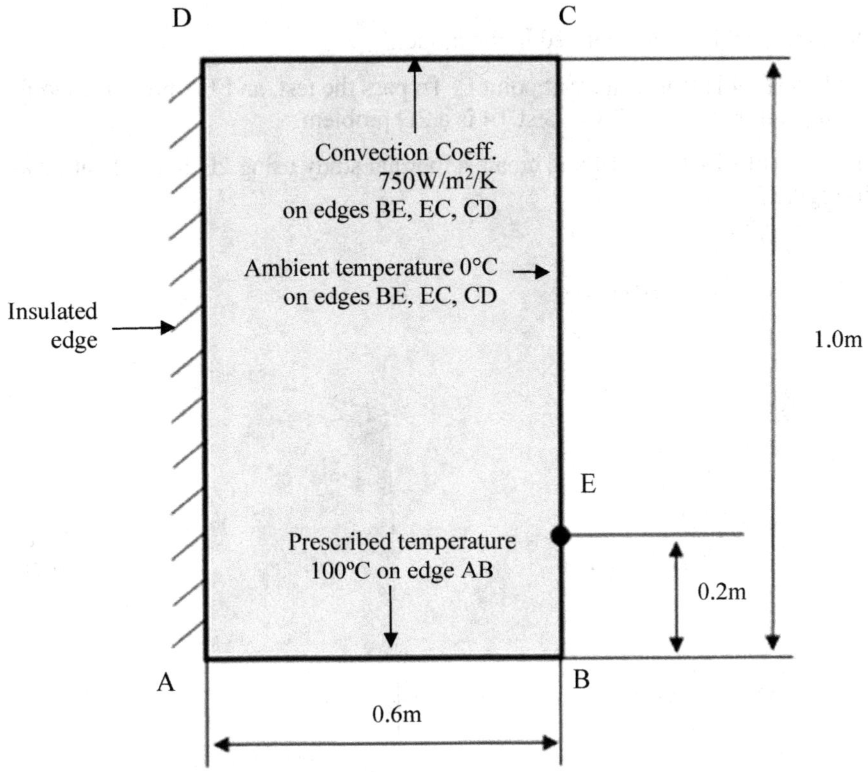

Figure 20-14: Geometry and boundary conditions in Test T4.

This is a 2D problem.

Benchmark test T4 specifies material conductivity and convection as follows:

Conductivity = 52.0W/m/K

Convection = 750W/m^2/K

The custom material has been defined in the model.

The target in test T4 is temperature at point E. To pass the test, an FEA program should find this temperature to be 18.3°C. Test T4 is a 2D problem.

Open model NAFEMS TEST T4 and create a thermal study using 2D Simplification as shown in Figure 20-15.

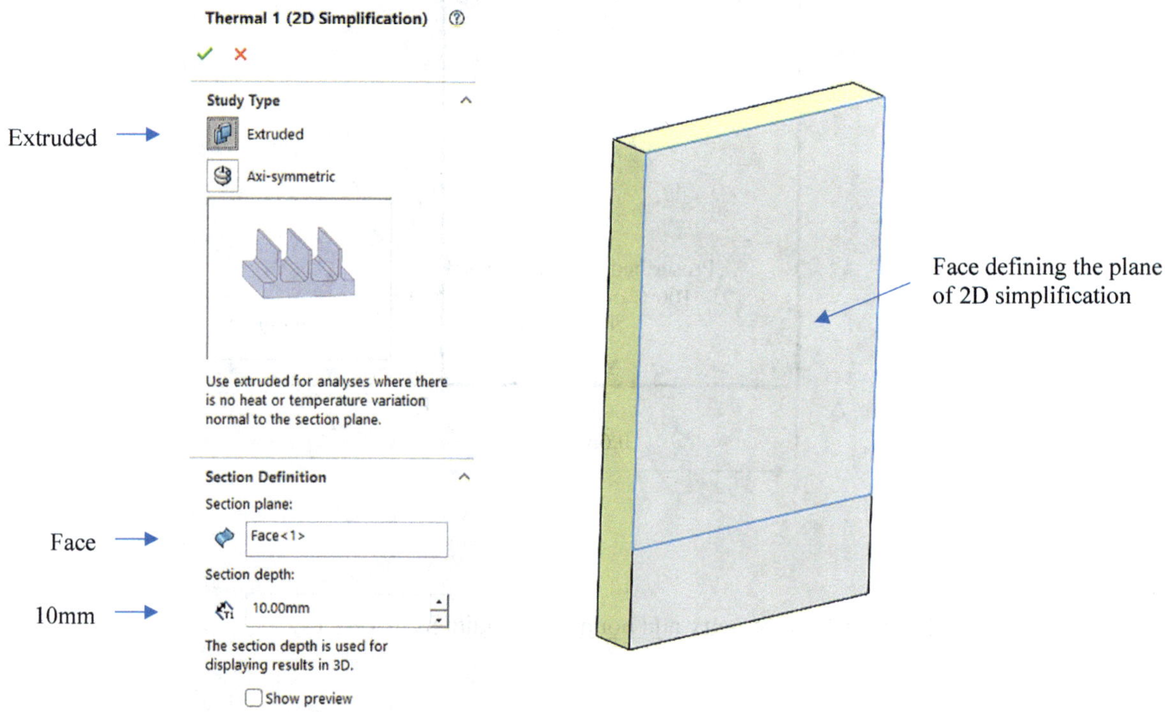

Figure 20-15: 2D Simplification uses Extruded 2D simplification.

This is a 2D extruded problem; the thickness is uniform. Any thickness may be used in this benchmark test.

Apply prescribed temperature (Figure 20-16).

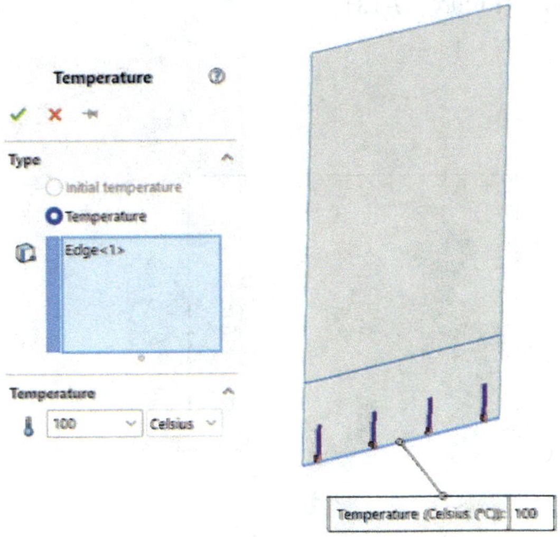

Figure 20-16: Definition of the Prescribed Temperature in test NAFEMS T4.

Apply a temperature of 100°C to the bottom edge. Prescribed temperature symbols are shown.

Apply convective boundary conditions (Figure 20-17).

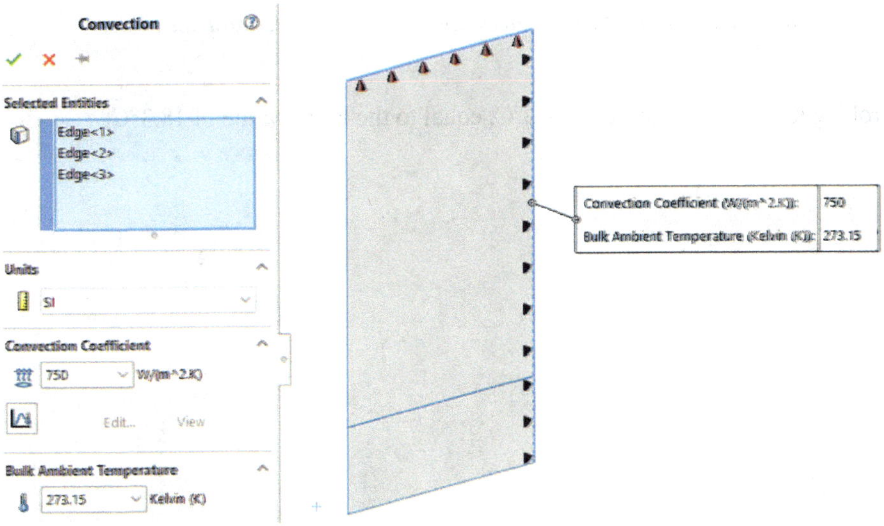

Figure 20-17: Definition of convection conditions in test T4.

Apply a convection of 750W/m²/K and an ambient temperature of 273.15K to the top and right edges. Convection symbols are shown.

Mesh the model with the default Standard mesh and obtain solution. Probe the Temperature plot in location E (Figure 20-18).

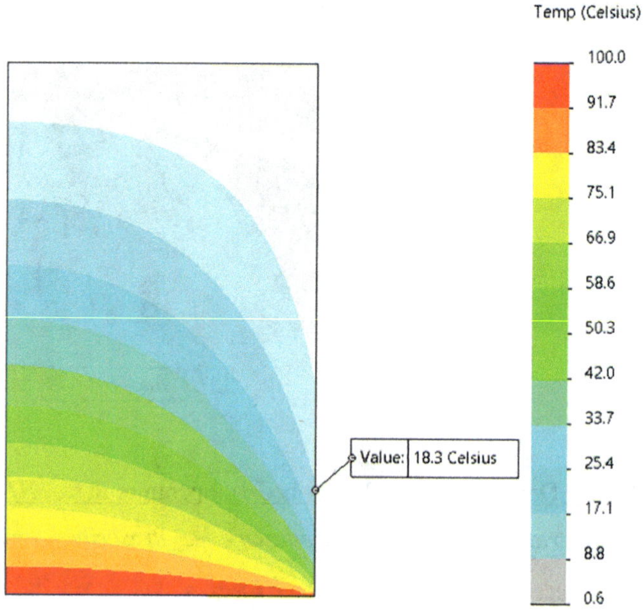

Figure 20-18: Probing temperature results in Test T4.

Probe at the intersection of the vertical edge with the horizontal split line.

Probing shows temperature of 18.3°C, equal to the target value of 18.3°C.

Summary of studies completed

Model	Configuration	Study Name	Study Type
TEST T2.sldprt	*Default*	*Thermal 1*	Thermal
TEST T3.sldprt	*Default*	*Thermal 1*	Thermal
TEST T4.sldprt	*Default*	*Thermal 1*	Thermal

Notes:

21: Glossary of terms

Boundary Condition
A specified condition at the boundary of the solution domain, such as temperature, heat flux, convection, or radiation. Boundary conditions define how the system interacts with its surroundings.

Buoyancy Flow (Natural Convection)
Fluid motion caused by temperature differences within a fluid. Warmer fluid becomes lighter and rises, while cooler fluid becomes heavier and sinks, creating circulation without a fan or pump.

Conduction
A mode of heat transfer in which energy moves through a material without bulk motion of the material itself. It occurs due to molecular interactions and is described by Fourier's law.

Conductivity (Thermal Conductivity)
A material property that measures how easily heat flows through a solid due to a temperature difference. It is usually denoted by k and has units of W/(m K).

Conjugate Heat Transfer (CHT)
A heat transfer process in which heat moves through solids by conduction and through fluids by convection at the same time. Temperature and heat flow must match at the solid–fluid interface.

Contact Resistance (Thermal Contact Resistance)
Resistance to heat flow at the interface between two solids in contact. It occurs due to surface roughness and imperfect contact and can significantly affect heat transfer.

Control Volume
A small region of space within the computational domain used in finite volume analysis. Conservation laws are applied to each control volume to compute temperature and fluid flow variables.

Convection
A mode of heat transfer between a solid surface and a moving fluid. Heat is carried away by the bulk motion of the fluid and is characterized by the convection heat transfer coefficient.

Density
The mass per unit volume of a material. In thermal analysis, density affects how much thermal energy a material can store during transient heating or cooling.

Element
A small subdivision of the model in a finite element mesh. Mathematical equations are applied over each element to approximate the physical behavior of the system.

Emissivity
A surface property that describes how effectively a material emits thermal radiation compared to a perfect black surface. Its value ranges from 0 to 1.

Finite Element Mesh
A division of a model into small, connected elements with nodes at their corners. The solution (such as temperature or displacement) is calculated at the nodes and approximated within each element.

Finite Volume Mesh
A division of the computational domain into small control volumes. The governing equations are applied to each volume to ensure conservation of energy and other physical quantities.

Grid Independence (Mesh Independence)
A condition in which further mesh refinement does not significantly change the simulation results. It indicates that the numerical solution is sufficiently accurate with respect to mesh size.

Heat
A form of energy that is transferred between systems due to a temperature difference.
Heat Flux
The rate of heat transfer per unit area. It represents how much heat passes through a surface per unit time and area.
Heat Transfer
The process by which thermal energy moves from one region or body to another due to a temperature difference.
Initial Condition
The specified state of the system at the start of a transient analysis, such as initial temperature distribution. It defines the starting point for time-dependent simulations.
Linear Analysis
An analysis in which material properties, boundary conditions, and loads do not depend on temperature or time. The governing equations remain linear.
Mesh Refinement
The process of reducing element or control volume size to improve solution accuracy. Refinement is often applied in regions with large temperature gradients.
Node
A point in a finite element mesh where solution variables such as temperature are calculated. Elements are connected to one another at nodes.
Nonlinear Analysis
An analysis in which at least one material property, boundary condition, or load depends on temperature or time, causing the governing equations to become nonlinear.
Radiation
A mode of heat transfer that occurs through electromagnetic waves. It does not require a material medium and can occur in vacuum.
Radiation Enclosure
A group of surfaces that exchange thermal radiation with each other. Radiation analysis within an enclosure accounts for view factors between all participating surfaces.
Solution (Computational) Domain
The region of space included in a simulation where the governing equations are solved. It may include solids, fluids, or both.
Specific Heat
The amount of energy required to raise the temperature of a unit mass of a substance by one degree Celsius (or one Kelvin).
Steady-State Analysis
An analysis in which temperatures and other conditions do not change with time.
Temperature
A measure of the thermal state of a body that determines the direction of heat transfer. It is measured in Kelvin (K), Celsius (°C), or Fahrenheit (°F).
Thermal Expansion
The tendency of a material to change its dimensions when its temperature changes. It is described by the coefficient of thermal expansion.
Thermal Stress
Stress that develops in a material due to temperature changes that cause expansion or contraction while movement is constrained.
Transient Analysis
An analysis in which temperatures or boundary conditions change with time.
View Factor
A geometric factor in radiative heat transfer that represents the fraction of radiation leaving one surface that reaches another surface.

Volumetric Heat Generation
Heat produced within a material per unit volume, typically expressed in W or W/m^3. It represents internal heat sources such as electrical resistance heating or chemical reactions.

Notes:

22: References

To review the fundamentals of the **Finite Element Method** and **Heat Transfer**, readers are referred to the following publications, listed in order of relevance. This list represents only a small sample of the extensive literature available on these topics.

1. **Kurowski, P.** *Finite Element Analysis for Mechanical Engineers*. Video course, SDC Publications.
2. **Kurowski, P.** *Engineering Analysis with SOLIDWORKS Simulation 2026*. SDC Publications, 2026.
3. **Kurowski, P.** *Finite Element Analysis for Design Engineers*. SAE International, 2023.
4. **NAFEMS.** *Background to Benchmarks*. NAFEMS, 1993.
5. **NAFEMS.** *How to Undertake Finite Element–Based Thermal Analysis*. NAFEMS, 2002.
6. **Incropera, F. P., DeWitt, D. P., Bergman, T. L., and Lavine, A. S.** *Fundamentals of Heat and Mass Transfer*. John Wiley & Sons, Inc.
7. **Logan, D. L.** *A First Course in the Finite Element Method.* Brooks/Cole.

Notes:

23: List of exercises

Solved models are underscored.

Chapter	Models
1	BRACKET TH.sldprt HEAT SINK01.sldprt PIPE 01.sldprt PIPE 02.sldprt
PART 1	
2	HOLLOW PLATE TH.sldprt CROSS.sldprt WAVE.sldprt
3	L BRACKET TH.sldprt BRACKET10.sldprt
4	STEEL ROD.sldprt TWO RODS.sldasm RECTANGULAR TUBES.sldasm
5	HEATING DUCTS.sldasm HEATING DUCTS ROUND.sldasm
6	HOT PLATE.sldasm HPLATE10.sldasm HPLATE SPIRAL.sldasm
7	MUG.sldprt POT10.sldprt POT20.sldprt
8	LINK03.sldprt PLATE20.sldprt ROD20.sldprt

9	HEAT SINK.sldasm HEAT SINK TH.xlsx Z80.sldasm Z85.sldasm
10	FURNACE.sldprt GLOBE.sldprt TORUS.sldprt
PART 2	
11	GRAPHITE BALL.sldprt DODECAHEDRON.sldprt TETRAHEDRON.sldprt
12	HEMISPHERE.sldprt TETRAHEDRON100.sldprt SPHERE100.sldprt
13	REFLECTOR.sldasm BLOCKS.sldprt ENCLOSURE.sldprt
PART 3	
14	ELBOW.sldprt COOLING TUBE.sldprt CHANNEL.sldprt SPIRAL.sldprt
15	BALL15.sldprt CYLINDER.sldprt WING.sldprt
16	MICROCHIP.sldasm HEAT SINK01.sldasm DOME.sldasm
17	LIGHT FIXTURE.sldasm CANDLE.sldasm GLASS PLATE.sldasm

18	PELLETS.sldasm CYLINDER.sldasm GEAR.sldasm
19	LOOP.sldasm HELIX.sldasm COOLING TUBE.sldasm
PART 4	
20	TEST T2.sldprt TEST T3.sldprt TEST T3.xlsx TEST T4.sldprt

Notes:

9781630577964